Guns and Contemporary Society

Guns and Contemporary Society

The Past, Present, and Future of Firearms and Firearm Policy

Volume 3: Current Controversies and Policy Recommendations

Glenn H. Utter, Editor

 PRAEGER™

An Imprint of ABC-CLIO, LLC

Santa Barbara, California • Denver, Colorado

Library of Congress Cataloging-in-Publication Data

Guns and contemporary society : the past, present, and future of firearms and firearm policy / Glenn H. Utter, editor.
    volumes cm
  Includes index.
  Contents: Volume 1. Background to the current debate over firearms — Volume 2. Cultural issues related to firearms in the United States — Volume 3. Current controversies and policy recommendations.
    ISBN 978-1-4408-3217-8 (3 volume set : alk. paper) — ISBN 978-1-4408-3218-5 (ebook) 1. Gun control—United States—History. 2. Firearms ownership—Government policy—United States—History. 3. Firearms—United States—History. 4. Firearms—Law and legislation—United States—History. I. Utter, Glenn H.
  HV7436.G877185 2016
  363.330973—dc23   2015018600

ISBN: 978-1-4408-3217-8
EISBN: 978-1-4408-3218-5

20 19 18 17 16   1 2 3 4 5

This book is also available on the World Wide Web as an eBook.
Visit www.abc-clio.com for details.

Praeger
An Imprint of ABC-CLIO, LLC

ABC-CLIO, LLC
130 Cremona Drive, P.O. Box 1911
Santa Barbara, California 93116-1911

This book is printed on acid-free paper ∞
Manufactured in the United States of America

Contents

Preface

The topic of gun rights and gun control continues to attract the attention of a large segment of the population, composed first of those who, motivated by self-defense concerns, interest in gun collecting, participation in sports and hunting, and the all-around love of firearms (so-called hoplophilia), avidly defend the right to keep and bear arms; and second of those who, due to their concern for such unfortunate consequences of the presence of firearms as accidental and intentional gun-related injuries and deaths, and perhaps a general dislike of firearms as dangerous instruments (often called "hoplophobia"), strive to place greater restrictions on firearm purchases and possession. The larger portion of the U.S. population tends to support, rather mildly (the percentage tends to wax and wane around such events as highly publicized shootings), various limitations on firearm ownership and use, although the proportion of the general population supporting gun rights has tended to increase in recent years.

Some individuals couldn't imagine owning, let alone carrying, a firearm, while others would reject any notion of being without their gun(s). Recently a friend commented that he wouldn't consider leaving home without a handgun (no wonder avid gun rights advocates are so concerned about instituting state reciprocity laws that recognize the concealed carry permits of other states). He mentioned his discomfort at social gatherings where others expressed a strong aversion to guns and support for gun control. He would remain silent, apparently content that as long as he wasn't hindered in possessing and carrying a firearm, he didn't feel compelled to disclose his own views about the advantages of gun ownership. Conversely, undoubtedly others with less attachment to firearms have experienced annoying conversations with highly committed gun rights supporters. In either circumstance, there is likely little worthwhile discussion.

Pro–gun rights advocates have come to abide by the adage that the best defense is a good offense. At the state level, legislatures continue to approve legislation, such as concealed carry provisions and stand-your-ground laws, that broadens gun rights. Recently legislators in several states have engaged in efforts to expand the locations, including university campuses, where concealed weapons may be carried. In Texas, for instance, newly elected governor Greg Abbott indicated his willingness to sign any concealed carry bill passed by the legislature even if the legislation does not grant individual universities the authority to prohibit concealed carry on campus. When the legislature in 2015 sent him a concealed carry bill, Abbott quickly signed it. The Florida legislature also has considered legislation to legalize concealed carry on state university campuses, and the Montana legislature has approved an on-campus gun bill. At the urging of gun rights groups, Texas legislators in the 2015 session debated a controversial bill to allow openly carrying firearms in public, a proposal about which gun control advocates as well as some gun rights supporters expressed reservations.

Groups advocating gun control measures, although usually being outspent and outmaneuvered by the National Rifle Association and its efficient lobbying structure, as well as by other gun rights organizations, have adapted their goals and strategies to increase the chance of victory. In the 2014 Washington State election, gun control organizations were able to place on the ballot—and 60 percent of voters approved—an initiative requiring criminal background checks on all firearms sales in the state. Organizations supporting gun control reportedly plan to use this state-by-state strategy, also employed successfully by the marriage equality (same-gender marriage) movement, to achieve further victories, especially in states like Nevada, Maine, and Oregon that allow policy measures on the ballot.

These instances of political action indicate that firearms policy continues to be a focus of interest groups and government officials, and that several issues remain at the forefront of policy making. The essays in these three volumes provide in-depth treatments of the more significant contemporary issues, including firearms trafficking (the illegal gun trade), recent court decisions involving the right to keep and bear arms, the import and export of firearms and the United Nations Small Arms Treaty, the relationship between suicide and the availability of firearms, guns in the public schools, proposals to permit concealed carry of firearms on college and university campuses, the legal use of firearms for self-defense (including stand-your-ground laws and their consequences), the domestic threat of terrorist attacks and the availability of firearms to those on the terrorist watch list, and the effectiveness of criminal background check policies in reducing crime rates.

A major objective of these essays is to encourage consideration of policies that may gain common agreement among gun rights supporters and those advocating certain additional gun control measures. These detailed treatments of important topics are valuable to a wide readership, including researchers; teachers; students at the high school, undergraduate, and graduate levels; public officials; law-enforcement personnel; and the general reader interested in gaining a further understanding of the issues. The contributors represent a wide variety of backgrounds, including various academic fields, constitutional law, and public policy. They focus on three basic subject areas: the historical background to the importance of guns in contemporary society and the significance of the so-called gun culture; the current political and cultural issues involving firearm policy; and policy recommendations. The authors offer detailed treatments of the subjects, providing a wealth of information that the reader will find useful. While recognizing the sobering reality of interest group politics, the authors provide new insights into the topics and offer novel perspectives from which to view issues and possible policy alternatives.

I wish to express my appreciation to all those who participated in preparing the individual chapters. They have done a masterful job in presenting the results of their investigations. I thank my editor, Jessica Gribble, who contributed immensely to preparing this work for publication, providing helpful assistance and offering valuable advice and encouragement. I also wish to express my appreciation to Mark A. Hazlip, who provided much-needed technical assistance in preparing the manuscript.

Glenn H. Utter

Introduction

Commentary on firearms and firearm research and policy analysis takes differing approaches and often begins either with the assumption that the possession of firearms is a basic right that should be protected, or that the presence of firearms contributes to crime and violence and therefore the right of ownership and use should be limited in various ways. One avenue of investigation involves the description of some instance in which the presence or use of guns led to a beneficial outcome, for instance when a potential victim of crime deterred a criminal by brandishing a firearm or by actually firing the weapon in self-defense. Alternatively, anecdotes describe situations in which the presence of firearms led to tragic outcomes, such as a child bringing a gun to school and shooting a classmate. Such descriptions, although compelling to the already committed, usually do not provide convincing evidence for or against any particular firearm policy.

Gun rights advocates can readily point to examples where victims of crime could have successfully warded off an attacker if only they had a firearm to use in self-defense. Gun control advocates can just as readily identify cases in which the presence of a firearm led to far greater injury than would otherwise have occurred. As an example of the former, Kate Pickert (2014) recounts an incident at Mercy Health System in Darby, Pennsylvania, that occurred in July 2014. A patient with a revolver had already shot and killed a colleague of Lee Silverman, a psychiatrist at the facility. Silverman, crouching behind an office chair, bullets having grazed his thumb and face, took a semiautomatic handgun from his pocket and shot the assailant several times. The assailant was discovered to have an additional 39 bullets still available, a strong indication that he would have continued searching for victims had not Silverman, who had a concealed weapons permit, violated Mercy Health's no-gun policy by having a handgun with him in the office.

Tom Diaz (2013), a gun control supporter, provides an example of the danger involved in the presence of firearms. He tells the story of Meleanie Hain, a Lebanon, Pennsylvania, mother and an avid supporter of gun rights, who in September 2008 caused concern among other parents when she openly carried a semiautomatic pistol to her five-year-old daughter's soccer game. Parents complained to the sheriff, who revoked Hain's concealed carry permit. Hain appealed the ruling in local court and the judge reinstated her permit, but cautioned her about the lack of common sense he perceived in her actions. Not satisfied with the restoration of her permit, Hain and her husband Scott initiated a lawsuit against the sheriff, claiming damages of $1 million for the harm done to her reputation. Apparently, all was not well with the Hain marriage. In October 2009 Scott shot and killed Meleanie and himself in a murder-suicide. Diaz states that "Meleanie's 'Baby' Glock 26 was found, fully loaded, in a backpack hanging on a hook on the back of the house's front door" (73). Diaz concludes that "Guns in the home are much more likely to be used against occupants of that home—especially women—than against invaders from the outside" (74).

Home invasions do occur, and they provide gun rights supporters with counter-examples. Mary E. Whitaker, a violinist from New York City, was a member of the symphony orchestra at Chautauqua Institution, a summer arts center in rural western New York State. In August 2014, at the end of the Chautauqua season, as she was preparing to return to New York, two men reportedly invaded Whitaker's rural summer home close to the cultural retreat (Khoury and Campbell 2014). The two men allegedly came to Mary's front door, asking to use the phone. When their true intent of robbery became clear, Whitaker resisted and one of the men, wielding a shotgun, shot her twice—in the leg and in the chest—killing the 61-year-old woman. Both men were subsequently arrested after they had already used Whitaker's credit cards about 50 miles away at stores in Erie, Pennsylvania. Residents in the area were appalled that such a crime could have occurred in the peaceful rural setting. One of the comments some residents made was that if only Mary had been armed, she could have resisted the home invasion much more successfully and possibly saved her life. Gun rights supporters use such examples to caution that anyone can end up the victim of vicious predators, and therefore the wisest strategy is to become armed and prepared to use a firearm in an emergency. Each side tends to dismiss or disregard the validity of the other's examples—which often are fraught with emotion—considering them irrelevant to the ultimate question of the place firearms do, or should, hold in contemporary society.

Comments on firearms at times originate from religious spokespersons, who also present conflicting views about the religious significance of firearms in American society. For instance, Peter W. Marty, an Evangelical Lutheran Church in America pastor and columnist for *The Lutheran* magazine, has criticized what he sees as the prevalence of a gun culture in the United States: "Among many Americans, the gun now claims nearly divine status. Our fascination with its powers has turned it into a small 'g' god. . . . You don't question a god that requires human sacrifice and guarantees your security and safety. You revere this god even when it can't sustain such guarantees. You enshrine its divinity in an impenetrable temple called 'my rights'" (Marty 2014, 3). Televangelist Pat Robertson expressed a very different view on his television program in September 2014: "Violent attacks and even deaths on church property occur far more often than people realize." But rather than calling for greater limitations on firearm ownership, Robertson advocated the arming of church members, stating: "What is the new beatitude? Blessed are the fully armed because theirs is the kingdom of Heaven" (Rothkopf 2014). Such views indicate the very different cultural perspectives that are expressed about the possession and use of firearms. When a young man fatally shot nine people (including Clementa C. Pinkney, who was the senior pastor and a state senator) at the Emanuel African Methodist Church in Charleston, South Carolina, those on opposing sides of the gun debate focused on different lessons. There was a call for greater security measures at churches but also the recognition that, were it not for a bureaucratic error, the shooter would have failed a background check and could not have purchased the handgun he used to kill nine innocent people.

An interesting tendency of both gun rights as well as gun control advocates is to assert that the other places far too much emphasis on the significance, either positive or negative, of firearms. From the perspective of gun rights supporters, gun control advocates blame firearms for much crime and violence, while from the point of view of gun control advocates, gun rights advocates consider firearms as the solution to crime against the individual. Alternatively, gun rights advocates argue that firearms are neutral instruments that can be used for good or ill, while gun control supporters claim that gun control measures, while they have been used arbitrarily to deny certain groups the right to possess firearms—as in the post–Civil War American South to deny firearm ownership to African Americans—can be instituted fairly and without adversely affecting the rights of law-abiding gun owners to reduce gun-related violent crime.

One approach to analyzing gun control and gun rights focuses on the history of firearms possession and use in the United States. Guns have played a significant role throughout the nation's history and firearms are deeply ingrained in various aspects of popular culture (Kopel 1992, 381–82). Some applaud the ways in which firearms have been interwoven with various aspects of American culture from the Revolutionary War to the present. Others recognize the violent traditions of the United States and conclude that people have as the most reasonable option to arm themselves for self-protection. A more violent society than other developed nations provides the context for the pragmatic defense strategy of firearm ownership. Alternatively, many bemoan the violence so often present in American history, which, they claim, the presence of firearms often intensified, and hence they call for a variety of restrictions in the hope of lowering the level of violence.

Gun Control and the "Slippery Slope"

In opposing further gun control legislation, gun rights advocates often invoke the "slippery slope" argument, which involves the belief that current proposals for firearm restrictions ultimately will lead to further calls for limitations and the implementation of ever more stringent controls that will inevitably end with a national gun registry and finally firearm confiscation. Hence, gun rights advocates speak of the opposition as "anti-gunners" and "gun banners" even though actual proposals fall far short of any intention to confiscate firearms from the law-abiding citizen. This slippery slope argument has at least some limited validity derived from the history of national firearms policy. The Brady Handgun Violence Prevention Act would have been far more difficult to implement had the Federal Firearms Act of 1938 and the Gun Control Act of 1968 not already established federal firearms licensees (FFLs), persons who are registered as firearms retailers to the general public. Those two prior laws initiated the standard that certain classes of people, including convicted felons and those involuntarily committed to a mental institution, should be prevented from acquiring and possessing firearms. Under the Brady Act, the federal government required these businesses to initiate background checks of potential gun purchasers in order to determine if they are restricted from acquiring a firearm.

A key to the "slippery slope" argument appears to be the fear that a regulation originally intended to limit access to firearms by certain groups of people, such as convicted felons, people who are under a court restraining order—those who both gun rights and gun control supporters agree are likely to harm themselves and others with a firearm—nonetheless not only inconveniences the law-abiding citizen, but also has the potential to be abused by restricting the right to gun ownership for groups considered "dangerous" because of their political or cultural preferences or ethnic or racial identification. For instance, William Vizzard (2000, 38) notes that early gun laws in the United States banned firearm ownership by African Americans. Charles C. W. Cooke (2014), a staff writer at the *National Review*, recently published an opinion piece claiming the importance of firearms to black liberation, and so Southern racists, recognizing the crucial value of firearms, attempted to disarm African Americans after the Civil War. New York's Sullivan Law, enacted in 1911, is often mentioned as an example of an attempt to limit gun possession among disfavored groups (in this case, especially Italian immigrants) by requiring a license to purchase and carry a handgun, a license that could be issued at the discretion of government officials. For many gun rights supporters, the establishment of background checks creates an apparatus that the unscrupulous potentially can employ to deny firearm possession to political opponents and "undesirables."

Organizations dedicated to firearm ownership have in recent decades placed increasing emphasis on firearms as a means of self-defense, not only against criminal acts but also as a protection against a tyrannical government. The history of Germany during the Weimar Republic and the Third Reich has often been cited as a caution against gun control measures in the United States. Therefore, an examination of Stephen P. Halbrook's historical analysis of gun control in Germany in the 1920s and 1930s may clarify a significant aspect of the gun rights movement's attitude toward gun control proposals in the United States, as well as the possible relevance of the German experience to the politics and culture of twenty-first-century America.

Gun Control and Nazi Germany

Halbrook's treatment (2013) of firearm policy in the Weimar Republic in Germany during the 1920s and early 1930s, and during the National Socialist regime that came to power in 1933, makes the same detailed argument that gun rights supporters have often made: gun control, however well (and perhaps naively) intentioned, can lead to disastrous consequences.

The specter of the German Third Reich often has been cited as a grave warning against gun control measures, which purportedly disarm law-abiding citizens but have little effect on gun possession among criminals and those who would threaten the liberty and independence of the general population. Halbrook, a legal expert on the Second Amendment, presents a detailed historical account of the Nazi campaign in Germany in the 1930s to disarm all who might oppose the totalitarian regime. He claims that the Nazis used the legal facade of firearm laws, enacted during the post–World War I Weimar Republic, beginning immediately after the war and continuing into the early 1930s, to accomplish their objective.

In January 1919, in the chaotic days following the armistice, the Council of People's Representatives issued the Weapons Possession Decree that called for the surrender of all firearms and ammunition (Halbrook 2013, 4), and in August 1920 the German Reichstag enacted the Law on the Disarmament of the People, which authorized a "Reichskommissar" to determine the class of military weapons that would be subject to confiscation (7). In 1928 the Weimar Republic enacted the Law on Firearms and Ammunition, the provisions of which Halbrook lists; the law "required a license to manufacture, assemble, or repair firearms and ammunition or even to reload cartridges" (16). In 1931 the German central government determined that all firearms must be registered. In March of that year, President Paul von Hindenburg signed the Law Against Unauthorized Use of Weapons, which prohibited being armed at public political assemblies and granted police wide discretion in enforcing the law (25). Halbrook concludes that this law, as did previous legislation, "served primarily to impact individual gun owners rather than to restrict politically motivated groups" (26). While citizens—including Jews—generally abided by the laws, armed groups often found it easy to circumvent the restrictions on firearm possession (13).

In January 1933 President Hindenburg, who was never a supporter of the democratic foundations of the Weimar Republic, appointed Adolf Hitler as chancellor, thus bringing the National Socialist German Workers (Nazi) party to power. The Nazis began a concerted effort to collect firearms from opponents of the new regime, including Jewish citizens, who, according to Nazi ideology, constituted a racial enemy of the German people. In March 1938 the Nazi-dominated Reichstag enacted the Weapons Law, which reinforced licensing requirements for gun possession (Halbrook 2013, 123). In October 1938 police forces throughout Germany began a campaign to disarm Jewish citizens. This process, Halbrook asserts, was made more manageable by the weapons laws instituted during the Weimar years that called for gun registration, a mandate that law-abiding citizens obeyed, but which extremist groups, including the National Socialists as well as the Communists, did not.

Given the civil disruption in Weimar Germany following World War I—including the lack of perceived legitimacy of the newly established regime; opposition to the Versailles Treaty that established the terms of peace but also placed huge financial burdens on Germany; economic hard times (inflation in the early 1920s and depression after 1929); significant support for anti-democratic political groups and deep political divisions; and an endemic anti-Semitism (Evans 2003, 93–94, 152)—the regime was unable to maintain domestic peace and grasped at ways in which to maintain order, including that passage of firearms legislation that, Halbrook, emphasizes, the National Socialist regime was able to employ in disarming political enemies after Adolf Hitler and the Nazi party took power in 1933.

Halbrook's research and analysis are well executed and deserve more detailed investigation, given the key role that conclusions drawn from historical research play in the current culture and politics of gun rights. Responding to Halbrook's discussion of gun control in the Weimar Republic and Nazi Germany, Philip J. Cook and Kristin A. Goss (2014, 172) acknowledge that, "Although historians have written volumes about the Nazi period, they have paid little or no attention to the role of gun laws in facilitating Hitler's rise and reign—a fact that is either a terrible oversight or a telling omission." Cook and Goss state that scholars and advocates on both sides of the gun debate "agree on the historical narrative" about firearms laws in pre–World War II Germany, but they draw different inferences from that narrative. For their part, Cook and Goss note that although Halbrook claims that the Nazis, using firearm registration lists developed during the Weimar Republic, were successful in disarming the regime's perceived worst enemy—Jews—Halbrook "provides no direct evidence for these assertions" (225, note 13). However, even if Halbrook's conclusion is correct about the Nazi use of firearm registration lists to disarm the population, the historical context of the Weimar Republic provides an important perspective from which to understand why political leaders instituted gun registration and why the regime ultimately failed to control the anti-democratic attacks from both right and left.

Cook and Goss comment that the extensive restrictions on gun ownership were liberalized, first in the late 1920s and subsequently by the Nazis, but that the National Socialist regime prohibited gun ownership by those considered enemies of the nation, most prominently Jews. When in 1938 a German Jewish refugee shot and killed a member of the German embassy delegation in Paris, Hitler used this event as a justification for completely prohibiting Jews from acquiring and possessing firearms. As Cook and Goss state, "Jews were ordered to surrender their weapons or be sent to a concentration camp for 20 years" (173). In fact, as Halbrook observes, even those who surrendered firearms were subject to arrest (Halbrook 2013, 147).

Cook and Goss observe that gun rights supporters draw a clear lesson—a corollary to the slippery slope argument—from the German experience:

if a democracy requires its citizens to register their firearms, a future dictatorial regime can use that information to disarm any individual or group opposing the government. The conclusion for gun rights advocates is that a key deterrent to authoritarian government is a populace that is armed and determined to protect their basic rights, and that the democratic nature of a government is no assurance that gun control measures will not be used at some future time to subjugate the population. Cook and Goss respond that a small minority, such as the Jewish residents in Nazi Germany, cannot defend themselves against the police, the army, and well-organized paramilitary groups if at least a significant segment of the overall population is unwilling to join the resistance. They further assert that "no direct evidence has been presented [by Halbrook] that the Nazis used a gun registry as a road map for raids on Jewish homes, which were often concentrated in Jewish quarters anyway and thus easily identified for mass sweeps" (174). They conclude that "a well-armed and vigilant citizenry" would likely not be able to compete against much better armed military and paramilitary groups (175). Nonetheless, organized paramilitary groups in various parts of the world have been able to employ tactics and use sophisticated weaponry to challenge the established military and police forces. Such successful opposition depends upon access to types of military hardware that any society might not wish to allow the general citizenry or any organized militia groups to possess, hardware that exceeds the potency of handguns and long guns that private citizens generally own.

Cook and Goss refer briefly to the context in which gun laws were enacted in Germany during the 1920s and early 1930s, which involved polarized political conflict, often accompanied by forms of violence such as assassination, that a weak governing system proved unable to control. This observation may be crucial to fully understanding the background to the firearms laws. The firearms restrictions did not arise *sui generis* but were obviously intended as an instrument for reducing the level of violent confrontation among groups opposed to the Weimar regime, and following the National Socialist rise to power, as a means of reducing the ability of enemies, real or concocted, to challenge the regime through the use of violence.

Reflecting on this cautionary history lesson—that "a well-meaning liberal republic enacted repressive firearm prohibitions that would be highly useful to dictatorship" (Halbrook 2013, 217)—it may be asked what policies might have been more effective in protecting an obviously highly tenuous democracy in defending the nation against extremists on the political right and left who were equally dedicated to the demise of the frail Weimar Republic. Weapons are the obvious means of participating effectively in violent conflict. It may be asked whether doing nothing about the possession of firearms except attempting to punish their violent use by extreme groups would have made a difference to the disintegration of German society and the descent of the political system into constant violent battles among competing anti-regime groups who were fighting the existing authorities as well as each other.

In order to understand the efforts of the Weimar Republic and the subsequent National Socialist regime to control firearm possession, it may help to focus on the historical context in which firearm policy was being made. Richard M. Watt (1968) provides a detailed account—coinciding in many respects to Halbrook's depiction—of the violent conflicts that occurred just following World War I that may help in understanding, if not justifying, the Weimar regime's desire to limit firearm possession, and to acquire, through registration, information about who owned guns.

In January 1919, following Germany's military surrender, various left-wing groups, including the Communists, concluded that the time was ripe for revolution. On the right, former army personnel formed Free Corps paramilitary groups, with little or no control from the new government that German officials were creating at Weimar (Watt 1968, 297). An insurrection developed in Bremen as well as other port cities in early January 1919. According to Watt's account, rebel leaders armed the revolutionary workers and called a general strike. Red Guards blocked the docks and refused to allow delivery of food shipments from the United States. To break the revolutionaries' hold on the city, on February 2 a small contingent of Free Corps troops began an attack. With superior equipment, the troops defeated the left government and reopened the port (299). The revolutionary forces around Germany continued their efforts to gain control of cities and local governments. According to Watt, workers in Halle established "a revolutionary council under an Independent Socialist leader, disarmed the police and distributed their weapons among the proletariat" (301). A Free Corps contingent entered the city, only to be confronted by workers, who fought with the troops and attempted to take their rifles and immobilize wagons that carried machine guns (301). After workers killed a Free Corps officer, Watt reports, the Free Corps leaders "ordered troops into the street to kill anyone caught with a firearm" (302).

Watt states that the Communist leadership concluded that, with the National Assembly progressing toward completion of work on the Weimar constitution, and with Free Corps units increasing in strength, the rebels should not attempt to use military action—which would only invite armed attacks—but should rely instead on the general strike—a strategy that communist leader Rosa Luxemburg initially formulated in 1906

(Luxemburg 1971)—as their main weapon, hoping that Free Corps units would not fire on unarmed workers. However, the Communist leadership had little control over the rebel workers, who took up arms, setting up machine guns at subway entrances in Berlin. Although Communist leaders tried to persuade the rebels to lay down their arms, the revolutionaries ignored the entreaties. Consequently, the government was presented with the justification they needed to act. Free Corps leader Gustav Noske received broad authority over Berlin, and as they advanced, Free Corps members fired on any workers who resisted. Noske declared that "Any person who bears arms against government troops will be shot on the spot" (quoted in Watt 1968, 307; Halbrook 2013, 4). Watt states that many German workers possessed firearms, acquired "more or less legitimately" immediately after the war, which made them targets of the Free Corps when the Guard Cavalry Rifle Division extended Noske's order to include "anyone who possessed a firearm, whether in rebellion or not" (Watt 1968, 307; Halbrook 2013, 5).

Historian Richard J. Evans (2003) also provides a detailed account of the tragic events in Germany following the nation's defeat in World War I that have a bearing on the policies instituted regarding firearm possession. The Communists under the leadership of Vladimir Ilyich Lenin had seized power in Russia, and the Communist party in Germany endeavored to do the same in Germany. Evans observes: "The middle and upper classes were alarmed by the radical rhetoric of the Communists and saw their counterparts in Russia lose their property and disappear into the torture chambers and prison camps of the Cheka" (Evans 2003, 57). Supporters of representative democracy were aware that the Russian Communists were engaged in "suppressing human rights, dismantling representative institutions, and abolishing civil freedoms" (57). Members of the Social Democratic Party, who played a major role in the formation of the new German government following the war, feared that the Communists would follow the same terror tactics being employed in Russia (74). The Social Democrats, "afraid for their lives" and wishing to prevent anarchy, supported the formation of "heavily armed paramilitary bands" known as the Free Corps (74). Evans comments that these paramilitary groups, although doing the bidding of the Social Democrats, also targeted the Social Democrats themselves, and were open to killing anyone considered a traitor to the nation (75).

Evans writes that both the Communists and the emerging National Socialists attempted to enforce a ban on the private possession of firearms. In Bavaria in 1919, the Communists attempted to establish the beginnings of the "Bolshevization" of Europe (159). They declared that workers were to receive military training and that "weapons in private possession had to be surrendered on pain of death" (159). In attempting to regain control, the Free Corps announced that "anyone in Munich found bearing arms would immediately be shot," a declaration that led the Munich workers' and soldiers' councils to pass a resolution of no-confidence in the Communists (159). Gun battles occurred in Munich and other cities.

The Communist Party failed to gain power, and as a result the leadership adopted a more moderate strategy during the mid-1920s. But by the end of the decade, Evans comments, the party returned to a more radical position and remained uncompromisingly opposed to the Weimar Republic, labeling it a fascist regime. The mainstream members of the dominant Social Democratic party continued to fear that the Communists would follow the same terror tactics being employed in Russia (74). As the Depression that began in 1929 grew worse, Communist groups established "red districts," such as in Wedding, an area of Berlin. Anyone who entered the district and was suspected of being a brownshirt (a member of Hitler's National Socialist party) could be beaten up and threatened with guns (237).

Although both Communist and Free Corps groups employed firearms in their violent clashes, Evans notes that the Communist movement, composed mainly of unemployed persons, lacked the financial resources to compete effectively with National Socialists and other conservative and nationalist groups in acquiring weaponry and other resources that could be used against the opposition. The Weimar Republic, supported by the Social Democrats, remained the enemy of both left and right. The passage of weapons laws can be understood in the context of this armed struggle over the control of the nation, with supporters of the existing regime attempting to deal with a political situation that at times closely resembled chaos. Adding to the impotence of the regime was what Evans terms "the ultra-conservative nationalist judiciary's refusal to pass meaningful sentences on stormtroopers arrested for acts of violence" (2015, 51). The regime often proved ineffective in attempting to maintain order when conservative judges handed down light sentences to those stormtroopers prosecuted for committing acts of violence. Adolf Hitler himself became a beneficiary of judicial leniency following his failed attempt to overthrow the German government in November 1923. Although participants had shot and killed four policemen in their treasonable revolt (an offense that could have meant the death penalty), Hitler served less than one year of a five-year sentence.

Had the Communists possessed greater resources to combat the government forces and right-wing militia groups, that situation might have resulted in even greater levels of violence and possibly the disarming of the right-wing groups and all those suspected of anti-Communist sympathies, for certainly disarming the enemy in an armed conflict constitutes a major goal of the victor.

The right of each citizen to possess firearms—for various reasons, including sport and self-protection as well as defense against a regime that attempts to violate the rights of the people—might possibly be most advantageous in a society in which competing political groups already accept the legitimacy of their political opponents and are willing to respect the rights of all, rather than in the turbulent conditions in Germany of the 1920s. Hans J. Morgenthau made the perceptive comment that a weak government can more easily lead to dictatorship than a more stable and authoritative governing system. Morgenthau, a Jewish scholar who fled Nazi Germany in the early 1930s, undoubtedly had in mind the rise of fascist regimes in Europe during the 1920s and early 1930s when he made that claim.

Morgenthau commented in a lecture on the consequences of a government that fails to govern effectively: "Totalitarianism, especially if you think of its German and Italian examples, has not grown out of a concentration of power in the hands of the government so that the government amasses more and more power until finally it is in the full possession of it. To the contrary, it has been the result of weak governments, of governments that were unable to govern and were replaced through the democratic process with people, with movements, and charismatic leaders who promised, first of all, that they would govern" (Lang 2004, 79–80). Morgenthau argued that societies in which the governing system is ineffective in controlling societal conflict will be susceptible to a dominant group that restores order on its own terms and with the blessing of a large portion of the population who fear a condition resembling Thomas Hobbes's state of nature, potentially a war of all against all, or more accurately a situation involving conflict among irreconcilable groups with the general population on the sidelines, suffering the consequences of armed conflict. Hobbes envisaged a slippery slope of another kind, in which the lack of a widely recognized sovereign authority would lead to the disintegration of the political system as well as the society it is supposed to protect and preserve (Hobbes 1958, 143).

Given the civil disruptions in Germany during the Weimar period, it should not be surprising that the Nazis, when they gained power, wished to disarm their enemies, real (the Communists) or fabricated (Jewish citizens). Far left and far right groups, certainly dedicated to destroying a government they despised, but also knowing that the government was too weak to maintain order, faced a classic case of the prisoner's dilemma

(Rapoport 1966, 128–132; Rapoport and Chamma 1965): to disarm, it could be argued, would likely be to the advantage of both left and right because they both would avoid the destructiveness of violent confrontation. But if one side decides to obey the government's edict to disarm, its enemies will acquire a major advantage in the struggle for power if they refuse to surrender their weapons. In order for disarmament to become a rational strategy, the governing authority would have to possess the ability and the will to enforce mutual disarmament, which was obviously not the case in post–World War I Germany. In such a deplorable situation, for the average citizen to obey a law that the regime could not enforce exposed them (especially Jewish citizens), as Halbrook details, to the whims of the ultimate winner of the battle between left and right. However, it is doubtful whether the uniquely extreme circumstances of Germany in the first half of the twentieth century can provide a guideline for weapons policy in the twenty-first century United States.

Gun Control Advocacy versus Gun Rights

Gun control advocates often focus on such issues as the potential danger of firearms in the home, including the greater probability of accidents and suicide. Although the number of firearm accidents, while often tragic, has declined significantly in recent years (National Shooting Sports Foundation 2013), suicides account for more than half and as many as two-thirds of firearm deaths each year (Nocera 2014, A21). However, gun rights advocates insist that a stored and locked gun—a condition that gun control advocates recommend—provides little protection if the resident faces intruders intent on doing harm. Also, a handgun provides little protection if the owner leaves the home without carrying the means of defense.

Jeffrey R. Snyder (1993) provides a classic example of the defense of the right to possess and especially to carry firearms (particularly handguns) for self-defense against criminal acts. Snyder offers an argument that sounds much like a variant of blaming the victim: "Crime is rampant because the law-abiding, each of us, condone it, excuse it, permit it, submit to it. We permit and encourage it because we do not fight back, immediately, then and there, where it happens. . . . We are a nation of cowards and shirkers" (Snyder 1993, 42). The responsibility for one's own self-defense is based on an essentially libertarian position that the police are not "personal body guards" and that ultimately we cannot expect other persons to risk their lives to protect us when we will not assume the moral duty to protect our own safety (43). How national defense coincides with this argument is not completely clear. A society expects military personnel to risk their lives for the safety of the country as a whole. Perhaps it can be argued that everyone (except the infirm and aged) can be called on to take up arms and therefore military service represents an exception to the libertarian position of limited government control over the lives of individual persons. However, such an argument would seem to carry less weight with the establishment of a professional military in that only a small minority of citizens risks their lives to the benefit of all others.

Snyder calls most gun control proposals "hokum," including the Brady Handgun Violence Prevention Act, which had just been passed when Snyder wrote his article. He dismisses the criminal background check policy as ineffective, in part because "medical records are not public documents" (45), although the states and the federal government more recently have attempted to institute procedures to determine those individuals who should be denied the right to acquire and possess firearms due to mental incapacity, procedures that nonetheless do not violate the privacy rights of individuals when weighed against the benefits for society as a whole.

Any person who fails to arm himself against possible criminal acts, Snyder asserts, "shows contempt of God's gift of life" (53) and fails to meet the duties to family and community. Such a person "proclaims himself mentally and morally deficient." Even though there is a wealth of firearms among the civilian population, Snyder argues that law-abiding citizens nonetheless "do not go about armed" (53). He ultimately recommends federal legislation that supersedes all state and local laws by establishing a "privilege and immunity of citizenship" to carry firearms—in other words, a law that establishes a national right to carry concealed weapons. Arguments such as that presented by Snyder have proliferated in recent years and are reflected in the U.S. Supreme Court decisions *District of Columbia v. Heller* (554 US 570; 2008) and *McDonald v. Chicago* (561 US 742; 2010), in which the Court, in 5–4 decisions, interpreted the Second Amendment as guaranteeing an individual the right to keep and bear arms.

Gun rights advocates, in addition to focusing on the self-protection value of firearms, take a lesson from such cases as Germany during the Weimar Republic and the National Socialist regime, further claiming that firearm ownership by the broad citizen population constitutes a crucial line of defense against a government that has become tyrannical. Some advocates even argue that the Second Amendment to the U.S. Constitution includes a right to insurrection against a government that no longer governs in the interests of the people. Certainly questions far beyond the right to keep and bear arms must be addressed when dealing not only with the right of self-defense against individual aggressors, but also the notion of a right to employ firearms to defend oneself against the government—in other words, the right to rebel. Critics of this view note the difficulties involved in determining what circumstances would justify such rebellion, especially if each individual retains the full gamut of rights claimed for the Second Amendment. English philosopher John Locke developed a theory of revolution that suggested a justified revolt against the sovereign required the support of a majority of the population (Lloyd Thomas 1995, 83–87). The American Civil War might be considered (and certainly is regarded by some, who term the conflict a war of Northern aggression) as a situation in which citizens supposedly took up arms against a government that was violating the rights (of at least a portion) of the population—Southern free whites.

As the Supreme Court decisions in *Heller* and *McDonald* indicate, recognizing an individual right to possess firearms leaves open the question of what limitations might be placed on that right, just as the protection of free speech rights in the First Amendment does not prohibit some level of restrictions on freedom of speech, as, for instance, in cases of libel and slander. Some gun rights advocates regard the Second Amendment, not the First, as the most important right contained in the Bill of Rights, for without the capacity for self-defense, they argue that freedom of speech, the press, and religion come to naught. A more circumspect gun rights supporter might consider that, without the First Amendment freedoms, the defense of the Second Amendment could prove to be extremely difficult. A quote from the Russian Communist leader Vladimir Ilyich Lenin, a supporter of neither free speech nor gun rights, is revealing: "Why should freedom of speech and freedom of the press be allowed? Why should a government which is doing what it believes to be right allow itself to be criticized? It would not allow opposition by lethal weapons. Ideas are much more fatal things than guns. Why should any man be allowed to buy a printing press and disseminate pernicious opinions calculated to embarrass the government?" (Quoted in Bettmann 1987, 102). Just as Halbrook has focused historical research on the limitation of firearm ownership in Germany during the 1920s and 1930s, historians could (as some researchers already have) focus attention on Nazi attempts to outlaw radios and radio transmitters as well as printing presses, and the sanctions suffered by those who violated such restrictions. The preeminent position of Joseph Goebbles as the minister of propaganda in Nazi Germany also indicates the importance of controlling expression in a totalitarian regime. The day-to-day inundation of the German population with the Nazi ideology of race, politics, and culture was considered vital to maintaining popular support for the regime.

Firearm policy certainly must take into account the notion of individual rights as well as the Second Amendment foundation, revered by many. But policy formation must also be informed by the context in which that right is exercised and the actual consequences of the right to possess firearms. However, measuring those consequences has not proved to be an easy task.

Empirical Research

Lewis F. Richardson (1960), a physicist who conducted research in mathematical physics and meteorology and was also committed to pacifism, extended his research interests to efforts to apply quantitative methods to gain an understanding of the causes of, and ultimately to control, violent conflict. His ultimate goal was to reduce the level of violence within societies as well as internationally. Through the use of quantitative methods, he strived to gain knowledge of the causes of conflict and possible ways of lessening violent events. He introduced his treatment of "deadly quarrels" with a Socratic dialogue:

POLITICUS: What are you trying to prove?
RESEARCHER: In social affairs it is immoral to try to prove.
FIDOR: Yes. One should have faith that God will provide. He that cometh to God must believe that he is and that he is a rewarder of them that diligently seek him.
RESEARCHER: I meant that in social affairs where proof is seldom rigid, and where prejudice so easily misleads, it is best not to start with a fixed opinion. He that comes to research must be in doubt, and must humble himself before the facts, earnestly desiring to know what they are, and what they signify.

Investigators of various aspects of firearm possession and use attempt to employ the sort of objective research techniques thought to characterize the scientific enterprise, but often scholars come to different conclusions about the benefits and dangers of firearms. Although guns can be employed to achieve good as well as evil ends, which can in part explain these conflicting results, this phenomenon also can result, in some cases, from the emphasis researchers place on topics that are determined by their interest in the right to own firearms for sport, self-defense, or the protection of liberty, or on the objective of limiting the perceived ill effects of the use of firearms-related violent acts such as physical assault, murder, or suicide.

Researchers have criticized others' research, criticism resulting in part from different emphases regarding the harmful or beneficial consequences of firearm ownership and use. The normative scientific goal of adhering to objective research methods arguably tends to become confounded with other preferences. Charges of dishonesty aside, researchers arrive at differing conclusions that place them on a continuum from avid supporters of the right to own firearms to advocates of stringent government control of firearm possession and use.

Measuring the effects of policy changes (such as the Brady Handgun Violence Prevention Act that mandated background checks of potential firearms purchasers, or state concealed carry laws) can be methodologically complex and difficult to confirm. Testing the null hypothesis of no effect is considered subject to two possible errors: (1) concluding that there actually is a positive effect when in fact there is none (type I, or α, error); and (2) failing to reject the null hypothesis when in fact the policy change did have a positive effect (type II, or β, error) (Blalock 1979, 109–110). Statisticians recognize a third kind of error: "the researcher rejects a false null hypothesis but improperly infers the relationship between the variables" (Zeller and Carmines 1978, 203). For instance, Ian Ayres and John J. Donohue III (2003) examine John Lott and David Mustard's (1997) conclusion from their investigation of data from counties across the United States that "state laws enabling citizens to carry concealed handguns had led to *reduced* crime." After re-analyzing the data, Ayres and Donohue conclude that "state-specific estimates generated on the 1977–1997 county data are more supportive of the view that shall-issue [concealed carry] laws increase crime than that they decrease it" (1286). Hence, Ayres and Donohue are claiming that Lott and Mustard have committed a type III error.

A related dilemma for researchers is that a discovered correlation (for instance, between liberalized concealed carry laws and an increase or decrease in violent crime) may prove to be spurious; there may be other variables that intervened, causing the effect, and therefore the correlation between the two initial variables does not reflect the true causal path. Researchers employ sophisticated statistical models in their search for causation in order to control for such intervening variables.

Arguments between gun rights supporters and gun control advocates tend to provide differing interpretations of the effects of current firearms laws. Dennis Henigan (2009, 144) quotes Wayne LaPierre, executive vice president of the National Rifle Association, as referring to "powerful, existing Federal firearms laws" (LaPierre 1997, 10), a position that clearly suggests that no additional legislation is needed to deal with the misuse of firearms. At other times, gun rights supporters argue that existing legislation is ineffective in keeping firearms out of the hands of criminals as well as those who would cause harm to themselves and to others, and that additional legislation would not fare any better than enforcing present laws in controlling the illegal use of firearms but would only add further restrictions on the Second Amendment rights of law-abiding citizens. Is it that firearm laws are ineffective in controlling criminal activity and therefore only limit the right of law-abiding citizens to acquire and possess firearms; or that firearms laws currently are sufficient, if properly enforced, to deal with criminal use of guns? In either case, additional legislation regulating firearms sales and possession are rejected as futile attempts to effect greater crime control, or are not required because existing laws and regulations, if properly enforced, will prove satisfactory. Gun control advocates respond that current laws are weakly written enforcement tools and are riddled with loopholes that result in inefficiency and limited effectiveness. Efforts to disentangle these arguments are certainly difficult, especially when policy affects the interests of groups within society that have conflicting goals and points of view.

Outline of the Book

The three volumes of this work are divided into three major categories: first, the historical and cultural background to the current policy debates over firearms; second, the current cultural issues related to firearms; and third, contemporary controversies over the place of firearms in the United States and policy recommendations for either limiting or expanding the right to possess and carry firearms.

The first volume begins with Tom Lansford's exploration of the place of guns in the United States from colonial times to the Civil War, focusing on the interaction between the presence of firearms and significant events in American history. Keith Rollin Eakins and Loren Gatch continue the background investigation, describing the introduction of gun control policy at the national level from the early twentieth century to the present, concluding that the results are "a murky clash of symbolisms driven by anecdote and periodic tragedies," with the effectiveness of measures at the national level difficult to determine. Robert H. Wood continues the discussion by analyzing the history of firearm policy at the state and local levels, where most of firearms legislation, such as concealed carry regulations, has been instituted. Wood also explores the influence that recent mass shootings have had on the willingness of state legislatures to introduce additional firearms-related measures. Nicholas J. Johnson, in his analysis of the potential effects of the *District of Columbia v. Heller* (2008) Supreme Court decision, provides a caution to gun rights advocates. Johnson argues that, given lower court interpretations of the right to keep and bear arms following the Court's decision in *United States v. Miller* (1939), lower federal and state courts may interpret the Supreme Court's decision in *Heller* in such a way as to allow gun restrictions. Zachary Elkins, in his comparative analysis of gun rights in national constitutions, concludes that constitutional gun rights are "near extinction" and that the U.S. Constitution's Second Amendment protection of the right to bear arms represents an exception, and perhaps an anachronism. Roger Pauly recounts the development of the firearms industry in the United States, focusing on the interaction between the "heroic" inventors of firearms and the generosity of the federal government in financially supporting the manufacture of firearms. Nonetheless, as Pauly emphasizes, firearms companies continue to advertize the individualistic spirit supposedly behind the development of firearms manufacturing in the United States. Along with the development of the firearms industry, the tradition of firearms ownership, and the emergence in the early twentieth century of concerns about the misuse of guns developed two opposing groups of organizations: those dedicated to the preservation of gun rights and those committed to placing controls on the possession and use of firearms. David T. Hardy recounts the evolution of the National Rifle Association from an organization originally concerned with improving marksmanship to a highly successful interest devoted to the Second Amendment right to keep and bear arms. Hardy also examines the development of other gun rights organizations that have arisen, some of which have attempted to challenge the position of the National Rifle Association as the preeminent protector of the rights of gun owners. Walter F. Carroll examines the development and activities of organizations that support greater controls on the purchase and possession of firearms. Although not nearly as well funded as the NRA, such organizations nonetheless have recorded some successes in instituting control measures, the most notable example being the Brady Campaign to Prevent Gun Violence and its efforts to pass the Brady Handgun Violence Protection Act of 1993. Carroll notes the shift in tactics that gun control groups have made by emphasizing gun violence as a public health issue (a topic that Matthew A. Butkus examines in detail in chapter 14). Jason Sides, James Vanderleeuw, and Joanna Joseph, in their chapter on the Bureau of Alcohol, Tobacco, Firearms, and Explosives, focus on the ATF's "Operation Fast and Furious," the failed attempt to track illegal transfer of firearms from U.S. dealers to Mexican drug trafficking networks. The authors conclude that more effective strategies must be developed by the U.S. and Mexican governments in order to stem the flow of illegal arms into Mexico.

The second volume begins with David B. Kopel's detailed examination of efforts of the international community to establish gun control measures. Kopel presents an extensive list of national protections of human rights, including the right to arms, the right to privacy and the protection of the home, and the right to defense against tyranny. Henry B. Sirgo discusses the involvement of the United States in the import and export of firearms, noting both the support for imports as well as opposition, in part to protect the domestic companies manufacturing firearms. Sirgo discusses the recent United Nations Arms Trade Treaty, which the NRA and other gun rights organizations have strongly opposed, and presents the major provisions of that international agreement. Ted G. Jelen investigates the level of firearm ownership in the United States. Jelen notes that although overall firearm ownership has declined in recent years, such ownership has increased slightly in the twenty-first century. He concludes that gun owners "are disproportionately likely to be male, older, and less educated, to live in the South, and in rural areas." Gun owners are also more likely to be political conservatives and hunters, and to be more concerned about personal safety than non-gun owners. Saundra J. Ribando and Amanda J. Reinke discuss the convoluted history of militia movements and their relationship to firearm ownership. Militias have a long tradition in the United States, and in the last 20 years such organizations have arisen that are willing to challenge the authority of government officials at all levels. The attachment of such groups to firearms raises fears among many about the potential for violence among those opposed to many of the cultural changes occurring in the country. Matthew A. Butkus deals with public health approaches to firearms, an area of gun violence investigation that is especially controversial among gun rights advocates, given that much of the research focuses on the deaths and injuries caused by firearms and on ways of reducing that violence through government action. Elizabeth Parks Aronson and Maxwell T. Smith provide an extensive treatment of suicide, the leading cause of firearm-related deaths. They note the need for further research into the possible impact that restrictions on the purchase and possession of firearms have on the rate of gun-related suicides. Simon J. Bronner offers a detailed discussion of hunting traditions and culture in the United States, and examines the cultural divisions between hunting enthusiasts and anti-hunting and animal rights advocates and groups. Bronner discerns a broader culture war between "tradition and local-centered worldviews" on the one hand and the "universalist, or cosmopolitan, call for change" on the other that parallels the opposing views of gun rights advocates and gun control supporters. Awareness of this "cultural confrontation" can aid in understanding the often deep divisions on the firearms issue. Bronner furnishes a post-script to this previously published chapter that deals with controversial policies that some state governments have instituted to encourage the sport of hunting.

Mary Zeiss Stange provides a detailed discussion of patterns of gun ownership among women and the benefits that women can achieve through firearm ownership, especially for self-defense and recreation. Although Bronner discusses hunting as primarily a male-dominated activity, Stange emphasizes the greater participation in recent years of women in the hunting culture. Stange suggests that, culturally and symbolically, guns are a "great equalizer" and a model for social and psychological empowerment. Joan Burbick presents reflections on the cultural implications of gun shows gleaned from visits to these highly popular marketing events in several states. Burbick identifies in the attraction of firearms a preference for individual rights interpreted as a patriotic duty that replaces the republican commitment to community, a theme on which she elaborates in *Gun Show Nation* (2006). Burbick provides a postscript to this chapter, which was originally published prior to the U.S. Supreme Court cases *District of Columbia v. Heller* (2008) and *McDonald v. City of Chicago* (2010) in which the Court ruled that the Second Amendment guarantees a private individual the right to possess firearms for self-protection.

The third volume begins with Ronald D. Stephens's (director of the National School Safety Center) discussion of firearms in schools. Stephens presents recommendations for preventing and dealing with gun-related incidents on school property. Robert L. Spinks and Michael C. Powell extend Ronald Stephens's discussion of guns in schools by investigating the topic of concealed carry of firearms on university campuses. They discuss concealed carry from the perspective of law enforcement officers, focusing especially on the difficulties that police officers may face in a possible "active shooter" incident on campus. Glenn E. Meyer presents the results of psychological experiments concerning the legal use of differing types of firearms in self-defense situations and emphasizes the possible defenses for such use in the court system. Saundra J. Ribando and Amanda J. Reinke examine the connection between terrorism and the acquisition and ownership of firearms. They discuss the advantages and disadvantages of introducing further policies to deal with the threat of terrorism, such as expanding the category of those prohibited from purchasing firearms to include individuals on the terrorist watch list in order to prevent those persons intent on committing terrorist acts from acquiring firearms. Mary Anne Franks examines the adoption in 33 states of so-called stand-your-ground laws, which, she notes, were intended to "clarify and strengthen the concept of justifiable self-defense and enhance public safety," but instead, she argues, promote "the use of deadly force as a first, instead of a last, resort." Franks states that such laws have been of no benefit to women, who are often the victims of rape, stalking, harassment, and various forms of abuse. Sean Maddan examines various strategies—some promising and others not so promising—to reduce firearm-related violence. Among possible policies that may be effective, Maddan mentions directed police patrols, tracking private sales of firearms, personalizing weapons, and improving the collection of data from criminal justice agencies. Glenn H. Utter examines the background check system established by the Brady Handgun Violence Prevention Act of 1993 and proposals for making the system more effective, including the improvement of data collection from the states and expanding background checks to cover not only sales by federally licensed firearms dealers but also private sales and transfers. The third volume concludes with a dialogue between a gun control supporter—Paul Helmke, former president of the Brady Campaign to Prevent Gun Violence—and Richard Feldman, president of the Independent Firearm Owners Association. Helmke and Feldman offer, from their differing perspectives, possible strategies to achieve agreement on the issues raised in the debate about firearms in American society.

References

Ayres, Ian, and John J. Donohue III. 2003. "Shooting Down the 'More Guns, Less Crime' Hypothesis." *Stanford Law Review* 55: 1193–1312.

Bettmann, Otto L. 1987. *The Delights of Reading: Quotes, Notes and Anecdotes*. Boston, MA: David R. Godine Publisher.

Blalock, Hubert M., Jr. 1979. *Social Statistics*. New York: McGraw Hill.

Burbick, Joan. 2006. *Gun Show Nation: Gun Culture and American Democracy*. New York: The Free Press.

Cook, Philip J., and Kristin A. Goss. 2014. *The Gun Debate: What Everybody Needs to Know*. New York, Oxford University Press.

Cooke, Charles C. W. 2014. "Do Black People Have Equal Gun Rights?" *New York Times* (October 26): SR4.

Diaz, Tom. 2013. *The Last Gun*. New York: The New Press.

Evans, Richard J. 2003. *The Coming of the Third Reich*. New York: Penguin Books.

Evans, Richard J. 2015. *The Third Reich in History and Memory*. New York: Oxford University Press.

Halbrook, Stephen P. 2013. *Gun Control in the Third Reich: Disarming the Jews and Enemies of the State*. Oakland, CA: The Independent Institute.

Henigan, Dennis A. 2009. *Lethal Logic: Exploding the Myths That Paralyze American Gun Policy*. Washington, DC: Potomac Books.

Hobbes, Thomas. 1958 (1651). *Leviathan, Parts I and II*. New York: Bobbs-Merrill.

Khoury, Lisa, and Shawn Campbell. 2014. "Two Arrested in Death of Chautauqua Violinist." *Buffalo News* (August 22). http://www.buffalonews.com/city-region/chautauqua-county/two-arrested-in-death-of-chautauqua-violinist-2014822 (accessed December 29, 2014).

Kopel, David B. 1992. *The Samuri, the Mountie, and the Cowboy: Should America Adopt the Gun Controls of Other Democracies?* Buffalo, NY: Prometheus Books.

Lang, Anthony F., Jr. 2004. *Political Theory and International Affairs: Hans J. Morgenthau on Aristotle's The Politics*. Westport, CT: Praeger.

LaPierre, Wayne. 1997. "Standing Guard." *The American Rifleman* (May), 10.

Lott, John R., Jr., and David B. Mustard. 1997. "Crime, Deterrence, and Right-to-Carry Concealed Weapons." *Journal of Legal Studies* 26(1).

Lloyd Thomas, David A. 1995. *Lock on Government*. London: Routledge.

Luxemburg, Rosa. 1971 (1906). *The Mass Strike, the Political Party, and the Trade Unions*. New York: Harper Torchbooks.

Marty, Peter W. 2014. "Guns in a Culture of Idolatry." *The Lutheran* (November): 3.

McGrath. 2014. "Confiscating Liberty: Review of Stephen P. Halbrook." *Chronicles* (September): 26–28.

National Shooting Sports Foundation. 2013. "Firearm-Related Injury Statistics: Highlighting Declining Trends in the United States." http://www.nssf.org/PDF/research/IIR_InjuryStatistics2013.pdf (accessed February 16, 2015).

Nocera, Joe. 2014. "Guns and Public Health." *New York Times* (November 4): A21.

Pickert, Kate. 2014. "Armed America." *Time* (September 29): 28–31.

Rapoport, Anatol. 1966. *Two-Person Game Theory: The Essential Ideas*. Ann Arbor: University of Michigan Press.

Rapoport, Anatol, and Albert M. Chamma. 1965. *Prisoner's Dilemma*. Ann Arbor: University of Michigan Press.

Richardson, Lewis F. 1960. *Statistics of Deadly Quarrels*. Chicago, IL: Quadrangle Books.

Rothkopf, Joanna. 2014. "Pat Robertson: 'Blessed Are the Fully Armed.'" http://www.salon.com/2014/09/09/pat_robertson_blessed_are_the_fully_armed. (accessed December 12, 2014).

Snyder, Jeffrey B. 1993. "A Nation of Cowards." *The Public Interest* 113 (Fall): 40–55.

Vizzard, William J. 2000. *Shots in the Dark: The Policy, Politics, and Symbolism of Gun Control*. New York: Rowman and Littlefield.

Watt, Richard M. 1968. *The Kings Depart: The German Revolution and the Treaty of Versailles 1918–19*. New York: Simon and Schuster.

Zeller, Richard A., and Edward G. Carmines. 1978. *Statistical Analysis of Social Data*. Chicago, IL: Rand McNally.

CHAPTER ONE

Weapons in School

Ronald D. Stephens

Reading, writing and retaliation has become a common theme on many of our nation's campuses. Far too often this retaliation involves ducking bullets and serious violence. Students are willing to take the risk of bringing a weapon to school simply for protection, to show off or to intimidate others. Many of the former fist fights are being replaced by gunfights. Former fire drills are being replaced by crisis drills.
> —*Congressional Testimony, opening statement by Dr. Ronald Stephens before the United States Congress, October 1, 1992*

Statement of the Problem

In many ways this statement is as relevant today as it was more than two decades ago. However, new factors have emerged with respect to the types of weapons that seem to be appearing more frequently in schools. In former times, the single-shot weapon or the six-shooter was common. Now it is much more likely to be semi-automatic or military-style weapons involved in school shootings, according to reports by the FBI and other law enforcement officials. And while most gunmen act alone, sometimes the organization of the assault is much more sophisticated and carefully orchestrated. Take for instance the 2003 shooting at John McDonough High School in New Orleans, where one of the local gangs used assault-style weapons to storm a gymnasium full of students. Ten individuals conspired together to develop their assault plan for the school, including their access route, their communications plan, the identification and location of their target, the actual shooting of the target, and their escape. Not only did they successfully kill their target with multiple rounds of ammunition, three additional innocent, collateral victims were shot in the process. The high school gymnasium assault was the first "conspiracy conviction killing" in the history of the City of New Orleans. Litigation against the New Orleans Parish School Board was not finalized until 2011.

Adam Lanza, the Sandy Hook shooter who killed twenty students, six teachers, his mother, and ultimately himself, according to police investigators had voluminous amounts of information about previous school shootings, including Columbine, the October 2006 Amish schoolhouse massacre, and the February 2008 Northern Illinois University shooting. He had compiled a spreadsheet listing mass murders throughout history, suggesting that these materials provided a backdrop for his planning and execution of the shooting. The shooter had also written a graphic essay about a woman who killed children. FBI officials recently released a report examining 160 mass shootings between 2000 and 2013, which indicated that there is a "copycat phenomenon" in many of these shootings. Andre Simons of the FBI's Behavioral Analysis Unit stated: "As more and more notable and tragic events occur . . . we are seeing more compromised, marginalized individuals who are seeking their inspiration from those past attacks." The report went on to state that the majority of these shootings are over in five minutes, one-fourth of the shooters committed suicide before the police arrived, and in all but two of the cases the gunman acted alone (Tucker 2014). These shootings have provided a riveting reminder of the violence and threats that continue to place our nation's schools and communities in jeopardy. There is a compelling need for every school and every community to take reasonable steps to prevent such acts of violence from occurring.

The Annual Youth Risk Behavior Survey conducted by the Centers for Disease Control and Prevention (CDC) in 2013 reported that the four leading causes of juvenile death include motor vehicle crashes (23 percent), unintentional injury (18 percent), homicide (15 percent), and suicide (15 percent). A key factor that contributes to the likelihood of violence toward young people, according to the CDC study, is whether young people routinely carry weapons such as a gun, a knife, or a club in their community or to school. The CDC's 2013 survey reported that 17.9 percent of students had carried a weapon at least one day during the past 30 days prior to the survey. Nationwide, male students were three times more likely to carry a weapon (28.1 percent) than female students (7.9 percent). White males (33.4 percent) were much more likely than black males (18.2 percent) or Hispanics (23.8 percent) to carry a weapon. Among tenth, eleventh, and twelfth graders, seniors were more likely to carry a weapon. Reasons that students frequently give for carrying weapons to school are for protection because they feel intimidated or threatened, to impress someone, to give them some form of status, and sometimes simply to use.

Nationwide, 5.2 percent of students had carried a weapon to school at least one day during the 30 days prior to the survey. Between 1993 and 2013 there was a significant linear reduction in the percentage of students carrying weapons to school, from 11.8 percent down to 5.2 percent—more than a 50 percent reduction. This trend would seem to indicate that schools and communities are doing a better job keeping guns away from school.

The CDC Survey reported that nationwide 6.9 percent of students had been threatened or injured with a weapon. The prevalence of having been threatened or injured with a weapon was higher among ninth graders (8.5 percent), declining to 4.9 percent among twelfth graders.

The Youth Risk Behavior Survey indicated that nationwide 24.7 percent of students had been in a physical fight one or more times during the twelve months before the survey. Of those involved in a physical fight, 3.1 percent had to be treated by a doctor or nurse. Between 1993 and 2013 there has been a linear reduction in injuries requiring treatment, from 4.4 percent to 3.1 percent. Nearly 8.1 percent of students reported being in a physical fight on school property. Males were twice as likely as females to be involved with such fights.

Violence and the fear of violence are facts of life in many of our nation's schools. The fears of students are genuine. Between 1993 and 2013 the CDC reported there has been a linear increase in the number of students who did not go to school because of fear or other safety concerns at least one day during the 30 days before the survey. For 2013 the percentage of students staying away from school because of fear rose to 7.1 percent from 4.4 percent in 1993.

This kind of increase is a national tragedy. The fear of violence is powerful, motivating some students to protect themselves with whatever is at their immediate disposal. Consequently, it is not surprising that some students stay away from school because of fear while other students carry weapons to school for protection to help counterbalance that fear. Statistics like these suggest the need to create comprehensive and systematic safe-school plans. Prior to creating and embracing appropriate crime prevention strategies it is first essential to articulate and acknowledge the scope and magnitude of school crime challenges that affect the presence of weapons in schools.

Generally, someone does not just start pulling the trigger of a gun for no reason; there is something that has happened first. Whenever one talks to youth about why they became involved in a fight, their answers are often intriguing. They frequently say things such as "he called me a name," "he looked at me funny," or "he yelled at me." According to the FBI's Behavioral

Analysis Unit "most shooters had a real or perceived, personally held grievance that they felt mandated an act of violence" (Tucker 2014). Attitudes precede actions. When one considers a "violence continuum," the items at the very bottom include such things as name calling, hard looks, cursing, yelling, cyber bullying, and threatening, followed by assault, battery, rape, homicide, and possibly suicide. If an individual is willing to commit suicide they may be willing to commit any other form of violence that appears at the lower level of misbehavior on the violence continuum. School-associated violent deaths have been tracked since 1992. It is interesting to observe that nearly one out of four of those incidents resulted in the shooters killing themselves after shooting their victim(s).

In studies and analyses done by the National School Safety Center, several interesting facts have been learned about school shooters. First, half of them had a record of juvenile misbehavior. Nearly half of them were under the influence of alcohol or illegal or prescription drugs at the time of the shooting. Forty-five percent were on the fringe of their peer social group. Nearly 80 percent were either bullies or victims of bullying. Ninety percent had previously brought a weapon to school. In most cases someone else knew about the planned shooting (National School Safety Center). For instance, in Bethel, Alaska, the shooter had arranged for a photographer to document the shooting. Another student who knew about the shooting slept in late on the morning of the attack and took a taxi to school to get him there on time so he could witness it. Many shooters displayed warning signs, some through essays, student projects, and unusual behavior before the event. But in many cases there were few visible warning signs.

To fully understand what needs to be done to address the weapons problem in schools it is necessary to consider the collective roles of students, parents, school officials, the community, juvenile courts, cyber bullying, alcohol and other drugs (including prescription drugs), as well as fear and avoidance factors, and easy access to guns without adult supervision.

Students in particular have a unique interest in reporting the presence of weapons in their school. In many cases it is an innocent bystander or an unintended victim that is shot and killed. Parents must take special care to limit their child's access to guns. In the vast majority of school shootings the weapons come from home. Communities and the courts have a role as well. We tend to get the kind of behavior that we tolerate as a society. It must be made clear that weapons have no place on the school campus.

It is a well-known phenomenon that the presence of violence in the community often breeds violence in the school. Safe schools and safe communities go together. Fighting is more likely to escalate when weapons are available or brought to school. When this happens students must face daily decisions regarding high-risk situations. Plotting a hallway route becomes a matter of survival; attending class depends upon the presence or absence of weapon carriers; and choices sometimes must be made as to whether or not to use the school restrooms, which are frequently places of student intimidation and violence.

Nationwide 14.8 percent of students reported being electronically bullied (Centers of Disease Control 2014). Females were three times more likely to be electronically bullied than males. Students reported being electronically bullied at school at even higher rates—19.6 percent. Bullying is a significant part of the weapons-in-school issue. The United States Secret Service Study found that bullying was involved in 80 percent of the nation's school shootings.

The most recent CDC survey sheds additional insights on the importance of providing support and protection for children at school. The 2013 survey indicated that during the twelve months prior to the survey, 29.9 percent of students nationwide had felt so sad or hopeless almost every day for two or more weeks in a row that they stopped doing usual activities. This was higher among females (39.1 percent) than males (20.8 percent) (Centers for Disease Control 2014, 11).

Nationwide, 17 percent of students had seriously considered attempting suicide. Females were twice as likely as males to consider suicide. The CDC study reported that 13.6 percent of students have created a suicide plan and 8 percent of students actually attempted suicide (Centers for Disease Control 2014, 11–12).

The 2013 survey also reported that 22.1 percent of students nationwide had been offered, sold, or given an illegal drug on school property. These numbers have remained fairly stable, from 24 percent in 1993 to 22.1 percent in 2013.

More than two decades ago Congress passed the Federal Gun-Free School Zones Act of 1994. The act prohibits anyone from bringing a firearm onto the campus unless the individual with the weapon is a sworn peace officer. In addition to the federal law, all states that wanted to continue receiving government funding were required to pass similar state legislation. However, the federal and state legislation alone clearly has not eliminated the problem of weapons in schools.

Since 1992, when the National School Safety Center began working with the U.S. Departments of Education and Justice and with the Centers for Disease Control and Prevention to track "School Associated Violent Deaths" in public and private K-12 schools, the nation has experienced more than 900 deaths on school campuses, caused primarily by firearms. This number includes the 863 recorded deaths from 1992 to the 2010–2011 school year.

When combined with subsequent shootings, including Sandy Hook and elsewhere, the numbers exceed 900. A school-associated violent death is defined by the CDC as "a homicide, suicide, or legal intervention (involving a law enforcement officer), in which the fatal injury occurred on the campus of a functioning elementary or secondary school in the United States" (Kemp and Truman 2013, 7).

So questions emerge: How do we keep guns, knives, and other dangerous weapons away from school and away from children? What steps should schools take to create campuses that are safe and weapon free? What is the role of students, parents, law enforcers, the local community, and the courts in keeping our campuses safe? What steps can schools take to make their campuses safe without turning them into armed camps of juvenile detention "look-alike" facilities?

At the vast majority of schools across the country, responding to a weapons incident has been left in the hands of either an academy-trained school resource officer (SRO) or to local law enforcement. Since the Sandy Hook shooting, several states have adopted legislation that permits the arming of staff in schools. These states include Ohio, Colorado, New Jersey, Pennsylvania, Connecticut, and Washington (Flock 2013). In some schools the message to would-be intruders is more striking. For instance, Perry Black, administrator of the Arkansas Christian Academy has signs posted on his campus that read: "Staff is armed and trained and any attempt to harm children will be met with deadly force." In Texas, just outside of Dallas, Harrold School District superintendent David Thweatt stated: "We are the first responders. We don't have five minutes to wait for law enforcement." Each staff member who carries a concealed weapon must be approved by the board and they must be trained. According to the superintendent, those with weapons are strategically placed throughout the school.

Clearly, no task is more important than creating safe schools for all of America's children. When schools are unsafe or perceived as unsafe it is difficult for children to learn and for teachers to teach. It should not require an act of courage for parents to send their children to school, nor should children feel that they must arm themselves for protection at school or on the way to and from school.

The National Center for Education Statistics released its annual report on June 10, 2014, entitled "Indicators of School Crime and Safety." The report stated that in 2011, 33 percent of ninth- through twelfth-grade students said they had been in a physical fight—one in twelve on school property. The highest percentage of students in a physical fight were ninth graders.

With respect to discipline and safety measures taken by schools, the survey reported that:

96 percent of students reported their school had a code of student conduct.

95 percent of schools required a visitor sign in.

89 percent of schools reported the presence of hallway and other adult supervision.

70 percent of schools acknowledged the presence of security guards.

11 percent said their school used metal detectors.

77 percent of schools used security cameras, an increase from 37 percent in 2001 to 70 percent in 2011. (Kemp and Truman 2013, viii)

An August 2014 report from the Child Trends Data Bank, reporting on the most recent CDC studies, observed that the proportion of students reporting that they carried a weapon to school within the past 30 days decreased from 26 percent in 1991 to 17 percent in 1999. Since 1999 Child Trends Data Bank observed that the percentage has not strayed far from 18 percent as of 2013. High school males in 2013 were more than three times as likely as females to carry a weapon (28 percent versus 8 percent).

In 2013 white male students (33 percent) [followed by Hispanics (24 percent) and blacks (18 percent)] were most likely to carry a weapon within the past 30 days. In 1991, black students were significantly more likely than white students to carry weapons (33 percent versus 25 percent) (Centers of Disease Control 2014).

After major school shooting events such as Sandy Hook; Columbine; Red Lake, Minnesota; West Nickel Mines, Lancaster, Pennsylvania; Paducah, Kentucky; Pearl, Missouri; and Moses Lake, Washington, the public perception of our school systems is that they are out of control and this is the message that is frequently conveyed. However, despite the cumulative effect of these tragic events, schools continue to be one of the safest places for our young people to be. A youngster is roughly 99.9 percent more likely to be a victim of assault or attack in the local community or at home than in our nation's schools.

Having said this, schools still must take proactive and reasonable steps to keep their campus free of weapons and keep children free of harm, from both students and staff and outsiders. Many schools are surrounded by a 360-degree perimeter of community crime. In such instances their challenges to keep their campuses safe is even greater. If these shooting incidents have taught us anything, they have emphasized the need for readiness, the importance of having broad, uniform protocols, the need to develop appropriate school crime prevention and school crisis preparation and response strategies, the need for standard nomenclature, an agreed-upon system of organization, a working communications network for emergency response, and the need for self-reliance. In legal circles, the previous school shootings are called "due notice." Public awareness of these shootings has diminished the validity of the excuse by school officials that "We never thought it would happen here." These events compel schools to prepare.

The prevalence of such problems suggests the need to develop a series of strategies to diminish, manage, and control the potential risks associated with weapons in school and to be able to respond in effective ways. Here are seven things that schools can do now to make a positive difference in promoting safe and welcoming schools.

1. **Take immediate action to secure your school.**
   As a minimum, use the following security measures to reduce the threat of harm and to enhance your school's safety. These measures may require that you review current practices, reassign personnel, and rethink and redeploy resources.

   - **Increase the visibility of the administrative team** during passing periods, school activities, and events. Visibility may be increased by wearing badges and designated items of clothing.
   - **Establish a "safety zone" around your school site and walk it periodically** to assess people, situations, or events that may present school security risks.
   - **Control access to your school.** Enforce sign in/out procedures. Monitor entrances to your campus. In addition, monitor the service calls of all vendors, maintenance, delivery, and other personnel. Screen and register all visitors.
   - **Design new campuses in ways that promote safe schools.**
     Ben Matthews, with the North Carolina State Department of Education's "Safe and Healthy Schools Support Division," is studying how to make schools intruder-proof. Clearly, this is a daunting, if not impossible task. However, we can clearly take some additional steps. His team is considering options like a vestibule inside the school's main entrance where all visitors must be "buzzed-in" to the school. Many schools have recently adopted features such as these.
     Strategies that were previously identified as recommended policies are now becoming legislated. For instance, the North Carolina State Assembly has mandated that all schools must have a panic alarm system by 2015.
   - **Require picture identification badges** for teachers, staff, authorized volunteers, and visitors. As appropriate for your school setting, size, and grade level, require students to wear or carry identification badges as well.
   - **Improve natural surveillance.** Remove physical barriers, overgrown vegetation, and visual obstacles that reduce the ability to observe

students and campus activities. Remove posters from all window glass in order to enhance natural supervision.

- **Appropriately utilize security technology** to enhance surveillance and supervision. Make certain that such equipment is appropriate to your school setting and is properly installed, used, and maintained.
- **Monitor repeat offenders** to discourage dangerous and disrespectful behavior as well as criminal acts.
- **Track and analyze crime patterns at your school** and in the community to make data-driven decisions about responses.
- **Create viable systems for reporting school safety concerns and threats.** Encourage the timely sharing of information about potential safety problems, risks, and dangers.
- **Carefully screen, select, and supervise employees and all volunteers, including parents.**
  School districts in places like Knoxville, Tennessee, have established electronic screening of all campus guests through their local law enforcement agency, which does an immediate criminal background check on visitors.

2. **Demonstrate school safety leadership.**
Institutionalize expectations, norms, knowledge, and practices that promote school safety. Integrate these concepts into the total educational mission.

- **Incorporate school safety language in the academic mission statement** as a means of validating the school's efforts to create and preserve a safe environment. Make the connection between high standards of academic achievement and high standards of safety and conduct.
- **Prepare a summary of federal, state, and local laws pertaining to school safety.** Make this information readily available to the school community to promote compliance.
- **Schedule a yearly review, evaluation, and update of safety plans, policies, discipline codes, management systems, rules, practices, and other related issues.**
- **Communicate your behavior expectations for students and staff.** Clearly articulate policies regarding:

  Weapons, searches and seizure;
  Bullying and harassment, gang activity;
  Alcohol, tobacco, and other drug use;
  Cell phones and pagers use;
  Tardiness and truancy;
  Dress code;
  Fighting;
  Profanity;

Appropriate use of the school's Internet, student lockers, parking
   privileges, and school property;
Mandated reporting of crime, sexual abuse, or child endangerment.

- **Market the school's safety expectations** in school publications, student handbooks, parent correspondence, letterhead, business cards, and web sites, and during school activities and major events.
- **Establish in written form a detailed safe school plan for the managing of people and resources to create and maintain a safe school. Steps include:**
   Enlist the involvement of stakeholders as members of your safe school
      planning team.
   Create a common focus and vision among members of your team.
   Establish memorandums of understanding with outside partners and
      agencies such as police, fire, paramedics, office of emergency services,
      and similar agencies in your community.
   Conduct school safety assessments, surveys, and audits. Conduct legal
      compliance reviews to make certain that school policies are in
      accordance with local, state, and federal regulations.
   Identify and prioritize safety needs, issues, concerns, and problems.
   Select and implement effective strategies, promising practices, and
      evidence-based programs that respond to your safety needs.
   Communicate safety plans with the entire school community as appropriate. Provide training as needed, keeping in mind that in a growing
      number of states all school personnel have been identified as emergency
      responders.
   Monitor and evaluate the effectiveness of the safe school plan on an
      annual basis, and refine as needed.

3. **Promote school safety partnerships**
   Adopt a partnership approach to school safety with the larger community.
   Enhance school safety perspectives, expertise, resources, and services by
   engaging representatives from all stakeholder groups.

- **Establish or expand school safety partnerships to include:**
   Students
   Parents
   Teachers and other staff
   Law enforcement and other first responders
   Mental health professionals
   Youth-serving agencies
   Business and civic leaders
   Faith community members

- **Involve partners in a variety of school safety activities,** including:
  Planning and decision making
  Policy development
  Needs assessment
  Information sharing
  Problem solving
  Prevention and mitigation
  Response and recovery
  Referrals for special services and support
  Threat assessment
  Program evaluation
  Training and cross training
  Resource development
  Testing the safety plan: drill, practice, and field exercises
- **Learn about and utilize the services, resources, and guidance of local, state, and federal emergency response agencies.**
- **Establish an interagency information sharing process for identifying troubled youth and referring them to special support services.**
- **Work with partners to provide support, special services, or alternative placement options for troubled youth.**
- **Recognize and publicize the accomplishments of partnership groups.**

4. **Anticipate and prepare for crisis response.**
   As a critical component of the comprehensive safe school plan, establish in written form a plan for managing people, skills, and resources during a crisis.

- **Identify the chain of command within the school and establish a school crisis response team.** Identify the areas of expertise—the talents and the tasks, delineating roles and responsibilities for each member.
- **Assess your school's vulnerabilities to domestic and international terrorism or natural disasters.** Identify your school's assets, risks, and hazards.
- Inventory the school community for the availability of skills, supplies, equipment, and resources related to emergency response, including:
  Equipment such as generators, communication devices, vehicles, and battery-operated equipment
  Mental health and counseling support services
  First aid supplies and skills
  Water, food, and other supplies
- **Seek information, resources, training, and tools within your community regarding coordinated response to disasters and terrorism.** Know your roles and responsibilities.

- **Coordinate with your local Emergency Operations Center (if available)** to gain understanding about how the Unified Command System will operate in your community when a major shooting or disaster strikes.
- **Develop policies and interagency agreements for crisis response, crisis management, and crisis resolution or recovery.**
- **Anticipate the possibility of terrorist acts** by monitoring current events, threat levels, and directives. Watch for and report suspicious activities.
- **Anticipate the onset of emerging natural disasters.** Keep open lines of communication with school district leaders and state and civic authorities.
- **Develop contingency plans** for evacuation, sheltering-in-place, communication systems, equipment, transportation, emergency responders, chain of command, and medical services.

  During any crisis the focus of the school must remain on one key responsibility—acting immediately to keep students and staff safe. When a serious crisis strikes at school, response options to be taken by school personnel are limited. With the safety of students and staff in mind, the most common emergency response options are founded on the following rationales:

1. Students and staff may be safer at home than they would be at school **(cancel school prior to the start of the day).**
2. Sending students home is safer than keeping them at school **(early dismissal).**
3. Students are safer inside buildings than they would be outside **(shelter in place).**
4. Students will be safer when they have been isolated from the threat **(lockdown or lockout).**
5. Students will be safer if they move to another area **(evacuation or reverse evacuation).**
6. Students must physically protect themselves from falling or flying debris **(duck and cover).**

Other rationales that drive emergency response options include:

1. People need to be kept away to preserve a crime scene and protect evidence **(restricted access).**
2. People need to be moved because there is an immediate need within the community to convert the school facility to a temporary emergency response center **(relocation).**

There are at least 10 basic response options that schools can use in an emergency situation. While school emergency operations plans often reflect unique situations, needs, and culture of the school community, the basic set of the response options are universal. Selecting which response to use depends on the nuances of the event. Some crisis events may require the use of a combination of response options. For instance, in Red Lake, Minnesota, when the shooter entered the school, he moved from classroom to classroom to shoot students. At the beginning of the crisis, when the shooting began, it made sense to go into a lockdown mode. However, the problem was that the shooter was going to the various classroom doors and shooting out the hardware, thereby gaining entrance to the classrooms. When this action was observed, one teacher had the good judgment of orchestrating a classroom evacuation at the first opportunity.

I am frequently asked the question what to do when a shooting incident takes place. The way this question is answered depends upon many factors: What is happening at the time? Is there a reasonable escape route? What is the demeanor of the shooter? Do you hide? Do you flee? Or do you try to fight? These are all difficult choices while you attempt to supervise and care for children.

1. **Shelter in place**—This emergency response action would be used when it is safer to "shelter" people inside a building rather than expose them to possible harm outside the building. Examples of events triggering this response might be a hazardous materials incident or a chemical attack. Shelter in place involves closing windows, doors, air ducts, and ventilation systems, and when possible, sealing the room. In the case of a terrorist attack, the school may be called upon to shelter people in place for an extended period of time. Long-term sheltering has planning implications for food, water, and emergency supplies.

2. **Lockdown**—This emergency response action would be used when isolating individuals from threat that will make them safer. Events triggering this response might be an armed intruder, a hostage situation, sniper activity, or police activity in or around the school. During a lockdown, all doors and windows are locked. Students and teachers remain in their classrooms and no one is allowed to enter or leave. No one is released until an "all clear" signal is given. Parents are not allowed to pick up children from school.

3. **Lockout**—This response action would be used to restrict campus access to unauthorized persons. Entrances and doors are locked and monitored. One event triggering this response could be the spillover of criminal activity in the community onto school grounds.

4. **Evacuation**—This response action would be used when students and staff need to be moved to a safe location. This response directs people to predetermined areas using established safe routes. Emergency operations plans typically have primary and secondary sites identified. Examples of events triggering this response might be serious violence, fires, explosions, earthquakes, or other natural disasters. During the

9/11 attacks on the World Trade Center there were nine schools within the boundaries of "ground zero." One of the elementary schools had an evacuation plan to move to the next nearest school, but that school was also within "ground zero." The back-up plan was to move the students to the next nearest school which was also at "ground zero." The principal had the good judgment to make an "on-the-spot" decision. She marched her students toward the Brooklyn Bridge and established a parent reunification point at that place. The point is, even with the best of comprehensive plans during a crisis there is a need for flexibility, common sense, and good judgment.

Evacuations can take place on-site or off-site. The most common on-site evacuation is similar to a fire drill where students are directed to leave the building and assemble at safe locations on or near the campus. An off-site evacuation utilizes a safe location outside the school, and may require transporting students and staff to the new location.

5. **Reverse Evacuation**—While similar to evacuation, this emergency response action moves students and staff from outdoors to indoors. If people are outside in an open area, they are directed to return to designated classrooms or other inside locations to avoid harm. Examples of events triggering this response might be a sudden electrical or hailstorm or when law enforcement or firefighting activity may be occurring in the immediate vicinity of the school.

6. **Duck and Cover**—This response directs people to immediately drop to the floor, take cover, and protect themselves as much as possible from flying objects and debris or even a shooter.

7. **Restricted Access**—This emergency response action would be used when people need to be kept away from the activity of emergency responders. For example, law enforcement personnel are working to preserve and investigate a crime scene.

8. **Relocation**—This action is triggered by the need of the larger community to respond to a wide-scale event by converting the school facility to a temporary emergency response center.

Crisis response options must take into consideration students who have disabilities or special needs, with special consideration given to specific evacuation procedures to students with mobility, visual, and hearing impairments including providing assistance to mentally impaired students to help them cope during crisis situations. It is important to maintain and transport back-up supplies or vital medications or equipment necessary for these students.

○ **Establish both district-level and school site plans for communication during a crisis** in the following areas:
Media protocols

Standardized response alerts, codes, and signals

Protocols for emergency contacts

Parent notification

Back-up systems

○ **Account for the special needs of disabled staff and students in all crisis response planning.** Pay special attention to issues regarding mobility, medication, and support equipment.

○ **Maintain accurate, current, and portable staff and student rosters and emergency contact data.**

○ **Create a plan for the reunification of families following a crisis.**

○ **Establish a "Threat Assessment Team"** and information-sharing protocols to monitor and assess early warning signs of potentially violent students and for referring troubled youth for special services.

○ **Share crisis response plans/procedures with the school community as appropriate.**

○ **Drill and practice with students, staff, and emergency responders as appropriate.**

5. **Train adults within the school community.**
   Prepare the administrative team, teachers, staff, parents, and school safety partners regarding critical school safety issues and practices.

   • **Include safety topics in the plan for annual leadership training and staff development.** Include both certified and classified staff as well as part-time and substitute employees.

   • **Train staff to distinguish between disciplinary matters and criminal offenses and to respond appropriately.**

   • **Provide teachers with instruction regarding effective classroom management and student discipline.**

   • **Increase the effectiveness of school resource officers, security staff, and campus supervisors by providing resources and training regarding school safety issues.**

   • **Provide training and outreach programs to enlist parent involvement and to help parents understand their role in keeping their children and schools safe.**

6. **Enlist the participation of students in school safety.**
   Involve students in planning and managing their personal and school safety. Let students know why it is in their self-interest to work closely with school officials in reporting suspicious activities or certain risks that may affect them. For instance, prior to a school shooting in Edinboro, Pennsylvania, two students were robbed at gunpoint in the school parking

lot the evening before the shooting. Neither of the students involved in the criminal act reported the matter to school officials or to law enforcement. The next day, the assailant who had robbed them in the parking lot came to school and shot another student and the school principal. Had the incident been reported it is more likely that the school shooting could have been prevented. Students need to understand why it is in their self-interest to report such crimes. In addition, school officials should include curriculums, support services, peer activities, and partnerships that promote school safety.

Several schools that have adopted a comprehensive bully prevention curriculum have witnessed positive by-products to the curriculum, not only among students but also the staff. Emphasizing simple courtesy and thoughtfulness can go a long way toward improving campus climate.

- **Seek perspectives, knowledge, and opinions of students in school safety surveys and focus groups.**
- **Engage students in the development and delivery of school safety policies and strategies.**
- **Educate students regarding their personal roles and responsibilities for maintaining a safe school for themselves and others.**
- **Implement research-based personal, social, and safety skills development programs and curriculums.**
- **Train students how to access and use available safety resources, programs, and personnel, such as:**
  Tip Lines
  Peer helper groups
  Counselors and counseling services
  School resource officers, security officers, and designated safety advocates

7. **Recognize the influence of culture and diversity on school safety.**
   Provide opportunities to increase the school community's understanding of culture and diversity. Expand your school's definition of diversity to include a range of characteristics beyond race, ethnicity, or national origin. Identify and validate the unique and varied cultures that comprise your school community.

   - **Recognize that diversity issues may be at the core of some school safety problems such as bullying, hate-motivated conduct, gang activity, and other harassment behaviors.** Provide staff and students with the opportunity to explore and develop respect for cultural differences.
   - **Recognize the importance of belonging to the school community.** Promote a sense of respect for all students, staff, parents, and families.

- **Be aware that the organizational cultures, priorities, and work styles of community agencies often challenge those of schools.** Identify and discuss these differences before conflict or crisis occurs.
- **Seek understanding about how culture and diversity issues will influence the ability of your school community to recover from a crisis.** Include this understanding in your crisis plans.

Additional strategies for minimizing weapon violence may include but are not necessarily limited to:

Placing school safety on the educational agenda

Conducting an annual school safety site assessment

Placing a sworn school peace officer on the campus

Considering the use of metal detectors when there is a compelling reason to do so

Employing the use of surveillance cameras

Establishing threat assessment protocols to help identify high risk situations before they escalate to major levels of violence

Employing positive student behavior curriculums to enhance school climate

Drilling and practicing with students, staff, and first responders to become familiar with various options

The Art of Safe School Planning

Safe school planning is a collaborative process that creates a framework for school safety assessment and action. Creating safe and orderly schools is about commitment and community will. It requires school and community leaders to articulate the quality of the educational climate and learning environment they want to provide for their children and then to collaboratively and cooperatively develop the strategies that will produce the desired results. It is about evaluating where you are, planning for where you want to be, and then implementing a series of comprehensive strategies to deal with the difference. Essential ingredients for creating safe schools include:

Establishing a safe school planning team

Developing a safe school vision

Assessing school safety

Identifying problems and areas of desired change

Setting goals to promote school safety

Exploring effective strategies, promising practices, and research-based programs

Selecting and implementing strategies

Developing a crisis response plan

Sharing the plan with the community

Evaluating and assessing progress annually

Safe school planning is about the art of the possible. Stakeholders who engage in the process use partnerships, collaboration, effective strategies, and innovation to develop and sustain ideal learning environments for students and staff, environments that are free from anxiety, fear, and intimidation. School officials are not expected to eliminate all school crime but they are compelled to take reasonable steps that will promote the safety and well-being of all students and those professionals who serve them.

References

Centers for Disease Control and Prevention. 2012. *School-Associated Violent Deaths Study*. http://nces.ed.gov/programs/digest/d13/tables/dt13_228.10.asp.

Department of Health and Human Services. 2013. "Youth Risk Behavior Surveillance, United States 2013." *Morbidity and Mortality Weekly Report* (June 13). Atlanta, GA: Centers for Disease Control.

Flock, Elizabeth. 2013. "At Least 7 States Now Have Armed Staff in Schools." *U.S. New and World Report* (July 30).

Matthews, Ben. 2014. "North Carolina Changing the Way Students Are Protected in the Classroom." WTVD News, I-Team (July 14). http://abc11.com/education/i-team-north-carolina-beefs-up-school-security/177560.

National School Safety Center. Westlake Village, CA. www.schoolsafety.us.

North Carolina Public Schools. 2014. *North Carolina Public Schools Facilities Guidelines*. http://schoolclearinghouse.org.

Robers, Simone, Jana Kemp, Jennifer Truman, and Thomas D. Snyder. 2013. *Indicators of School Crime and Safety: 2012*. National Center for Education Statistics, US Department of Education, and Bureau of Justice Statistics, Office of Justice Programs, US Department of Justice, Washington, D.C.

Tucker, Eric. 2014. "FBI Releases Report Examining Mass Shootings." Associated Press (September 25). http://news.yahoo.com/fbi-releases-report-mann-shootings-us-160247334—politics.html.

CHAPTER TWO

Concealed Carry of Firearms on University Campuses

Robert L. Spinks and Michael C. Powell

Introduction

Perceptions easily become the misinformed realities of the public who are bombarded with news stories flooding radio, television, and cable network channels 24 hours a day that indicate that crime is rising and that there is a need to have access to a concealed carry firearm at all times. But is a university more like a mall or a public library, or is it a public school? The Gun-Free School Zones Act of 1990 [(18 USC, Section 922(q)] and 1996 is a federal statute that clearly makes all K-12 schools into gun-free zones. Although open or concealed carry might be lawfully permitted at a mall or at many libraries, there are notable exceptions about which many state legislatures and the public generally agree where the presence of a firearm would be potentially disruptive, such as schools, courthouses, and airports. Even Students for Concealed Carry on Campus (SCCC) recognizes that the open carry of holstered firearms on a university campus "would compromise the learning environment" (Swenson 2013).

Concealed carry of handguns on university campuses raises a host of questions about liability and risk management concerns on many levels. State laws vary greatly in defining university campuses as gun-free zones, allowing legal concealed carry and in giving institutions control to ban or allow weapons. There is also the ongoing debate involving the Second Amendment and the U.S. Supreme Court's interpretation of gun rights plus the different states' rights issues that provide different restrictions on both open carry and permitted concealed gun carry by the general public across the United States.

University campuses are often their own self-contained community within a larger city that includes not just classrooms and research facilities, but bookstores, cafeterias, food establishments, counseling centers, study halls, libraries, fitness facilities, theaters, sports complexes, and parking facilities. Aside from students, staff, and faculty who use these campuses on a daily basis, hundreds of thousands of visitors attend public events and sporting contests annually at even the smaller institutions. As with any large institution or facility that allows access to the public, university campuses can also be a magnet for criminals looking for opportunities to steal, stalk, and assault.

Crime on university campuses is significantly less than in the surrounding cities and counties. With nearly 16 million students attending any one of the nation's approximately 4,200 degree-granting post-secondary institutions (Federal Bureau of Investigation 2014), the risk of being a crime victim is roughly one-tenth that of being a victim off campus (Birnbaum 2013). Birnbaum notes that in 2010 campus murder and manslaughter comprised a mere 0.05 percent, of all reported campus crimes and that 79.16 percent of campus crimes were non-violent in nature. Burglary constituted roughly two-thirds of all reported campus crime; forcible sexual offenses totaled 9 percent and aggravated assault totaled 7.18 percent. Yet, when comparing campus violent-crime rates (which include murder, rape, robbery, aggravated assault) with those in the general population, campuses were clearly significantly safer venues.

A 2001 U.S. Department of Education (DOE) study found that in 1999 the overall homicide rate at university campuses was 0.07 per 100,000 students, while the homicide rate in the United States was 5.7 per 100,000 persons and 14.1 per 100,000 for persons aged 17 to 29 (Armed Campuses 2014).

American Gun Culture and the Militarization of the American Public

There has been a growing discussion about the militarization of the police, which was triggered in part by the shooting of Michael Brown by local police in Ferguson, Missouri, and the police response to the resulting protests and rioting. This discussion about the police, recently triggered by the media coverage in Ferguson, did not start there. The challenges of President Nixon's declaration of a "war on drugs" in June 1971 (Drug Policy Alliance 2014) and increasingly violent criminal acts led to the creation of police

Table 2.1 Comparative Violent Crime Rates, 1997–2010 (Birnbaum 2013)

	1997	1998	1999	2000	2001	2002	2003	2004	2005	2006	2007	2008	2009	2010
Violent crimes per 100,000 FTE students	68.6	70.3	66.5	65.0	61.9	60.9	60.3	58.0	59.1	58.3	55.8	52.2	46.8	47.3
Violent crimes/100,000 of U.S. Population	611.0	567.6	523.0	506.5	504.4	494.4	475.8	463.2	469.0	473.6	466.9	457.5	431.9	403.6
College rate as a percent of U.S. population rate	11.2%	12.4	12.7	12.8	12.3	12.4	12.7	12.5	12.6	12.3	12.0	11.4	10.8	11.7

Special Weapons and Tactics (SWAT) groups. The Philadelphia Police Department, Stakeout Unit was formed in 1963 by Commissioner Bell to quash a rash of bank holdups (Philadelphia Police Department 2012). But SWAT is most often connected with the Los Angeles Police Department with the formation of a structured police tactical unit in 1967 by then-inspector Daryl Gates (later to become the Chief of Police in Los Angeles) in part as a response to the Watts Riots of 1965 (Los Angeles Police Department 2014; Clinton 2010). In the post–9/11 world under Bush and Obama the police have been granted additional risk management duties.

Some civil libertarians believe that there is an evolving style of aggressive policing associated with tactical training and arming of the police (Balko 2013). They have equated the use of military-style tactics and equipment in both correctional and policing venues as a negative evolution toward a paramilitary state (Kraska 2001).

What has been notably left out of that discussion is the militarization of the American public, the para-military capabilities of organized criminal gangs, and narco-terrorism especially in southern border states, and the presence of career and violent criminals. American policing has long been reactionary in its evolution, which has been true of responding with new tactics and policies to a rising challenge of criminal activity.

Community Oriented Policing and Problem Solving (COPPS) came into being in the 1980s as a way to examine root causes of crime, authorize patrol officers to develop community partnerships, and develop better police connections with citizens and neighborhoods. However, in many locations this strategy remains a philosophy rather than a structured change in police responses. Although more than 80 percent of local law enforcement agencies across the country say that they employ COPPS (Bureau of Justice Statistics 2014) and train officers in COPPS (Hickman and Reaves 2001), many citizens might be hard pressed to identify specific examples of improved customer service, community outreach programming, or crime prevention services that are well marketed by their local police or sheriff's office.

University Policing

Just as the law provides for many shades of gray in order to allow discretion in its application because no two criminal situations are entirely the same—and each has unique issues, factors, and circumstances that can come into play—law enforcement agencies also are not the same. With more than 17,000 state and local law enforcement agencies in the United States, there is a variance in staffing, training, and resources.

According to the Bureau of Justice Statistics (2011):"State and local law enforcement officers nationwide total about 765,000 (those with general arrest powers), representing 17,985 state and local law enforcement agencies with at least one full-time officer or the equivalent in part-time officers, including:

- 12,501 local police departments
- 3,063 sheriffs' offices
- 50 primary state law enforcement agencies
- 1,733 special jurisdiction agencies
- 683 other agencies, primarily county constable offices in Texas."

Special jurisdiction agencies include university and college police departments, but civilian security forces that do not have the power of arrest and therefore in most cases the security and public safety agencies of private universities and colleges are not included in this count. A few states including California and Louisiana do extend general policing powers to private universities in their states (such is the case with the University of Southern California police and with the Tulane University police in New Orleans). Special jurisdiction agencies in the BJS Report (Bureau of Justice Statistics 2008) included 503 four-year education campuses with about 11,000 full-time sworn officers and 253 two-year education campuses with more than 2,600 sworn officers. Yet, the Department of Justice (DOJ) recognizes that there are 4,000 post-secondary institutions serving 15 million students and several million faculty, staff, and visitors (Department of Justice 2005). Other types of special jurisdictions are public buildings and facilities (for instance, education and medical campuses), natural resources, transportation systems and facilities, criminal investigations, and special enforcement (alcohol and tobacco, narcotics, gaming, racing, and agriculture).

Policing in America is largely dependent on small police agencies, about half (49 percent) of which employ fewer than ten full-time officers. Nearly two-thirds (64 percent) of sworn officers work for an agency that employs 100 or more officers (Reaves 2011). The vast majority of all university and college police agencies fall into the small- or medium-size category.

University and college campuses are the equivalent of a city within a city. Small colleges usually have only a few thousand students, while the nation's largest campuses have student populations larger than significant sized cities: Arizona State University, 70,440 students; Miami Dade College, 61,674 students; Houston Community College, 60,303 students;

University of Central Florida, 56,106 students; Ohio State University, 56,064 students; Lone Star College, 54,412 students; University of Minnesota–Twin Cities, 51,721 students; University of Texas at Austin 51,195, students; University of Florida, 49,827 students; and Texas A&M University, 49,129 students. These institutions are the 10 largest universities and colleges in the United States (MatchCollege.com 2014). Whether a campus is large or small, these self-integrated communities include both residents and commuters, including students, staff, faculty, and the general visiting population attending not just education courses but also the fine arts, general enrichment programs, and many athletic events.

University campuses experience varied types of crime, involving thefts, burglaries, and other property crimes as well as crimes against persons, including homicides, aggravated assaults, rapes, sex crimes, and more. The biggest differences between university police and traditional city and county law enforcement is that the university police agency is often expected to be a helping agency first and an enforcement agency second. More so than many city and county law enforcement departments, university policy agencies commonly involve service functions and prevention programming.

University Shootings—Background

Concern over the safety of all educational institutions has increased over the past two decades as the threat of active shooter* incidents has risen. First, these shootings were initially seen as being a high school–centered issue that targeted a specific individual against whom a shooter had a grudge or other complaint. But beginning with the 1996 school shooting at Frontier Middle School in Moses Lake, Washington, where a student shot and killed his algebra teacher and two students, the idea of mass killings began to evolve. School violence is not a new phenomenon, and the earliest known school shooting in the United States occurred on July 26, 1764, in Greencastle, Pennsylvania, when four armed men entered the schoolhouse and shot and killed schoolmaster Enoch Brownalong with nine or ten children (K12 Academics 2014a). Violence on university campuses was a fairly rare occurrence in comparison to general community violence well into the late twentieth century. While history provides a handful of violent campus-based shootings, such March 11, 1908, when two individuals at the Laurens Finishing School in Boston, Massachusetts, were murdered; April 2, 1921, when a professor at Syracuse University was shot and killed in his office; and June 7, 1925, in Baton Rouge, Louisiana, when a professor was murdered by an axe-wielding assailant on the Louisiana State University campus. Other target-specific killings occurred infrequently over the next forty years on the campuses of higher education in the United States (K12 Academics 2014b). These university campus attacks were not mass shooting incidents that are presently of major concern.

The University of Texas at Austin "Clock Tower shooting" is often viewed as the initial incident of a mass shooting on a university campus. On November 12, 1966, Charles Whitman, at the age of 25, killed his wife and mother and then went to the observation deck of the campus tower building and began shooting a rifle. In just 96 minutes he killed fifteen people and wounded 31 others before police shot and killed him. It was determined during the autopsy that Whitman had a brain tumor. Whitman was not a student at the university, but he like others was drawn to educational institutions which are a significant representation of the entire community (K12 Academics 2014b).

The year 1999 was a turning point for police response to an active shooter incident, triggered by two students at Columbine High School in the suburb of Denver, Colorado, who shot and killed 12 students and wounded 24 others. Both Columbine shooters committed suicide. Columbine captured the nation's attention because it was broadcast live as breaking news on a host of television and cable news networks. This violence did not involve foreign terrorists, bank robbers, or political radicals. The motives of the shooters were not those of traditional criminals. While a subsequent review of the killers' motivation revealed some pre-attack indicators, the nation was immediately struck by the venue of the shootings: an upper-middle-class suburban high school with a high graduation rate and with many of the graduates going on to college. Unlike many other types of crime, the average American could not dismiss it as something that could never happen in their community. The Columbine incident was something new; it prompted fresh thinking by police departments about how to respond. At the time, police routinely were trained to respond to a critical incident, contain it, possibly negotiate with the gunman, and make a tactical entry as a last resort. This strategy meant that the first police entry into Columbine High School did not begin until 30 minutes into the killing spree. Nationwide, patrol-level officers did not have the equipment (tactical-level bullet-resistant vests, ballistic helmets, and entry tools) to advance immediately into an in-progress active shooter situation.

More than 15 years later, active shooter response training for law enforcement continues to expand across the nation. And more and more law enforcement agencies provide advanced level equipment in order for patrol officers to advance quickly into an active-shooter environment. Although some have responded negatively to this equipment, claiming that local police agencies are "militarizing" (Baur 2014), the discussion should focus on deploying the appropriate equipment and utilizing the appropriate tactics for the specific type of policing event faced by law enforcement.

The Federal Bureau of Investigation (FBI) published *A Study of Active Shooter Incidents in the United States Between 2000 and 2013,* that reviewed 160 "active shooter" incidents involving 1,043 casualties. These shootings included a cross section of locations which were not merely centered on school or university campuses (Federal Bureau of Investigation 2013, 13).

The FBI study concluded with the following findings regarding the review of 160 active shooter incidents that were reviewed:

> The FBI identified 160 active shooter incidents, noting they occurred in small and large towns, in urban and rural areas, and in 40 of 50 states and the District of Columbia. Though incidents occurred primarily in commerce and educational environments (70.0 percent), they also occurred on city streets, on military and other government properties, and in private residences, health care facilities, and houses of worship. The shooters victimized young and old, male and female, family members, and people of all races, cultures, and religions.

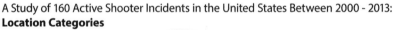

A Study of 160 Active Shooter Incidents in the United States Between 2000 - 2013: Location Categories

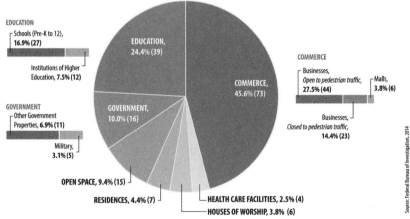

Figure 2.1   A Study of 160 Active Shooter Incidents in the United States Between 2000–2013 (Federal Bureau of Investigation, 2014)

Snapshot

The following characteristics of the 160 active shooter incidents
identified between 2000 and 2013 are noted:

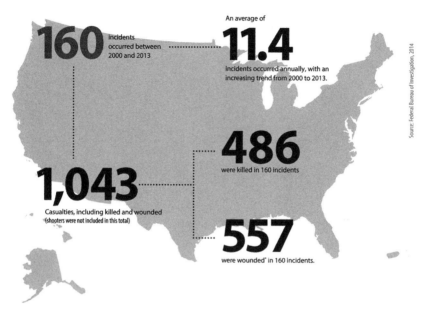

Figure 2.2 Snapshot (Federal Bureau of Investigation, 2014)

The findings establish an increasing frequency of incidents annually.
During the first 7 years included in the study, an average of 6.4 incidents
occurred annually. In the last 7 years of the study, that average increased
to 16.4 incidents annually. This trend reinforces the need to remain vigilant regarding prevention efforts and for law enforcement to aggressively
train to better respond to—and help communities recover from—active
shooter incidents.

The findings also reflect the damage that can occur in a matter of
minutes. In 64 incidents where the duration of the incident could
be ascertained, 44 (69.0 percent) of 64 incidents ended in 5 minutes or
less, with 23 ending in 2 minutes or less. Even when law enforcement
was present or able to respond within minutes, civilians often had
to make life and death decisions, and, therefore, should be engaged
in training and discussions on decisions they may face. (FBI 2013, 8)

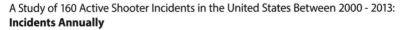

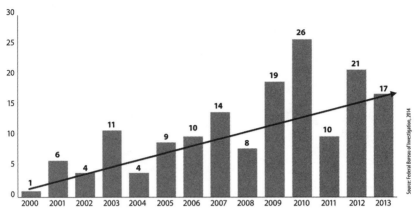

Figure 2.3   A Study of 160 Active Shooter Incidents in the United States, 2000–2013 (Federal Bureau of Investigation, 2014)

The trend for active shooting incidents of all types has continued to grow since 2000 as the FBI-generated graph indicates (FBI 2013, 8) (Figure 20.3).

In 2013 President Obama signed into law the Investigative Assistance for Violent Crimes Act (IAVCA) of 2012 [28 USC 530 C(b)(1)(m)(i)], which granted the attorney general the authority to assist in the investigation of "violent acts and shootings occurring in a place of public use" and in the investigation of "mass killings and attempted mass killings at the request of an appropriate law enforcement official of a state or political subdivision" (Investigative Assistance for Violent Crimes Act 2012).

The majority of active shooter incidents or mass killings have involved off-campus locations. Although in some instances open carry and concealed carry of a firearm are a lawful option, citizen intervention has been rare. The FBI study showed that only 3.1 percent (5 incidents out of 160 that were studied) of the shooting incidents ended after armed individuals who were not law enforcement officers exchanged gunfire with the shooter(s). In these incidents, three shooters were killed, one was wounded, and one committed suicide. However, only one incident involved a citizen with a valid firearm permit, while the other four incidents involved a security officer at a church, an airline counter, a federal museum, and a school board meeting (FBI 2013, 11).

If citizens have largely been ineffective in terminating active shooters in non-educational venues, would having armed students, staff, faculty, or visitors on a university campus pose a greater risk than any possible benefit that their addition on campus could offer? Firearms and their use likely will continue to be a controversial issue in the United States. However, everyone should be on the side of safety and security along with being responsible in the possession and use of firearms, including the addition of firearms to traditionally gun-free areas such as university campuses.

Police officers respond on a daily basis to violent crime scenes and engage suspects using various options up to and including deadly force. The FBI estimates that approximately 400 violent offenders are shot by the police nationwide annually. Conversely the average number of police officers killed in the line of duty has averaged 150 per year with an average of 58,261 assaults against law enforcement annually that result in 15,658 serious injuries each year (National Law Enforcement Officers Memorial Fund 2014). The police are trained to use the lowest level of force to gain the highest level of voluntary compliance. Many conditions come into play in a violent or armed confrontation, including the suspect's actions, the type of call, lighting, weather conditions, experience under stress, the time of day, length of shift and possible fatigue, how many participants are at the scene, and many other factors. Police train under all these conditions to better prepare for a violent armed confrontation, including having the ability to communicate and coordinate a response to an active shooter situation on a university campus. When officers are moving swiftly to engage a violent individual or an active shooter, they must engage that potential suspect in the appropriate manner. If a plainclothes officer or armed off-duty police officer enters the scene and acts in such a way that responding officers perceive as a threat, an "unidentified friendly" possibly can be injured. An armed faculty or staff member, a student, or concealed carry permit holder may suffer the same fate by displaying a weapon. These civilians will not have the same training or experience and competency as a police officer would and would not be readily recognizable as a "friendly" armed person.

Protected or Prohibited Locations Apply to Permitted Concealed Carry

The concept of weapon-free zones or properties where firearms are prohibited is not new. Various state and federal laws make it illegal for both a concealed carry permit holder and the general public to bring guns and other weapons—such as knives, OC (oleoresin capsicum, or pepper) sprays, and tasers—onto certain properties and into certain facilities and businesses. These restrictions are uniform for federal facilities, but vary from state to state.

Federal facilities have long had restrictions on having firearms in post offices, in federal buildings, on military reservations (by civilians), at prisons, on trains, or on property controlled by the U.S. Army Corps of Engineers. Although as of 2010, firearms are allowed in national parks, there are still restrictions.

Other prohibited carry locations vary widely from state to state, but may include (Louisiana Revisited Statute Title 40, Section 1379.3):

- State government facilities, including courthouses, police stations, or correctional facilities
- Polling places
- Educational institutions including elementary and secondary schools and colleges
- School or professional sporting events and venues
- Amusement parks, fairs, parades, and carnivals
- Businesses that sell alcohol
- Hospitals, many of which are educational teaching hospitals
- Churches, mosques, and other "houses of worship," at the discretion of the church clergy
- Municipal mass transit vehicles or facilities
- Airports, especially beyond the security check points and on aircraft or ships
- Private property where the owner or lessee has posted a sign or verbally stated that firearms are not permitted
- Any public place, while under the influence of alcohol or drugs

"Gun-free zones" continue to be debated over their effectiveness. OpenCarry.org takes the position that laws banning gun carrying on a state university campus will only keep the law abiding citizens unarmed. Individuals or groups who have the determined intent to commit far more serious crimes, including murder, robbery, rape, and stalking, will never be deterred by merely formally prohibiting weapons. According to that reasoning, those wishing to commit mass murder may intentionally choose gun-free venues like shopping malls, schools, and churches (where weapon carrying is generally prohibited) because the population inside is disarmed and thus less able to stop them (Deakins 2008; Hetzner 2011).

Concealed carry restrictions offer a patchwork of limitations from state to state. This issue of states' rights allows states the opportunity to regulate the concealed carry of firearms. Private businesses can also restrict the open carry or concealed carry of guns on their private property. There have been some notable examples of businesses discouraging or prohibiting the carrying of weapons in their establishments; Whole Food Markets,

IKEA, Peet's Coffee & Tea, AMC Theaters, California Pizza Kitchen, Toys R Us, Buffalo Wild Wings, Disney World, and Disney Land have banned guns from their establishments. Starbucks has asked customers to leave their guns at home (Huffington Post 2013).

Rise in Perception of Active Shooters on Campus

While the number of active shooter incidents has risen and are highly publicized, they occur more often away from schools and universities. However, there has been a noticeable reaction in some states to authorize K-12 and university staff to carry concealed guns because they are perceived as a deterrent and valuable as a first responder. Some states require employees to notify school administrators if they intend to arm themselves according to firearm statutes, while other states require no notification at all of school administrators. Firearm training and qualification standards range from non-existent to just a few hours in length.

The proposal to add guns, or more guns, to the university environment has scant research to validate the presumption that there would be a reduction in the risk of an active shooter incident occurring on a university campus or that other violent crime would be reduced. Many of these incidents involve determined individuals who plan their assaults and would not necessarily be deterred by the knowledge that there could be a concealed carry individual (either a civilian or a staff member) in their path. Having more guns on a campus carried by civilians does raise the risk of accidental discharges, gun thefts, and the potential for a misidentification by police of a civic-minded citizen as an active shooter.

Risk and Responsibility Factors on a University Campus

The National Summit on Campus Safety published report (2005) identified a range of potential risks that are specific to the unique venues of college campuses (Department of Justice 2005):

- Many universities function as full-scale towns, with permanent and transient populations that often exceed 25,000 people. For example, the University of California, Los Angeles; University of Maryland, College Park; and many others are self-contained entities with large residential populations, shops, recreational facilities, and full-service police and fire departments. They are located within major metropolitan centers. Cities such as Lawrence, Kansas, and Madison, Wisconsin, are dependent on local university campuses for their economic survival. Smaller colleges and universities, including the nation's two-year institutions (community colleges, technical colleges, junior colleges), serve large transient populations.

- In some jurisdictions, threat assessments have cited colleges and universities as potential primary targets of terrorist activity, while in other jurisdictions they have been ignored in homeland security planning and activities.
- Many campuses house sensitive materials and information and sponsor activities and events that increase their vulnerability. It is common for major universities to employ people and establish facilities dedicated to research in the following areas:

  - Nuclear—Engineering
  - Biochemical—Communication
  - Medical—Public safety
  - Defense—Transportation
  - Technology–Intelligence
  - International affairs—Aerospace

- In addition, many universities house historic and classified documents. They also serve as homes to scholars and researchers who comprise a notable segment of the nation's intellectual talent. Major universities also serve as contractors to government agencies such as the Department of Defense (DOD), Department of Justice (DOJ), National Security Agency (NSA), FBI, and the National Aeronautics and Space Administration (NASA), as well as to the nation's largest corporations.
- Colleges and universities have extensive international connections. Many have a substantial number of international students on campus who sometimes account for up to half of the full-time student body. They enter the country through student visas to pursue their education.
- Many of the nation's major universities maintain campuses overseas and have close ties with countries in Eastern and Western Europe, the Middle East, the Far East, and Latin America. Campuses abroad include small enclaves focusing on specific areas of research or academic study to large multipurpose centers serving hundreds or thousands of students.
- As with most communities, campuses in the United States are open environments in which students, faculty, and others move about freely with few security restrictions. Freedom of movement is encouraged. Restrictions are seen as contrary to the core mission of most universities, which generally embodies an environment of intellectual and physical openness. On many campuses, libraries, laboratories, and student lounges remain open 24 hours a day.
- University campuses are large workplaces. In several major cities, the university is the largest nongovernment employer in the jurisdiction. Most

people who live and work on campuses assume that they are safe and give little thought to risk. Their freedom of movement is closely linked to the freedom of expression and the freedom to explore and share ideas fostered in academic environments. For generations, college and university campuses have been hubs of divergent views, which are expressed without interference, fear, or retaliation.

- Other issues, too, should be considered in focusing on security, safety, and problem solving on college and university campuses. New students, for example, arrive on campus each semester and few universities have systems in place to routinely check their background.

- Further, there is little or no joint or cross-sector training for municipal, county, or state police officers and security personnel who serve on college and university campuses. In some cases, there is little or no cross training among police and security personnel who serve on different campuses of the same university.

While the real-world risk to educational environments exists, the risk to K-12 schools based on research involving active shooting incidents is over double that which universities have experienced over the last decade. The 39 incidents in the FBI study that occurred in educational environments (27 schools, 12 Institutions of Higher Education [IHE's]) resulted in 117 individuals killed and 120 wounded. In this study, schools are defined as pre-kindergarten through twelfth grade (Pre-K-12) educational facilities; incidents that occurred at school-related facilities such as school administration buildings are also included in this category. Incidents in educational facilities account for some of the higher casualty counts. For example, the highest death tolls among the 160 incidents occurred at Virginia Polytechnic Institute and State University in Blacksburg, Virginia (32 killed, 17 wounded), and Sandy Hook Elementary School in Newtown, Connecticut (26 killed, 2 wounded [1 additional death at a residence]). Other high casualty counts occurred during the shootings at Northern Illinois University in DeKalb, Illinois (5 killed, 16 wounded), and Santana High School in Santee, California (2 killed, 13 wounded). No law enforcement officers were killed or wounded in school incidents, and no officers were killed in incidents at IHEs. One officer was wounded in one incident at an IHE; however, it occurred at a medical facility on the campus and not in a campus residence or classroom" (Federal Bureau of Investigation 2013, 15).

The twelve active shooter incidents on university campuses that occurred during the 2000–2013 period that the FBI examined in their study resulted in 60 individuals killed and 60 others wounded. The shooters, two of whom were female, ranged in age from 18 to 62. The shooters included five former students, four current students, two employees, and one patient visiting a medical center. The most incidents occurred on Fridays (five) with others occurring on Mondays (two), Thursdays (two), a Sunday (one), a Tuesday (one), and a Wednesday (one).

These incidents ended when:

- ■■ Five shooters were apprehended by police at the scene (one after two off-duty officers and a citizen restrained him, and one after a being restrained by an off-duty mall security officer);
- ■■ Four shooters committed suicide at the scene (three before police arrived, one after);
- ■■ Two shooters were killed by police at the scene; and
- ■■ One shooter fled the scene and was apprehended by police at another location (Federal Bureau of Investigation 2013, 16).

University Environments: What Role Do Guns Have on a Campus?

The militarization of elements of the American populus through the survival movement, the shift in hunting from traditional rifles to assault weapons, and the rise in civilian purchases of such items as night vision equipment and body armor has contributed to a mindset that deploying armed and minimally trained citizens to school or university campuses will provide a new wall of security against active shooters, lone wolf terrorists, or other felony attacks.

A non-scientific poll conducted by the student newspaper *The Equinox* at Kent State University (with an enrollment of over 29,000 students) that was published in 2011 reported that students responded negatively to having more guns on campus (Nathan 2011):

Question 1: Do you think that gun carry policies should be allowed on college campuses?
No: 72.5%   Concealed Carry: 13.8%   Open Carry: 13.6%
Question 2: Would you feel more or less comfortable with your professors carrying a gun during class?
Less: 90.4%   More: 9.6%
Question 3: Have you or anyone you know ever been the victim of gun violence?
No: 91.8%   Yes: 8.2%

The American Association of State Colleges and Universities (AASCU) stated in a 2008 policy brief that the Association discourages legislation that would overturn or weaken concealed weapons bans on university campuses (Harnisch 2008). A survey of Missouri State University students, conducted in April 2008, found that only 24 percent of respondents believed students should be allowed to carry guns on the Missouri State campus. Mike Robinson, Oklahoma State University director of public safety, supported this view in comments he made regarding a state measure to ease campus gun laws: "Students don't want it. Faculty doesn't want it. Administration doesn't want it. Campuses are one of the safest places you can be. I am certain that campuses will be less safe if we allow guns" (Harnisch 2008).

A 2012 survey at the University of Toledo found that 94 percent of responding professors at 15 randomly selected universities in the Great Lakes states were against permitting concealed weapons on campus. Students also felt strongly and weighed in with 79 percent of those interviewed expressing opposition to concealed weapons on campus (Swenson 2013).

Campus law enforcement and safety services vary significantly from state-to-state. While many campuses have a full-service police department, other institutions may be limited by state statute to use public safety officers (having only detention authority or limited arrest powers), have a civilian security department, contract with a private security company, or have a contractual relationship for local or state police to provide policing services.

The Unstable, Immature, and Risky Personalities in a University Environment

Are university campuses at any higher risk than the general community in having more unstable, immature, or at-risk personalities? The answer is potentially yes, since the demographic of many campuses is not reflective of the larger surrounding community. The university experience largely caters to a younger and less mature demographic that includes the 18-to 24-year-old segment of society. Many campuses face the reality of a "party atmosphere" where experimentation with alcohol and drugs can be greater than in the general population. Physiologically the human brain has not yet fully developed until about the age of 24 and younger individuals are more prone to engage in risky behaviors and activities. Adding a firearm into such a mix certainly carries significant risk.

Laurence Steinberg, a Temple University psychology professor, helped draft an American Psychological Association (APA) brief for a 2005 case in which the U.S. Supreme Court outlawed the death penalty for crimes committed by juveniles before the age of 18. That ruling relies on research on the adolescent brain that indicates the brain is still maturing in the teen years and reasoning and judgment are developing well into the early to mid-20s. Brain scans have given biological support to observations about teenage behavior, such as impulsiveness and vulnerability to peer pressure. Brain scans indicate that the frontal lobe does not mature until age 25, and its connection to other parts of the brain continues to develop to at least that age (Ritter 2007).

Experts state that individuals in their later teens and early 20s, when compared to adults, are more:

- Impulsive
- Aggressive
- Emotionally volatile
- Likely to take risks
- Reactive to stress
- Vulnerable to peer pressure
- Prone to focus on and overestimate short-term payoffs and underplay longer-term consequences of what they do
- Likely to overlook alternative courses of action

According to the Suicide Prevention Network (SPN), the second leading cause of death after accidents at American colleges and universities is suicide, with many more attempted suicides that were not successful. With the introduction of more firearms to university campuses there is a definite possibility of many more attempted suicides that could be completed due to the greater ease of access to firearms (Harnisch 2008). These findings will continue to inform the discussion regarding the best policy in balancing the right to keep and bear arms with the overall public safety concerns about lack of training, mental preparation, and the vulnerability of an unarmed populus.

When a gun is used in an attempted suicide there is an 85 percent chance that death will occur, compared to 2 percent of the attempts involving drug overdose, a far more common method. If firearms are more readily available on a university campus, there is the likelihood that more suicide attempts would also succeed (Skorton and Altschuler 2013).

Concealed Carry Permits and Licensing

There is not a national standard for issuing a concealed carry permit, but there are conditions that generally will lead to prohibiting a person from obtaining the concealed carry permit. For example, in the nine states reviewed in a 2012 Government Accountability Office (GAO) report, all nine will reject an applicant for the following reasons: abuse of controlled substances, felony conviction, mental deficiencies or psychiatric disorder, and involvement as the respondent to a protection or restraining order (Government Accountability Office 2012). Each state has a wide range of other disqualifications specific to that state. An applicant might not be allowed a concealed carry permit in one state, yet be eligible in another. Some states are mandated by state law to issue concealed carry permits, others are "may issue" states, and very few are "shall not issue" states. The diagram (Figure 2.4) indicates the status of each state through 2012. The map illustrates the increase in "must issue" states since 2002.

Those states identified as "shall issue" generally grant more concealed carry permits than the "may issue" states, controlling for population. Not all states recognize the concealed carry permits of other states. It is the responsibility of the concealed carry permit holder to know the laws of reciprocity of states through which or to which they may be traveling. If a state does not recognize the permit, it is incumbent upon the permit holder to obtain a nonresident permit by the state that does not honor their state concealed carry permit. The laws regarding concealed carry may change often. The most up-to-date laws governing a particular state are usually on the state website and should be checked prior to traveling through and to other state jurisdictions.

Controversy continues on the right to carry firearms on university campuses. A student-organized gun advocacy group, Students for Concealed Carry on Campus (SCCC), supports the rights of those students who are legally able to carry a concealed weapon elsewhere, arguing that these students should also be allowed to carry firearms on university campuses just as they are allowed to legally carry a concealed firearm elsewhere in their state. One example cited by SCCC is that faculty and students on college and university campuses are often working, studying, or participating in activities late into the night. They then must walk to their vehicle, public transportation, and home or dormitory, sometimes in unsafe neighborhoods. The student gun rights group maintains that not allowing legally owned and carried firearms to this group of people exposes them to danger and denies them the ability to defend themselves in violent encounters (Harnisch 2008, 3–5).

SCCC holds that students should be able to use firearms to be able to defend themselves on university campuses. The group refers to the Virginia Tech shooting, stating that if the students were allowed to carry firearms, some of those students would still be alive, as other students watched helplessly as the events unfolded. This is an unsubstantiated claim; there is no way to determine if any student witnessing the shooting would have exercised their right to carry a firearm on campus

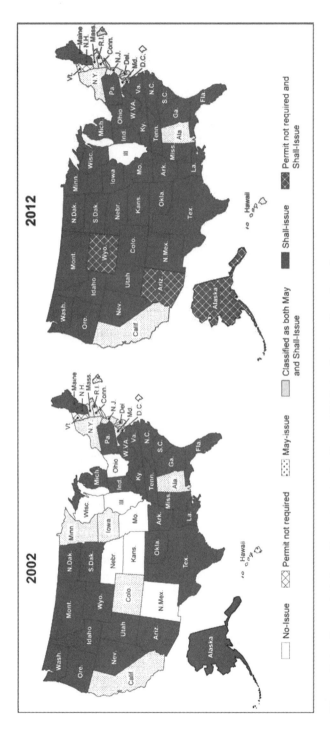

Figure 2.4 Concealed Carry Provisions in the States (GAO Analysis on State Laws)

(if allowed), or that their efficiency in firearms handling would have been effective, or if instead, other firearms carriers would have increased the injury and death toll. Louisiana State Representative Ernest Whooten stated, "We've got a problem and maybe it'll be a deterrent if one of those disturbed persons or wackos thinks 'if I go shooting, they may shoot back'" (Harnisch 2008, 4). However, those with mental deficiencies or overtaken by passion perhaps rarely think rationally about the consequences of their actions at the time that these heinous crimes are committed.

As the balance of Second Amendment rights and general safety concerns, such as issues involving firearms training and licensing, are weighed, college and university administrators and lawmakers in all fifty states find it difficult to agree on what actions to take. Professional associations, including the American Association of State Colleges and Schools (AASCU) and the International Association for Campus Law Enforcement Administrators (IACLEA), and policing professionals agree that relaxing current laws to expand concealed carry of firearms on university campuses would be an unwise policy change.

The IACLEA issued a position paper (Sprague 2008) on recommendations for dealing with concealed firearms carrying on college campuses, which concluded that concealed carry initiatives do not make campuses safer. The statement cited multiple sources and concluded that current evidence suggests that concealed carry laws generally will increase crime; that lives would not be saved by allowing concealed carry on college campuses; and that the use of a gun by a civilian in a self-defense action is a rare occurrence (approximately .004 percent in 2005). The position paper further identified additional risks with concealed carry laws on college campuses:

- One study cited that two-thirds of gun-owning college students engage in binge drinking and are more prone to engage in risky activities.
- Another study discovered that college student gun owners engaged in activities, including reckless behavior involving alcohol, that put themselves and others at risk for severe or life-threatening injuries.
- Guns in a college dormitory room open the possibility for increased risk of firearm-related death or injury to another resident rather than protection against intruders.
- University police may not be able to distinguish between an active shooter and others with firearms.
- There is a risk of on-campus accidental discharges or misuse of firearms at on-campus or off-campus parties and events, which may also involve alcohol or drug use.

Currently, 19 out of the 50 states and District of Columbia ban concealed firearms carry on college campuses: California, Florida, Georgia, Illinois, Louisiana, Massachusetts, Michigan, Missouri, Nebraska, Nevada, New Jersey, New Mexico, New York, North Carolina, North Dakota, Ohio, South Carolina, Tennessee, and Wyoming. In 23 states the decision to ban or allow the concealed carry of firearms on college campuses is made by each institution: Alabama, Alaska, Arizona, Arkansas, Connecticut, Delaware, Hawaii, Indiana, Iowa, Kentucky, Maine, Maryland, Minnesota, Montana, New Hampshire, Oklahoma, Pennsylvania, Rhode Island, South Dakota, Vermont, Virginia, Washington, and West Virginia (National Conference of State Legislatures 2014). On the other end of the spectrum, one state, Nebraska, introduced legislation to add more restrictions with respect to the carrying of concealed weapons on campuses during the same time that other states were attempting, without success, to lessen the restrictions on carrying firearms on campuses (Harnisch 2008). Due to state legislation and court rulings, eight states now allow the carrying of concealed firearms on public college campuses: Colorado, Idaho, Kansas, Mississippi, Oregon, Texas, Utah, and Wisconsin.

Equipment Selection and Carrying Options

Merely allowing concealed carry on a university campus is just one of several issues that face a civilian. The selection of the firearm is no easy task. Individuals, should they decide to carry a firearm, are faced with some important equipment decisions and carrying options if concealed carry were to occur at their university campus. Bigger is not always better. The weight, recoil, and ammunition selection are important factors. The weight of the firearm for concealed carry must be examined carefully. How will the firearm be carried? If the weight is too uncomfortable, or bulky, the weapon will not be carried. If the weapon is not carried, but at home locked away, the idea of having a firearm for protection is defeated. The weapon must be light enough to carry comfortably concealed. The larger the caliber of the weapon, the more recoil there is. For every forward motion there is an equal and opposition reaction. If there is too much firepower, the recoil is such that the owner will not want to practice shooting the weapon. Any follow-up shots will be compromised due to being off target and will require more time to come back on target. This comes back to the training issue of civilians and the amount of time, expense, and commitment that is devoted to being effective and efficient with the firearm. Good marksmanship and the reliable placement of the shots can help alleviate the felt need for a larger-caliber firearm. Using a smaller firearm, with less recoil and accurate shot placement, will be more effective.

The next piece of equipment, almost as important as the firearm, is the method of carrying a concealed firearm. The whole concept of carrying a concealed weapon is to keep the firearm out of sight and unnoticed until it is needed. The stature of an individual will dictate effective means of carrying a firearm concealed, such as in a purse, fanny pack, back pack, or holster. The firearm is carried for self-defense, not a shootout at the OK Corral, so care should be taken in the method of carry. Reaction is always slower than action, but a quick draw is not the only consideration. Hip or waist holster carry is probably the most common, as the firearm is near the hands and easily obtainable. Weather may be a factor when deciding to carry on the waist. Ankle holsters are another popular carry method. The ankle holster can allow for quick access to the firearm, but also includes the added step of bending over or kneeling to retrieve the weapon. When using the ankle holster, the individual's size and weight are major factors. Using tactical advantages when drawing may involve searching for cover or concealment prior to engaging the threat. Another method of carry that was made popular in the 1980s by the television program *Miami Vice* is the shoulder holster. This method offers the advantage that the weapon is easily retrievable and often there is built into the harness an ammunition pouch of the type needed for the firearm. With this type of carry, a coat or shirt is required to conceal the firearm. Size and weight play an important role in this method of carry, along with stature. A tall person with a barrel chest may be large enough to easily conceal the firearm in a shoulder holster, but may be too large in the upper body to retrieve the firearm effectively when needed.

Responsibilities of Firearms Carry and Civil Liability Concerns

Carrying and using a weapon comes with both criminal and civil liability risks about which many citizens have little understanding. Although the idea of using deadly force to save the life of an innocent bystander or oneself may seem obvious, it becomes much more complicated under the pressure of an emergency situation that may occur only once in a lifetime for private individuals. The Civil Rights Act of 1871 may be unfamiliar to most citizens; enacted after the Civil War, it was designed to combat the illegal actions of the Ku Klux Klan. However, today this statute applies to all agents of the state and would presumably apply to a school or university employee who is now armed on a campus. Title 42, Section 1983 of the U.S. Code reads:

Every person who under color of any statute, ordinance, regulation, custom, or usage, of any State or Territory or the District of Columbia, subjects, or causes to be subjected, any citizen of the United States or other person within the jurisdiction thereof to the deprivation of any rights, privileges, or immunities secured by the Constitution and laws, shall be liable to the party injured in an action at law, Suit in equity, or other proper proceeding for redress, except that in any action brought against a judicial officer for an act or omission taken in such officer's judicial capacity, injunctive relief shall not be granted unless a declaratory decree was violated or declaratory relief was unavailable. For the purposes of this section, any Act of Congress applicable exclusively to the District of Columbia shall be considered to be a statute of the District of Columbia.

In some jurisdictions, Section 1983 has been applied directly to private employers when litigants have sued under this act. It can also be applied in virtually all jurisdictions in a more indirect manner to private employers if they are acting under state or federal authority. Today, the Civil Rights Act can be invoked whenever a state or local government official violates a federally guaranteed right. Can civilian school or university employees who may be government employees have liability under USC 42, Section 1983 by taking action that deprives a person of their rights through the misapplication of deadly force?

Police Training versus Citizen Requirements for Training

If the trend is to add new numbers of private persons carrying concealed handguns on university campuses, perhaps these same institutions should strengthen the training of their police, review staffing levels of law enforcement officers on campus, enhance resources, improve physical barriers, and introduce closed circuit television resources as other deterrents to crime and to increase the tactical advantage of campus law enforcement. Of course these steps have costs associated with them and retrofitting campuses with locking class doors, classroom phones, electronic locks, perimeter controls and warning systems is a costly investment in an era with tight budgets.

Basic Weapons Handling and Training for Civilians

Basic weapons handling means different things to different people, depending on training or experience, and often on what an individual has seen on television. Some may have a realistic idea of what weapons can and cannot do, while others' perceptions may be based on the sensationalism of Hollywood. Once an individual makes the decision to purchase a firearm, they also must take legal responsibility, including potential civil and criminal liability. With the acceptance of those responsibilities also comes the obligation to be proficient in the use of the firearm. Many states, but not all, require some type of firearms training in order to be granted a concealed carry permit. Of the nine states considered here as examples in the 2012 GAO Report, seven require some type of firearms training, and two do not. The training varies from state to state as depicted in Table 2.2. Of the selected nine, three states require some type of live fire on the range, with only one state, Tennessee, having a range requirement of scoring 70 percent on a written and shooting portion in order to pass and be eligible for a concealed carry license. On the other end of the spectrum Arizona requires training, but there is no state standard for proficiency. In the nine selected states, Texas and Tennessee have the most comprehensive requirements, with California third. The actual training, shooting range time (if any), and a written test (if any) are decided by the individual instructor. Washington and Oregon do not require any testing or range qualifications to obtain a concealed carry permit. Only a handful of states require any classroom or range training as part of the concealed carry permit process.

Based on these examples, how prepared is the average university faculty and staff member or student for a violent armed encounter? Training requirements are not standardized for all states. The Supreme Court has upheld the position that the U.S. citizen has an individual right to keep and bear arms. Having the right to arm oneself is an important freedom, but being able to use a firearm effectively and efficiently is a responsibility. If an armed citizen believes they must use the weapon, they are held accountable for the use, including possible civil and criminal liabilities, even if the person is justified in using the weapon. Has the civilian population been trained mentally and physically for the confrontation? Or have they been trained just enough to fall into the "Tombstone Courage" mind set; trained just enough that they believe they are ready, but with little to no tactical training or survival skills? Based on the nine-state sampling and references to Washington and Oregon, should faculty, staff, and students be allowed to carry firearms on campus?

Range Training and the Use of Simulators

The training, licensing, and equipment have been discussed for the civilian. But what about the training police officers receive? Each state mandates specific training for police cadets. Officers are trained in the firearms their

Table 2.2. Case Study of States' Training Requirements to Qualify for a Concealed Carry Permit[i]

State	Training required	Live fire required	Hours of instruction required	Proficiency requirementent (written or shooting)	Specific topics as prescribed by state regulations/laws covered
Tennessee	Yes	Yes: 48 rounds (12 rounds each at 3, 7, and 15 yards, as well as a distance between 2 and 25 yards specified by the instructor)	8 (4 hours of classroom and 4 hours of firing range)	70% on both written and shooting exams	Handgun nomenclature, function, and operation; handgun safety, cleaning, and storage; legal liabilities of carrying a handgun
Texas	Yes	Yes	Between 10 and 15	70% on both written and shooting exams	Use of deadly force; handgun use, proficiency, and safety; nonviolent dispute resolution; proper storage practices with an emphasis on child access prevention
Arizona[a]	Yes	Not specified[b]	No	No	Not specified[b]
California	Yes	Not specified[b]	Up to 16 hours	75% on both written and shooting exams	Firearm safety; and permissible use of a firearm laws

[i]Gun Control: States' Laws and Requirements for Concealed Carry Permits Vary across the Nation. United States Government Accountability Office (GAO): Washington, D.C., 2012.

Florida[a]	Yes	Yes	Not specified[b]	Yes	Not specified[b]
Louisiana[a]	Yes	Not specified[b]	Not specified[b]	No	Child access prevention
Virginia[a]	Yes	Not specified[b]	Not specified[b]	No	Not specified[b]
Georgia	No	Not applicable	Not applicable	Not applicable	Not applicable
Maryland[c]	No	Not applicable	Not applicable	Not applicable	Not applicable

Source: GAO analysis of state information (2012).

[a] Applicants in these states can fulfill their training requirement by taking a state-approved National Rifle Association, law enforcement, or other firearms safety-training course, or by presenting evidence of experience with a firearm through participation in current military service or proof of an honorable discharge from any branch of the armed services. In Florida, an applicant may also demonstrate firearm proficiency by presenting evidence of equivalent experience with a firearm through participation in organized shooting competition. Fla. Stat. Ann. § 790.06(2)(h)5.

[b] For certain states, the amount of training and the specific topics are not specified in their state laws.

[c] Maryland does not require training for applicants wishing to obtain a permit for personal protection. However, other applicants (e.g., security guards) have to show evidence of training completion to qualify for a permit.

agency authorizes for duty. Most agencies have moved to semi-automatic handguns ranging from 9mm to 45ACP (automatic Colt pistol). The brand, make, and model differ within and among agencies. Firearms should be fitted to the officer's hands since not all firearms have the same size grip. Officers must shoot and pass an initial qualification course as outlined by the state and must pass the state standards. Most academy firearms training for officers is at least 40 hours. Officers must pass written tests demonstrating competency in state and federal laws regarding the legality of justified use of deadly force and what may constitute civil rights violations. Most officers also shoot under stressful conditions, time constraints, reloading tactics under time stress situations, and night and low light shooting conditions. Many academies require officers to shoot from varying positions, including leaning, prone, kneeling, and shooting from various distances. Officers may also have to run or jog before and during live fire exercises to experience the effects that shortness of breath and muscle fatigue will have on the ability to control fine motor skills needed to accurately shoot a firearm. Being subject to this type of endurance training gives officers an understanding of the physiological effects of shortness of breath and an adrenaline surge and know what to expect with a reduction in fine motor skills. These physiological effects are part of the basic fight or flight self-preservation reaction; people do not have complete control over their actions.

Intense training can give officers the ability to recognize their physical and emotional state, and acquire skills to compensate for some of the effects. Officers work through shoot-don't-shoot scenarios during live-fire training, honing their ability for split-second decision making and marksmanship. With some of the latest technology has come the ability to train with multiple projection screens ranging from 90 to 360 degree field of vision using laser-equipped firearms to track the accuracy of the officers' shot placement. Such systems include full size, actual people to interact with the officer. Some of the training opportunities include real time, fast-paced shoot-don't-shoot scenarios. The scenes may be manipulated so that the same situations can have multiple outcomes, from a shoot situation to a no-shoot option. There are also noises the officers must contend with, hearing loud screams, people running by the officer or across their path, in order to replicate actual situations. This type of training is very beneficial for placing a great deal of stress on the officer who must make multiple decisions just as in potential actual circumstances.

The McNeese State University Police Department (MSUPD) in Lake Charles, Louisiana, has utilized its 90-degree theater, a force simulator, as an educational tool outside the traditional police environment. Partnering with the university's Criminal Justice Program, the MSUPD provides simulator access to criminal justice majors as well as to faculty, staff, and the general student population. This is done as an educational experience, but also as an opportunity for the university community to grasp the physical and mental skills required in the use of force in a situation utilizing a firearm, a Taser, OC spray, and possibly a flashlight.

There is generally a distinct difference in the basic training in the use of a firearm received by civilians and by police officers. Police officers receive additional career training and yearly or quarterly qualifications in firearms. Many agencies shoot quarterly to keep their accuracy level high, while other agencies allow for monthly training. Officers also receive weapon retention training and many train in ground fighting techniques to protect the firearm from being used against the officer. Agencies also issue different gun holster designs to heighten security levels, making it more difficult for a gun to be taken from the officer. The vast majority of holsters purchased by private individuals involve considerations of price rather than security. A single holster retention snap is not a security holster; the snap is added to hold the weapon in place, not to secure it from someone trying to actively take a firearm away from the carrier.

Comparing the state-required civilian training for carrying a concealed weapon, the typical types of civilian holsters, and no standardization of ammunition, contrasted to the continued training that police officers are required to attend, along with testing, qualifications to be met, high-quality equipment, and teamwork, is it advisable to integrate civilians (faculty, staff, and students) with police officers in carrying concealed weapons on campus? In responding to an active shooter or a violent crime, the task of university police is to save lives by assembling a team of officers and quickly locating the threat. A quick search for the active shooter to terminate the threat can be a highly risky operation. Officers are looking for a person with a gun. They may or may not have an accurate description based on a report from an eyewitness, who is very likely under stress. Outside agencies will be responding and entering buildings searching for the active shooter. If police enter a hallway and see a person standing over someone, or walking in the hallway armed with a gun, the officers will verbally engage the person. However, this situation may end badly if the person does not immediately do exactly as they are ordered. Even if the person is identified as a faculty or staff member, or student, protocol would be to search and secure. This protective tactic for the officers also slows down the response to the actual active shooter if a concealed carry individual is encountered. Should the right of a private individual to carry a firearm outweigh the additional danger such a person may create during a shooting incident when the responding officers do not know who the "bad guy" is?

Civilian Situational Awareness

How situationally aware are students, staff, faculty, and visitors on a university campus? Today college campuses are overrun with people wearing expensive headphones or simple ear-buds plugged into cell phones. Individuals wandering to classes, meetings, meals, and club get-togethers are often engrossed in listening to music or talking on their cell phones, oblivious to the environment around them. Without being aware of one's environment, it is nearly impossible to identify a potential threat, describe a threat to summon help, or have a plan to quickly react in a sudden and violent encounter.

Mixing Off-Duty Law Enforcement with Unidentified Armed Civilians

There is ongoing debate about the arming of teachers and administrators, and in allowing concealed permit holders, including students, to be armed on university campuses. Law enforcement officers attend stringent training in firearms in the police academy, and attend annual in-service training in order to maintain their proficiency. But there are no such requirements for ongoing training for concealed carry permit holders. Officers are trained under high-stress environments, using movement in their shooting exercises and scenarios, and also learning tactics, communications, and first aid. This training culminates when officers are faced with a hostile situation. With the changes in tactical responses after Columbine, officers no longer wait for a SWAT (special weapons and tactics) team to arrive when an active shooting situation presents itself; many lives have been lost waiting for such a response. Officers from differing jurisdictions may arrive first, team up, and start the armed emergency response to the threat. With proper communication as other officers arrive and deploy, each unit will be able to know where other officers are converging on a shooter. Under these circumstances, if a person is not immediately identified as a "friendly," the person runs a high risk of being engaged with deadly force if officers see a firearm. Civilian concealed carry permit holders receive none of this rigorous and ongoing training and practice.

Police officers, as with military personnel, are at risk of friendly fire during a violent armed confrontation in which officers are moving into an active shooting situation, seeking out those who are armed, and those who are not readily identified as police officers. The current 24-hour news cycle magnifies situations where police officers must quickly make decisions when they find their life, or the life of another, is in danger, and are prepared to use deadly force. They might shoot an unarmed person, a suspect, an armed citizen, or even another police officer. One such incident occurred in Lynchburg, Massachusetts, in 2013. A plainclothes police officer was chasing a suspect, and was shot once by a uniformed officer (Tumblr.com 2011). Fortunately the officer survived. In New York City, an off-duty police officer was chasing a suspect who had attempted to break into the officer's car. The officer, in regular street clothes, pulled his weapon and gave chase. Other plainclothes on-duty officers saw the men running and saw that the pursuer was armed. When the plainclothes officers yelled for the men to halt, the off-duty officer stopped and turned around, holding his department weapon. One of the officers shot him three times. When medical assistance arrived, the victim was identified as a police officer (Long 2011). These two examples demonstrate the volatile situations in which mistakes can be made. Even though these two officers were carrying police identification, their identity was not apparent at the time of the shooting.

According to the 2014 Police Executive Research Forum (PERF) report on active shooter incidents, a number of police policies note that plainclothes or off-duty officers who respond to an active shooter incident should remember that other responding officers may mistake them for a perpetrator. Ideally, police agencies could work together regionally and issue special apparel that can be recognized from a distance (such as brightly colored baseball caps or windbreakers) that plainclothes and off-duty officers can keep handy in case they respond to an unexpected event so that officers can recognize other officers at a glance. Uniform tactics for plainclothes and off-duty officers at an active shooting incident might include immediately holstering their weapons after stopping a shooter, identifying themselves, and complying with instructions from other responding officers. Civilians do not engage in police active shooter training, do not have badges or special clothing to identify themselves to the police, and thus may be viewed as another armed suspect by multiple teams of first responders who could easily identify the good-intentioned armed civilian as an active shooter.

Is there time for the armed citizen to react with any certainty in an active shooter situation, which is one of the major arguments that citizen right-to-carry advocates use in their arguments for being armed on a university campus? Is there truly a benefit above the risk for citizens to carry a handgun on a university campus? The level of police presence is usually higher on a university campus than in the general community, the rate of crime on campuses is substantially below that of the surrounding community, and by having university police on-duty the response time to prevent or interdict in-progress crimes or workplace violence is usually much faster than that of other local law enforcement agencies. The key value of citizens to the police in an active shooter situation and in many other criminal incidents is to be a situationally aware witness who is on a cell phone providing descriptions of suspects, information about possible weapons, and casualty updates. The "good witness" also becomes invaluable in debriefing with the police in the aftermath of a major event and in future criminal prosecutions.

Magazines for the civilian gun enthusiast abound with articles on home safety, wilderness survival techniques, concealed carry, suggested training, and even topics such as "Active Shooter Takedowns: Lifesaving Tips and Tactics to Neutralize a Gunman in a 'Gun-Free' Zone" (Janich 2014). This article identifies weapon disarming techniques, which require a tremendous amount of dedicated on-going practice to even consider using. While police officers may receive some level of defensive tactics training that may include weapons disarming, it is a very risky strategy to employ. For the average citizen to engage in this level of training to become proficient would be the rare exception. It is the rare voice that focuses on citizens managing and weighing their vulnerability and risk against the need to carry a firearm at one's place of work or at an educational institution (Janich 2013).

Target-Rich Environments for Criminals and Armed Citizens

The term target-rich environments refers to the ease with which criminals may commit crimes with expected high returns for little risk. This may also be referred to as "gun-free zones" by those who support the concealed carry of firearms on school and university campuses. In discussions that were held after the Virginia Tech shooting, some argued that if students had been allowed to carry firearms on campus they may have been able to protect themselves. However, arming faculty, staff, and students does not appear to be in the best interest of the civilian population. The lack of training, practice, and specialized equipment such as tactical bullet resistant vests, radios for communication and coordinating tactical responses, and responding officers' inability to distinguish armed students and faculty from shooters may result in a "friendly fire" situation. When considering the pros and cons of allowing firearms on campuses, it is not just a concern of the active shooter, who receives the majority of news coverage. With an increase of firearms on campuses, the possible stress revolving especially around final examinations, and living in close proximity to others in dormitories, arguments may easily erupt into violence. The general safety of students and the public can be needlessly threatened by student firearm owners. One study revealed that two-thirds of college students who own firearms also engage in binge drinking. Students who own firearms are more likely than those students who do not to consume alcohol "frequently and excessively," to make poor choices such as driving while intoxicated, to engage in property damage activities, and to have negative encounters with police (Sprague 2008). Introducing firearms into the university, a setting in which young, relatively immature adults have left home for the first time, experience new freedoms, and encounter the stress of higher education, can sometimes lead to disastrous consequences.

What Should the General Public Do to Protect Themselves?

The 2014 Police Executive Research Forum (PERF) study does not endorse concealed carry of firearms on university campuses, but notes that "it is important for people to think in advance about how they would respond, because the extremely high stress of an active shooter incident tends to cause people to freeze. Taking action quickly, and taking the right kinds of actions, is critical to saving lives" (PERF 2014, 37). The Department of Homeland Security (DHS) has published pocket cards (Figure 2.6) providing guidance to civilians about active shooter incidents. "The effectiveness of these principles was demonstrated in [the] analysis of the Virginia Tech active shooter event of 2007. In that incident, the shooter attacked or attempted to attack five classrooms. The people in each classroom responded in different ways. In the room that was attacked first and where no defensive actions were taken, 92 percent of the people were shot. In another room, where students had time to push a large desk against the door and hold it there, the shooter fired through the door, but no one was shot" (PERF 2014, 39).

While violence or an active shooter situation can occur on a university campus, the risk of such occurrences is not limited only to institutions of higher education. According to the 2013 FBI Study, 73 (45.6 percent) of 160 incidents that were reviewed occurred in areas other than schools or universities. These included businesses open to pedestrian traffic [44 (27.5 percent)], businesses closed to pedestrian traffic [23 (14.3 percent)], and malls [6 (3.8 percent)]. These distinctions were made in order to determine whether the public was more at-risk in areas where pedestrian traffic was likely. Educational environments were identified as the second-largest location

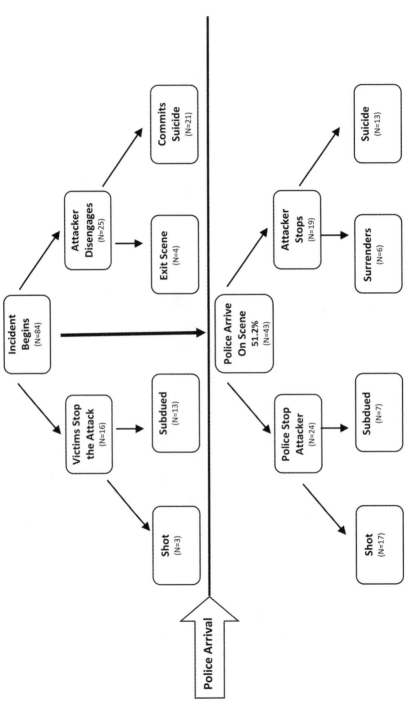

Figure 2.5 Resolution of Active Shooter Events in the United States, 2000–2010 (Active Shooter Events, CRC Press, 2013)

HOW TO RESPOND	HOW TO RESPOND
WHEN AN ACTIVE SHOOTER IS IN YOUR VICINITY	WHEN LAW ENFORCEMENT ARRIVES

	• Remain calm and follow instructions
1. EVACUATE	• Put down any items in your hands (i.e., bags, jackets)
• Have an escape route and plan in mind	• Raise hands and spread fingers
• Leave your belongings behind	• Keep hands visible at all times
• Keep your hands visible	• Avoid quick movements toward officers such as holding on to them for safety
2. HIDE OUT	• Avoid pointing, screaming or yelling
• Hide in an area out of the shooter's view	• Do not stop to ask officers for help or direction when evacuating
• Block entry to your hiding place and lock the doors	
• Silence your cell phone and/or pager	**INFORMATION**
	YOU SHOULD PROVIDE TO LAW ENFORCEMENT OR 911 OPERATOR
3. TAKE ACTION	
• As a last resort and only when your life is in imminent danger	• Location of the active shooter
• Attempt to incapacitate the shooter	• Number of shooters
• Act with physical aggression and throw items at the active shooter	• Physical description of shooters
	• Number and type of weapons held by shooters
CALL 911 WHEN IT IS SAFE TO DO SO	• Number of potential victims at the location

Figure 2.6 U.S. Department of Homeland Security Brochure Educates the Public about Active Shooter Incidents (http://www.dhs.gov/xlibrary/assets/active_shooter_pocket_card.pdf)

category [39 (24.4 percent)]. These incidents were further broken down into those occurring in schools [27 (16.9 percent), including two school board meetings], and higher education institutions [12 (7.5 percent)].

Other incidents, in descending order, were located in:

- Open spaces [15 (9.4 percent)]
- Government properties [16 (10.0 percent)]
- Other (non-military) government properties [11 (6.9 percent)]
- Military properties [5 (3.1 percent)]
- Residences [7 (4.4 percent)]
- Houses of worship [6 (3.8 percent)]
- Health care facilities [4 (2.5 percent)]

Armed citizens have taken action in some active shooting incidents, but it is a very small impact given the potential risk associated with increasing the number of weapons on the street in general and especially on university campuses. Of the majority of the 160 incidents reviewed in the 2013 FBI Study, 90 (56.3 percent) ended on the shooter's initiative—sometimes when the shooter committed suicide or stopped shooting, and other times when the shooter fled the scene:

1. There were at least 25 incidents where the shooter fled the scene before police arrived. In 4 additional incidents, at least 5 shooters fled the scene and were still at large at the time the study results were released.
2. In other incidents, it was a combination of actions by citizens and/or law enforcement that ended the shootings. In at least 65 (40.6 percent) of the 160 incidents, citizen engagement or the shooter committing suicide ended the shooting at the scene before law enforcement arrived.
3. Of those:

   - In 37 incidents (23.1 percent), the shooter committed suicide at the scene before police arrived.
   - In 21 incidents (13.1 percent), the situation ended after unarmed citizens safely and successfully restrained the shooter. In two of those incidents, three off-duty law enforcement officers were present and assisted.
   - Of note, eleven of the incidents involved unarmed principals, teachers, other school staff, and students who confronted shooters to end the threat (nine of those shooters were students).
   - In five incidents (3.1 percent), the shooting ended after armed individuals who were not law enforcement personnel exchanged gunfire with the shooters. In these incidents, three shooters were killed, one was wounded, and one committed suicide.
   - The individuals involved in these shootings included a citizen with a valid firearms permit and armed security guards at a church, an airline counter, a federally managed museum, and a school board meeting.
   - In two incidents (1.3 percent), two armed, off-duty police officers engaged the shooters, resulting in the death of the shooters. In one of those incidents, the off-duty officer assisted a responding officer to end the threat.

     Even when law enforcement arrived quickly, many times the shooter still chose to end his life. In 17 (10.6 percent) of the 160 incidents, the shooter committed suicide at the scene after law enforcement arrived but before officers could act.

     In 45 (28.1 percent) of the 160 incidents, law enforcement and the shooter exchanged gunfire. Of those 45 incidents, the shooter was killed at the scene in 21, killed at another location in 4, wounded in 9, committed suicide in 9, and surrendered in 2 (Federal Bureau of Investigation 2013, 11).

Conclusion

Higher education institutions have always been viewed as being protected, calm, and inviting bastions that encourage research, exploration, and intellectual growth. Colleges and universities are comparable to a small town with housing, theaters, sports complexes, laboratories, libraries, eating establishments, and parking facilities. These support functions all contribute to an institution's primary mission of research and education. These institutions are generally safer, with less crime, than surrounding communities. Universities provide emergency first responders that offer quick reaction to emergencies, medical calls, and criminal incidents, often much faster than traditional local law enforcement agencies.

If civilian concealed carry of firearms on university campuses became a nationwide standard this would mean that instructors might be carrying a firearm while counseling or directing a student or during classroom lectures. Could students and faculty end up armed during a counseling or disciplinary session? How productive could any of these types of meetings remain when one or both parties are armed?

Investing in additional training, equipment, and staffing for university policing provides a greater return in maintaining and enhancing campus-wide safety in a coordinated and professional manner instead of relaxing weapons laws which will unnecessarily increase the number of firearms on campuses. Institutions of higher learning remain unique facilities that are deserving of continued protected status.

Note

* The agreed-upon definition of an "active shooter" by U.S. government agencies— including the White House, Department of Justice/FBI, Department of Education, and Department of Homeland Security/Federal Emergency Management Agency— is "an individual actively engaged in killing or attempting to kill people in a confined and populated area" (A Study of Active Shooter Incidents in the United States between 2000 and 2013 by the FBI). Implicit in this definition is that the subject's criminal actions involve the use of firearms. Mass killings or mass shootings may not always involve an "active shooter," which is a specific type of shooting situation law enforcement and the public may face.

References

Armed Campuses. 2014. "Guns on Campus Laws for Public Colleges and Universities." http://www.armedcampuses.org (accessed November 1, 2014).

Balko, Radley. 2013. "Rise of the Warrior Cop: Is It Time to Reconsider the Militarization of American Policing?" *Wall Street Journal* (August 7). http://online.wsj.com/articles/SB10001424127887323848804578080407805199904 (accessed November 1, 2014).

Baur, Shane. 2014. "The Warrior Cops Suit Up." *Mother Jones* (November/December).

Birnbaum, Robert. 2013. "Ready, Fire, Aim: The College Campus Gun Fight." *Change: The Magazine of Higher Learning* (September-October), 5–6. http://www.changemag.org/Archives/Back%20issues/2013/September-October%202013/gun-fight-full.html (accessed September 22, 2014).

Bureau of Justice Statistics. 2001. "Community Policing." http://bjs.gov/index/cfm?ty=tp&tid=81 (accessed October 15, 2014).

Clinton, Paul. 2010. "Daryl Gates and the Origins of LAPD SWAT." *Police—The Law Enforcement Magazine* (April 16). http://www.policemag.com/blog/swat/story/2010/04/daryl-gates-and-the-origins-of-lapd-swat.aspx.

Deakins, Jacob. 2008. "Guns, Truth, Medicine, and the Constitution." *Journal of American Physicians and Surgeons* 13 (2). http://www.jpands.org/vol13no2.deakins.pdf (accessed October 13, 2014).

Department of Justice. 2005. "National Summit on Campus Public Safety." Office of Community Oriented Policing Services. http://www.cops.usdoj.gov/publications/nationalsummitoncampuspublicsafety.pdf.

Drug Policy Alliance. 2014. "A Brief History of the Drug War." http://www.drugpolicy.org/new-solutions-drug-policy/brief-history-drug-war (accessed October 30, 2014).

Federal Bureau of Investigation. 2013. *A Study of Active Shooter Incidents in the United States Between 2000 and 2013.* Washington, DC.

Federal Bureau of Investigation. 2014. *Crime in Schools and Colleges: A Study of Offenders and Arrestees Reported via National Incident-Based Reporting System Data.* Washington, DC. http://www.fbi.gov/about-us/cjis/nibrs/crime-in-schools-and-colleges (accessed October 16, 2014).

Government Accountability Office. 2012. *Gun Control: States' Laws and Requirements for Concealed Carry Permits Vary Across the Nation.* GAO-12-717.

Harnisch, Thomas. 2008. "A Higher Education Policy Brief, Concealed Weapons on State College Campuses: In Pursuit of Individual Liberty and Collective Security." Washington, DC: American Association of State Colleges and Universities.

Hetznere, Amy. 2011. "Where Angels Tread: Gun-Free School Zone Laws and an Individual Right to Bear Arms." *Marquette Law Review* 95: 359–398.

Hickman, Matthew, and Brian Reaves. 2003. "Community Policing in Local Police Departments, 1997 and 1999." Bureau of Justice Statistics. http://www.bjs.gov/content/pub/pdf (accessed October 20, 2014).

Huffington Post. 2013. "8 Companies That Have Actually Banned Guns." (September 18). http://huffingtonpost.com/2013/09/18/company-gun-bans_n_3948309.html.

Janich, Michael. 2013. "Workplace Violence: Defend and Escape an Active Shooter at the Office." *Personal and Home Defense* (November 21).

Janich, Michael. 2014. "Active Shooter Takedowns." *Personal and Home Defense* (March 27), 14–17.

K12 Academics. 2014. "School Shootings: College and University School Incidents." http://www.k12academics.com/school-shootings/history-school.shootings-united-states/college-university-school-incidents#VHnv_X7naUk.

Kraska, Peter. 2001. *Militarizing the American Criminal Justice System: The Changing Roles of the Armed Forces and the Police.* Evanston, IL: Northwestern University Press.

Long, C. 2011. "Omar Edwards Shot by Fellow Officer Andrew Dunton." *Huffpost Good News* (May 25). http://www.huffingpost.com/2009/05/31/omar-edwards-shot-by-fell_n_209447.html.

Los Angeles Police Department. 2014. "History of SWAT." http://www.lapdonline.org/metropolitan_division/content_basic_view/849 (accessed November 5, 2014).

Matchcollege.com. 2014. "Top Largest Colleges and Universities." http://www.matchcollege.com/top-colleges (accessed October 20, 2014).

Nathan, Tara. 2011. "Carrying on Campus." *The Equinox: Student Newspaper of Kent State University* (March 24). http://keene-equinox.com/2011/03/carrying-on-campus (accessed November 25, 2014).

National Conference of State Legislatures. 2014. "Guns on Campus: Overview." http://ncsl.org/research/education/guns-on-campus-overview.aspx (accessed November 4, 2014).

National Law Enforcement Officers Memorial Fund. 2014. "Law Enforcement Facts." http://www.nleomf.org/facts/enforcement (accessed November 28, 2014).

Philadelphia Police Department. 2012. "Philly Police Unit Profile: Special Weapons and Tactics." http://blog.phillypolice.com/2012/05/phillypolice-unit-profile-special-weapons-and-tactics-swat.

Police Executive Research Forum. 2014. *Critical Issues in Policing Series: The Police Response to Active Shooting Incidents.* Washington, DC.

Reaves, Brian. 2011. *Census of State and Local Law Enforcement Agencies, 2008.* Bureau of Justice Statistics. http://www.gov/index.cfm?ty=pbdetail&iid=2216 (accessed October 3, 2014).

Ritter, Malcolm. 2007. "Experts Link Teen Brains' Immaturity, Juvenile Crime." *USA Today* (December 2). http://usatoday30.usatoday.com/tech/science/2007-12-02-teenbrains_n.htm (accessed September 18, 2014).

Skorton, David, and Glenn Altschuler. 2013. "Do We Really Need More Guns on Campus?" *Forbes* (February 21). http://www.forbes.com/sites/collegeprose/2013/02/21/guns-on-campus (accessed November 29, 2014).

Sprague, Lisa. 2008. "Position Statement: Concealed Carrying of Firearms Proposals on College Campuses." West Hartford, CT: International Association of Campus Law Enforcement Administrators.

Swenson, Ben. 2013. "Weapons 101." *Coastal Virginia Magazine* (May–June). http://www.coastalvirginiamag.com/May-June-2013/Weapons-101 (accessed September 30, 2014).

Tumblr.com. 2013. "Maine Plain Clothes Police Officer Accidently Shot." http://accidentalgunshots.tumblr.com/post/48488244429/maine-plain-clothes-police-officer-accidently-shot.

CHAPTER THREE

Psychological Factors in Legal Firearms Usage

Glenn E. Meyer

Background

Firearms are a common possession in American households. However, their legal usage is not a subject of intensive psychological research. Psychological researchers and organizations may view firearms as inherently unpleasant, reducing interest in studying them in anything but a negative light (Redding 2001; Cornell and Khasawneh 2008; Inbar and Lammers 2012). Since the psychological community is seen as politically liberal in most analyses (Duarte et al. 2014), interest in firearms research is minimal except in some focused legal and psychopathological domains. When discussing ergonomic issues in gun design, Cornell and Khasawneh (2008) put it well: "Virtually no ergonomic investigations have been undertaken regarding firearm safety mechanism design and operation. The desire to avoid political confrontation or the reluctance to be associated with one side or the other in one of the most hotly and emotionally debated issues of the last four decades might account for much of the academic neglect on the topic of firearm safety mechanism design."

However, there is a body of research to be examined. The issues involved can be the psychological factors that influence juries regarding firearm usage: gender, aggressive priming by weapons, memory effects, interactions of race and shooting decisions by police and civilians, bystander intervention, and ergonomic factors in the misuse of firearms. Each of these points will be touched on.

There has been a good deal of discussion in the legal literature of the standards for the use of lethal force in self-defense (Leverick 2007) and factors that influence juries (Devine 2012; Klein and Mitchell 2010). The starting point for this discussion is whether characteristics of firearms and related issues can influence jury decisions. Such issues can include the gender of the firearm user, the race and ethnicity of the participants in the critical incident, firearm experience and training of the gun user, and other human factors. Related problems can be the memory of witnesses to a firearm-related event.

One may predict an increase in self-defense shootings as concealed carry laws have spread across the United States. Roughly, every other household may possess at least one gun (Saad 2011). Gun sales have dramatically increased in recent years (Thurman 2012). For example, federal background checks to purchase firearms increased by 25 percent from 2010 to 2011. Laws have eased the carrying of concealed handguns with 43 states having easily obtained permits or no permits needed for carrying a handgun. In some states, one out of eleven people are able to carry a handgun on the street legally (Jonsson 2012). At least 118 million handguns are in civilian hands and 8 million people have obtained the above-mentioned permits (Government Accounting Office 2012). Studies have indicated that citizens use privately owned firearms more often than thought in self-defense situations (Kleck 1997; Tark and Kleck 2004).

There is a tendency of the naive self-defense oriented user to assume that they will always engage in a "good shoot." It will be judged as such and thus they will be praised. Issues such as gun choice, ammunition choice, and posturing to friends or on the Internet about shooting to kill will not even come into play because shooters supposedly will never see the inside of a courtroom. The discussion rages on the Internet among gun enthusiasts and law enforcement. Here are some fairly typical interchanges. The first is from AR15.com, a popular forum discussing the firearm (http://ar15.com/archive/topic.html?b=1&f=5&t=1445493):

"I read a post a year or so ago regarding the potential for getting into deep poop for using a registered SBR in a self-defense situation."

Reply: "I'll use mine if needed. A good shoot is a good shoot."

Reply: "While a good shoot is a good shoot regardless of the firearm used, juries are stupid and impressionable. The 'ZOMG! Sawed-off Rifle bullet hose of death' would not be my first choice to see as Exhibit A. IOW, I could see a questionable shoot being labeled a bad shoot if an SBR is used."

From a police forum discussing the risk of modified weapons (http://forums.officer.com/forums/archive/index.php/t-129352.html):

"In the 30+ years that I have been hearing this, NO ONE has been able to produce a court case where this was a factor. I carried modified or custom guns for all but the first 2 years of my career. As I used to teach, if it's a good shoot (per your report and witnesses), using a modified gun and oddball ammo does not matter. If it's a bad shoot, having used your issued gun/ammo, with your entire chain of command standing there telling you to 'shoot him' is not going to help."

The idea of a good shoot and finding a case misses several points. Given that a person is going to trial means that the state does not think it is a "good shoot." The influence of weapons-related issues may not make it into legal databases as they affect the mind of a jury in a way that does not necessarily lead to an issue that such data bases will report. Yes, if it is a "good shoot" it won't matter. But you are not the one deciding if your intentional act of extreme violence against another person was justified. If the district attorney and grand jury do not agree with you that it was justified, it won't be a justified shooting unless your trial jury decides it was (Frank Ettin—attorney http://thefiringline.com/forums/showthread.php?t=501122&highlight=suppressed).

Certainly the discussion of George Zimmerman's shooting of Trayvon Martin in Florida in February 2012 demonstrates that one cannot count on a defendant's claim that it was a "good shoot."

Anecdotally, we can see appearance issues operating. In a recent Court TV televised trial (*Florida v. Roten* 2000); the defendant was accused of a hate crime shooting. Roten used a modified SKS (an older Soviet pattern 7.62-mm semiautomatic military rifle) with accessories that might make the rifle appear fiercer than some. The commentator asked why anyone would need such a weapon. During the District of Columbia sniper trial, the district attorney, James A. Willett "dramatized the importance of the weapon" (Dao 2003) by assembling over a period of several minutes the assault rifle used in the attacks. Many people believe that certain types of guns are "good for only one thing—to kill" (Kleck 1997, 16).

From the psychological literature, the operative principle seems to be the "priming of aggressive ideation." The exposure to images of weapons or the weapons themselves can lead people to act aggressively. The first major proponent of the concept was Berkowitz (1993, 70), who stated: "If we tend to think of guns . . . as instruments that are deliberately used to hurt others, rather than as objects of sport and enjoyment, the mere presence of a gun may stimulate us to assault others more severely than we intend."

Such attitudes may be formed by media presentations of violent crimes and military conflicts in news and fictional portrayals. Aggressive thoughts can influence one's view of a social interaction or make an aggressive resolution to a dispute seem more appropriate (Berkowitz and LePage 1967; Bartholow et al. 2005).

Typical studies present images of weapons, weapons themselves, or models of weapons to experimental subjects (usually college students) and operationally defined measures of aggression or negative affect are collected (Anderson et al. 1998). Such studies, use measures of reaction time to words; Bartholow et al. (2005, 49) employ a computer to prime participants with weapon words or weapon pictures, as well as non-weapon stimuli (for instance, plants and animals). Each of these primes was followed by either an aggressive or nonaggressive target word. The participants' task was to read the word aloud as soon as they recognized it. The relative accessibility of aggressive thoughts was assessed by comparing participants' response times to aggressive and nonaggressive target words following both weapon and non-weapon primes. The findings indicated that identifying a weapon increases the accessibility to aggressive thoughts. Such articles may have overreaching but attractive anti-firearms titles, such as: "Does the Gun Pull the Trigger? Automatic Priming Effects of Weapon Pictures and Weapon Names" (Anderson et al. 1998).

Other studies use an analog of aggressive behavior. In an experiment developed by Lieberman et al. (1999), a participant is presented a stimulus that may prime aggression and then is given the opportunity to add anonymously various amounts of hot sauce to another person's drink. While the ecological validity of the lab measure can be debated, it is standard. Klinesmith et al. (2006) used the technique to study weapons-based aggressive priming. Male participants interacted with a pellet gun model of a Desert Eagle handgun or a children's toy. They then were given the opportunity to add as much hot sauce as they wanted to someone else's drink. Participants manipulating the gun added more hot sauce and this was correlated with an increase in testosterone (which mediates aggressive behavior). It was speculated that for males, the presence of guns may increase societal violent behavior.

Thus, the weapon and related issues may make a juror be more punitive towards a defendant as negative affect accrues to the weapon user and the juror feels more aggressive to the defendant. Another suggested effect is that exposure to a weapon influences the emotional aspect of decision and the cognitive construction of a critical incident.

There are various models of jury decisions (Devine 2012):

1. Bayesian and Stochastic postulates that jurors use weighted models and probabilities to come to a decision. It is not seen as a likely psychological process.
2. Story model: Jurors are active information processors that impose a chronological narrative organization on the issues. Information used includes cognitive and emotional schema, stereotypes, scripts, and sequences of events. An example from Devine (2012) would be:

   - David insults Sheila at a bar (initial event).
   - She becomes upset (psychological reaction).
   - She picks a fight outside the bar for revenge (goal).
   - Haymaker thrown (action).
   - She breaks his jaw (consequence).

   The story is used to explain why he is suing her to recover medical costs. There are two criteria for evaluating a story.

   A. Coverage: evidence and facts
   B. Coherence: logical flow based on consistency, completeness, plausibility

The mental state of the actors is important and the story model is seen as the leading paradigm of decision making. Mental state as indicated by the presentation of weapons indicating to the jury something about the defendant can be important. Various social decision processes have been postulated to drive how the story is constructed.

The juror strives to construct a coherent view of the critical incident very early on—perhaps in the opening statements. Presentations of witnesses and exhibits are evaluated as they fit into the story or are discarded. Weapons characteristics and related issues can help form a story that indicates the defendant was irresponsible or "blood lusted." The defendant had the weapons and wanted to use them. Certainly, the Trayvon Martin case is an example with George Zimmerman portrayed as a want-to-be cop. Media "experts" on the Headline News channel speculated that because he had a round chambered in his gun he was "ready to go." If such a presentation is effective, then the jurors will interpret the case through that filter. A "bad" gun—one that is designed primarily to kill—would help to form a story of firearms misuse.

Initial Laboratory Studies on Weapons Effects

Laboratory research supports this view. Two early studies are informative.

First, Dienstbeir et al. (1998) hypothesized that handling or observing weapons would influence criminal proceedings. In their first experiment, participants were assigned prison sentences for first offenses ranging from drunk driving through drug offenses, vandalism, arson, robbery, rape, and manslaughter. Participants chose a specific sentencing option from a 14-point scale, with sentences ranging from no prison time (1) to a death sentence (14). The participants either watched a sports presentation and handled a football or watched a target shooting presentation and then handled a .22 rifle and a Ruger Super Black Hawk .44-magnum pistol while simulating target-shooting for two minutes (96). The weapons participants assigned significantly longer sentences than the sports participants.

In their second experiment, the authors postulated that greater salience of a weapon to a crime would lead to longer recommended sentencing. Two different crimes were presented to groups of four to ten subjects acting as jurors. One crime was a burglary of a gas station and the other was a burglary of a department store. The first crime was associated with burglary tools and the second with a gun (99). There were videotaped depositions by a police officer concerning the crimes. The salience of the gun was varied, with some mock jurors being given only a detailed verbal description of a "Tech-9 machine gun," others seeing the gun that was then placed on the evidence table, and the last group passing the gun from juror to juror before its being placed on the evidence table. Recommended sentence increased from a mean of 5.47 years to 6.60 years as the jurors had more gun exposure. The effect was more pronounced for women than for men. Women with lower gun familiarity gave longer sentences, but the trend was in the opposite direction for men. The authors discuss the implications for the balance between probative and prejudicial effects of how weapons are presented and how appearance issues might influence (at that time) the debate about automatic assault weapons. (I note that many of the researchers in the field are not really conversant with correct firearms nomenclature.)

A second critical study in this area was conducted by Branscombe and colleagues (1993). The goal was to examine gender stereotypes and social inferences about a homeowner who shoots an intruder. They hypothesized that those who violated stereotypical gender norms would be perceived more negatively. In their first study, a homeowner (male or female) heard a noise downstairs, and saw a masked intruder carrying the stereo. A shot was fired that either hit the intruder or the wall. The participants had to vote guilty or not guilty if the homeowner was charged with criminal assault (this being before the current Castle Doctrine paradigm), give a confidence rating, and select a sentence. Thus the person could be a competent or incompetent shooter, male or female defendant. Lenient sentencing and not guilty decisions were the norm. However, subjects were less confident that the incompetent shooter who missed the intruder was innocent compared to the competent male shooter who succeeded. The opposite tendency was observed for female shooters. Competent female shooters created more doubt about their innocence than did incompetent female shooters.

In their second study, there was a strong manipulation of competency (118). A male or female observed their car being broken into by a teenager and went outside with a .38 SPL revolver. The teenager was told to freeze but started to run. The homeowner fires and hits the teenager, but in two different circumstances. One is competent, as an officer states: ". . . she/he meant to shoot the kid, and the bullet hit its target. She/he definitely knew how to use a gun!" In the incompetent condition, the statement was: "She/he meant to shoot the kid, and the bullet ricocheted off the ground. She/he definitely did not know how to use a gun!" The officer adds that, "while I sympathize with Mr./Ms. Crane's desire to protect his/her property, I cannot condone his/her actions. Because his/her life was not threatened, we are considering the possibility of charging him/her with armed criminal assault. At this time, we haven't decided whether or not to file charges against Mr./Ms. Crane." Participants were asked to judge the actions of the homeowner by assigning blame, deciding whether to charge the homeowner, and considering punishment options.

The results demonstrate that as subjects' adherence to the belief that guns provide protection increases, so too does their desire to punish a skillful female shooter, while the desire to punish a skillful male or unskillful female decreases. When the respondents strongly disagree with the notion that guns provide protection, the stereotype-inconsistent homeowners are treated more leniently than those who behave according to normative expectations. For those who do not believe guns protect, the skilled male is perceived as deserving particularly severe punishment. The authors conclude: "For those individuals, who believe that guns will protect their owners, stereotype-inconsistent targets, especially skilled female shooters, were evaluated less positively, were considered more to blame for the outcome, and as deserving greater punishment than stereotype-consistent targets. Less dramatic differences on these dependent measures were observed for those persons who do not believe that guns provide protection. In fact, there was a tendency for those who do not believe that guns provide protection to perceive the stereotype-inconsistent targets more positively, blame them less, and advocate less punishment relative to the stereotype-consistent targets." (121).

They note that previous research indicates that feminist views and viewing guns as protective are negatively related. It appears that violating stereotypical norms can dramatically influence a juror's judgment.

Specific Firearms Issues

The above studies were rather general in nature. What about more specific and technical aspects of firearms usage? Defendants may be evaluated on the basis of the actual firearm and ammunition used, their training, and firearms usage history. Three cases are informative and suggest that such considerations matter. They certainly negate the mantra that in a "good shoot," the truth will out.

Harold Fish

http://www.nbcnews.com/id/15199221/ns/dateline_nbc-crime_reports /t/trail-evidence/

Mr. Fish was involved in an altercation with a man and his dog. The interaction led to Mr. Fish shooting the gentleman. The firearm used was a 10mm semiautomatic pistol. This caliber is a powerful one for a hand-gun. It was pointed out at trial that this is more powerful than the police generally use and that it was loaded with hollow-point ammunition. Mr. Fish's use of this combination of firearm and ammunition in a shooting likely would result in serious injury or death. It was reported that the jury may have viewed this information negatively.

Larry Hickey

http://www.armedcitizensnetwork.org/images/stories/Hickey%20 Booklet.pdf

Mr. Hickey was involved in a physical altercation with three individuals, which ended in gunfire. Hickey claimed that disparity in physical force necessitated using a firearm. He had significant firearms training, which was brought up by the prosecution. A mock jury had a negative reaction and said he had a great deal of training and should have known better. Interestingly, many firearms trainers use catchy phrases as mnemonic devices, perhaps to get a manly chortle out of a class. Two of the classics, "Always cheat, always win" and "One should treat everyone else in a polite manner while simultaneously having a plan to kill them," were brought up by the prosecution. The defense emphasized that the same instructors also taught de-escalation and avoidance. In closing arguments, the negative statements were seen as powerful. From the jury research, they would support a negative construction of Hickey's actions.

Most quality firearms instructors will teach avoidance (Gochenour 2006), as does Massad Ayoob. Steele (2007) suggests that quality training will make it easier to defend a client. However, it may be a double-edged sword if a defendant seems to have ignored that part of class.

Gabriel R. Drennen

http://billingsgazette.com/news/state-and-regional/wyoming/wyoming -supreme-court-hears-riverton-killing-appeal/article_9a1007be-e3b8 -5c88-a9c0-fe36b32d7eea.html

Mr. Drennen was involved in a shooting with a friend and renter. Pushed off a porch and fearing a continued assault, he fired several shots. A relevant issue was that at trial it was mentioned that he was a competitive shooter and engaged in open carry, thus demonstrating a murderous mindset and a tendency to use a firearm. There was a further mindset issue given that the last shot was delayed, which suggested premeditation.

These examples demonstrate that in the real world, issues concerning firearms can be presented to a jury. They are certainly relevant in court if the defendant did not pass over the magic "good shoot" paradigm. I began a research program to investigate some of the issues about how weapons type, gender, and incident interact.

The Effect of Type of Weapons Used in Various Civilian Scenarios

The type of weapons that a U.S. citizen and a resident of a particular state can possess is a matter of much controversy. Bans on various types of semi-automatic weapons have been passed by both the national and state governments and that discussion is well known. However, these bans appear to have had little effect on crime (Koper and Roth 2001).

There is significant negative animus towards what are seen as firearms too dangerous for civilian use, a view that can even extend to police usage. Many people believe that certain types of guns are "good for only one thing—to kill" (Kleck 1997, 16). Ayoob (2000) and Rauch (2004), as well as law enforcement authorities, have commented on how juries can be influenced by media impressions of assault rifles. Media outlets portray gun owners as deranged and demonize military-appearing weapons. There has been significant debate over whether military-style weapons are appropriate for civilian law enforcement (for instance, Associated Press 2002). In San Francisco, a police request for assault rifles led a councilperson to comment : ". . . do we want our officers walking around with M-16s? It sends the wrong message to the community, which is already not trusting police officers and is frankly very fearful of them" (Soltau 2004). Some firearms companies try to sell pump action 5.56 mm rifles or Ruger's 9mm and 40 SW line to police departments because those weapons do not look like military guns (http://www.remingtonle.com/rifles/7615.htm). The inability of the latter to penetrate body armor led reviewers to speculate that, at least, you would be more accurate if you shot violent perpetrators in the leg.

Nor is the gun universe completely satisfied with the AR-15 platform. In the gun media, there is the well-known Zumbo incident. Mr. Zumbo, a well-known hunting expert, opined in 2007: "Excuse me, maybe I'm a traditionalist, but I see no place for these weapons among our hunting fraternity. I'll go so far as to call them 'terrorist' rifles. They tell me that some companies are producing assault rifles that are 'tack drivers.' Sorry, folks, in my humble opinion, these things have no place in hunting. We don't need to be lumped into the group of people who terrorize the world with them, which is an obvious concern." Bill Ruger, manufacturer of a competitive but more sporting appearing rifle, previously aided in denouncing the military derivative guns (Speir 2004). Such sentiments are congruent with those of failed presidential candidate Mitt Romney in earlier days: These guns are not made for recreation or self-defense. They are instruments of destruction with the sole purpose of hunting down and killing people.

Psychological research, using the techniques discussed earlier, confirms that a hunter or gun owner does not necessarily have positive attitudes about "assault" weapons. Bartholow, Anderson, Carnagey, and Benjamin (2005) found that assault weapons prompted more aggressive attitudes than did sporting firearms in gun-knowledgeable individuals, as compared to less knowledgeable participants. The former are more aware of their presumed more "lethal" purpose.

However, these authors are overly general in their definition of "assault weapons" by gun world standards: "Assault guns included both handguns and assault rifles (semi-automatic and fully automatic 'machine guns'). Assault guns differ in appearance from hunting guns in several ways, including black or gray coloration, short barrels, and large ammunition magazines or 'clips.'"

Defining what is an assault rifle or weapon is an ever popular topic on the Internet and in the gun media. The term "assault" is seen as a pejorative term and various gun world entities proposed the use of "modern sporting rifles" for AR-15 types of weapons to distinguish them from fully automatic M-4 or M-16 firearms used by the military and police. It is thought that such palliatives and pointing out that they are definitely not machine guns will soothe the savage breast of people who have negative attitudes toward these guns. We decided to study the effect of assault rifle usage using juror decisions in an ambiguous homeowner defensive situation and in a police incident.

Defense against a Burglar: G. E. Meyer, A. S. Baños, T. Gerondale, K. Kiriazes, C. M. Lakin, and A. C. Rinker (2009)

We conducted three experiments on whether the type of weapons used in a home defense scenario would influence a jury, and one experiment with a police incident. The first three used the same classic defensive gun use conundrum that is ubiquitous in firearms training and similar to that used by Branscombe and colleagues (1993) and Dienstbier and colleagues (1998). Mock juror participants were presented with detailed written descriptions of a burglary scenario including defensive gun usage. The written presentations were created with the input of legal and law enforcement professionals to ensure that the arguments were valid and are comparable to other jury simulation methodologies (Bornstein 1999; Roesch, Hart, and Ogloff 1999). The scenarios also contained additional factual descriptions of the firearm (Figure 3.1), the layout of the home (Figure 3.2 for a version of the layout), the fatal injuries, and other details. No pejorative remarks were made about the guns.

First, the written presentation described the incident in factual terms: At night a homeowner hears a sound from downstairs, and investigates. The homeowner, who is armed, goes to the foot of the stairs and discovers a burglar in the act of stealing a VCR. The homeowner challenges the burglar by pointing the firearm at him and yells, "Don't move!" The burglar responds with a curse and a threat to kill the homeowner. The burglar does not have a visible weapon. The homeowner then shoots the burglar twice, killing him. Immediately after the shooting, the homeowner calls 911 and informs the police of the actions of the burglar as described above.

The scenario is ambiguous with regard to the need of the homeowner to shoot. While laws may vary (Kleck 1991, 1997), in many states this would

Figure 3.1   Firearms Images Used in the Scenarios

be a defensible shooting if the homeowner saw the threat as credible. However, the homeowner did have the burglar at a disadvantage and another jurisdiction might indict and try the homeowner.

Second, mock jurors read the prosecution's and the defendant's portrayal of the incident. The prosecution emphasized that there was no need to engage or shoot the burglar and there was the possibility of retreat. The district attorney brought the charges of second degree murder with a

ATTRACTIVENESS SCENARIO

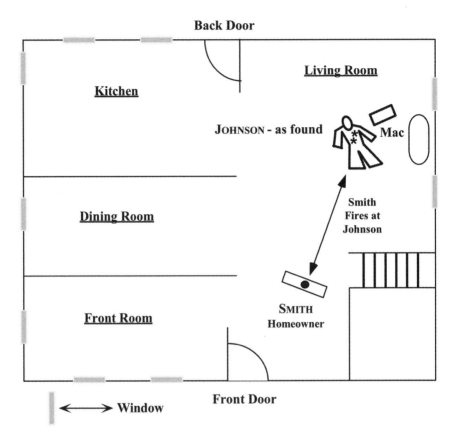

Figure 3.2 Attractiveness Burglary Layout: Similar Versions Used in Experiments Using the Burglar Scenario

possible penalty of up to a 25-year sentence against the defendant and argued the defendant was never truly in danger of grievous bodily harm, could have retreated, or at least waited before firing the weapon.

The defense emphasized that the homeowner feared for his or her life or felt in danger of grievous bodily harm and did not have the duty to retreat. When the burglar turned, he feared that this younger man might rush him. The distance of 15 feet could be closed in a second's time. Thus, the defendant felt there was sufficient disparity of force (difference in physical abilities) and the burglar could quickly put him at risk of significant harm. The defendant was also operating under the "Castle Doctrine": A person's home is his or her castle and one does not have to retreat in one's own home nor should one be compelled to hide if one suspects an intruder is present.

The first study used a male defendant and six possible weapons as seen in Figure 3.1 (these pictures were used in subsequent studies). The guns were a mixture of sporting guns and what might be classified as tactical or assault weapons by people not familiar with appropriate terminology. Women decided on higher sentences than men for the homeowner defendants (male average = 3.9 years and female average = 5.7 years). Importantly, the average recommended sentence when the homeowner used the AR-15 weapon was 7.2 years for male subjects and 8.5 for females. This was significantly higher than any of the other gun types. The handguns had the lowest recommended sentences (in the two to four year range).

We replicated the experiment with students from the local community college who were older and had different socio-economic status and life experiences than liberal arts students. We focused on two gun scenarios, the AR-15 and the Ruger Mini-14. Both are equally potent but the latter looks less aggressive to some. The Mini-14 was explicitly excluded in the original assault weapons ban, perhaps due to its appearance and manufacturer demonizing of the AR-15 and higher capacity magazines (Speir 2004). We analyzed judgment of guilt versus innocence. In direct comparison, the AR-15 yielded significantly longer mean recommended sentences in the order of seven to nine years as compared to the Ruger (approximately two and a half years). With regard to the verdict, the percent of guilty judgments was approximately 65 percent for the AR-15 versus 45 percent for the Ruger.

The third experiment added the significant factor of defendant gender. From the previously cited research, a female using a weapon of war, assault rifle, or "evil black gun" might represent an added burden for the defense. Thus, we tested the same burglary scenario with a female homeowner/shooter in addition to a male. Based on Branscombe and colleagues (1993) we expected mock jurors to judge female shooters more harshly. Interactions with weapon type might be expected because using the AR-15 might violate gender stereotype more than the Mini-14.

Participants in this study were students in introductory psychology classes. The same materials and procedure were used again in this experiment. Participants were asked to make a guilty/not guilty judgment. Next, participants were asked to assign a penalty, assuming the defendant was found guilty, that could range up to 25 years. Except for the mention of the homeowner's gender, no specific remarks about risk based on gender were made. Each participant saw only one scenario.

We found the overall effect of gun type was significant. AR-15 shooters were given longer sentences. The most telling finding was that female mock jurors gave female AR-15 shooters the harshest sentences—a mean of approximately eight years as compared to a male average of five and a half years. In comparison, the lowest average recommended sentence was for a male shooting a Ruger Mini—about two and a half years. Thus, gun type and gender could be a potent combination in sentencing. See the summarized data presented in Figure 3.3. Assault rifles were again seen negatively and women using them were penalized. The violation of gender stereotypes and societal norms was detrimental to their defense. We evaluate other gender-specific issues later.

It is important to note that the AR-15 was not specifically discussed as being an assault rifle or in some way unusual but only in technical terms and matched with equally lethal weapons. A law enforcement officer suggested that for the issue of weapons type to be important at trial, an attorney would have to bring it up and a judge might not allow that. However, our studies as well as earlier investigations indicate that the simple presence of a weapon can be influential. Attorneys should be cognizant of the gun presence, gender, and gun type effects/gender interactions so as to mount an effective defense for their client.

Police Perceptions of Weapon Types

An intentional but mistaken shooting of civilians by police is traumatic for all involved. The best known case is that of Amadou Diallo who on February 4, 1999, was shot 19 times and killed near his Bronx apartment building when police mistook his wallet for a gun (Cooper 1999). Police use of assault rifles like the AR-15 is also controversial—and has increased after notorious shootouts (such as the February 1997 North Hollywood shootout with two heavily-armed bank robbers) and as a response to terrorism and rampage shootings. Politicians and citizen groups express negative attitudes toward militarization trends in police departments. Sachs (2008) refers to a Chicago citizen's group protesting a plan for the police department to buy such guns and the militarization of police. The issue has been investigated, such as the police response to the Michael Brown shooting in Ferguson, Missouri (Boule 2014).

Police themselves may have negative attitudes toward various weapon types. An informal experiment was conducted at a recent Force-on-Force police training exercise, dealing with traffic stops in which a civilian is found to have a firearm. The training officer was aware of the preliminary results of our investigation and was curious as to how they would apply to officers. The type of firearm was varied between an AR-15, a handgun, and a pump-action shotgun. The gun was stored in a manner that was a minor violation of the law, and the officer might have some discretion in dealing with the situation. All of the officers (N = 45) in the exercise stated that they would arrest the driver with the AR-15. Only two said that they

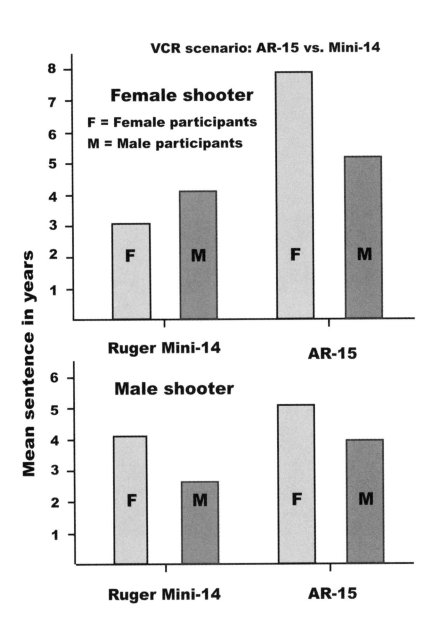

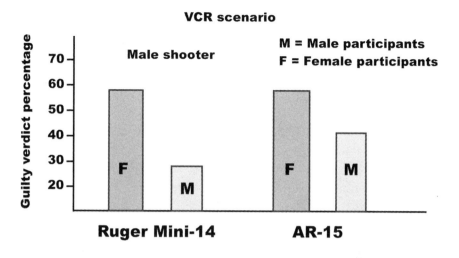

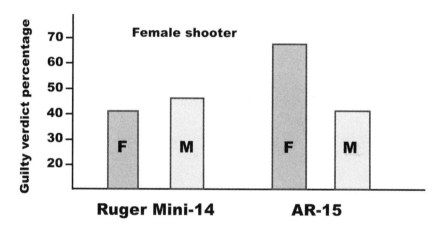

Figure 3.3a and b Judgment of Guilt vs. Innocence (Results from Meyer et al. 2009)

would arrest the shotgun-carrying driver, and 75 percent said they would not arrest the driver with the handgun. A typical comment was that anyone carrying an assault rifle was looking for trouble. The training officer was surprised, as the officers were usually "gun friendly," and some carried assault rifles in their own cars.

Overall, this study found a powerful effect for the appearance of assault rifles. Strategies to make them seem less dangerous, such as arguing about terminology, emphasizing recreational usage or the constitutional right to possess such weapons have not yet been explored in the jury setting. We next explored other scenarios to determine the weapons effect depending on the situation.

Accidental Shootings and "It Just Went Off"

This experiment dealt with a classic excuse for a shooting: "The gun just went off and I thought there was a bad guy out there." In 1993, 30 people were accidentally killed by private citizens who mistook them for an intruder. In contrast, police accidentally killed 330 innocent individuals in the same year (Lott and Mustard 1997, 1–2). For example, the case in which a Louisiana homeowner shot a Japanese exchange student Yoshihiro Hattori in 1992 made national and international news and led to protests and petitions from the Japanese government and citizenry (Ayoob 1998). The student, along with a friend, was looking for a party. They went to the wrong house and approached the homeowner who, along with his wife, was frightened by the seemingly threatening behavior of the student. The victim's refusal to stop at a verbal command (perhaps due to language difficulties) led to his being shot and killed. The homeowner was acquitted but later had a large judgment against him in civil court. Sometimes the homeowner claims that the gun just went off. Factors that cause accidental or negligent discharges will be discussed below.

A trial similar to the Hattori case but not as well known involves Todd Vriesenga, who had an initial run-in with young people engaged in a Halloween prank at his home (CourtTV, 1993, *Minnesota v. Vriesenga*— http://www.nytimes.com/1992/11/19/us/no-headline-969692.html). Vriesenga chased them away by waving a canoe paddle and shouting some obscenities. Later, a young man from the group decided to go up to the house to apologize. At this point, accounts diverge. Vriesenga claimed the young man was trying to enter through the front door. Vriesenga retrieved a shotgun from the closet to defend himself and as he pushed against the door, he claimed the gun fired accidentally. Forensics suggested that he actually raised the gun to his shoulder and fired through the door. Testimony from the other young people contradicted Vriesenga. In any case, Vriesenga was found guilty of a misdemeanor use of a firearm to cause death and was given a two-year sentence. Interestingly, in his testimony, Vriesenga seemed to try to minimize the aggressive aspect of the shotgun. He stated that when he saw someone approaching: "I reached in that closet for what I thought was nothing but some steel and some wood that would intimidate these people away," which seems to be a less than credible statement or one calculated not to give the impression of going for a powerful weapon.

We switched to the tape methodology as the case fell into our paradigm to study and because of evidence that making the firearm more salient can influence sentencing (Dienstbier et al. 1998). While controversial, studies of the effect of violent games suggest that exposure to violence may key aggressive attitudes (Anderson and Dill 2000). Bornstein (1999) reported that it is ambiguous whether video demonstrations in court increase guilty sentences. If there is an effect it is probably not much (Bright and Goodman-Delahunty 2006; Feigenson and Dunn 2003). Kassin and Garfield (1991) reported that viewing a tape of a murder scene leads to lower conviction standards than non-video or irrelevant video conditions. Bernhardt, Sorenson, and Brown (2001) report that televised presentations about gun violence can key negative attitudes about gun usage. Kassin and Dunn (1997) found that computer-animated displays can influence juries. Thus, we decided to try a more visual medium. However, because we used a real trial, we could not study shooter gender.

We obtained a one-hour summary of the *Michigan v. Vriesenga* trial from CourtTV with permission to use it in our experiment (Court TV 1993). The tape was edited in two ways. First, the length was cut to twenty minutes as we edited out irrelevant breaks, testimony not felt essential, and commentary from Court TV reporters. We also removed footage of the state's forensic expert who described the shotgun that Vriesenga used. Instead, at the end of the video, we added a segment of an expert (Karl Rehn from KRTraining of Austin, Texas) demonstrating one of four firearms. The expert described the gun in non-pejorative terms and then fired two shots from the firearm at a target. There was then a close-up of the target.

The firearms used were the AR-15, a Ruger 10/22 22LR rifle, a Winchester Defender shotgun, and a Winchester over and under shotgun (see Figure 3.1). The AR-15 was the operationally defined "evil" gun. The Winchester Defender 12 gauge shotgun, similarly, is a gun more designed for tactical use and not a sporting arm. It has a high capacity for a shotgun of eight rounds. It is black and anecdotally impressive to our students. Depending on jurisdiction, such shotguns have been subject to various legal strictures (Kleck 1997). The Ruger 10/22, while a semiautomatic rifle with a black synthetic stock, is not particularly impressive in appearance. It is a common "plinker" and can be found sitting benignly in Walmart stores across the country. Although all firearms are weapons of lethal force, this gun would not be seen as being close in lethality to the other weapons used. Legal bans on this type of firearm are not common in the United States (Kleck 1997). The last firearm was a sporting shotgun

(Winchester over and under) and very commonly in use for hunting and various competitions. As a 12-gauge firearm, it is a very lethal instrument. However, this type of gun is usually not specifically recommended in the firearms literature for self-defense use. It is however recommended by Vice President Biden and should be shot in the air or through the door (Calmes 2013).

Each gun was fired at standard B-27 targets. This target is a black, 25-inches-by-45-inches, human male silhouette that is portrayed from the head to just below the hands. It is a commonly used law enforcement range target and is also used for civilian practice. The center of the target was covered with a Birchwood-Casey Shoot n c B24-10 seven-inch circle to provide greater visibility. When hit by a round, the Shoot n c leaves the bullet hole with a brilliant yellow ring to emphasize the placement of the shot.

The rifles each fired a small caliber round of approximately .22 inch in diameter, so that the two holes in the target were relatively small. The shotguns were loaded with 00 buckshot that consisted of nine pellets, each .33 inch in diameter. The two shots fired from each gun essentially vaporized the center of the targets with an approximately four-inch wide hole. In pre-testing the videos, observers were most impressed with the shotguns. It made some subjects wince when they saw the damage inflicted on the targets. After presentations of the video, subjects were asked to decide between guilty and not guilty, and if a sentence was given, select a prison term from 2 to 25 years.

In this case, there were no significant effects for gun type and participant gender. Mean sentences ranged from 6 to 11 years with no discernible pattern. Guilty rates ranged from 50 percent to 80 percent. The AR-15 generated 80 percent guilty ratings, as did the Ruger 10/22.

Overview of Issues

Our results pull together various threads in the professional and popular literatures. Gender main effects in several of the experiments were significant with women subjects judging shooters more harshly than the male subjects did. This is congruent with the literature. We found a gun type risk in the burglary scenario—the classic assault rifle, for both men and women. Interestingly, the three-way interaction between gun type, shooter gender, and subject was significant. The locus of the prison sentence interaction was due to women subjects giving the longest sentence to woman shooters who used the assault rifle. These results are in accord with previous findings of harsher judgments for women who break gender-biased weapon use stereotypes (Branscombe et al. 1993) and suggest that such a woman might be seen as more inherently culpable than a man if she used a weapon that was seen as inappropriate for the "gentler sex." If one violates role stereotype in a confrontation, then blame can be shifted more to the violator, which in this case is the woman. Branscombe et al. (1993) found that women who violate gender stereotypes in a shooting situation (shooting competence) are judged more harshly. Using an AR-15 is likely to be such a violation and led to the harsher sentence. Similarly, this supports Dienstbier and colleagues (1998) that women tended to give longer sentences to women who used the AR-15. McCaughey (1997), in an analysis of women who train in self-defense tactics, suggests that they are at risk at trial for not appearing womanly and like a victim. Branscombe and Weir (1992) found that a strong physical defense against a rapist led to shorter sentences for the attacker. They state that behavior which does not fit classic schema of the female stereotype will be construed as abnormal. It is then easier to assign alternate outcomes. Using an AR-15 may make the shooter open to violating the norms of someone exercising self-defense. Does the gun mean that you are more prone to go on the offense? This may be even more damaging for women. Kazan (1997) states that in battered women cases, those who are active in protecting themselves may not be seen as truly battered. Some women may feel less safe around guns in the community (Miller et al. 2001) and thus regard gun users in general as contributing to their lack of safety.

No scale really can measure psychometrically the need to shoot at this time, but such scenarios are qualitatively judged no-shoots in my experience and research with the self-defense training communities and some legal scholarship (Heller 1998). Branscombe and Weir (1992) report that changing the scenario can weaken the effects as one moves toward a ceiling or floor. Finkel, Meister, and Lightfoot (1991) found wide variations in not guilty verdicts by reason of self-defense (NGRSD) with women defendants in battered women, rape, and a Goetz-like subway shooting. Branscombe and colleagues (1993) found similar ceiling effects in one of their studies similar to ours. Darley, Carlsmith, and Robinson (2000) found that sentencing behavior seems motivated by a need to give the guilty party their just deserts. The scenarios with no gun-type risk may have been ones where the moral nature of the act (an unnecessary shooting) led to the shooters being found guilty independent of the gun used; the gun was not part of the motivational evaluation of our subjects.

Olson and Darley (1999) found that lower sentences were given to persons who in self-defense situations killed someone who was stealing a car, was an unarmed attacker, or could safely retreat as compared to those who kill in response to a trivial threat. Failure to believe in the justice system led to longer sentences that may be related to our attitude findings. They further suggest that legal codes should be more in accord with community standards than those suggested in the MPC when determining self-defense standards. However, some of their scenarios were not in accord with modern self-defense training. Perhaps scaling approaches could be developed to scale defensive gun use scenarios and punishments, as Harlow, Darley, and Robinson (1995) did for intermediate penal sanctions.

Training and Its Influence on Jurors

Training in firearms usage would seem to be an obvious positive. In a critical incident, one wants to act correctly and efficaciously. Realistic firearms training increases situational awareness: the ability to marshal useful cognitive and perceptual processes. Experts have automated the technical aspects of firearms usage (gun manipulation, stance, commands, evaluation of stimulus relevance) and need less mental effort for these processes (Johnson et al. 2014). Training has been shown in many critical incidents (fires, accidents, plane disasters) to mitigate the crippling effects of a crisis situation, providing a perceptual and cognitive schema, paradigm, heuristic, or unified pattern with which to understand and select relevant stimuli of the incident. Training can provide a person:

- Habituation to the fearful nature of stimuli.
- Confidence that one can handle a situation.
- A perceptual and cognitive schema, paradigm, heuristic, or unified pattern to understand and pick out relevant stimuli of the incident.
- An available set of automatic and cognitive responses to move into working memory; unconscious competence.

The firearms training community has recognized a tendency particularly in males not to train with their firearms (Werner 2014—http://tacticalprofessor.wordpress.com/2014/11/09/what-is-the-value-of-training/comment-page-1/#comment-750). Werner believes that the Dunning-Kruger effect—the tendency to regard oneself as more competent than is justified—leads many to think that they are competent combatants without formal gun usage training and education.

How does training influence jury views of a shooter? Steele (2007), in an article for attorneys, states that "Ideally, the client will also have some formal training in the use of deadly force which will allow the client's teacher to testify about the client's training in order to show that the client's actions were subjectively reasonable."

In this study, we evaluated whether training might be a negative factor, as suggested anecdotally. Thus, we presented the participants a Kitty Genovese scenario (Manning et al. 2007) with the bystander using lethal force. We are also interested in bystander effects. All participants first received a variant of the same scenario in written form. A 51-year-old male (intervener—Mr. Smith) enters a parking structure and sees a male (Johnson) in his twenties kicking, yelling at, and hitting a woman. The woman seems to be a stranger to her attacker. The bystander kills the attacker and then is brought to trial. Defense and prosecution present arguments about a charge of second degree murder (Good Samaritan versus crazed vigilante). Our focus is how participants actually view the use of lethal force in the bystander situation. Did they think it was justified? We also want to examine whether weapons priming would negatively or positively affect the jury decision. Thus, we varied the prosecution's presentation, the defendant's level of training in firearms usage, and the vividness of the portrayal of the gun used. It is possible that a defendant with more training will be judged more negatively than one without such training and that a portrayal of a trained defendant using a weapon would be damaging to his case. There are three conditions in the presentation of the case: (1) a simple presentation of the incident without a detailed description of the weapon or a description of advanced handgun training; (2) a presentation of the incident plus a description of the defendant's intensive handgun training and a photograph of him at the training venue along with a humanoid target that has bullet holes in the center and head; and (3) all the same descriptors as before in addition to a video presentation of the defendant in a series of training exercises. In these videos, the defendant is engaged in shooting at a series of humanoid cardboard targets with a Glock handgun in scenarios that duplicate typical defensive handgun usage. Training was described as a typical series of courses:

- The First Pistol Course
- Beginning Defensive Tactics
- Intermediate Tactics
- Extreme Defensive Techniques
- Intensive Handgun Usage

A rating of guilt was used, from 1 (sure of innocence) to 7 (sure of guilt). The participants also completed a self-rating of knowledge about firearms on a scale from 1 (not knowledgeable at all) to 7 (very knowledgeable). The subjects were assigned to two groups based on their self-perception of gun knowledge. Self-reports of 1 to 4 (lower knowledge) were in the first category (N = 192) and reports of 5 to 7 (higher knowledge) were in the second category (N = 67).

Results

There were significant differences according to participant gender, with males being more likely to self-report high levels of knowledge (males = 47.9 percent versus females = 7.7 percent). Participant gender had no effect or interaction. Gun knowledge did have an effect but appears most dramatically in the drop in the guilt ratings for the knowledgeable subjects presented with the most detailed description that included the video presentation, as shown in Figure 3.4. Thus for gun-friendly people, being

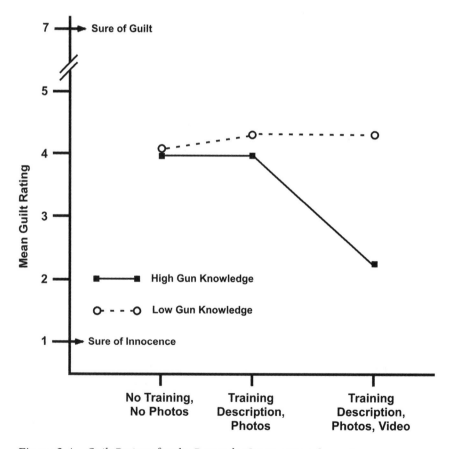

Figure 3.4   Guilt Ratings for the Bystander Intervention Scenario

more knowledgeable was evaluated more positively. Anecdotally, a female who was skilled in the martial arts said the video convinced her that the shooter knew what he was doing. Although training might seem a negative to some, Nagtegaal and colleagues (2009) did not find that members of a Netherlands shooting association displayed necessarily higher levels of aggression.

Gender Issues, Training, and Attitudes toward Firearms

Much of the discussion of self-defense can encompass issues specific to women and how gender attitudes influence the legal process (Barrow and Mauser 2002; Branscombe and Owen 1991; Branscombe and Weir 1992; Branscombe, Crosby, and Weir 1993; Kazan 1997). There is significant female and feminist literature that is positively oriented toward self-defense (Farnam and Nicholl 2002; Hayes 2010; Jackson 2010; McCaughey 1997; Stange and Oyster 2000). McCaughey (1997) recounts that unprecedented numbers of women are learning to maim, shoot, and disable men who assault them.

However, not all view favorably women's use of guns. Gender differences can be potent and controversial in firearms-based societal attitudes toward women's use of force (Homsher 2001; McCaughey 1997; Stange and Oyster 2000). Homsher (2001) critiqued *Ms. Magazine*'s proposition that gaining equal rights did not include the Second Amendment right to keep and bear arms and that adopting a male view of firearms usage was abhorrent. Dole (2000, 11) states in analyzing the mass media: "Despite widespread support for strong images of women in the media, mainstream film viewers and academic feminists alike have hesitated to celebrate cinematic women with guns, even those who are upholders of law." In film, "women using guns" tests the cultural and masculine meaning of firearms, and gender barriers might be fundamentally altered (19). This can be threatening to both men and women. One component of the feminist debates over the movie *Thelma and Louise* might be their violent behavior involving guns (Keating 2000). Active self-defense by women may be viewed negatively as a violation of a gender stereotype of the passive woman. Hollander (2009) summarizes the negative attitudes to women's self-defense: (1) women's active resistance to attack is improbable; (2) it is too dangerous; and (3) the victim is often blamed. Marsh and Goldberg (1996) discovered the general attitude that women should comply in a robbery attempt, which leads to the question of whether firearms are seen as appropriate self-defense tools for women. Anderson (2001), in reviewing Stange and Oyster (2000), expressed the view that teaching women to use guns disempowers them. Women are capable of being trained to physically resist men and do not need a firearm. Using guns should not be part of the female resistance paradigm because firearms are more appropriately a male instrument. Barrow and Mauser (2002) hold that such a view may be common in the legal literature and precedents.

The present study attempts to explore further the issues revolving around the use of firearms in self-defense scenarios concerning women in jury scenarios. In the first study, the situation involves a response to a stalker. The second is that of a classic battered wife. How would the use of a firearm be perceived in a situation that was not immediately defensive? The third concerns whether a female shooter's attractiveness would influence a verdict in a home defense scenario. Also explored is how attitudes toward firearms and participant gender may influence the jury. Negative attitudes toward firearms may lead predictably to harsher views of women using guns. However, the gender of the participant may interact with views of firearms. A pro-gun male might be more conservative in his view of female empowerment and thus have a negative view of women using firearms. However, a pro-gun attitude might lead men to celebrate the gun usage by a woman who is breaking gender stereotypes. Similar positive or negative predictions could be made for antigun males that lead to a set of empirical questions.

Shooting a Stalker

Stalking can be "generally defined as an intentional pattern of repeated intrusive and intimidating behaviors toward a specific person that causes the target to feel harassed, threatened, and fearful, or that a reasonable person would regard as being so" (Miller 2012).

Questions about attitudes toward firearms in Table 3.1 (based on Branscombe, Weir, and Crosby 1991) concern age and gender. The four questions were also related to popular concerns of the firearms-using public. The responses were used to classify the participants into gun-positive and gun-negative groups. Using a median split of the summed responses (a maximum score of 28, a score of 18 being the median), the participants were categorized as being positive or negative on gun-related attitudes. We found the median of 18 to be remarkably stable in other laboratory studies involving hundreds of participants.

Participants were presented with a laminated card describing a stalker's shooting and the court consequences. In one version, the woman simply bought a Glock handgun. In the other, she bought the handgun and

Table 3.1 Firearms Attitude Questions

1. Do you think adult law-abiding citizens should be able to possess firearms?

1	2	3	4	5	6	7
Strongly Disagree						Strongly Agree

2. Do you think that people have the right to use lethal force to protect themselves?

1	2	3	4	5	6	7
Strongly Disagree						Strongly Agree

3. Do you think that people have the right to use lethal force to protect their property?

1	2	3	4	5	6	7
Strongly Disagree						Strongly Agree

4. Rate your knowledge of firearms:

1	2	3	4	5	6	7
Not Very Knowledgeable						Very Knowledgeable

Procedure: Sum scores and those scoring 18 and above are classified as pro-gun. Below as anti-gun. Based on a stable median split with hundreds of participants.

proceeded to take a set of advanced firearms training courses. Participants provided a rating from "not guilty" to "guilty" (1 to 7) and, if guilty, recommended a sentence for second degree murder of 2 to 25 years.

Results

As might be expected, the victim who shot the stalker was viewed more negatively by those with unfavorable firearms attitudes. In general, ratings to convict were in the middle range, perhaps expressing doubt as to guilt (Figure 3.5).

The effects of firearms training, participant gender, firearms attitudes, and gender by firearms attitudes are significant for the recommended sentence. As seen in Figure 3.5, negative attitudes toward guns clearly led to longer sentences and this was due to the males with negative gun

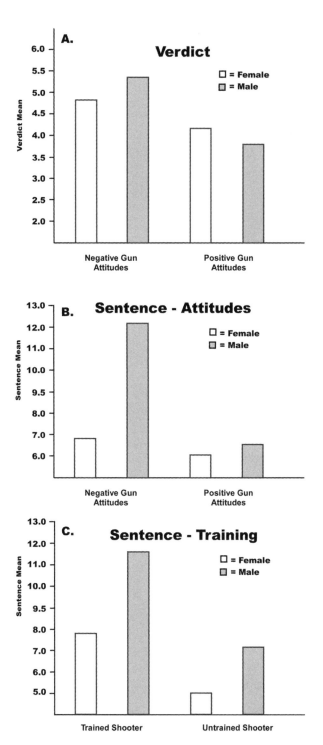

Figure 3.5 Stalker Verdict and Sentence: Attitudes and Training

attitudes. Male participants recommended longer sentences and training was seen as a negative factor. The trained female stalking victim was particularly disliked by male participants. These results correspond with the idea that females should be passive victims and not engage in a proactive defense, and males would be more likely to hold such beliefs. Antigun males were particularly judgmental against female use of firearms. These results are in accord with other studies showing greater animus against females who act against gender stereotypes (Branscombe et al. 1993; Meyer et al. 2009).

Battered Wife Uses a Firearm

Can a woman use lethal force against a partner or spouse who has a long-term history of battering when she is not under immediate threat of physical attack? There seem to be two central aspects to the issue. First, is it legitimate to use lethal force to prevent further attacks that may or not occur? Is the probability of a later attack enough to warrant the use of lethal force and thus a claim of self-defense? The use of preventive lethal force is not accepted legal doctrine nor is it recommended by self-defense experts (Leverick 2007; Ayoob 2014). The second main issue is whether the psychological consequences of being physically abused, such as the controversial battered woman syndrome as a subset of the post-traumatic stress disorder (PTSD) can serve as a justifying or mitigating factor at trial (Leverick 2007). Since its first use, the battered woman syndrome has been quite controversial (McCaughey 1997).

In this experiment, a woman shoots and kills an abusing spouse who is sleeping (a scenario used in research—Greenwald et al. 1990; Terrance and Matheson 2003). Previous studies found that simulated juries were not overly sympathetic to the defendant spouse. We focused on whether gun type (revolver, AR-15, or sporting shotgun) and participants' firearms attitudes would influence verdict and sentence judgments. The guns included a Smith and Wesson 642 and an AR-15. One might predict that the type of gun would influence these decisions with the AR-15 leading to the battered spouse being treated more harshly. Kazan (1997) states that in battered women cases, those who are active in protecting themselves may not be seen as truly battered. Using a weapon with negative animus might fit into that belief structure.

Participants were presented with the battered wife scenario based on Terrance and Matheson (2003). Divided into three gun type groups, they were presented with a videotape of an expert firing the firearms used in this study. Participants made a dichotomous guilty/not guilty judgment as well as a sentence recommendation (2 to 50 years) for second degree murder.

The battered wife was found guilty by a substantial majority of participants (82 percent), a result that agreed with past studies. Terrance and Matheson (2003) state that juries overwhelmingly produced guilty verdicts. Similarly, Greenwald and colleagues (1990) found 69 percent guilty verdicts. None of the factors of participant gender, gun attitudes, or gun type had any significant effect (see Figure 3.6).

With regard to sentencing, the participants were not lenient on the defendant, recommending an average sentence of 9.6 years (MSE = .58). The firearms attitude effect clearly shows that positive firearms participants recommend a lower sentence (M = 7.9, MSE = .84) than those with negative firearms attitudes (M =10.9, MSE - .77).

The high rate of juror displeasure seems to have eliminated a gun type effect.

Defendant Attractiveness in a Home Defense Scenario

Attractiveness of a trial participant is one factor that can influence juries. One can consider whether the attractiveness of a victim influences the sentencing of the attacker or one can consider whether the attractiveness of a defendant committing a crime influences how the jury considers the defendant. A defensive gun user may be seen as an attractive victim and/or attractive defendant.

Devine (2012) reviews the literature on the issue of defendant attractiveness. The typical conclusion is that the hypothesis that an attractive defendant is treated better is either rejected or weakly supported. Many other factors were poorly controlled or might have moderated the reported findings, such as the definition of attractiveness and unmeasured jury attitudes.

With regard to victims, some suggestive evidence may come from the literature regarding sexual assault, rape myths, and jury views. Clarke and Lawson (2009) report that the attackers of attractive women are treated less harshly than those of overweight and seemingly unattractive women. Jurors can "understand" why one would attack an attractive woman. Thus, an attacker of an unattractive woman is viewed as more deviant and deserving of punishment. Clarke and Stemac (2011) discovered that males who accepted rape myths made more negative evaluations of the victim and more positive evaluations of the perpetrator. Similarly, Ryckman and colleagues (1998) reported more negative attitudes toward

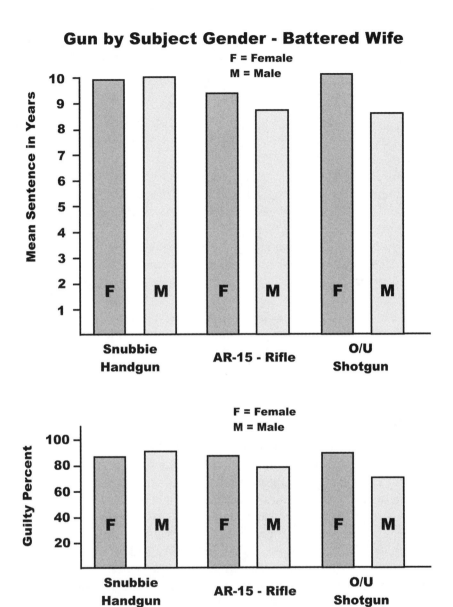

Figure 3.6 Mean Sentences and Guilt Verdict Percentages in Battered Wife Scenario

a sexual assault victim who was larger than the attacker. It was felt that a large woman should be able to defend herself against the smaller male. Branscombe and Weir (1992) report that strong resistance to rape increased sympathy for the attacker. Herrera and colleagues (2012) found that in a battered woman scenario the competent and attractive woman defendant was viewed more harshly by a sample of police officers. Such women were seen as capable of handling themselves better and were less likely to be a victim.

In this experiment, we used the scenario in which the female defendant hears a burglar downstairs, as in Meyer and colleagues (2009). The burglar is carrying the defendant's laptop computer, and the defendant challenges the burglar. The defendant varies in attractiveness. The questions under consideration are the possibilities that being attractive would either aid or hurt a defendant's case. Possibly being attractive and using a firearm would be seen as reasonable because an attractive woman is at greater risk of sexual assault and hence is more fearful. On the other hand, an attractive woman might be seen as violating a gender stereotype by being armed, which would be detrimental to her case. Such factors might interact with participant gender and firearms attitudes.

Results

Verdict

The results for the verdict ratings data are presented in Figure 3.7. The analysis is straightforward. Attractiveness was a significant effect, as was gun attitude. Most important is that the effects seem driven by the males with negative firearm attitudes (as seen in the significant three way interaction of participant gender, firearms attitude, and attractiveness). For all the cells except that of negative firearms males judging attractive defendants, the verdict ratings were towards the not guilty end of the continuum. There are small differences toward guilt for the attractive conditions than the others, but only the negative males/attractive defendant cell was clearly in the more guilty range.

Sentence

Firearms attitude was clearly significant in that the participants with negative gun attitudes suggested much stiffer sentences than those who were positive (Figure 3.8). This result is clearly driven by males with negative gun attitudes being particularly harsh on attractive women.

Verdict

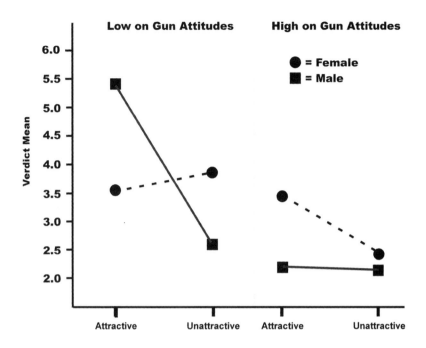

Sentence

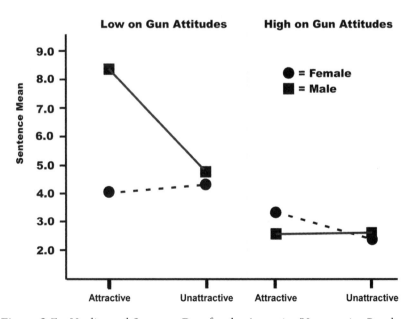

Figure 3.7 Verdict and Sentence Data for the Attractive/Unattractive Burglary Scenario

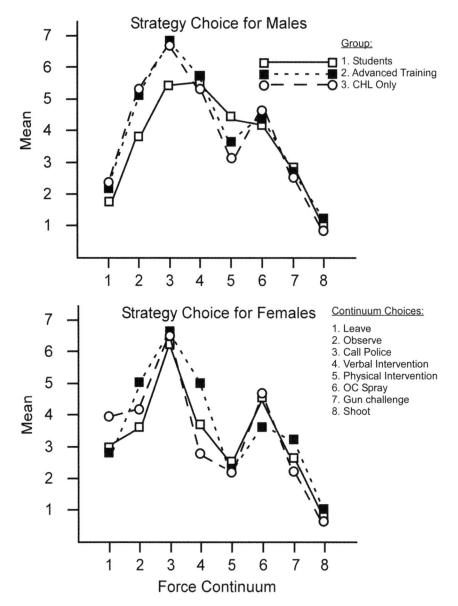

Figure 3.8 Verdict and Sentence Data for the Attractive/Unattractive Burglary Scenario

General Discussion

"Historically, girls and women have been considered deviants or criminals for behaving in a variety of ways legally permitted for males" (McCaughey, 1997, 22). One most fascinating aspect of the results is the particularly strong negative view of males with negative attitudes toward firearms. As seen in the stalker scenario, that male group recommended sentences approximately seven years longer than the female participants of either gun attitude or the positive attitude males. In Figure 3.8 (attractiveness/burglar scenario), the anti-gun males stood out from all other groups. Sentence recommendations increased by approximately five years and guilt recommendations increased from the not guilty or neutral range into the clearly guilty range. Previous literature, as mentioned above, has demonstrated that attractive women are seen almost as excusable targets for attack and not seen as ones who should be physically competent in defense. Why should antigun males be more prone to these attitudes? One might expect that antigun males would be liberal in social attitudes because liberal attitudes are commonly associated with negative gun attitudes (Schlenker et al. 2012), which might be expected to accompany a celebration of strong women who defend themselves. However, if the negative attitude toward guns links conservative values with gun ownership, the female defendant is perceived as violating a basic premise of female behavior and thus she would not be supported. Violating a liberal female stereotype would be as bad as adopting a conservative stance. This is an interesting finding because usually more liberal males are less accepting of rape myths (Hammond, Berry, and Rodriguez 2011). Did gun usage reverse the usual supportive views toward women?

One answer might be found in the idea of prototypicality. Herrera and colleagues (2012) concluded that their finding of negative attitudes toward attractive women was related to the perception of competent and attractive women not being compatible with a prototype of a female victim. In our experiments, it is plausible that males with negative gun attitudes would have a prototypical view of women as not being gun users. Thus, such a use would produce quite negative evaluations by these male participants.

Branscombe and Weir (1992) came to an interesting conclusion on analyzing their results, which may apply to ours:

> Despite this, we are in no way suggesting that women should not attempt to prevent or resist victimization attempts. Rather, we have contributed to the literature indicating how cognitive processes influence judgments of victims. (Branscombe and Weir 1992, 99)

Gun users and defense lawyers need to be aware of such issues for voir dire (jury selection) and case presentation. The seemingly contradictory attitudes of some males toward women considered inappropriately strong are something also to be explored further.

Other Firearms-Relevant Psychological and Human Factor Issues

Negligent Discharges

There are quite a few factors that might lead to a gun that "just went off" (Norman 2013; Hendrik, Paradis, and Hornick 2008).

1. Finger on the trigger and affordances. An affordance is a quality of an object, or an environment, that allows an individual to perform an action. For example, a knob affords twisting, and perhaps pushing, while a cord affords pulling. Thus, when a person grabs a gun, the weapon is designed to guide the index finger to the trigger. The finger seeks the trigger as it is a natural hold position; the finger extended is not a "normal" grip position.

   A study reported on Policeone.com (http://www.policeone.com/police-products/firearms/articles/94371-Can-you-really-prevent-unintentional-discharges/) had police enter a room to make an arrest. Thirty-four officers drew their gun and all said they kept their fingers off the triggers, which was not true for seven of them. The officers also engaged in physical activities to see if they would pull the trigger during activity. Twenty percent of those with single action triggers did activate the trigger. Six percent with double action guns did so.

2. Reholstering the gun. Rushing the reholstering or being under stress can cause one to forget to remove the finger from the trigger and the finger hits the holster. Certain holsters may promote errors due to slips manipulating retention devices.

3. Forgetting to check the gun. The individual may not remember or know that a semi-automatic handgun may have a round in the chamber and ready to fire—even when the magazine is out.

4. Physical activity can activate single action and even double action guns. Similarly, specifically lightened trigger pulls on guns (the Glock 3.5-pound trigger) or competition guns with very light triggers are prone to accidental firing.

5. Not being able to stop shooting and continuing fire when a person should not. Research with simulators found that 68 percent of police fired an extra shot after the stop signal, which may occur because of perceptual narrowing (tunnel vision) that causes the shooter to miss the signal, or because reaction to the signal is not fast enough to inhibit the fast trigger pull motor response.

Because handgun rounds are not guaranteed to instantly drop a target, many shots can be fired, which can lead to the perception of excessive use of force.

6. Startles can generate 14 pounds of trigger pull, which is enough force to activate most guns, even double action ones.

7. Moving firearms can exert forces with a starting or stopping movement, which can cause the firearm to fire if the finger is on the trigger. Swinging a Colt 1911 a few feet in one-quarter of second can generate about 17 pounds of force, well above what is needed to pull most triggers.

8. Other movement-based causes include:

- Jumping motions, losing balance, leg kicks, and stress or fright.
- Contralateral or sympathetic contraction: the hand gripping the gun is affected by "sympathetic" reflexive reactions to the movement of other limbs, causing uncontrollable contraction of gun hand fingers.
- Naïve shooters: Drawing a handgun and extending it out to a shooting position; one in five individuals unintentionally fires a weapon as it is brought up to eye level and pushed forward.
- Yips: "uncontrollable, forceful spasmodic jerks" that are associated with an abnormally high heart rate or other possible physical causes.
- "Hand confusion": Which hand has the light? Is it a taser? The individual activates the gadget and pulls the trigger.
- Trying to catch a falling gun. Affordance gets the finger on the trigger and the gun fires. A modern handgun is probably drop safe—let it fall.

Race and Appearance

Race is a central focus in many discussions in the United States, and certainly influences firearms issues. Clearly, in the history of firearms laws, restricting firearms was first seen as a way to prevent violence and revolt by African Americans during slavery and after emancipation. This point has been documented strongly by scholars of slave rebellions and the Civil Rights movement (Umoja 2013; Cobb 2014; Johnson 2014). Cities with large minority populations can have Caucasian mayors such as Rahm Emanuel (Bosman 2014) and Michael Bloomberg (Schouten 2014) who are strong advocates of strict gun control measures. The latter has gone as far as supporting what appears to be clear racial profiling in his "stop and risk" program. Bloomberg has stated: "We disproportionately stop whites too much and minorities too little" in stop-frisk checks (Gonen 2013). The purpose of the policy was to reduce guns on the street, but led to successful court challenges. Bloomberg's claim has not been supported by his successor, Mayor Bill deBlasio. A report from his office found that "the likelihood a stop of an African American New Yorker yielded a weapon was half that of white New Yorkers stopped" (Office of Bill de Blasio, Public Advocate for the City of New York 2013, 2). The role of prejudice in promoting gun control is a topic not much touched on in psychological analyses of racism. However, much research has been done on how race influences who is shot. People of color may be more likely to be shot by police, which suggests racial bias. However, others suggest that the differential rate is due to differing rates of criminal activity (see review by Correll et al. 2014).

Race may influence legal firearms usage by police and citizens. Are people of color at more risk of being shot in a critical incident? Attention from social scientists and law enforcement came to the fore after the well-known Amadou Diallo case where an unarmed African immigrant was mistaken for a rapist. When challenged by police, Diallo pulled out his wallet and was shot 19 times (Cooper 1999). Why the police opened fire at that moment is debated still. Police might have perceived a gun. An intentional but mistaken shooting of civilians by police is traumatic for all involved. What a person perceives is a combination of what is there and an interaction with a cognitive hypothesis. Would someone be more likely to shoot at a person for whom they hold racial or ethnic animus?

The shooting of Michael Brown in Ferguson, Missouri, has reignited the debate about police shootings (Clarke and Lett 2014). There is also the issue of whether civilian self-defense shootings are influenced by race. Certainly, prejudice has overt (explicit) and covert (implicit) components. Because a person did not utter racist comments does not mean that in emotional and stressful situations someone will not decide to act against persons of certain races or ethnicities. For example, research has shown that Caucasians tend to judge minority facial expressions as angrier than the corresponding facial expression on whites (Hugenberg and Bodenhausen 2003). In the world of the armed citizen, incidents like those of the Trayvon Martin shooting by George Zimmerman, Renisha McBride by Theodore Wafer (Hopkins 2014), and Jordan Davis by Michael Dunn may have had a racial aspect. Martin was stopped by George Zimmerman for looking suspicious. McBride was shot by Wafer as she pounded on his door, and Dunn shot Davis over a dispute involving loud music. In the latter two cases, there was no physical assault on the shooters: one could ask if race made them overreact and see a need for lethal self-defense, but those claims did not convince the juries. Zimmerman was engaged in physical combat but did he choose to follow Martin based on race? Most analyses have been superficial and driven by social and political views.

There was little referencing of what is known about the interactions of race and firearms. Analyses of determining prejudice have been naïve, even from seemingly knowledgeable commentators. Charles Krauthammer (a psychiatrist and columnist) said: "In doing so, Obama was following the overwhelming evidence. A concurrent FBI investigation, which involved interviewing more than 30 of Zimmerman's acquaintances, found zero evidence of Zimmerman harboring racial animus. Nor did he even mention race when first describing Martin to the police dispatcher. Race was elicited only by a subsequent direct question from the dispatcher" (2013).

The Diallo incident generated a tremendous amount of follow-up research (Payne 2001; Payne et al. 2002; Correll et al. 2002). Payne's participants identified guns faster and more accurately after introducing a black face even though the task was simple computer-based recognition of gun and non-gun pictures. To increase ecological validity, Correll, Park, Judd, and Wittenbrink (2002) used a first person shooter task using key presses for a shoot-don't-shoot decision. The participants erroneously "shot" black targets more than white, were faster at shooting blacks, and quick at deciding not to shoot an unarmed white target. Signal detection analyses suggest that the operative effect was on criterion (a more lenient one being used for blacks) rather than sensitivity changes (being able to distinguish unarmed from armed targets). Similar effects have been found for targets identified as Islamic or Arabic in both the United States and Germany (Unkelbach et al. 2008; Fleming, Brady, and Kimble 2009; Mange et al. 2012), which has been called the "turban effect." Bias against Hispanics but not Asians has also been reported (Sandler et al. 2012). Gender can have an effect, with participants hesitant to shoot white and black females (Plant et al. 2011). Thus, it was found initially that civilian and police subjects tended to misidentify common objects as firearms in the hands of African Americans. They were more likely to "shoot" them in computer simulations.

Several other major research themes have emerged. They revolve around the ecological validity of previous testing and whether training and expertise influence the biases suggested by the early research. Ecological validity is a problem for many of the firearms related studies (as seen in the aggression priming literature). As Cox and colleagues summarize, the extant research used undergraduate participants who lacked the training and experience of police officers and the stimuli were static pictures and key press responses. These studies lack the dynamic nature and responses (aimed, trigger pull) of an actual shooting, and also did not consider the effect of neighborhood and local crime statistics as a biasing factor in shoot or no shoot decisions. Thus, several more ecologically valid studies alter the original picture.

James and colleagues (2013) tested military, civilian, and police participants in realistic computerized training simulators. These have a level of ecological verisimilitude superior to earlier studies. Participants took longer to shoot black suspects than whites or Hispanics. The delay based on race was from .68 to 1.34 seconds. They were more likely to shoot unarmed whites and more likely to fail to shoot armed blacks. Participants were five to six times less likely to shoot black subjects. Thus, a bias favoring blacks was found. With a realistic test, bias was not found and also civilians trained up to police standards demonstrated less bias. The authors have yet to determine the reason for this reversal finding, which might be a cultural counter bias related to public disapproval of past shootings. Plant and colleagues (2005, 2011) also found that training reduced bias in undergraduate participants in a key press shooting task.

Sim and colleagues (2013) and Correll and colleagues (2014) report that first person shooter simulations found police officers were unlike untrained students or community members in that they made more correct decisions, could more effectively tell armed from unarmed stimuli, and did not show a pattern of bias. Thus, evidence for biased decision criteria was not found in the officers, but they were faster to shoot armed black targets than white. This result was more pronounced in those from dangerous urban areas. Bias in undergraduates could be reduced by training. The authors postulate that cognitive control with training overrides the biased tendency to shoot. However, officers from more dangerous areas show more signal detection bias, which might be seen as a reasonable cognitive appraisal of their exposure to threats. Also, fatigue and arousal can possibly increase bias in the shoot-no-shoot decision. A tendency to try not to be biased might also be a factor.

Cox and colleagues (2014), also using a realistic simulation scenario with officers, found a tendency not to shoot armed suspects, and no racial bias in errors. Neighborhood did interact with race, possibly due to the stress and risk in such areas. Latency data demonstrated that armed blacks were correctly shot faster than whites. Exposure to stories about black criminals increased the bias in the decision to shoot (Correll et al. 2007).

Blanket statements that police and civilians are fundamentally biased in shooting incidents involving people of color cannot be supported by recent studies. Untrained undergraduates cannot be taken as a model for trained officers. Neighborhood and area crime rates co-vary with race and influence decision making. Levels of stress in unrealistic simulations cannot be generalized to actual high stress situations. In real world incidents, these studies are of interest but cannot show conclusively that a particular shooting was a product of bias.

Mental Health, the Prediction of Violence, and Firearms Acquisition

The interaction of mental health and firearms has been dominated by recent rampage shootings. The act of mass killing is so extreme that the mental stability of the shooter is suspect. On the surface, shooters such as Seung-Hui Cho (Virginia Polytechnic Institute), Adam Lanza (Sandy Hook Elementary School in Newtown, Connecticut), James Holmes (Aurora, Colorado, movie theatre), and Jared Loughner (the shooting of Representative Gabby Giffords in Tucson, Arizona) have psychiatric impairment such that, if they survive the incident, they may be found not guilty by reason of insanity (depending on individual state statutes). Hindsight bias, of course, would suggest to many that the shooters should have been identified and prevented from acquiring firearms, if the acquisition occurred legally. As Swanson and colleagues (2014) point out, controlling access to firearms by the mentally ill appears to be the only issue agreed upon by gun rights and gun control advocacy groups. Disagreement occurs on how this prohibition should be accomplished and whether a given procedure violates the right to keep and bear arms (assuming one thinks that right does or should exist).

When considering mental disabilities and guns, the core questions include:

(1) Do some forms of mental illness or disability predict that a gun will be misused as compared to the rates of misuse in a control population?
(2) Should past history of mental illness be used to screen gun purchases?
(3) Are there any measures with sufficient predictive validity to suggest their use for screening the general population and the gun owning population?
(4) Would any existent measures produce so many false positives or negatives as to render them useless?
(5) If a person has a firearm, will a developing mental illness make it more likely for the gun to be used against others and/or oneself as compared to a control population?

(6) Will the presence of a gun be a stressor according to the modern diathesis-stress models of mental illness (in other words, whether the presence of the gun is a causal factor in bringing about a violent act)?

No one would want a person who is *non compos mentis* (not of sound mind) to have an instrument of lethal force, but it must be noted that the determination of mental status is a most controversial issue in the mental health professions and the law. The *Diagnostic and Statistical Manual of Mental Disorders 5*, published by the American Psychiatric Association, contains the current set of accepted diagnostic criteria. The volume makes no explicit mention of firearm ownership or use in connection with any indicator of mental illness. It is also true that mass killings have been conducted by individuals who seemingly are stable and well liked. The case of Jaylen Fryberg is a clear example of a popular young man and high school homecoming king who planned the execution of his best friends and then committed suicide (Johnson and Dewan 2014). It is hard to imagine a psychiatric procedure that could have discerned his intents.

Nevertheless, mental status is used in state and federal regulations to determine worthiness to own or purchase a firearm. On the federal level, the Federal Firearms Act of 1938 did not specifically prohibit purchase by the mentally ill. However, it set the conceptual groundwork for future federal gun control legislation. The issue surfaced in the Gun Control Act of 1968, which banned federal firearm licensees from transferring a gun or ammunition to someone who "has been adjudicated as a mental defective or has been committed to any mental institution." Such individuals also could not receive a firearm from interstate or foreign commerce. The act itself was not clear in several sections. "Mental defective" is not a term used by the contemporary mental health community. Continuing in this vein, the Firearms Owners' Protection Act of 1986 denies anyone who is or has been adjudicated as a mental incompetent or committed to any mental institution the privilege of owning firearms (Edwards 1993, 409–412).

Such blanket provisions have been challenged on constitutional grounds. A case was brought to the U.S. Supreme Court challenging the law (*Department of Treasury v. Galioto*, 477 U.S. 556; 1986). Several mental health organizations—including the American Psychological Association (APA)—filed amicus briefs in the case. Of several points made by the APA, these two stand out: "(4) the statute did not prevent firearm abuse because individuals with no history of arrest prior to commitment are no more likely than the general population to commit violent acts; and (5) administrative convenience alone did not constitutionally justify permanent disqualification under an overbroad classification based on false, stigmatizing stereotypes." The issue was resolved when Congress amended the provisions of the Omnibus Crime Control and Safe Streets Act of 1968, as amended by the Gun Control Act of 1968, to afford administrative relief (by application to the secretary of the treasury) to those held ineligible to possess and purchase firearms.

However, the issue and terminology remain. Many states have adopted similar standards. Norris and colleagues (2006) summarized state firearms prohibitions for persons with mental illness, stating that "forty-three states, the District of Columbia, and Puerto Rico have prohibitions for persons with mental illness. Thirty-six states and Puerto Rico have prohibitions for drug abuse. Thirty-one states, the District of Columbia, and Puerto Rico have prohibitions for alcohol abuse. Twenty states and the District of Columbia have databases tracking individuals with mental illness." Similarly, Swanson and colleagues (2014, 9) summarize that California prohibits firearm purchase and possession for five years for individuals subjected to short-term emergency involuntary hospitalizations (Health and Safety Code sections 8100 and 8105), in addition to those subject to full involuntary commitments, while Florida prohibits people from accessing firearms if they have been initially admitted involuntarily to a psychiatric hospital, even if they subsequently agree to remain in the hospital voluntarily. The firearms statutes are not uniform; they vary considerably in ownership and/or carry restrictions and the manner in which restricted individuals are defined. Prohibited persons range in various states from those who receive outpatient psychiatric treatment to persons who have been civilly committed to treatment or found not guilty by reason of insanity. Some statutes restrict individuals with a history of alcohol or substance abuse (with different criteria for inclusion in this restricted class).

The horror of the Newtown and Aurora mass shootings has led to another wave of state legislative actions, which primarily occur in states with a history of being pro-gun control. There are attempts to limit weapons characteristics to reduce the amount of damage done but this is of doubtful utility. More of interest is legislation concerning mental health. For instance, Governor Andrew Cuomo rushed the New York Safe Ammunition and Firearms Enforcement (SAFE) Act through the state legislature in what seemed to be a moral panic. Some of its provisions turned out to be technically flawed (such as the seven round magazine fiasco). Its main provision (New MHL 9.46) regarding mental health is as follows:

- A "mental health professional" must report a person who "is likely to engage in conduct that would result in serious harm to self or others" to the County Director of Community Services (DCS) or designee as soon as practicable.

- If the Director of Community Services or designee agrees that the person is likely to engage in such conduct, he/she fills out and submits a secure on-line form to the NYS Division of Criminal Justice Services (DCJS).
- DCJS determines if the subject of report has or has applied for a firearms license or has registered an assault weapon, and works with the State Police, which notifies the appropriate county firearms licensing official.
- The county licensing official must suspend or revoke the license as soon as practicable.
- Licensing official notifies local law enforcement to remove gun(s) (https://www.omh.ny.gov/omhweb/safe_act/nysafe.pdf).

On the federal level, the passage of the Brady Handgun Violence Prevention Act and implementation of its final version on November 30, 1998, put in place an instant background check for firearm purchases. As part of this process (the National Instant Criminal Background Check System), purchasers fill out ATF Form 4473—Firearms Transaction Record. Question F on the form asks: "Have you ever been adjudicated mentally defective or have you been committed to a mental institution?"

The vivid instances of rampage shootings have led to some new measures. The Virginia Tech massacre might have been prevented if Seung Hui Cho's psychiatric problems were reported promptly and his ability to purchase firearms limited. This led to the passage of H.R.2640 – the NICS Improvement Amendments Act of 2007. The legislation provided for aid to states for cor-rectly reporting disqualifying mental disabilities to the National Instant Criminal Background Check System in determining eligibility for firearms purchases. It also had important provisions for relief if a person (1) has had such information set aside or expunged or the person involved has been fully released or discharged from all mandatory treatment, supervision, or moni-toring; (2) the person has been found to no longer suffer from a mental health condition or has been found to be rehabilitated; or (3) the adjudica-tion or commitment is based solely on a medical finding of disability with-out a hearing and there has been no adjudication under the federal criminal code of mental defectiveness. Appeals and review channels were required. Voluntarily getting treatment would not be a disqualifier in most cases for firearms ownership. These provisions were added because of the criticisms of gun rights organizations such as the National Rifle Association. The bill was a rare collaboration between opposing sides in the gun debate.

Vagueness about mental health status, firearms ownership, and receiv-ing a concealed carry license can occur also on the state level. For example, the Michigan concealed pistol license application contains the following question: "Do you have a diagnosed mental illness, regardless of whether you are receiving treatment for that illness?" Because of that provision, Joseph Heindmeyer was denied a license by an Ottawa County board because of an early history of diagnosed mental problems. However, at the time of application Heindmeyer was seen as healthy. The Michigan Court of Appeals mandated that the older history was not a disqualifier given his current mental status and that a license be granted. A proposed ballot initiative in Oregon stated that an applicant for a concealed carry license "submit a mental health report from their physicians as part of conditions to qualify to hold a concealed handgun permit" (Oregon Secretary of State Elections Division, 2014). It is difficult for anyone knowledgeable in the field to see how a physician could supply such a report.

Do legislative actions have any utility or down sides? Does the psychiatric or psychological technology exist to predict and prevent violent gun usage? Would such technology generate significant violations of the constitutional right to keep and bear arms? This problem might not bother those who do not believe in such a right or think that saving a life trumps any gun ownership or gun usage. Proposals with surface validity abound. For instance, Senator Dianne Feinstein, in 2013, proposed a new and stricter assault weapons ban (http://www.feinstein.senate.gov/public/index.cfm/assault-weapons-ban-summary). When Senator Cornyn of Texas suggested a modification to exempt veterans, Feinstein objected because many veterans may be subject to post-traumatic stress disorder (PTSD), which she regarded as a phenomenon related to the Iraq war. She pondered how mentally incapacitated veterans should be evaluated. However, veterans' organizations would object to such a sweeping evaluation.

Similarly, mental health professionals have found fault with the New York SAFE Act. As Hartocollis (2014) reports, there are concerns that the homeless are over-reported and stigmatized. Thirty five thousand reports do not mesh with the actual number of shootings in the United States. The number of rampage shootings numbers in the two-digit realm for a given year. The false positive problem is evident. The reporting criteria are ill applied by those without reasonable diagnostic procedures and who are swamped by reports, producing many false positives. The database does not apply to long guns. Mental health professionals clearly fear that gun owners will avoid seeking help because they do not want to lose gun rights or have their names placed into a data base. That argument is countered by the view that all these problems and risks are acceptable if it saves a life—a position often expressed by gun control activists.

Recent reviews by noted experts are not sanguine about mental health checks (perhaps as part of universal background checks for gun sales) being particularly useful. Fox and Delateur (2013) point out that:

1. Mass murderers are not mentally deranged individuals who suddenly snap.
2. Mass shootings are not on the rise, despite media portrayals or unsophisticated analyses.
3. Video games have not been causally linked to mass murder.
4. There are not clear telltale warning signs of a mass killer. Most of the proposed signs are applied to far too many people and are only clear signs after the fact.
5. Expanding mental health treatment may not reach the alienated potential shooter and forced interactions may actually increase the risk from some of these individuals.
6. Universal background checks as currently proposed would not have deterred the rampage shooters in past incidents.

Fox and Delateur conclude that Second Amendment rights should not be limited simply because someone looks strange or acts in an odd manner (135).

Several analyses have concluded that predicting violence is a complex issue and quick clinical assessments are not seen as useful for predicting violent behavior (Swanson et al. 2014; Skeem and Monahan 2011; Bartol and Bartol 2015). One might propose an evaluation for gun ownership or purchase based on more extensive psychological and psychiatric techniques. Specific purpose testing or actuarial predictive measures could be proposed, but they would be very time consuming and expensive for a simple gun purchase. Tests such as the Historical Clinical/Risk Management Scale, Classification of Violent Risk instrument or Violent Risk Appraisal Guide can take hours to administer with little guarantee of useful information. The predictive power in such tests seems to reside in a history of violence. It is hard to see how such tests could be mandated for the millions of gun sales that occur in the United States. The number of skilled professionals needed to perform such evaluations does not exist and few would be willing to take on the burden of denying Second Amendment rights to those not already involved in the criminal justice system.

Even if mandated, the utility of such tests and of actuarial techniques is not precise enough to be useful. Wong, Wong, and Coid (2010) reviewed nine risk assessment tools to determine if they would be useful in proactive measures such as preventive detention. They concluded: "Because of their moderate level of predictive efficacy, they [the risk assessment tools] should not be used as the sole or primary means for clinical or criminal justice decision making that is contingent on a high level of predictive accuracy, such as preventive detention" (761). Using such assessments to screen gun owners does not appear useful. Such a mandated exercise would amount to a measure to prevent legal gun purchases by throwing expensive obstacles in the way of the prospective gun owner and might even increase illegal ownership. The vast majority of violent crime (96 percent) is related to poverty, lower socioeconomic status, and substance abuse and not mental illness (Swanson et al. 2014), so general mental status screening would not influence the majority of violent gun crimes. The factors mentioned are predictive whether or not a person is determined to be mentally ill.

Of those with diagnosed problems, Swanson and colleagues indicate that higher violence odds are found with those persons diagnosed with delusions and psychoses (2 to 10 percent), personality disorders (20 percent), and substance abuse (20 percent). Thus, the majority of the mentally ill are not at risk and even in these categories they are the minority. A general screening would be unacceptable in our civil liberties environment. Nor are the mentally ill more likely to have access to firearms when compared to the general population (Ilgen et al. 2008).

Suicide

Much controversy swirls around other issues of mental status and gun possession. There is much concern that possession of a gun is a causal factor in suicide. Early population-wide analyses in the United States and comparisons with other countries indicate that this is not the case. There seems to be almost complete substitution of other means of suicide where strict firearm regulations are instituted. Also, countries with low firearm-ownership rates can have substantial suicide rates (Kleck 1997). However, some argue for a relationship based on other population survey studies (for instance, Wintemute and colleagues 1999). Thus, the subject is not without controversy and the analyses are situated in a polarized research universe that may influence result interpretations (Vizzard 2000). Clinicians inquire about gun possession in cases where suicide is feared and advocate their removal. However, compliance is problematic (Brent and colleagues 2000) and whether it really would prevent a suicide is still debatable. Some analyses and literature summaries have found little effect of gun control measures on suicide rates in some locales (Klieve, Barnes, and De Leo 2009; Kates and Mauser 2006) while others suggest a relationship (Miller and Hemenway 2008). A recent review by Swanson and colleagues (2014) promotes the view that gun restrictions do reduce suicide risk as observed in Switzerland and Australia. Similar effects were seen in some parts of the United States. One issue is whether gun restrictions lead to substitution of methods and Swanson reports this is not the case. The issue is not resolved.

Threat Assessment

Another approach to the problem comes from the threat-assessment literature. Given the recent spate of school and workplace shootings, much effort has gone into identifying persons who might be at risk of committing violent acts. Weapons interest would have surface validity and some gun control interests have characterized weapons enthusiasts as "gun nuts." However, studies sponsored by the Federal Bureau of Investigation (O'Toole 2000) and the Secret Service (Reddy et al. 2001) do not find that owning weapons per se has any predictive or prospective usefulness before serious threats have been received and other personality and social factors have been examined. Too many Americans have firearms to make this approach useful. After a significant and specific threat is received, a serious suspect who possesses weaponry, demonstrates unusual fascination with weapons and violence, and has received firearm training might be a greater risk. Reddy and colleagues (2001, 163) observe that "there are no data that demonstrate the validity of effectiveness of prospective profiling to identify potential perpetrators for any type of crime." They give as an example Sara Jane Moore, who in 1975 attempted to shoot President Gerald Ford, as someone who did not fit any accepted profile. Given the general failure of many prospective profiles, weapon ownership or interest by itself has little predictive power if there is not a specific threat.

Reviews of the relationship of mental health and violence are a mixed bag. A significant portion of the country thinks that serious mental illness predicts violence (Swanson et al. 2014) but the issue is more complex. Major psychosis is related to an increase in violent behavior (Douglas et al. 2009), but not all forms of psychosis are strong predictors. The causality is not clear. For example, co-morbidity with substance abuse might be more causal. Also, the size of the effect is small and of the same order as some other factors such as nonviolent criminal history or marital status. Antisocial personality disorder and psychopathy were found to be stronger predictors. Not all forms of psychosis were strong predictors. Schizophrenia was found to be significant but affective disorders were not. However, Douglas and colleagues (2009) conclude that an evaluation of psychosis is important in risk assessment but must be linked to evaluations of past violence and substance abuse. It should not be the sole factor in determining risk. This finding suggests that banning firearms ownership solely on diagnosis might not be supported if one does not want to be over-inclusive, although some gun control advocates might want to err on the side of caution.

The current state of psychiatric and psychological science does not suggest that weapon ownership or interest is predictive of violent behavior; that the mental-status questions required by federal, state, and local regulations for screening gun purchasers are strongly predictive; that guns are a causal factor in suicide; or that gun ownership per se is indicative of any sort of mental disorder. Surface validity is the main appeal of these measures. Tightening up regulations for the most seriously disturbed, given appropriate safeguards against overreach, may have validity but it is too early to tell.

Video Games, Social Media, and Priming Aggression

Another question is whether guns are the stressor that will provoke violence, assuming the diathesis-stress model of abnormal behavior. Certainly, there cannot be gun violence if there are no guns. This is a different question from whether the presence of a gun leads to mental illness or aggressive behavior. Given the high rate of gun ownership in the United States, if guns were a causal factor in violence, we would expect more violence than we actually observe. A more reasonable analysis is that social factors lead to most of the gun violence (for instance, gang and drug-related gun use in some milieus). The gun is an instrumentality used in committing violence that society generates. It is not causal. However, some research suggests that weapons can prime aggressive thoughts (Berkowitz 1993). Whether owning firearms leads to actual violence has not been truly tested at the human-subject level (as compared to population-based studies). The best analogy might be to the issue of whether exposure to violent television or video-game images leads to violent acts. Laboratory experiments using weapons priming with images of guns or handling replicas and dependent variables such as pepper sauce addition to drinks, verdicts in jury simulations, and noise surrogates suggest firearms may lead to aggression (Anderson, Benjamin, and Bartholow 1998; Berkowitz 1993; Berkowitz and LePage 1967; Dienstbier et al. 1998; Branscombe, Crosby, and Weir 1993; Klinesmith, Kasser, and McAndrew 2006; Meyer et al. 2009). However, that view has not gone without challenges (Buss, Booker, and Buss 1972; Ellis, Weinir, and Miller, 1971). Anderson and Dill (2000) make such a claim, while Felson's (1996) review of the literature finds the evidence inconsistent. The debate continues as to whether video games prime aggression. Some disagree (Ferguson, Cruz, Ferguson, and Smith 2008; Fox and Delateur 2013) while others that such games can directly lead disturbed people to engage in gun violence (Grossman 2009).

Real World Gun Users and Bystander Intervention

In more ecologically valid tests of weapons priming of aggression (with real weapons users), priming was not seen as that potent. Nagetegaal and colleagues (2009) adminstered a series of personality measures to shooting association memberships and surprisingly (from a standard aggressive priming model) found that they were less aggressive and impulsive than non-members. Phillips and Maume (2007) interviewed one hundred men imprisoned for aggravated assault or homicide. The goal was to determine whether guns contributed to escalating the violent act as compared to the violent intentions of the actor. They concluded (291): "The relationship between guns and violence is not spurious, but does attenuate considerably after eliminating intentional cases and controlling for the respondent's level of anger." Markey and colleagues (2014) examined actual violent crime statistics as compared to violent video game releases. They report that there were not increases in crime and perhaps even a decrease in violence, suggesting the laboratory correlations are suspect when applied to the real world.

In a series of tests, we asked three groups of participants about their reaction to a woman being assaulted (the classic Kitty Genovese scenario). The question was what would be the level of force used in the intervention. They ranged from leaving the scene, observing, calling the police, verbal intervention, physical interaction, oleoresin capsicum (OC) spray, challenging with a firearm (if legally carried), and shooting the attacker. The options were rated on a 1 to 7 scale from most unlikely to most likely. The three participant groups were:

1. Males and females with significant firearms training (far beyond that needed for a concealed carry license).
2. Males and females with a concealed carry permit or license but with no significant firearms training.
3. Undergraduate participants (as a control group) who did not have a concealed handgun permit or license.

It was hypothesized that Groups 1 and 2 who possess weapons for their specific lethal value might be primed to consider their use, especially to defend a victim. Such everyday priming of concealed carry and the intensive priming of Group 1 would appear to promote their aggressive use, seeing the situation was pro-social behavior.

The results are seen in Figure 3.8 above. Males were more likely to suggest physical intervention than females but none of the groups were likely to shoot the attacker and even challenging with a gun was not rated highly. Thus, having access to and practice with real world weapons did not produce a priming effect that might have been predicted from studies using toy guns as stimuli and hot sauce as an indicator of aggression.

Nagetegaal and colleagues argued, as we do, that the controlled and educational exposure to firearms did not have such a priming effect. Thus, our results plus those of Buss and colleagues (1972), Ellis, Weinir, and Miller (1971), Nagetegaal and colleagues (2009), and Phillips and Maume (2007) are unexpected from some laboratory tested theory but congruent with actual situations. They are not congruent with the seeming surface validity of guns "causing" violence in common parlance. Our conjecture is that these results are due to the powerful cognitive constraints that become part of these legal weapons users' makeup and the processes involved in judging blame and moral responsibility.

Memory and the Weapons Focus Effect

Since the 1980s it has been known that the presence of a weapon can interfere with eyewitness memory (Pickel 1998; Steblay 1992). Eyewitnesses seem to concentrate on the weapon more than on the perpetrator and the victim. This is especially true if shots are fired. For example, Stanny and Johnson (2000) found that memory about the perpetrator was about 45 percent as compared to 70 percent about the weapon. These rates dropped to about 35 percent and 50 percent respectively if a weapon was fired. Gender schemas were potent; Pickel (2009) found a greater memory decrement for the perpetrator if a woman held the weapon. Thus, testimony about the weapon might be more useful in identifying individuals if the weapon has been found and linked to a person.

Conclusions

Psychology has a place in examining the roles and usage of firearms in modern society. Because lives are at stake, more research should be encouraged. Our findings would have an impact for several areas of study. It confirms the general role of gender stereotype in decision making. Also, the effects of weapons priming negative attributions seem supported. Legal applications may be two-fold. Prosecuting and defense attorneys may want to take the weapons and gender interactions into account during jury selection. Prosecutors may want to construct alternatives for the shooter to suggest that they did not have to shoot and especially with such a powerful weapon. Homeowners, seeking to defend themselves, may want to consider their selection of weapons based on research and their gender. The significant effects appear to focus on the AR-15 versus other weapons. This is, of course, dependent on the scenario as discussed above. In fact, we did not find that video presentations could overcome the scenario effect. Subjects seemed quite impressed by the appearance of the "evil" guns (race gun, AR-15, Defender, shotgun and the destructive nature of the Defender). When observing the impact of the buckshot rounds on the B-27 highlighted target, many spontaneous exclamations were heard.

One important point in our study is that the weapons are not specifically discussed as being assault rifles or in some way unusual. They are described in technical terms. A law enforcement officer commented to us that for the issue of weapons type to be important, an attorney would have to bring it up and a judge might not allow that. However, as earlier studies indicated, the simple presence of the weapon can be influential. As Branscombe and colleagues (1993) point out in response to suggestions that females not use guns because they may be at differential risk, a defense attorney should be cognizant of such risks because persuasive techniques may be used to diffuse them. The attorney might construct counterfactuals that indicate no matter what the defendant did, the same results would have occurred, if she or he had a "nice" gun.

Attorneys may also consider how modern human factors operate and how cognitive science can influence evaluations of gun issues. Perceptual constructive processes were potent in the Diallo case. Implicit and explicit prejudicial factors affect shoot-no-shoot decisions. Gender stereotypes and attractiveness (variables from social psychology) can influence jury decisions. At the time of writing, the country is transfixed by the interactions of race and police shooting behavior in Ferguson, Missouri, and other cities. Many of the factors discussed in this piece have come into play in the national discussion. Naïve assertions, based on social and political beliefs and not on empirical investigations, are not sufficient in dealing with the issues treated in this chapter.

References

Anderson, C. A., A. J. Benjamin Jr., and B. O. Bartholow. 1998. "Does the Gun Pull the Trigger? Automatic Priming Effects of Weapon Pictures and Weapon Names." *Psychological Science* 9 (4), 308-314. doi: 10.1111/1467-9280.00061.

Anderson, C. A., and K. E. Dill. 2000. "Video Games and Aggressive Thoughts, Feelings, and Behavior in the Laboratory and in Life." *Journal of Personality and Social Psychology* 78 (4), 772–790.

Anderson, M. 2001. "Guns against Rape? A Critique of Gun Women: Firearms and Feminism in Contemporary America." *Villanova Women's Law Forum.* http://vls.law.vill.edu/publications/womenslawforum/articles.htm (accessed November 20, 2002).

Associated Press. 2002. "Erie Police to Carry Assault Rifles." *Pittsburgh Post-Gazette.* www.post-gazette.com/localnews/20020428erie0428p8.asp (accessed February 23, 2014).

Ayoob, M. 1998. "Mistaken Identity Shooting: The Death of an Exchange Student." *American Handgunner* 23: 46, 82–87, 133.

Ayoob, M. 2000. "Firepower: How Much Is Too Much?" *Combat Handguns* 21 (4), 8–9, 90–91.

Ayoob, M. 2014. *Deadly Force: Understanding Your Right to Self-Defense.* Iola, WI: Gun Digest Books.

Barrow, R. L., and G. M. Mauser. 2002. "Dangerous Women: Feminism, Self-Defense and Civil Rights." http://www.sfu.ca/~mauser/papers/women/Law-review-abstract.pdf (accessed September 30, 2002).

Bartholow, B. D., C. A. Anderson, N. L. Carnagey, and A. Benjamin. 2005. "Interactive Effects of Life Experience and Situational Cues on Aggression: The Weapons Priming Effect in Hunters and Nonhunters." *Journal of Experimental Social Psychology* 41: 48–60. doi: 10.1016/j.jesp.2004.05.005.

Bartol, C. R., and A. M. Bartol. 2015. *Psychology and Law.* Thousand Oaks, CA: Sage Publications.

Berkowitz, L. 1993. *Aggression: Its Causes, Consequences, and Control.* New York: McGraw-Hill.

Berkowitz, L., and A. LePage. 1967. "Weapons as Aggression-Eliciting Stimuli." *Journal of Personality and Social Psychology* 7: 202-207. doi: 10.1037/h0025008.

Bernhardt, J. M., J. R. Sorenson, and J. D. Brown. 2001. "When the Perpetrator Gets Killed: Effects of Observing the Death of a Handgun User in a Televised Public Service Announcement." *Health Education & Behavior* 28 (1), 81–94.

Bornstein, B. H. 1999. "The Ecological Validity of Jury Simulations: Is the Jury Still Out?" *Law and Human Behavior Special Issue: The First 20 Years of Law and Human Behavior.* 23 (1), 75–91. doi: 10.1023/A:1022326807441.

Bosman, J. 2014. "Mayor of Chicago Seeks to Further Tighten Gun Laws." http://www.nytimes.com/2014/05/29/us/mayor-rahm-emanuel-proposes-chicago-gun-restrictions.html. (accessed October 20, 2014).

Boule, J. 2014. "The Militarization of the Police." *Slate.* http://www.slate.com/articles/news_and_politics/politics/2014/08/police_in_ferguson_military_weapons_threaten_protesters.html (accessed November 16, 2014).

Branscombe, N., P. Crosby, and J. A. Weir. 1993. "Social Inferences Concerning Male and Female Homeowners Who Use a Gun to Shoot an Intruder." *Aggressive Behavior* 19 (2), 113–124. doi: 10.1002/1098-2337(1993)19:2<113::AID-AB2480190204>3.0.CO;2-B.

Branscombe, N., and S. Owen. 1991. "Influence of Gun Ownership on Social Inferences about Women and Men." *Journal of Applied Social Psychology* 21 (19), 1567–1589.

Branscombe, N., and J. A. Weir. 1992. "Resistance as Stereotype-Inconsistency: Consequences for Judgments of Rape Victims." *Journal of Social and Clinical Psychology* 11: 80–102.

Branscombe, N., J. A. Weir, and P. Crosby. 1991. "A Three-Factor Scale of Attitudes toward Guns." *Aggressive Behavior* 17: 261–273.

Brent, D. A., M. Baugher, B. Birmaher, D. J. Kolko, and J. Bridge. 2000. "Compliance with Recommendations to Remove Firearms in Families Participating in a Clinical Trial for Adolescent Depression." *Journal of the American Academy of Child and Adolescent Psychiatry* 39 (10), 1220–1226.

Bright, D., and J. Goodman-Delahunty. 2006. "Gruesome Evidence and Emotion: Anger, Blame, and Jury Decision-Making." *Law and Human Behavior* 30:183–202. doi: 10.1007/s10979-006-9027-y.

Clarke, A. K., and K. L. Lawson. 2009. "Women's Judgments of a Sexual Assault Scenario: The Role of Prejudicial Attitudes and Victim Weight." *Violence & Victims* 24: 248–264.

Clarke, A. K., and L. Stermac. 2011. "The Influence of Stereotypical Beliefs, Participant Gender, and Survivor Weight on Sexual Assault Response." *Journal of Interpersonal Violence* 26: 2285–2302.

Clarke, R., and C. Lett. 2014. "What Happened When Michael Brown Met Officer Darren Wilson?" http://edition.cnn.com/interactive/2014/08/us/ferguson-brown -timeline. (accessed August 28, 2014).

Cobb, C. E. 2014. *This Nonviolent Stuff'll Get You Killed: How Guns Made the Civil Rights Movement Possible*. New York: Basic Books.

Cornell, C.A., and M. T. Khasawneh. 2008. "An Ergonomic Comparison of Firearm Safety Mechanisms." *Ergonomics* 51: 1394–1406.

Correll, J., S. M. Hudson, S. Guillermo, and D. S. Ma. 2014. "The Police Officer's Dilemma: A Decade of Research on Racial Bias in the Decision to Shoot." *Social and Personality Psychology Compass* 8, 201–203.

Correll, J., B. Park, and C. M. Judd. 2002. "The Police Officer's Dilemma: Using Ethnicity to Disambiguate Potentially Threatening Individuals." *Journal of Personality and Social Psychology.* 83: 1314–1329.

Correll, J., B. Park, C. M. Judd, and B. Wittenbrink. 2007. "The Influence of Stereotypes on Decisions to Shoot." *European Journal of Psychology* 37: 1102–1107.

CourtTV. 1993. "*Michigan v. Vriesenga* Was It An Accident? A Death on Halloween." (August). http://www.courttv.com/onair/shows/thesystem/episode_k_s.html. New York: Courtroom Television Network LLC (accessed September 30, 2002).

Cox, W. T., P. G. Devine, E. Ashby, and L. L. Schwartz. 2014. "Understanding of Officers Shooting Decisions: No Simple Answers to This Complex Problem." *Basic and Applied Social Psychology* 36 (4), 356–364. doi: 10.1080/01973533.2014.923312

Dao, J. 2003. "Sniper Suspect Is Own Lawyer as Trial Opens." *New York Times.* (October 23). www.nytimes.com (accessed October 23, 2003).

Devine, D. J. 2012. *Jury Decision Making: The State of the Science.* New York: New York University Press.

Dienstbier, R. A., S. C. Roesch, A. Mizumoto, S. H. Hemenover, R. C. Lott, and G. Carlo. 1998. "Effects of Weapons on Guilt Judgments and Sentencing Recommendations for Criminals." *Basic and Applied Social Psychology* 20: 93–102.

Dole, C. M. 2000. "Women with a Gun." In M. Pomerance and J. Sakeris, editors. *Bang, Bang, Shoot, Shoot: Essays on Guns and Popular Culture.* Second edition. (11–21). Needham Heights, MA: Pearson Education.

Douglas, K.S., L. S. Guy, and S. D. Hart. 2009. "Psychosis as a Risk Factor for Violence to Others: A Meta-Analysis." *Psychological Bulletin* 135: 679–706. doi: 10.1037/a0016311

Duarte, J. L., J. T. Crawford, C. Stern, J. Haidt, L. Jussim, and P. E. Tetlock. 2014. "Political Diversity Will Improve Social Psychological Science." *Behavioral and Brain Sciences*. http://journals.cambridge.org/images/fileUpload/documents /Duarte-Haidt_BBS-D-14-00108_preprint.pdf (accessed November 26, 2014).

Ellis, Desmond P., Paul Weinir, and Louie Miller. 1971. "Does the Trigger Pull the Finger? An Experimental Test of Weapons as Aggression-Enhancing Stimuli." *Sociometry* 34: 453-465.

Farnam, V., and V. Nicholl. 2002. *Teaching Women to Shoot: A Law Enforcement Instructor's Guide*. Boulder, CO: DTI Publications.

Feigenson, N., and M. A. Dunn. 2003. "New Visual Technologies in Court: Directions for Research." *Law and Human Behavior* 27:109–126. doi: 10.1023/A: 1021683013042.

Finkel, N. J., K. H. Meister, and D. M. Lightfoot. 1991. "The Self-Defense Defense and Community Sentiment." *Law & Human Behavior* 15 (6), 585–602.

Florida v. Roten. 2000. "Racially Motivated or Sheer Coincidence?" http://www .courttv.com/trials/roten/background_ctv.html (accessed February 28, 2002).

Fox, J., and M. J. Delateur. 2014. "Mass Shootings in America: Moving Beyond Newtown." *Homicide Studies* 18: 125-145.

Gochenour, S. 2006. "Legal Principles in the Justification of the Use of Force." American Tactical Shooting Association. http://www.teddytactical.com/archive /MonthlyStudy/2006/02_StudyDay.htm (accessed September 22, 2010).

Gonen, Y. 2013. "Bloomberg: 'We Disproportionately Stop Whites Too Much and Minorities Too Little' in Stop-Frisk Checks." http://nypost.com/2013/06/28 /bloomberg-we-disproportionately-stop-whites-too-much-and-minorities-too -little-in-stop-frisk-checks (accessed October 20, 2012).

Government Accountability Office. 2012. *States' Laws and Requirements for Concealed Carry Permits Vary Across the Nation*. GAO-12-717. Washington, DC: United States Government Accountability Office.

Greenwald, J. P., A. J. Tomkins, M. Kenning, and D. Zavodny. 1990. "Psychological Self-Defense Jury Instructions: Influences on Verdicts for Battered Women Defendants." *Behavioral Sciences and the Law* 8: 171–180.

Grossman, D., and L. Christensen. 2004. *On Combat: The Psychology and Physiology of Deadly Conflict in War and in Peace*. Belleville, IL: PPCT Research Publications.

Halpern, D. F. 2000. *Sex Differences in Cognitive Abilities*. Third edition. Mahwah, NJ: L. Erlbaum Associates.

Hammond, E. M, M. A. Berry, and D. N. Rodriguez. 2011. "Influence of Rape Myth Acceptance, Sexual Attitudes, and Belief in a Just World on Attributions of Responsibility in a Date Rape Scenario." *Legal and Criminological Psychology* 35: 242–252.

Harlow, R. E., J. M. Darley, and P. H. Robinson. 1995. "The Severity of Intermediate Penal Sanctions: A Psychophysical Scaling Approach for Obtaining Community Perceptions." *Journal of Quantitative Criminology* 11: 71–95.

Hartocollis, A. 2014. "Mental Health Issues Put 34,500 on New York's No-Guns List." *New York Times*. (October 19). http://www.nytimes.com/2014/10/19 /nyregion/mental-reports-put-34500-on-new-yorks-no-guns-list.html (accessed October 19, 2014).

Hayes, G. 2010. *Personal Defense for Women.* Iola, WI: Gun Digest Press.

Heller, K. J. 1998. "Beyond the Reasonable Man? A Sympathetic but Critical Assessment of the Use of Subjective Standards of Reasonableness in Self-Defense and Provocation Cases." *American Journal of Criminal Law* 26 (1), 1–120.

Hendrik, H. W., P. Paradis, and R. Homick. 2007. *Human Factors in Handgun Safety and Forensics.* Boca Raton, FL: CRC Press.

Herrera, A., I. Valor-Segura, and F. Expósito. 2012. "Is Miss Sympathy a Credible Defendant Alleging Intimate Partner Violence in a Trial for Murder?" *The European Journal of Psychology Applied to Legal Context* 4 (2): 179–196.

Hollander, J. A. 2009. "The Roots of Resistance to Women's Self-Defense." *Violence Against Women* 15: 574–594.

Homsher, D. 2001. *Women and Guns: Politics and Culture of Firearms in America.* Armonk, NY: M. E. Sharpe.

Hopkins, C. 2014. "Michigan Man Found Guilty in Shooting Death of Girl on His Porch." National Public Radio. http://www.npr.org/blogs/thetwo-way/2014 /08/07/338600637/detroit-man-found-guilty-in-shooting-death-of-girl-on -his-porch. (accessed November 16, 2014).

Hugenberg, K., and G. V. Bodenhausen. 2004. "Ambiguity in Social Categorization: The Role of Prejudice and Facial Affect in Race Categorization." *Psychological Science* 15: 342–345.

Ilgen, M. A., K. Zivin, R. J. McCammon, and M. Valenstein. 2008. "Mental Illness, Previous Suicidality, and Access to Guns in the United States." *Psychiatric Services 2008* 59: 198-200.

Jackson, K. 2010. *The Cornered Cat: A Woman's Guide to Concealed Carry.* Hamilton, MI: White Feather Press.

James, L., B. Vila, and K. Daratha. 2011. "Selective Responses to Threat: The Roles of Race and Gender in Decisions to Shoot." *Journal of Experimental Criminology* 9: 189–212.

Johnson, K., and S. Dewan. 2014. "Tangled Portrait of a Student Emerges in Washington Shooting." *New York Times* (October 26). http://www.nytimes .com/2014/10/26/us/contrasting-portraits-emerge-of-jaylen-ray-fryberg -shooter-at-washington-school.html (accessed November 16, 2014).

Johnson, N. 2014. *Negroes and the Gun: The Black Tradition of Arms.* New York: Prometheus Books.

Jonsson, P. 2012. "Gun Nation: Inside America's Gun-Carry Culture." *Christian Science Monitor.* http://www.csmonitor.com/USA/Society/2012/0311/Gun-nation -Inside-America-s-gun-carry-culture (accessed September 2, 2012).

Kassin, S. M., and M. A. Dunn. 1997. "Computer-Animated Displays and the Jury: Facilitative and Prejudicial Effects." *Law and Human Behavior* 21 (3), 269–281.

Kassin, S. M., and D. Garfield. 1991. "Blood and Guts: General and Trial-Specific Effects of Videotaped Crime Scenes on Mock Jurors." *Journal of Applied Social Psychology* 21: 1459-1472. doi: 10.1111/j.1559-1816.1991.tb00481.x.

Kazan, P. 1997. "Reasonableness, Gender Difference, and Self-Defense Law." *Manitoba Law Journal* 24: 549–575.

Keating, N. M. 2000. "If Looks Could Kill: Female Gazes as Guns in *Thelma and Louise.*" In M. Pomerance and J. Sakeris, editors. *Bang, Bang, Shoot, Shoot: Essays on Guns and Popular Culture.* Second edition. (95–105). Needham Heights, MA: Pearson Education.

Kleck, G. 1991. *Point Blank.* New York: Aldine de Gruyter.

Kleck, G. 1997. *Targeting Guns: Firearms and Their Control.* New York: Aldine de Gruyter.

Klein, D., and D. Mitchell, editors. 2010. *The Psychology of Judicial Decision Making.* New York: Oxford University Press.

Klinesmith, J., T. Kasser, and F. T. McAndrew. 2006. "Guns, Testosterone, and Aggression: An Experimental Test of a Mediational Hypothesis." *Psychological Science* 17: 568-571. doi: 10.1111/j.1467-9280.2006.01745.x.

Koper, C., and J. A. Roth. 2001. "The Impact of the 1994 Federal Assault Weapons Ban on Gun Violence Outcomes: An Assessment of Multiple Outcome Measures and Some Lessons for Policy Evaluation." *Journal of Quantitative Criminology* 17 (1), 33–74.

Krauthammer, C. 2013. "The Zimmerman Case: A Touch of Sanity." http://articles .washingtonpost.com/2013-07-18/opinions/40655110_1_zimmerman-trial -george-zimmerman-zimmerman-case.

Lee, C. 2013. "Making Race Salient: Trayvon Martin and Implicit Bias in a Not Yet Post-Racial Society." *North Carolina Law Review.* http://scholarship.law.gwu .edu/faculty_publications/728.

Leverick, F. 2007. *Killing in Self-Defense.* New York: Oxford University Press.

Levett. L. M., E. M. Danielson, M. B. Kovera, and B. L. Cutler. 2005. "The Psychology of Jury and Juror Decision Making." In N. Brewer and K. D. Williams, editors. *Psychology and Law: An Empirical Perspective* (365–406). New York: Guilford Press.

Lieberman, J. D., S. Solomon, J. Greenberg, and H. A. McGregor. 1999. "A Hot New Measure of Aggression: Hot Sauce Allocation. *Aggressive Behavior* 25: 331–348.

Lott, J. R., and D. B. Mustard. 1997. "Crime, Deterrence, and Right-to-Carry Concealed Handguns." *Journal of Legal Studies* 26: 1–68.

Manning, R., M. Levine, and A. Collins. 2007. "The Kitty Genovese Murder and the Social Psychology of Helping: The Parable of the 38 Witnesses." *American Psychologist* 62: 555-562. doi: 0.1037/0003-066X.62.6.555.

Markey, P. M, C. N. Markey, and J. E. French. 2014. "Violent Video Games and Real-World Violence: Rhetoric versus Data." *Psychology of Popular Media Culture.* http://dx.doi.org/10.1037/ppm0000030.

Marsh, D. P., and M. S. Goldberg. 1996. "Evaluation of a Victim's Response to an Attempted Robbery: The Effect of Victim Gender." *Legal and Criminological Psychology* 1: 211–218.

McCaughey, M. 1997. *Real Knockouts*. New York: New York University Press.

Meyer, G. E., A. S. Baños, T. Gerondale, K. Kiriazes, C. M. Lakin, and A. C. Rinker. 2009. "Juries, Gender, and Assault Weapons." *Journal of Applied Social Psychology* 39: 945–972.

Meyer, G. E., H. M. Nguyen, K. L. Whitehouse, and J. R. Houchins. 2008. "Armed: Aggressive or Altruistic?" Presented at the Annual Meeting of American Psychology Association, Boston, MA.

Meyer, G. E. A. T. Gruber, K. M. Wallace, M. Robertson, V. Q. Nguyen, M. E. Murphy, and C. Raymond. 2012. "Does the Bystander Pull the Trigger?" Presented at the annual meeting of the Association for Psychological Science, Chicago, IL.

Miller, L. 2012. "Stalking: Patterns, Motives, and Intervention Strategies." *Aggression and Violent Behavior*. doi: 10.1016/j.avb.2012.07.001.

Miller, M., D. Azrael, and D. Hemenway. 2001. "Community Firearms, Community Fear." *Epidemiology* 11 (6), 709–715.

Minnesota v. Vriesenga. 1992. http://www.nytimes.com/1992/11/19/us/no-head line-969692.html.

Min Yang, M., C. P. Wong, and J. Coid. 2010. "The Efficacy of Violence Prediction: A Meta-Analytic Comparison of Nine Risk Assessment Tools." *Psychological Bulletin* 136: 740 –767. doi: 10.1037/a0020473.

Nagtegaal, M. H., E. Rassin, and P. E. H. M. Muris. 2009. "Do Members of Shooting Associations Display Higher Levels of Aggression?" *Psychology, Crime & Law* 15: 313–325. doi: 10.1080/10683160802241682.

Norman, D. A. 2002. *The Design of Everyday Things*. New York: Basic Books.

Office of Bill de Blasio, Public Advocate for the City of New York. 2013. *Stop and Frisk: The Urgent Need for Reform*. New York. Office of the Public Advocate. http://advocate.nyc.gov/sites/advocate.nyc.gov/files/DeBlasioStopFriskReform .pdf (accessed November 14, 2014).

Olson, K. C., and J. M. Darley. 1999. "Community Perceptions of Allowable Counterforce in Self-Defense and Defense of Property." *Law and Human Behavior* 23 (6), 629–651.

Oregon Secretary of State Elections Division. 2014. *Initiative 13*. http://egov .sos.state.or.us/elec/web_irr_search.record_detail?p_reference=20160000 ..LSCYYYHANDGUN (accessed November 26, 2014).

O'Toole, M. E. 2000. "The School Shooter: A Threat Assessment Perspective." http://www.fbi.gov/stats-services/publications/school-shooter (accessed March 17, 2015).

Owen, W. 1996. "Matte Black, Plastic, Stocky and Mean Design for Killing: The Aesthetic of Menace Sells Guns to the Masses." *I.D. Magazine* 43 (5), 54–61.

Padilla, G. 1996. "DA Won't Prosecute Teen in Roof Shooting." *San Antonio Express-News*. (May 24). http://www.mysanantonio.com/expressnews (accessed March 1, 2002).

Payne, B. K., A. J. Lambert, and L. L. Jacoby. 2002. "Best Laid Plans: Effects of Goals on Accessibility Bias and Cognitive Control in Race-Based Misperceptions of Weapons." *Journal of Experimental Social Psychology* 38: 384–396.

Payne, B. K. 2001. "Prejudice and Perception: The Role of Automatic and Controlled Processes in Misperceiving a Weapon." *Journal of Personality and Social Psychology* 81: 181-192.

Phillips, S., and M. O. Maume. 2007. "Have Gun Will Shoot? Weapons Instrumentality, Intent, and the Violent Escalation of Conflict." *Homicide Studies* 11 (4), 272–294.

Pickel, K. L. 1998. "Unusualness and Threat as Possible Causes of 'Weapon Focus.'" *Memory* 6: 277–295.

Plant, E. A., J. Goplen, and J. W. Kunstman. 2012. "Selective Responses to Threat: The Roles of Race and Gender in Decisions to Shoot." *Personality and Social Psychology Bulletin* 37: 1274-1281.

Plant, E. A., B. M. Peruche, and D. A. Butz. 2005. "Eliminating Automatic Racial Bias: Making Race Non-Diagnostic for Responses to Criminal Suspects." *Journal of Experimental Social Psychology* 41: 141–156.

Rauch, W. 2004. "A Rifle for Home Defense." *S.W.A.T.* 23: 74–76.

Reddy, M., R. Borum, J. Berglund, B. Vossekuil, R. Fein, and W. Modzeleski. 2001. "Evaluating Risk for Target Violence in Schools: Comparing Risk Assessment, Threat Assessment and Other Approaches." *Psychology in the Schools* 38 (2), 157–172.

Roesch, R., S. D. Hart, and J. R. P. Ogloff, editors. 1999. *Psychology and Law: The State of the Discipline.* New York: Klumer Academic/Plenum Publishers.

Ryckman, R. M., S. S. Graham, B. Thornton, J. A. Gold, J., and M. A. Lindner. 1998. "Physical Size Stereotyping as a Mediator of Attributions of Responsibility in an Alleged Date-Rape Situation." *Journal of Applied Social Psychology* 28: 1876–1888.

Saad, L. 2011. "Self-Reported Gun Ownership in the U.S. is Highest Since 1993." Gallup Politics. http://www.gallup.com/poll/150353/self-reported-gun-ownership-highest-1993.aspx (accessed September 2, 2012).

Sachs, P. 2008. "Protest Slated over Police Assault Plan." *Chi Town Daily News.* http://www.chitowndailynews.org/Chicago_news/Protest_slated_over_police_assault_rifle_plan,17272 (accessed November 16, 2014).

Schouten, F. 2014. "Bloomberg Group Launches Midterm Campaign for Gun Control." *USA Today.* http://www.usatoday.com/story/news/politics/2014/09/22/mike-bloomberg-gun-control-group-launches-new-ads-makes-endorsements/16069445 (accessed October 20, 2014).

Schlenker, B. R., J. R. Chambers, and B. M. Le. 2012. "Conservatives Are Happier than Liberals, But Why? Political Ideology, Personality, and Life Satisfaction." *Journal of Research in Personality* 46 (2), 127–146.

Sim, J. J., J. Correl, and M. S. Sadler. 2013. "Understanding Police and Expert Performance: When Training Attenuates (vs. Exacerbates) Stereotypic Bias in the Decision to Shoot." *Personality and Social Psychology Bulletin* 39: 291–304.

Skeem, J. L., and J. Monoahan. 2011. "Current Directions in Violence Risk Assessment." *Current Directions in Psychological Science* 20: 38–42. doi: 10.1177/0963721410397271.

Soltau, A. 2004. "Cops Outgunned by Thugs: Union Wants Better Firepower for Officers." *San Francisco Examiner.* http://www.examiner.com/article/index.cfm /i/070604n_guns (accessed August 25, 2004).

Speir, D. 2004. *William Batterman Ruger, Sr.: "Father" of the Clinton Administration's High Capacity Magazine Ban.* http://www.thegunzone.com/rkba/papabill.html (accessed February 23, 20014).

Stange, M. Z., and C. K. Oyster. 2000. *Gun Women: Firearms and Feminism in Contemporary America.* New York: New York University Press.

Stanny, C. J., and T. C. Johnson. 2000. "Effects of Stress Induced By a Simulated Shooting on Recall by Police and Citizen Witnesses." *American Journal of Psychology* 113: 359–386.

State of Texas. 2009. *Penal code, Chapter 9. Justification Excluding Criminal Responsibility.* http://www.statutes.legis.state.tx.us/Docs/PE/htm/PE.9.htm#9.32 (accessed September 23, 2010).

Steblay, N. M. 1992. "A Meta-Analytic Review of the Weapon Focus Effect." *Law and Human Behavior* 16 (4), 413–424.

Steele, L. 2007. "Defending the Self-Defense Case." *Champion Magazine* (March), 34.

Sunstein, C. 2005. "Moral Heuristics." *Behavioral and Brain Sciences* 28: 531-573. doi: 10.1017/S0140525X05000099.

Swanson, J. W., E. E. McGinty, S. Fazel, and V. M. Mays. 2014. "Mental Illness and Reduction of Gun Violence and Suicide: Bringing Epidemiologic Research to Policy." *Annals of Epidemiology.* http://dx.doi.org/10.1016/j.annepidem.2014.03.004.

Tark, J., and G. Kleck. 2004. "Resisting Crime: The Effects of Victim Action on the Outcomes of Crimes." *Criminology* 42: 861-909. doi: 10.1111/j.1745-9125 .2004.tb00539.x.

Terrance, C., and K. Matheson. 2003. "Undermining Reasonableness: Expert Testimony in a Case Involving a Battered Woman Who Kills." *Psychology of Women Quarterly* 27: 34–45.

Thurman, R. 2012. "U.S. Firearms Industry Today: Industry Enters Golden Era, Firearms Sales Set Records." *Shooting Industry* 57: 36–44.

Umoja, A. O. 2014. *We Will Shoot Back: Armed Resistance in the Mississippi Freedom Movement.* New York: NYU Press.

Unkelbach C., J. P. Forgas, and T. F. Denson. 2008. "The Turban Effect: The Influence of Muslim Headgear and Induced Affect on Aggressive Responses in the Shooter Bias Paradigm." *Journal of Experimental Social Psychology* 44 (5), 1409–1413. doi:10.1016/j.jesp.2008.04.003.

Werner, C. 2014. "What Is the Value of Training?" http://tacticalprofessor.word press.com/2014/11/09/what-is-the-value-of-training/comment-page -1/#comment-750 (accessed November 15, 2014).

Wintemute, G. J., C. A. Parham, J. J. Beaumont, M. Wright, and C. Drake. 1999. "Mortality among Recent Purchasers of Handguns." *New England Journal of Medicine* 341 (21), 1583–15893.

CHAPTER FOUR

Terrorism and the Ownership of Firearms

Saundra J. Ribando and Amanda J. Reinke

What Is Terrorism?

Although there is no universally accepted definition of terrorism, agreement does exist about its broad outlines. Generally, terrorism definitions include the use of violence (or threat of violence) directed at a broad audience and with a political goal. Such goals often include redistributing power, influence, or wealth that are not achievable within the constraints of the normal political process (Krieger and Meierrieks 2011). Since perpetrators cannot use the political process, they resort to terrorism as the only mechanism for drawing attention to their cause.

The U.S. Code defines terrorism as an offense that "is calculated to influence or affect the conduct of government by intimidation or coercion, or to retaliate against government conduct" and involves a violent crime (18 U.S.C. §232b). Domestic terrorism refers to activities that have three characteristics: (1) involve acts dangerous to human life that violate federal or state law; (2) appear intended to intimidate or coerce the population, government policy, or affect the conduct of government; and (3) occur primarily within U.S. territory (18 U.S.C. §2331).

Unfortunately, these legal definitions raise a number of questions and concerns. For example, Gage (2011) argues that many acts in American history that are viewed positively would be labeled terrorism today. She cites such activities as the Boston Tea Party, which involved no casualties but property was destroyed (similar to today's ecoterrorism), as just one of many examples. Amster (2006) argues that the definition in use, which includes property damage, is overly broad. In his view, including property damage in the definition results in subsuming constitutionally protected protest activity into terrorist activity.

Problems with the legal definition also create curious anomalies within the U.S. government. For example, the FBI has historically operated with the understanding that domestic terrorists not only operate inside the United States, but also lack foreign direction. Bjelopera (2013, 4), in a Congressional Research Service report, asserts that the FBI's shorthand definition of terrorism is "Americans attacking Americans based on U.S.–based extremist ideologies." Using this definition, the 1993 bombing of the World Trade Center, the attacks on 9/11, and the bombing of the Boston Marathon in 2013 were not domestic terrorism incidents, even though all three occurred within U.S. territory and meet the legal definition outlined in the U.S. Code.

One outgrowth of the definitional issue is the difficulty in getting a sense of the scope of the domestic terrorism threat. First, there is evidence that the federal courts and the Department of Justice use different criteria when sorting, counting, and categorizing terrorist prosecutions in general (Transactional Records Access Clearinghouse 2009), which opens the possibility that what one agency refers to as "terrorism" is not counted as such by another agency (Bjelopera 2013).

Complicating matters further, domestic terrorism incidents typically involve federal, state, and local law enforcement and multiple crimes. Incidents often encompass firearms, arson, or explosive offenses, fraud, vandalism, property damage, threats, and hoaxes. In some cases, what the FBI describes as a domestic terrorism suspect may not be charged with committing a federal crime. As a result, "individuals considered domestic terrorists by federal law enforcement may not necessarily be federally charged as terrorists" (Bjelopera 2013, 6). Instead, the suspect may be charged under state law for crimes committed as part of a terrorist incident.

Given that terrorism is by definition a political act, law enforcement officials may not be able or willing to label an act as "terrorism" early in an investigation. It can be challenging for investigators to distinguish between political motives and personal malice (Bjelopera 2013). For example, consider violent acts committed by white supremacist groups. Are their violent actions driven by political motivations such as a desire to set up an apartheid system, or simply hate?

Finally, Bjelopera (2013) points out that the FBI often uses the terms "extremism" and "terrorism" interchangeably. In part, this may be due to a desire to reconcile the FBI's traditional definition of terrorism as American-based and originated with the reality of individuals on U.S. soil conducting terrorist operations under the direction or influence of overseas parties. Alternatively, this could be an outgrowth of the government's possible reluctance to label domestic groups as terrorist groups due to civil liberties concerns.

Domestic Terrorism since 1970

Given the definitional and legal difficulties noted earlier, it is not surprising that sources vary concerning the number of domestic terrorist events. For example, the FBI counted 308 domestic terrorist events between 1980 and 2005 (FBI 2005). But the National Consortium for the Study of Terrorism and Response to Terrorism (hereinafter, START) recorded 1,058 such incidents. START conducts content analysis of media reports rather than formal prosecutions to develop its data set. In addition, it includes all terrorist incidents occurring in U.S. territories, regardless of whether or not the attack had an international connection. For purposes of this essay, and in light of the concerns raised earlier about government data, we will use the START data set, known as the Global Terrorism Dataset, as the source for this section.

From 1970 through 2012, there were 2,611 domestic terrorism incidents. The United States accounts for just 2.3 percent of 113,113 reported worldwide. As shown in Figure 4.1, domestic terrorism has decreased significantly over time from its high of 468 incidents in 1970 to just 13 in 2012. Over this time period, 2,652 individuals were killed and another 2,613 wounded. The states that were most often targeted for terrorist attacks were California (568, or 21.8 percent of all attacks) and New York (498, 19.1 percent). Although not a state, Puerto Rico has endured 246 terrorist attacks (9.4 percent). The most common type of attack was a bombing or explosion (1,352 or 51.8 percent of all attacks), followed by sabotage/vandalism of a facility or infrastructure (791, 30.3 percent). Suicide attacks are extremely rare—just 9 domestic terrorism incidents were classified as a suicide attack.

In the 1970s, domestic terrorism incidents originated primarily from the left wing of the political spectrum. There were 1,470 attacks (56.3 percent of all attacks between 1970 and 2012), resulting in 185 deaths and 616 wounded. Table 4.1 summarizes the types of groups involved with terrorist activities during this decade.

Groups inspired by left-wing ideologies such as communism and socialism clearly dominated the 1970s. Of the 1,470 terrorist incidents in

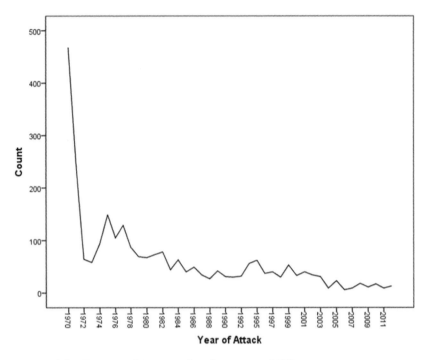

Figure 4.1 Domestic Terrorism Incidents since 1970

Table 4.1 Terrorist Attacks in the 1970s by Type of Group

	Number of Attacks	**Percent**
Black nationalists	173	11.8
Left-wing radicals	498	33.9
Environmentalists	2	.1
Puerto Rican nationalists	220	15.0
Other nationalists	254	17.3
White supremacists	56	3.8
Right-wing radicals	12	.8
Islamic fundamentalists	3	.2
Other[1]	33	2.2
Unknown[2]	218	14.8

1. "Other" refers to individual attacks.

2. "Unknown" attacks are those where no group was ever identified as being responsible.

the 1970s, 498 (33.9 percent) were perpetrated by left-wing radical groups such as the New World Liberation Front (86) and the Weathermen (44). Another 173 were associated with Black Nationalist groups. Those groups were also heavily influenced by left-wing ideology (Rosenau 2013) as were Puerto Rican and other nationalist groups.

The number of terrorism incidents began plummeting in the mid-1970s as the energy began to leave left-wing organizations, and law enforcement became more effective in infiltrating groups and prosecuting their members (Rosenau 2013). In the 1980s, there were 517 attacks, 54 persons killed, and 924 wounded. As illustrated in Table 4.2, nationalism was the driving force behind much of the terrorism during the 1980s. Groups such as the Jewish Defense League (30 attacks, 5.8 percent of the total) were joined by Puerto Rican groups such as the Macheteros (31.6 percent) in using violence as a way to bring attention to their cause.

In this decade, white supremacist groups such as the Ku Klux Klan, the Order, and Aryan Nations were responsible for 39 (7.5 percent) incidents. This was also the decade that witnessed the emergence of the violent anti-abortion movement. Of the 97 domestic terrorism incidents identified as right wing but not white supremacist, 90 (93 percent) were attributed to anti-abortion individuals or groups.

During the 1990s Puerto Rican and other nationalist groups moved away from terrorism and the overall number of attacks continued to decline. There were just 371 attacks; however, there were 219 killed and

Table 4.2 Terrorist Attacks in the 1980s by Type of Group

	Number of Attacks	Percent
Black nationalists	6	1.2
Left-wing radicals	34	6.6
Animal rights	6	1.2
Environmentalists	8	1.5
Puerto Rican nationalists	94	18.2
Other nationalists	112	21.7
White supremacists	39	7.5
Right-wing radicals	97	18.8
Islamic fundamentalists	5	1.0
Other	29	5.6
Unknown	87	16.8

945 wounded. In this decade, terrorism continued to originate from the right wing (Table 4.3), anti-abortion extremists accounting for 79 attacks (21.3 percent). A new cause emerged—animal rights. The Animal Liberation Front was responsible for 33 (8.9 percent) of the domestic terrorism incidents. With that emergence came a shift in the type of weapon preferred in attacks. For the first time, incendiary devices were used more frequently than explosives in terrorist attacks.

While the decade 2000 to 2009 will no doubt be most remembered for the 9/11 attacks, Islamic extremism was responsible for just 5 terrorism incidents in the United States. Driven by the 9/11 attacks, the casualty rate from domestic terrorism skyrocketed to 1,555 dead and 104 wounded. Domestic terrorism took a decidedly left-wing turn as animal rights and environmentalism emerged as the major contributors (Table 4.4). Of the 214 terrorism incidents in the United States, 57 (26.6 percent) were attributed to the Environmental Liberation Front and 29 (13.6 percent) to the Animal Liberation Front. Overall, 46.3 percent of terrorism incidents were attributed to such left-wing groups.

Just as the origination of the incidents has shifted with time, so has the level of violence. In the 1970s the largest number of deaths associated with a single incident was 11 compared with the 168 associated with the Oklahoma City bombing in the 1990s, and 1,381 attributed to the 9/11 attacks in New York City. Table 4.5 summarizes the results from conducting one-way analysis of variance.

Table 4.3   Terrorist Attacks in the 1990s by Type of Group

	Number of Attacks	Percent
Black nationalists	0	0
Left-wing radicals	1	.3
Animal rights	49	.32
Environmentalists	12	3.2
Puerto Rican nationalists	14	3.8
Other nationalists	12	3.2
White supremacists	37	10.0
Right-wing radicals	84	22.6
Islamic fundamentalists	3	.8
Other	54	14.6
Unknown	105	28.3

Table 4.4   Terrorist Attacks 2000–2009 by Type of Group

	Number of Attacks	Percent
Black nationalists	0	0
Left-wing radicals	0	0
Animal rights	31	14.5
Environmentalists	66	30.8
Puerto Rican nationalists	0	0
Other nationalists	0	0
White supremacists	5	2.3
Right-wing radicals	16	7.5
Islamic fundamentalists	5	2,3
Other	42	19.6
Unknown	49	22.9

Table 4.5   Results of One-Way ANOVA, Decade of Attack, and Number of Persons Killed

	Mean	Maximum	F	Sig.
1970s	.1298	11		
1980s	.1109	2		
1990s	.6000	168		
2000s	14.216	1382		
Overall			5.044	.000

However, if we exclude the Oklahoma City and the 9/11 attacks as outliers, the mean number of deaths continues to increase slightly over time, but the difference between the decades is no longer statistically significant.

This suggests that the increase in violence over time is attributable to the type of group or individual responsible. Some groups, such as the Animal Liberation Front and the Environmental Liberation Front, deliberately plan attacks to avoid human casualties. There have been no deaths attributed to any of their attacks. On the other hand, some groups plan attacks in ways designed not only to ensure casualties, but to maximize them. Such was clearly the case with Timothy McVeigh's truck bombing

Table 4.6   Results of One-Way ANOVA, Type of Group, and Number of Persons Killed

	Mean	Maximum	F	Sig.
Black nationalists	.4722	8		
Left-wing radicals	.0250	2		
Animal rights	0	0		
Environmentalists	0	0		
Puerto Rican nationalists	.0717	4		
Other nationalists	.1288	11		
White supremacists	.1926	5		
Right-wing radicals	.0529	2		
Islamic terrorists	199.8667	1382		
Other	1.4826	168		
Unknown	.0895	2		
			45.619	.000

in Oklahoma City and al Qaeda's 9/11 attacks on office buildings. Both attacks took place during a business day, using a weapon that was guaranteed to kill large numbers of people. In fact, when using one-way ANOVA to compare the number of persons killed by group category, Islamic fundamentalists emerge as the most violent (Table 4.6). In other words, as the perpetrators' identity has changed, so has the casualty rate.

What Causes Terrorism?

What separates terrorism from criminal behavior is motive. Terrorism is by definition a political act. As such, the general public and political leaders tend to ascribe the emergence of terrorism to some sort of political grievance. This suggests that addressing the underlying grievances would end terrorism. But researchers are learning that terrorism is a more complicated phenomenon than a simple reading of a terrorist group's manifestos would suggest.

Economic deprivation is often cited as a causal factor behind terrorist activities. According to this school of thought, violence is used when individuals believe there is a discrepancy between what they believe they deserve and what they actually receive (Gurr 1970). Known as "relative deprivation," this framework suggests that addressing economic inequality or causes of economic deprivation is the most effective counter-terrorism approach.

An alternative to this viewpoint suggests that modernization, and the economic and social change that comes with it, are major contributors to the emergence of terrorist groups. The transition from a traditional to a modern society often results in major shifts in labor markets which can create grievances (Robison, Crenshaw, and Jenkins 2006). Outside the United States, that same transition carries with it moves to more Western (secular, modern) ways of living and thinking that conflict with traditional ways. The conflict between the "old" and the "new" sparks resistance and, potentially, terrorist activity (Ross 1993).

The political order is often considered to be a contributing factor to terrorism. Academics disagree about whether certain political systems are better prepared to cope with terrorism. Some argue that democracy, because of its commitment to civil liberties, is ill prepared to handle terrorism outbreaks. On the other hand, because democracy provides more opportunities for disaffected groups to dissent, it may be more resistant to terrorism. Others argue that autocratic regimes, because of their repression, may create grievances, but are also more capable of tracking down and eliminating terrorist threats (Krieger and Meierrieks 2011).

Another purported cause of terrorism is regime instability. Essentially, instability creates power vacuums within which terrorist groups may emerge. Failed states are the most extreme example of this situation. In such environments, it becomes much easier for groups on the radical fringe to operate without fear of state action, creating a "safe space" where terrorist groups can train and operate (Krieger and Meierrieks 2011).

Identity clashes have also been put forward as causes of terrorism. While Huntington's "clash of civilizations" may be the most well-known explanation, other terrorism theorists have noted that terrorists often build on ethnocentric ideologies, stressing the superiority of "their group" over others or the threat that other forces pose to their own ethnic or religious group's survival. Bernholz (2006) notes that such conflict often involves the claim of absolute values, which has tremendous power for motivating individuals to join terrorist groups and justifying their extreme actions.

Eitan (2011) suggests that terrorism is not the product of broad societal factors such as poverty, but terrorist groups emerge out of social relationships. Specifically, terrorist groups emerge when radicalization happens, that is, when a faction splinters from a larger oppositional group. This emergence occurs primarily as a result of social interactions. Eitan's research suggests these social interactions include three important dynamics. The first is competition for power among leaders within the opposition movement. The second and third dynamics link the group to the broader society. When the group is "losing" in its struggle for change, it is more likely that a faction advocating radical action will emerge. In addition, when the movement's actions and state counteractions begin to escalate, splintering of the oppositional group is more likely.

Krieger and Meierrieks (2011) conclude that transnational terrorism largely emerges in settings where political institutions are authoritarian in nature, but largely unstable. There is little evidence in their study that economic conditions, in and of themselves, cause terrorism. But their work addresses only transnational terrorism such as that conducted by al Qaeda.

In the United States, which of these theories appears most relevant? Clearly, there is at least some evidence in favor of Gurr's relative deprivation theory. For example, the Black Panthers and their more radical offshoot, the Black Liberation Army, aimed their attacks primarily at law enforcement to combat what they perceived as white oppression expressed through police harassment and violence (Rosenau 2013). Similarly, Freilich and Pridemore (2005) demonstrated that economic deprivation, as measured by the number of farming and rural jobs lost, was positively related to the number of militia groups in a given U.S. state.

There is also some evidence in support of the identity clash theory. Terrorist groups in the United States that have been nationalist or white supremacist in nature provide excellent examples in support of this theory. For example, Vertigans (2007) traces the development of the radical right and notes the strong thread of defending the "American way of life" that runs through the literature produced by such groups. The statement of purpose put forward by one right wing terrorist group, the Covenant, the Sword, and the Arm of the Lord, includes references to the superiority of the white race and its endangered status in contemporary America (anon. 1995). The sense of threat and imminent collapse is also strong in publications from ecoterrorism groups. These groups believe that human activity, particularly in the form of capitalist economic activity, is destroying the earth and that for its survival, humanity must greatly reduce its numbers and return to subsistence living (Eagan 1996; Lange 1990).

Finally, we can also see evidence for Eitan's theory of relational dynamics. For example, the Earth Liberation Front (ELF) was a splinter group from Earth First!, which was itself founded by disaffected members of the Wilderness Society (Eagan 1996). The Black Liberation Front in the 1970s was a splinter group from the Black Panthers that emerged as a result of leadership struggles and the escalation and counter-escalation Eitan describes (Rosenau 2013). Eitan (2011) uses the Weathermen, a splinter group from Students for a Democratic Society, as a case study in his research, tracing the leadership fights, increasing sense of failure within SDS, and the escalation of confrontation and violence between the SDS and law enforcement as principal causes for the emergence of the Weathermen in the 1970s.

While no one theory appears to comprehensively explain the emergence of terrorism in the United States, several offer valuable insights. There appears to be some evidence for the applicability of relative deprivation theory, along with theories concerning identity clash and relational dynamics. Finally, although not a theory about terrorism's causation, the widespread ownership of weapons in American society makes resorting to violence an easy step to take for both groups and individuals wanting to intimidate the public.

Why Do People Become Terrorists?

One of the biggest challenges for researchers and governments in dealing with terrorism is learning why individuals join such groups. As an example, consider African Americans. Although as a group they have experienced slavery, racism, economic deprivation, and social isolation, relatively few have turned to terrorism as a way to redress grievances. The theories presented in the previous section help us understand the emergence of groups, but what leads individuals to join such groups?

Many researchers use rational choice theory, based in neoclassical microeconomics, to explain why individuals become terrorists. Rational choice theory includes these core assumptions: economic phenomena result from autonomous individual decision makers; individuals understand their preferences and have knowledge of the resources at their disposal; individuals maximize utility (satisfaction) by allocating resources optimally; individuals are capable of figuring out how to optimize their resources; individuals are concerned about maximizing their individual utility and are unconcerned with others (Kuznar 2007, 320). Bryan Caplan (2006), focusing on suicidal terrorist acts, uses rational choice modeling to understand why some individuals become terrorists while others are content to be sympathizers. He uses three types of rationality—responsiveness to incentives, narrow selfishness, and rational expectations—to explain why some individuals engage in terrorist acts, but the overwhelming majority of individuals never become active terrorists themselves. Caplan uses rational choice theory to critique scholars basing understandings of suicidal terrorist acts on religious doctrine, by pointing out that the majority of individuals never engage in terrorist acts; this fact clearly indicates their adherence to central principles of rational choice theory (2006, 92). In short, it simply is not in the best interest of most individuals to actively participate in terrorist acts. However, Caplan also recognizes that if all individuals followed rational choice theory constructs, suicidal terrorism would not exist at any level (2006). This conclusion highlights the primary limitation of rational choice theory: it presumes all individuals to be rational, knowledgeable about their own resources and potential, independent, and unconcerned about the welfare of others.

If rational choice theorists are correct in their assumptions about the push and pull factors influencing individual decision making, then the future of terrorist action depends upon the self-interest of individuals. This self-interest includes economic factors, preferences, and resources, and the ability of individuals to maximize utility through non-terrorist activities. This theory also presumes that all individuals are self-interested and are not concerned about others, which means that efforts to curtail terrorism must be targeted at the individual level rather than focusing on groups or communities.

Another suggestion is that individuals who become terrorists are somewhat similar to those who join cults—persons with low self-esteem in search of a sense of purpose and belonging. Rosenau (2013) documents how the Black Panthers deliberately targeted "street kids" for recruitment into the group. More recently, the recruitment efforts of the Islamist military group ISIS have attracted disaffected youths in the United States and other Western countries to engage in terrorist acts. Shapira (2012), in her participant-observer research on right-wing groups monitoring the U.S.–Mexico border, found that individuals joined because it gave them a sense of meaning. Drawing on strain theory, Blazak's (2001) study of white supremacist recruiting tactics concluded that recruiters deliberately targeted youths that were confused, uncertain, or defensive about feminist activism, in schools where minority populations had grown or the curriculum had shifted to being multicultural, and communities where competition for manual labor jobs was high. These studies often draw upon work by Robert K. Merton (1938) and Albert Cohen (1955), in which the researchers postulate that social deviance, including the emergence and popularity of gangs and juvenile delinquent behavior, stems from rapid social change that creates an actual or perceived breakdown of community control and social disorganization.

Similarly, researchers, such as Blazak (2001), often draw on Emile Durkheim's concept of anomie, combining it with strain theory to explain how youth are targeted for terrorist initiatives. The concept of anomie references an individual's psychological feelings of distress or instability based upon an actual or perceived breakdown of cultural standards, norms and values, a sense of lack of purpose, or feelings of alienation. In contrast to rational choice theory, strain theory and perspectives based on anomie focus attention on the sociocultural factors pushing individuals to join terrorist groups, rather than on individual resources, decision making, and rationality.

When framed by strain theory and anomic understandings of terrorist recruitment, stemming terrorist activity must involve targeting at-risk individuals, such as white youth in areas where multiculturalism is burgeoning or economic opportunities are scarce. In this case, identifying the straining and social exclusionary factors is key to identifying at-risk individuals. Curtailing terrorist activity therefore relies upon incorporating mechanisms of social inclusion and addressing concerns about employment opportunities and rapid social change.

Aho's (1990) study of radical right-wing groups in Idaho found that individuals joined because someone they knew was a member. In other words, the social bond connecting individuals preceded membership for individuals in these groups. Evolutionary psychologists take a similar approach, favoring a focus on small-group dynamics and the influence of charismatic leaders drawing individuals in by invoking nepotism, fictive kin relations, and developing relationships with potential recruits (Kuznar 2007, 319). Individuals are likely to join terrorist groups if they live in tight-knit, marginalized social groups, where others are members of the terrorist group. In this context, terrorist groups often emphasize the family-like nature of the organization, highlighting its potential as a support network and place for social bonding, or use peer pressure as a recruitment tool (Atran 2003; Atran and Stern 2005; Kuznar 2007). If Aho and others are correct, then if the state adopts repressive measures against the group, such as torture of captured members, such actions are likely to harden the resolve of the individual members and the group as a whole (Munger 2006).

Following evolutionary psychological theory, mechanisms used to curtail terrorist activity must focus on marginalized groups, such as immigrants looking for guidance and assistance or white youth in areas where employment opportunities are scarce and competition with minorities is high. This method contrasts with approaches based on rational choice modeling, which are individual-centric rather than focusing on groups or communities, and fail to account for social exclusion. It also diverges from strain theory in that it focuses on at-risk groups rather than the individual level.

Kuznar (2007) emphasizes the importance of macro and micro understandings of push and pull factors influencing whether individuals become terrorists. Although past understandings of education, poverty, rationality, and evolutionary psychology are all important considerations, Kuznar points to broader trends these approaches fail to account for. For example, new global structures and animosities have emerged in response to expansion of Western economic institutions and political agendas (2007, 322). Researchers cite this as a possible place where humiliation and resentment emerges for populations such as radical Muslims (Habeck 2006). Recognition of broader, potentially global, push and pull factors led Kuznar (2007) to apply sigmoid-utility theory and sigmoid function modeling to terrorism. As a theory, simoid-utility predicts potentially adaptive behavior by operationalizing status (for instance, wealth and social network analysis), by ranking individuals from lowest to highest, and determining social-status function (2007, 322). This model bases operationalization of concepts and components of the modeling function on cultural understandings of status, wealth, and social rank, but also models adaptive behavior, because individuals may change their decision making as the potential to gain utility changes (Kuznar 2002). For example, sigmoid-utility theory has been used to model utility, as a measure of wealth and status, for low status and middle class individuals in two population groups. The lower status individuals had the least utility to lose from risky activities, and were therefore more risk prone. Conversely, middle class individuals were more risk averse, because there was little to gain, but more to lose. As status changes, utility changes, and sigmoid-utility can therefore account for change over time. This model and theoretical approach can also be used to account for other risk-taking activities, such as participation in a terrorist group, by drawing upon data that accounts for social standing, material resources, and inequality.

Drawing upon sigmoid-utility theory, terrorism can be curtailed by identifying groups that are risk-prone and thus highly likely to engage in terrorist activity. The model could also be used to track change in that group over time in response to outreach initiatives directed at preventing terrorist activity among risk-prone groups.

Current Domestic Terrorism Concerns

Contemporary terrorism concerns in the United States can be broken down into three broad categories: threats from the left, threats from the right, and Islamic fundamentalism.

From the Left

Radical environmental and animal rights groups currently are the only significant terrorism concern from the left end of the political spectrum. Some argue that ecoterrorism is not "terrorism" at all (see Amster 2006), because humans are not targeted. In fact, the most prominent of these groups, the Environmental Liberation Front (ELF) and the Animal Liberation Front (ALF) plan and carry out their attacks in ways that are designed to avoid human casualties. Nonetheless, the activities of these groups meet the legal definition of domestic terrorism.

Ecoterrorist groups emerged out of the belief that mainstream environmentalist groups compromised too much as they participated in the political process (Eagan 2006). Thus, as Eitan (2011) predicts, these groups were splinters from more mainstream groups. The common threads in these groups are an unwillingness to compromise on environmental/animal rights issues, a focus on "direct action" as opposed to participation in the political process, and grass roots organizational structure that deliberately avoids any form of hierarchy (Eagan 1996).

These groups focus their activities on targeting property, typically using incendiaries, or the releasing of animals from "captivity." Common targets for the ELF include newly built subdivisions, car dealerships (especially those selling SUVs), and other corporately owned structures. The ALF is routinely involved in activities that release animals from laboratories or farms (Eagan 1996; FBI 2007; Bjelopera 2013).

The ideological basis for ecoterrorism comes from "deep ecology." According to this viewpoint, humans are simply another part of the biological community. Humans are not special, nor do they have a right to use other species except for the purposes of subsistence. According to "Principles of the Left Green Network" (1995, 356), such groups "oppose all forms of domination, of both human and nonhuman nature." Since the capitalist economic system is seen as the primary cause of environmental degradation, ecoterrorist and animal rights groups deliberately target businesses, laboratories that use animals in experimentation, and symbols of humanity's "excessive" growth such as subdivisions emblematic of urban sprawl and SUV dealerships (FBI 2007; Bjelopera 2013).

From the Right

Two movements on the right end of the political spectrum have raised concerns at the national level: militias and sovereign citizens. The militia and the sovereign citizens movement share much of the same ideology, an ideology that poses a direct challenge to the legitimacy of government. The principal difference between them is organization. Militias are paramilitary groups that organize and train together in military-style operations. Sovereign citizens are individuals, who operate independently of each other (Bjelopera 2013).

Militia groups and sovereign citizens share a deep distrust of government, especially the federal level of government. Both share a belief that government above the local level is either illegitimate (sovereign citizens) or limited to only those functions specifically mentioned in the Constitution (militias). Militia groups band together based on a common belief that there is a vast conspiracy to destroy what they see as the "American way of life." The conspiracy is variously claimed to come from the United Nations, or sometimes ZOG, the Zionist Occupation Government. With this in mind, militia groups and their members stockpile weapons and supplies to be ready for either a full-scale rebellion against the government or to defend themselves from government "overstepping" its authority (Vertigans 2007; FBI 2011a).

Sovereign citizens, on the other hand, operate alone. They declare themselves "sovereign," and claim immunity from the legal system. These individuals are, therefore, often involved in what has been referred to as "paper terrorism"—the filing of frivolous lawsuits and false liens—as means of extorting money from other individuals and tying up the legal system. They also commonly fail to pay taxes, register vehicles, get and maintain valid drivers' licenses, and have been known to produce false warrants and other legal documents (FBI 2011b; Bjelopera 2013).

Although the militia movement may seem to be the bigger threat, they have not been responsible for any terrorist attacks in the United States. Their tendency to stockpile weapons, however, and their involvement in *planning* attacks on law enforcement and government facilities have earned them the attention of the FBI and other government agencies (FBI 2011a). Sovereign citizens have also been known to become violent. Since 2000, they have killed six law enforcement officers (FBI 2011b).

Islamic Fundamentalism

Much of the media's interest in "homegrown" terrorism has been focused on the Muslim community in the United States. Well-publicized events, such as Major Nidal Hassan's attack at Fort Hood, have led many to conclude that the American Muslim community may become a source for a new generation of terrorists. Such concerns appear, however, to be somewhat exaggerated (Bjelopera 2013; Brooks 2011).

The Muslim community in the United States has not been a source of terrorists in the past primarily because the community is well-integrated into U.S. society and largely middle-class. As a result, there have been just a few cases of American Muslims participating in terrorist attacks. Moreover, the Muslim community has been instrumental in providing tips to law enforcement that have led to the arrest of individuals and the prevention of attacks (Brooks 2011). According to one report, Muslims have been involved in 60 terrorist plots in the United States since 9/11; 53 have been thwarted. In virtually every case, cooperation with the Muslim community was an integral part of law enforcement's operations (Zuckerman, Bucci, and Carafano 2013; Brooks 2011).

Law enforcement agencies are engaged in a delicate process with the Muslim community. It is clearly critically important to keep a good relationship with the community because it is the source of much valuable information about would-be jihadists. On the other hand, the availability of radical material through the internet, and the proliferation of jihadist activities overseas, makes it easier than ever for young Muslims to be radicalized and then gain training and experience in places such as Afghanistan, Pakistan, Somalia, and Syria (Bjelopera 2013). The fact that, historically, the most violent attacks have been associated with jihadist individuals and groups makes it critically important for government agencies to stay alert to this potential threat.

Domestic Terrorism and Firearms

The widespread ownership of weapons in the United States is a source of concern for those involved in the prevention of domestic terrorism. The 2014 confrontation between the Bureau of Land Management and a Nevada rancher, Cliven Bundy, who had been illegally grazing his cattle on federally-owned land, offered a powerful glimpse into the tendency of right-wing groups to stockpile weapons. Bundy, using typical sovereign citizen language, alleged that the federal government had no authority over the land since land management was not specifically in the U.S. Constitution as a federal responsibility. Supporters of Bundy, many of them well-armed members of militia groups, rallied from around the nation. The local sheriff, Doug Gillespie, in an interview, said, "I've never seen so many guns" (Ralston 2014, paragraph 5). The ensuing standoff, during which law enforcement found itself in the crosshairs of militia members with sniper weapons and outnumbered and outgunned, is but the latest reminder that gun ownership in the United States and domestic terrorism threats are genuine concerns.

Policymakers have attempted to respond to these potential threats in three distinctive ways: limiting the types of weapons that may be legally owned, attempting to crack down on "strawman" purchases, and including the terrorist watch list in the background check process to keep weapons out of the hands of potential terrorists. Given recent Supreme Court rulings in *District of Columbia v. Heller* (2008) and *McDonald v. City of Chicago* (2010) that established an individual right to own a weapon for self-defense, any attempts to limit gun ownership must respect the individual right while assisting the government's efforts to keep weapons out of the hands of potential domestic terrorists (Krouse 2012).

Attempts to limit the types of weapons available for legal purchase in the United States began in the 1930s with the National Firearms Act of 1934, which restricted the ownership of machine guns. The primary motivation behind such legislation is to ensure law enforcement is not outgunned by criminal elements. However, legislative efforts to restrict private ownership of military-style weapons (such as semi-automatic weapons) are often derailed by resistance from the National Rifle Association and other gun rights organizations (Krouse 2012). In addition, such legislative efforts are often portrayed by militia groups as evidence of government tyranny (Vertigans 2007; FBI 2011a) and are used as justification for purchasing and retaining even more weapons.

Trafficking firearms in the United States is diverting weapons from legal to illegal markets. The most common way to do this is through the use of a "strawman," someone who can legally purchase weapons and does so with the intent of passing it on to someone who cannot legally purchase them or to someone who could do so but does not wish to have a paper trail linking them to the purchase. Such actions are quite hard to detect. Large-scale straw purchasing schemes have historically been associated primarily with drug trafficking, particularly in the southwestern United States (Krouse 2012). Nonetheless, this is also often how weapons are stockpiled by militia groups (Stern 1996). Although Congress has repeatedly increased the ATF's budget specifically to assist in combating gun trafficking, federal prosecutions have dropped significantly. Between 2004 and 2010, the number of defendants charged for trafficking dropped by 52.5 percent, the number convicted declined by 58.16 percent, and over one-third of individuals convicted received no prison term (Krouse 2012).

As part of the Brady Handgun Violence Prevention Act, which went into effect in 1994, all licensed sellers of weapons must request a criminal background check on purchasers to ensure the purchaser is not a prohibited person. The FBI, through its National Instant Criminal Background

Check System (NICS), is the agency that conducts the check. Prior to 2004, terrorist watch list checks were not part of this criminal background check. That changed in February 2004, when the FBI began to screen prospective weapons purchasers against the "known and suspected terrorist (KST)" list. The FBI has no statutory authority to do this, which is something Congress should address by amending the Brady law (Krouse 2012). The terrorist watch list, however, has been subjected to significant criticism. Critics have claimed that the process for putting an individual's name on the list is "haphazard" and obtuse, and anyone whose name is incorrectly placed on the list finds it very difficult to have it removed (Savage 2011). This is a particular concern in the Muslim community given traditional patterns for naming children (resulting in many people with the same names) and multiple ways of translating those names from Arabic to English (ACLU 2014).

The Future of Terrorism in the United States

As this essay has shown, the United States has not been free of terrorism in the past. Terrorist tactics have been used by groups from both the left and the right end of the political spectrum as ways to gain attention, publicize a cause, and spark political change. Consequently, we should expect terrorist attacks in the future.

The increase in government surveillance and the claimed erosion of civil liberties associated with the USA PATRIOT (Uniting and Strengthening America by Providing Appropriate Tools Required to Intercept and Obstruct Terrorism) Act of 2001 have made government's task of tracking and apprehending terrorists and preventing their attacks easier and have has led to a number of well-publicized successes, such as Farooque Ahmed's attempt to bomb the Washington, D.C., subway system in 2010 (Zuckerman, Bucci, and Carafano 2013). In 2015, following contentious debate, Congress passed the USA Freedom Act, which renewed many of the key provisions of the USA Patriot Act. Ironically, however, as a nation we do not feel safer. If anything, we feel ever more uneasy as terrorist groups increasingly use violent tactics to gain the attention of the media, and these attacks continue to increase in lethality.

References

American Civil Liberties Union (ACLU). n.d. "Mapping the FBI: Uncovering Abusive Surveillance and Racial Profiling." https://www.aclu.org/mapping-fbi-uncovering-abusive-surveillance-and-racial-profiling (accessed January 4, 2015).

Amster, Randall. 2006. "Perspectives on Ecoterrorism: Catalysts, Conflations, and Casualties." *Contemporary Justice Review* 9 (3): 287–301.

Atran, Scott. 2003. "Genesis of Suicide Terrorism." *Science* 299 (5612): 1534–1539.

Atran, Scott, and Jessica Stern. 2005. "Small Groups Find Fatal Purpose Through the Web." *Nature* 437 (7059): 620.

Bernholz, P. 2006. "International Political System, Supreme Values and Terrorism." *Public Choice* 128: 221–231.

Bjelopera, Jerome P. 2013. *The Domestic Terrorist Threat: Background and Issues for Congress.* CRS Report R42536. Washington, DC: Congressional Research Service.

Blazak, Randy. 2001. "White Boys to Terrorist Men: Target Recruitment of Nazi Skinheads." *American Behavioral Scientist* 44: 982–1000.

Brooks, Risa. 2011. "Muslim 'Homegrown' Terrorism in the United States: How Serious is the Threat?" *International Security* 36 (2): 7–47.

Caplan, Bryan. 2006. "Terrorism: The Relevance of the Rational Choice Model." *Public Choice* 128 (1, 2): 91–107.

"The Covenant, the Sword, and the Arm of the Lord: Statement of Purpose." In *Extremism in America: A Reader,* edited by Lyman Tower Sargent, 326–332. New York: New York University Press, 1995.

Eagan, Sean P. 1996. "From Spikes to Bombs: The Rise of Eco-Terrorism." *Studies in Conflict and Terrorism* 19: 1–18.

Eitan, Alimi. 2011. "Relational Dynamics in Factional Adoption of Terrorist Tactics: A Comparative Perspective." *Theoretical Sociology* 40: 95–118.

Federal Bureau of Investigation. 2005. *Terrorism 2002-2005.* http://www.fbi.gov /stats-services/publications/terrorism-2002–2005 (accessed June 16, 2014).

Federal Bureau of Investigation. 2007. *A Threat Assessment for Domestic Terrorism, 2005-2006.* https://www.documentcloud.org/documents/402525-doc-30-threat -assessment-domestic-terrorism.html (accessed June 16, 2014).

Federal Bureau of Investigation. 2011a. "Domestic Terrorism: Focus on Militia Extremism." http://www.fbi.gov/news/stories/2011/september/militia_092211 (accessed June 17, 2014)

Federal Bureau of Investigation. 2011b. "Sovereign Citizens: A Growing Domestic Threat to Law Enforcement." *FBI Law Enforcement Bulletin 80* (9): 20–24.

Freilich, Joshua D., and William A. Pridemore. 2005. "A Reassessment of State-level Covariates of Militia Groups." *Behavioral Sciences and the Law* 23: 527–546.

Gage, Beverly. 2011. "Terrorism and the American Experience: A State of the Field." *The Journal of American History* June: 73–94.

Gurr, Ted. 1970. *Why Men Rebel.* Princeton, NJ: Princeton University Press.

Habeck, Mary R. 2006. *Knowing the Enemy: Jihadist Ideology and the War on Terror.* New Haven, CT: Yale University Press.

Krieger, Tim, and Daniel Meierrieks. 2011. "What Causes Terrorism?" *Public Choice* 147: 3–27.

Krouse, William J. 2012. *Gun Control Legislation.* CRS Report RL32842. Washington, D.C.: Congressional Research Service.

Kuznar, Lawrence A. 2002. "On Risk-Prone Peasants: Cultural Transmission or Sigmoid Utility Maximization?" *Current Anthropology* 43 (5): 787–789.

Kuznar, Lawrence A. 2007. "Rationality Wars and the War on Terror: Explaining Terrorism and Social Unrest." *American Anthropologist* 109 (2): 318–329.

Lange, Jonathan. 1990. "Refusal to Compromise: The Case of Earth First!" *Western Journal of Speech Communication* 54: 473–494.

Munger, Michael. 2006. "Preference Modification vs. Incentive Manipulation as Tools of Terrorist Recruitment: Role of Culture." *Public Choice* 128 (1, 2): 131–146.

National Consortium for the Study of Terrorism and Responses to Terrorism (START). 2012. *Global Terrorism Database.* http://www.start.umd.edu/gtd/ (accessed July 3, 2014).

"Principles of the Left Green Network." In *Extremism in America: A Reader,* edited by Lyman Tower Sargent, 351-358. New York: New York University Press, 1995.

Ralston, Jon. 2014. The Not-so-Jolly Rancher: How Federal Officials Botched the Bundy Cattle Roundup." *Politico Magazine* (4). http://www.politico.com/magazine/story/2014/04/the-not-so-jolly-rancher-106117.html#.U6 BcTpQ7vTo (accessed April 30, 2014).

Robison, K. K., E. M. Crenshaw, and J. C. Jenkins. 2006. "Ideologies of Violence: The Social Origins of Islamist and Leftist Transnational Terrorism." *Social Forces* 84 (4): 2009–2026.

Rosenau, William. 2013. "'Our Backs are Against the Wall': The Black Liberation Army and Domestic Terrorism in 1970s America." *Studies in Conflict and Terrorism* 36: 176–192.

Ross, J. I. 1993. "Structural Causes of Oppositional Political Terrorism: Towards a Causal Model." *Journal of Peace Research* 30 (3): 317–329.

Savage, Charlie. 2011. "Even Those Cleared of Crimes Can Stay on F.B.I.'s Watch List." *New York Times* (September 27). http://www.nytimes.com/2011/09/28/us/even-those-cleared-of-crimes-can-stay-on-fbis-terrorist-watch-list.html?pagewanted=all&_r=0 (accessed January 4, 2015).

Shapira, Harel. 2012. "From the Nativist's Point of View: How Ethnography Can Enrich Our Understanding of Political Identity." *The Sociological Quarterly* 54: 35–50.

Stern, Kenneth. 1996. *A Force upon the Plain.* New York: Simon and Schuster.

Transactional Records Clearing House. 2009. *Who is a Terrorist? Government Failure to Define Terrorism Undermines Enforcement, Puts Civil Liberties at Risk.* http://trac.syr.edu/tracreports/terrorism/215 (accessed July 15, 2014).

Vertigans, Stephen. 2007. "Beyond the Fringe? Radicalisation within the American Far-Right." *Totalitarian Movements and Political Religions* 8 (3–4): 641–659.

Zuckerman, Jessica, Steven Bucci, and James J. Carafano. 2013. *60 Terrorist Plots Since 9/11: Continued Lessons in Counterterrorism.* http://www.heritage.org/research/reports/2013/07/60-terrorist-plots-since-911-continued-lessons-in-domestic-counterterrorism (accessed October 22, 2014).

CHAPTER FIVE

How Stand-Your-Ground Laws Hijacked Self-Defense

Mary Anne Franks

Introduction

In 2005 Florida passed the nation's first so-called stand-your-ground law. By 2014 stand-your-ground laws had been passed in 33 states, transforming the legal landscape of self-defense. These laws significantly alter the historical understanding of justifiable force, ostensibly in order to clarify and strengthen the concept of justifiable self-defense and enhance public safety. The real accomplishment of these laws, however, has been to encourage the use of deadly force as a first, instead of a last, resort. Not only have these laws failed to deter crime, they have encouraged the escalation to deadly force in situations that do not call for it. Homicide rates increased in states with stand-your-ground laws after passing the legislation, and these states have higher homicide rates than states without stand-your-ground laws. The laws have encouraged the unnecessary use of deadly force on the part of those who have least reason to use it and inhibited the use of deadly force by those most vulnerable to attack. These laws have undermined the limited protections victims of domestic violence have achieved after decades of reform efforts and worsened existing racial disparities in the criminal justice system.

What stand-your-ground proponents get right is that self-defense doctrine in the United States has serious deficiencies, including a lack of clarity and arbitrary enforcement. What they ignore is that these deficiencies stem primarily from the conflation of the right to self-defense with gun rights as well as distortions created by race, gender, and class bias. Self-defense doctrine has historically stacked the deck against vulnerable populations and granted a virtual monopoly on deadly force to those with power. The stand-your-ground movement is thus not only a shameless exploitation of Americans' fear of crime, but also a missed opportunity to address these legitimate problems. Driven by elitist, profit-focused, ideological interests, these laws are long on feel-good rhetoric and short on political, social, or cultural analysis of the reality of crime and violence.

A society that takes the right of self-defense seriously should focus its reform efforts on developing consistent and just principles of self-defense and ensuring equality of access to this right. Stand-your-ground laws, created and promoted by lobbyists for the National Rifle Association and gun manufacturers, do the opposite of this. The laws encourage people to resolve conflicts with weapons, an encouragement that has unequal effects on populations most vulnerable to violence, including women and minorities. White men far outstrip both women and minority men in gun ownership and so are already better equipped and more willing to use deadly force. Black men are more likely to be perceived as suspicious or dangerous than other groups and are subsequently more likely to suffer the consequences of deadly force, while the possession of firearms (or even perceived possession) by minority men is often treated as grounds for suspicion, leading to violence. Women are most likely to face violent attack from someone they know and trust, and firearms are a poor fit for such confrontations. Women in domestic violence situations are far more likely to be the targets of deadly force than the agents of it, and the presence of a firearm in the home greatly increases rather than decreases a woman's chance of being killed. Firearm use generally is inherently unpredictable and imprecise, posing high risks to bystanders and the general public. The net effect of stand-your-ground laws is clear: increased danger to the public generally and increased endangerment of women and minority men particularly.

Stand-your-ground laws, taken as a whole, do violence to the very concept of self-defense. They conflate self-defense with gun use, encourage vigilantism and violent escalation, and exploit delusional hero fantasies. All of these effects undermine equality in the right to self-defense, privileging the powerful at the expense of the marginalized. True reform of the legal and social concept of self-defense would strive to correct these inefficient and unjust outcomes. Specifically, a legitimate reform effort should focus on clarifying when deadly force is truly necessary and reasonable. Such a reform effort should expand protections for women defending themselves against abusers, critically evaluate the disproportionate use of deadly force against unarmed minorities, and encourage training in and access to non-fatal methods of self-defense.

The Push for Stand-Your-Ground Laws

"Stand your ground" is an evocative phrase. It has a power-to-the-people, rugged individualism ring to it that is appealing on many levels. The Florida lawmakers who passed the country's first stand-your-ground law like to tell the tale of James Workman, "an old man from Pensacola [who] shot an intruder who tried to loot his hurricane-ravaged home" (Montgomery 2012). According to the proponents of the stand-your-ground bill, Workman and his wife spent months in legal limbo, anxiously awaiting the prosecutor's decision about whether to charge him in the shooting. Senator Durell Peaden, who introduced the stand-your-ground bill, said, "You're entitled to protect your castle. Why should you have to hire a lawyer to say, 'This guy is innocent'?" (Montgomery 2012). Using Workman's story proved extremely effective; the law passed unanimously in the state senate and 94–20 in the house. It was signed by Governor Jeb Bush in 2005 and quickly inspired similar legislation across the country. But the sponsors' version of what happened in Workman's recreational vehicle was incomplete, to say the least.

It was 2004, and Hurricane Ivan had devastated much of Florida's "Emerald Coast" on the Gulf of Mexico. Rodney Cox was a married father of two from North Carolina who had come to Florida in search of work with the Federal Emergency Management Agency (FEMA). On November 2, a disoriented and possibly intoxicated Cox called 911 to report "violence to myself." He attempted to give the operator his location, but couldn't figure out where he was. Cox eventually flagged down a sheriff's deputy, who thought Cox seemed intoxicated. Cox told the deputy someone had tried to break into his trailer. At some point, another man offered to take Cox to a hotel.

That same night, James Workman and his wife were sleeping in an RV outside their house, which had been severely damaged by Hurricane Ivan. Around 2:00 a.m., Workman's wife woke up, looked out the RV window, and saw what appeared to be a man trying to enter the couple's house. She woke up Workman, who got his gun and went outside. When Workman's wife called 911, she said that the intruder "just kept walking around and wanted a glass of water." Then she screamed. When the operator asked her to describe what was happening, she said that the man had gotten inside the house. Workman had fired a warning shot, but the man had entered the trailer, and Workman shot him. Rodney Cox was dead on arrival at the hospital (Montgomery 2012).

Senator Peaden and Representative Dennis Baxley invoked Workman's story in numerous media interviews, claiming that Workman had to wait six months and hire a lawyer before learning that he would not be prosecuted for the shooting. In fact, it was three months, and Workman never hired a lawyer. He was never arrested or charged for the shooting. Workman was also at best ambivalent about becoming "the poster child for a bill he was uncertain about at the time." Asked about the event, Workman said, "I had his blood on my chest. I hate it."

The appropriation of Workman's story also obscures the fact that the stand-your-ground law was hardly the product of a populist movement demanding changes in self-defense law. Rather, the law was the product of National Rifle Association (NRA) lobbyists and of the American Legislative Exchange Council (ALEC), "the shadowy Koch brothers-funded network that brings together right-wing legislators with corporate interests and pressure groups to craft so-called 'model legislation'" (Nichols 2012). The language of the bill was developed by Marion Hammer, a former president of the NRA and founder of one of the NRA's Florida affiliate organizations, the Unified Sportsmen of Florida (Weinstein 2012). "There is no single individual responsible for enacting more pro-gun legislation in the states than Marion Hammer," says Richard Feldman, a former political organizer for the NRA (Bender 2012).

Hammer's advocacy for the stand-your-ground bill was built on what the *Rolling Stone* characterized as a "convenient tale": "Hammer claimed to have been stalked in a parking garage by six men, one of whom wielded a 'long-necked beer bottle' before she pulled out her .38 and aimed—gave anyone who deemed himself under attack the right to fire first and explain later" (Solotaroff 2013). Hammer did not file a police report, but, she asserts, a police chief told her that had she shot the men, she could have been arrested (Weinstein 2012). One could hardly have invented a more compelling story to illustrate the need for stand-your-ground laws.

In 2005 Hammer gave an interview with the Center for Individual Freedom about the recently enacted law. In this interview, Hammer claimed that before 2005, the duty to retreat in Florida meant that "if someone had tried to drag a woman into an alley to rape her, the women [sic]—even though she might be licensed to carry concealed and ready to protect herself, the law would not allow her to do it. It required her to try to get away and run and be chased down by the perpetrator before she could then use force to protect herself" (Center for Individual Freedom 2005). Several years later, after the shooting of Travyon Martin prompted scrutiny of the law, Florida politicians Don and Matt Gaetz (father and son) railed against critics of the law by parroting Hammer:

> Consider an elderly woman in a dimly lit parking lot or a college girl walking to her dorm at night. If either was attacked, her duty was to turn her back and try to flee, probably be overcome and raped or killed. Prior to "Stand Your Ground," that victim didn't have the choice to defend herself, to meet force with force. (Schorsch, Gaetz, and Gaetz 2012)

Other stand-your-ground proponents have made similar claims:

> Clearly we have an inalienable right to our own preservation and with that comes the right to protect those that cannot defend themselves. Without such right we would have to stand idly by or even possibly retreat when we witness a neighbor being raped or an active shooter in our mall. Those of us who take our responsibility to our families and fellow citizens seriously will not stand idly by and watch those that we love, support, and in some occasions do not even know die at the hands of a criminal or a deranged assailant. (ABA 2014)

As an initial matter, it is notable how the examples used by stand-your-ground proponents so often focus on confrontations with violent strangers, and in particular stranger rape. This is notable not only for the fact that conservative politicians tend to ignore or downplay the existence of sexual assault in almost every context other than armed self-defense (Franks 2014), but also because sexual assault is overwhelmingly a crime perpetrated in private by people known to the victim (Rape, Abuse and Incest National Network 2014). Similarly, the "active shooter in the mall" scenario is incredibly rare,[1] and one that does not readily lend itself to resolution by an individual "standing his ground."[2]

Regardless, the claim that stand-your-ground laws are essential to an effective right of self-defense and that the "duty to retreat" is practically a death (or at least a rape) sentence bears closer examination. There are considerable variations across the stand-your-ground laws of the 33 states that have them, but their common characteristics are the elimination of the "duty to retreat" from confrontations anywhere a person has the right to be—hence the reference to "standing one's ground."

Prior to the rise of these laws, traditional self-defense doctrine in the United States and England included a "duty to retreat" from confrontations outside the home. By emphasizing that deadly force should only be used as a last resort, the duty to retreat rule reflected the value of preserving human life. The duty to retreat has never been absolute, however. First, the duty to retreat generally did not apply inside the home—the so-called "castle doctrine" (Gardner and Anderson 2014). Secondly, the duty to retreat was generally considered only to apply when an individual could retreat in "complete safety." That is, one was not required to flee from a confrontation if a person did not reasonably believe he could do so without risking serious injury or death. In Florida specifically, a person was required, before 2005, to use "every *reasonable* means" to avoid danger before resorting to deadly force: "[A] person may not resort to deadly force without first using every reasonable means within his or her power to avoid the danger, including retreat" (*Weiand v. State* 732 So. 2d 1044, Fla. 1999).

These longstanding qualifications of the duty to retreat rule are significant because they contradict the excitable claims of stand-your-ground proponents that the rule condemned law-abiding citizens to being shot down or raped in alleyways. A "college girl" attacked on her way to her dorm would not likely have been forced, pre-2005, to "turn her back and try to flee, probably be overcome and raped or killed." If a victim reasonably feared that she would be raped or killed, and that fleeing would not prevent her from being raped or killed, then fleeing would not be a "reasonable means" of avoiding danger. Such a victim would have been within her rights before 2005 to stand and fight.

With regard to immunity, proponents of stand-your-ground laws insist that citizens using justifiable force are required to languish in legal limbo. The Florida politicians who introduced the state's stand-your-ground bill claimed that Workman's case illustrated the dire need for radical reform. As one legal scholar pointed out, however,

> Workman did not need Stand Your Ground to be safe and secure in Florida, as evidenced by the fact that he was not charged for contributing to Cox's death. Yet his story created a powerful narrative instigating a revolutionary change in the law. His story remains influential, though many may not know or recall any specific details. In fact, it is powerful enough to drown out the voices of opposition and other counter-narratives warning of the dangers of an expansive permission to kill. (Megale 2013)

There is scant evidence, in other words, to support the proposition that stand-your-ground laws were necessary to solve what proponents claimed were serious problems with self-defense doctrine. It is significant that neither the Gaetzes nor Hammer cite any actual cases in which a victim used deadly force against a rapist or murderer and was denied a self-defense instruction on the basis of a duty to retreat. They instead resort to unchallengeable hypotheticals or bowdlerized versions of cases like James Workman's, a case that resulted in no charges against the law-abiding citizen using deadly force or even a protracted legal battle over the question. A 2014 report by the American Bar Association Task Force on stand-your-ground noted that "proponents of Stand Your Ground laws could point to no examples of cases wherein traditional self-defense law would not have protected a law-abiding individual operating in justified self-defense" (American Bar Association Report 2014). As Pennsylvania District Attorney Edward Marsico Jr. characterized it, stand-your-ground "is a solution looking for a problem" (ABA Report 2014).

Missed Opportunity: The Real Need for Self-Defense Reform

If stand-your-ground proponents had truly been looking for a problem to solve in self-defense doctrine in 2005, they would have easily found one— or several. The contemporary right of self-defense is marked by a skewed focus on gun rights as well as by a lack of protection for the most vulnerable. Efforts by the NRA and gun manufacturers to conflate self-defense with gun rights is so widespread and so effective that it has become difficult to think of the two as distinct concepts. But firearm use in modern times has never been proven to be particularly effective for self-defense or for deterring crime,[3] and the cost (financial, labor, medical, psychological) of fatalities and injuries caused by guns is staggering—between 100 and 174 billion dollars a year (Cook and Ludwig 2000). The Children's Safety Network Injury and Violence Prevention Center (2010) reports that "Firearms injuries cost $174 billion in the United States in 2010 and the government's firearm injury bill alone exceeded $12 billion. . . . The costs include medical and mental health care costs, criminal justice costs, wage losses, and the value of pain, suffering and lost quality of life."

To point this out is not to ignore or refute the Supreme Court's ruling in *District of Columbia v. Heller* (128 S. Ct. 2783, 2008) that the Second Amendment confers an individual "right to bear arms," or to argue that guns cannot or should not be used defensively. It is to point out that the right to self-defense is broader, richer, and more essential than a right to any particular instrument of self-defense. Those who believe that the right to defend ourselves and our loved ones is fundamental should be deeply concerned with the effectiveness of defensive methods and their likely consequences. There is no ignoring the fact that guns are difficult to use, control, and store safely. Any responsible gun owner knows that safe, effective gun use requires intensive education and training. Any person who has ever killed or seriously injured another human being—no matter the circumstances—knows of the heavy psychological burden this imposes. Even seasoned soldiers have been known to struggle with nightmares, depression, and post-traumatic stress disorder in the wake of justified killings on the battlefield (Grossman 1996, 86–92).

Guns leave little time for deliberation, investigation, or hesitation. In clear-cut situations of kill-or-be-killed, this makes them superior tools of self-defense. Far too often, however, the split-second, all-or-nothing nature of guns transforms an ambiguous situation into a fatal encounter. That is a fact to be mourned, not celebrated. There is, too, a circularity in the insistence on increased accessibility to weapons, as this helps create the very threat giving rise to the need for defensive force. Keeping weapons out of the hands of individuals with a history of violence would be a more effective means of reducing violence than arming every law-abiding citizen.

When the right to self-defense is dominated by access to and willingness to use firearms, it disproportionately favors the relatively powerful over the relatively powerless. The groups most likely to be victimized by crime generally are adolescents, the disabled, the poor, and minorities. Those most likely to be victimized by intimate partner crime and sexual assault are women. None of these groups is well-served by the emphasis on gun rights or by the changes in self-defense law produced by the stand-your-ground movement. In fact, the gun rights movement in general and the stand-your-ground movement in particular increase the vulnerability of these groups and undermine their ability to exert their right to self-defense. If self-defense truly is a fundamental right, these are the types of inequalities that reformers should address.

Adolescents are more than twice as likely to be victimized by crime as adults (Baum 2003). They are also the only population demographic that is categorically barred from gun ownership. Their other options for self-defense are constrained by their disadvantages in age, experience, and size. Disabled individuals similarly are at far greater risk of victimization than non-disabled individuals. The rate of violent victimization of the disabled population was three times the rate of the non-disabled population in 2012 (Harrell 2012). They are similarly disadvantaged with regard to their ability to physically defend themselves, whether with weapons or by other means. Poorer households are more likely to experience criminal victimization than more well-off households,[4] and they also have fewer resources to spend on firearms, alarm systems, or self-defense training. They are also less likely to be able to depend on reliable and efficient support from law enforcement.

Members of racial minorities, in particular black men, are placed at a considerable disadvantage when the right to self-defense is conflated with the right to be armed. Blacks experience more crime victimization than any other racial group (Bureau of Justice Statistics 2013) and yet their ability to defend themselves—whether with guns or not—is gravely undermined by racial bias in the general public, law enforcement, and the criminal justice system as a whole. The United States has a long and shameful history of depriving black people of their right to self-defense (see Johnson 2014), from slavery to the Black Codes to lynchings to modern-day racialized violence (see Lee 2003). The argument that the Second Amendment ensured an individual right to bear arms for self-defense was made on behalf of fugitive slaves long before the NRA took it up as a rallying cry, but it went unheeded (Johnson 2014, 50–51). The NRA did not begin pushing an individual right to bear arms theory of the Second Amendment until the 1970s (Waldman 2014, 87–102). While white open-carry activists march unmolested through town squares and grocery stores with loaded rifles slung across their backs, black men and boys with toy guns (and sometimes no guns at all) are gunned down by police officers and neighborhood watchmen (Lopez 2014). Racial bias—conscious and unconscious—leads people to perceive black men as more suspicious or dangerous than other groups (Richardson and Goff 2012; Lee 2013; Bernstein 2013). Black men's attempts to exercise self-defense—or even merely to stand up for themselves—are accordingly often perceived as unlawful force, with deadly results. This occurs even in the absence of conscious racial bias. According to one study of race and firearms, "Race stereotypes can lead people to claim to see a weapon where there is none. Split-second decisions magnify the bias by limiting people's ability to control responses. Such a bias could have important consequences for decision making by police officers and other authorities interacting with racial minorities. The bias requires no intentional racial animus, occurring even for those who are actively trying to avoid it" (Payne 2006). The role of racial bias in the perception of threats is at least one factor in the extraordinarily high rates of extrajudicial killings of black men, which one study reports as occurring once every twenty-eight hours (Malcolm X Grassroots Movement 2013).

While men are more likely to be victimized by crime generally than women, women are far more likely to face sexual assault and intimate partner violence, primarily at the hands of men. Women account for 84 percent of domestic violence victims (Department of Justice, Bureau of Justice Statistics 2005). In the United States, more than three women a day are murdered by current or former intimate partners (Catalano 2007). Nearly one in four women has experienced violence by a current or former intimate partner (Centers for Disease Control and Prevention 2008). According to a study by the Centers for Disease Control and Prevention, there were nearly 1.3 million rapes of women in the United States in 2010.[5] The general disparities in height, weight, and strength between men and women place women at a significant disadvantage in violent confrontations.

Firearms are, first, ill-suited for the kinds of violent confrontations women are most likely to face, as they often involve aggressors that the victims love and trust. As Gerney and Parsons (2014) comment, "Women are much more likely to be victimized by people they know, while men are more likely to be victims of violent crime at the hands of strangers." Few people have their weapons at the ready when they are at home with a partner, visiting a friend, or on a date (Franks 2014, 1108–1109). What is more, men's rates of gun ownership are three times that of women's (Jones 2013). One study revealed in a significant number of gun-owning households, only the male member of the household knew about the existence of the gun (Ludwig et al. 1998). Given these factors, it is unsurprising that the presence of a firearm in the home greatly increases rather than decreases a woman's chance of being killed.[6]

Women who do use deadly force against abusive partners frequently face the kind of legal uncertainty and punishment that stand-your-ground proponents claim to care about. The effect of bias and ignorance regarding domestic violence combined with long-held, unexamined, and deeply gendered assumptions about "reasonableness" and "imminence" has been to consign women to lengthy prison sentences for defending themselves. The 1989 North Carolina case of Judy Norman is only one example. For more than twenty years, John Thomas Norman ("J. T.") beat, raped, threatened, and tortured his wife, Judy. He forced her to perform sexual acts with strangers for money, to bark like a dog and eat out of dog bowls, and to sleep on the floor. After Judy attempted suicide, J. T. tried to prevent paramedics from coming to her aid and insisted that they "let the bitch die." During two days of particularly vicious beatings, J. T. told Judy that if she ever tried to have him taken into custody, "I'll see them coming and before they get here, I'll cut your throat." One day in June 1985 while J. T. was taking a nap, Judy visited her mother and took a gun from her mother's purse. When she returned home, she shot her sleeping husband three times in the back of the head.

According to the common law, deadly force can be used in self-defense only when it is necessary, proportionate, and in response to imminent danger. The Supreme Court of North Carolina overturned a lower court ruling that had allowed Judy to receive a jury instruction on self-defense, holding that Judy did not have "a reasonable fear of imminent death or great bodily injury." The court found that Judy was "not faced with an instantaneous choice between killing her husband or being killed or seriously injured. . . . she had ample time and opportunity to resort to other means of preventing further abuse of her husband," despite the fact that her husband had warned her that he would kill her "before they get here," had threatened her family, had escalated his violence toward Judy following his arrest for a DUI, and that Norman's mother had called the police the day of the shooting but they never arrived (Franks 2014, 1125–1126).

Judy Norman's case is all too typical for women who have used defensive force against abusive partners. According to one source, between 40 percent and 80 percent of women convicted of murder were acting in self-defense against abusers (Jacobsen). As Cynthia Gillespie argued in her influential book *Justifiable Homicide: Battered Women, Self Defense, and the Law*, self-defense laws were written with men's conflicts in mind (Gillespie 1990). The dynamics of a battering situation are very different from a one-off confrontation between two men, as it often involves two individuals of disparate size and strength, one of whom has repeatedly threatened and done violence to the other. Courts have interpreted self-defense laws to essentially impose a duty to retreat—and an *unreasonable* duty to retreat at that—upon domestic violence victims, despite the fact that they are often attacked in the home, the one place where individuals (men) have historically had the right to stand and fight.

Stand-your-ground laws do nothing to address the deep problems with the doctrine of self-defense. In fact, the cumulative effect of these laws has been an increase in violence generally, a burden that falls more heavily on already vulnerable populations. Those who are in most need of a robust defense of their right to protect themselves are the ones least well served by the stand-your-ground movement.

The Substance of Stand-Your-Ground Laws

The power of stand-your-ground as a concept lies not only in the way it conjures up courageous individuals fighting the good fight against dark criminal forces, but also in its slipperiness. The law came under criticism following George Zimmerman's shooting of unarmed black teenager Trayvon Martin (Jonsson 2014b), which was followed only a few months later by Michael Dunn's shooting of unarmed black teenager Jordan Davis (Jonsson 2014a), prompting many proponents of Florida's law to insist that such cases had "nothing to do" with stand-your-ground (Kopel 2014). Compelling, reassuring scenarios such as the elderly James Workman defending his home from an invader or Marion Hammer single-handedly fending off a gang of violent men are presented as true stand-your-ground cases; any case that plays less well or raises uncomfortable questions is dismissed as not being about stand-your-ground at all. But this posturing is unintelligible when one considers, first, that all the amendments made to Florida's self-defense law in 2005 are considered part of stand-your-ground. Second, the mere fact that a defendant might not explicitly characterize his own case as being about stand-your-ground—or may not prevail using its immunity provisions—does not mean the case does not in fact implicate Florida's self-defense law. Laws are as much about their impact on the general public as they are about specific legal outcomes, and it is quite clear that many people *believe* that stand-your-ground laws give them rights to use deadly force in a wide variety of situations and act accordingly. Whether a court ultimately rules in their favor is a secondary point to the dead bodies they leave behind.

There is indeed, however, considerable confusion about what precisely Florida's Stand-Your-Ground actually says and does, not only by the general public but also by legal actors. Accordingly, it is important to identify precisely what changed in Florida's law of self-defense in 2005.

a. **Florida's Stand-Your-Ground Law: Expansions, Presumptions, Immunity**
   Florida's law, which served as a model for legislation across the country, offers some of the more expansive protections for the use of deadly force (although some, such as Texas's, might be considered more extreme in some respects). In addition to eliminating the duty to retreat and providing criminal and civil immunity provisions, Florida's law includes presumptions of reasonableness that all but eliminate any obligation of a person using deadly force to demonstrate the necessity of that force as well as expressly allowing for the use of deadly force to defend one's property—a radical departure from traditional principles of self-defense.[7] While most of the substantive changes to Florida's justifiable force law occurred in 2005, the legislature amended the law again in 2014, adding language that makes clear that "threatening" to use force, and not just the actual use of force, is also covered by the statute as well as adding an expungement provision, both of which will be discussed in more detail below.

   i. **Duty to Retreat**
      According to Florida's "Justifiable Use of Force" provision:

   > A person is justified in using or threatening to use deadly force
   > if he or she reasonably believes that using or threatening to use
   > such force is necessary to prevent imminent death or great
   > bodily harm to himself or herself or another or to prevent the

imminent commission of a forcible felony. A person who uses or threatens to use deadly force in accordance with this subsection does not have a duty to retreat and has the right to stand his or her ground if the person using or threatening to use the deadly force is not engaged in a criminal activity and is in a place where he or she has a right to be [776.012 (2)].

As noted above, this law explicitly removes the duty to retreat from "any place" a person "has a right to be." As will be explained in more detail below, however, this aspect of the law is not necessarily a significant departure from traditional self-defense principles. The inclusion of the phrase "to prevent the imminent commission of a forcible felony," however, is. According to s. 776.08, forcible felonies include—in addition to murder, manslaughter, and sexual battery—carjacking, robbery, and burglary (776.08). This is a significant departure from the long-held belief that the use of deadly force should not be used to protect mere property. This long-held belief reflects a judgment that deadly force to protect property violates the supreme value of human life. Put another way, to kill or seriously injure a person because of a threat to property violates the proportionality principle that undergirds the concept of justifiable force. "Reasonable use of nonlethal force to protect property is acceptable under certain circumstances, but most, if not all, jurisdictions now hold that deadly force is never reasonable for the protection of mere property. Our society values human life above property" (Hickey 2003). Florida's dubious decision to make defense of mere property an adequate grounds for the use of deadly force is rendered explicit in 776.031, titled "Use or threatened use of force in defense of property," which restates that a person is justified in using deadly force and has no duty to retreat if he reasonably believes such force is necessary to prevent the commission of a forcible felony.

The list of forcible felonies also includes, bizarrely, "treason," which is defined under Florida law as "levying war against the [state], or in adhering to the enemies thereof, or giving them aid and comfort" (876.32). Such a crime is somewhat hard to parse, and "giving aid and comfort" is a remarkably broad formulation implicating speech rights. That treason is considered a "forcible felony" along with "any other felony which involves the use of a threat of physical force or violence against any individual" that can give rise to justifiable use of deadly force is peculiar, to say the least. One hopes that this does not grant a license to shoot a person ranting on a street corner about overthrowing the state or killing the president. At the very least, the inclusion of preventing "an imminent commission of a forcible felony" as grounds for deadly force when forcible felonies include property and speech crimes raises serious questions about proportionality.

ii. **Presumptions**

According to Florida law (and the law of most states), deadly force is only considered justified if the person using it "reasonably believed" it was necessary. The "reasonable man" or "reasonable person" standard wields tremendous influence in criminal and civil law, but establishing what this standard means is notoriously difficult. Florida's law offers considerable clarity here by including several stated presumptions of reasonableness in the use of deadly force, though whether such clarity is advisable is debatable. Florida's law states that a person "is presumed to have held a reasonable fear of imminent peril of death or great bodily harm" if the person against whom the deadly force was used:

(a) was in the process of unlawfully and forcefully entering, or had unlawfully and forcibly entered, a dwelling, residence, or occupied vehicle, or if that person had removed or was attempting to remove another against that person's will from the dwelling, residence, or occupied vehicle; and

(b) The person who uses or threatens to use defensive force knew or had reason to believe that an unlawful or forcible entry or unlawful and forcible act was occurring or had occurred [776.013 (1)].

Granting a presumption of reasonable fear to people who discover an intruder in their home makes sense. People expect their homes to be places of refuge, and the home is supposed to be the one place where people can relax and not be on their guard. The sudden appearance of a stranger in one's place of refuge is an alarming sight, and presuming that it is reasonable for a person to use deadly force without investigating further at such a sight seems justified.

However, Florida's law does much more than this. First, it expands the presumption to apply not only in homes, but also in "dwellings," expansively defined as "a building or conveyance of any kind, including any attached porch, whether the building or conveyance is temporary or permanent, mobile or immobile, which has a roof over it, including a tent, and is designed to be occupied by people lodging therein at night" as well as to "occupied vehicles" (even if the individual using force is not the occupant). Second, the generous use of the past tense—"had unlawfully or forcibly entered"; "had removed . . . another against that person's will"; "that an unlawful or forcible entry. . . had occurred"—strongly suggests that people have the right to use deadly force against individuals who are fleeing. This, again, violates longstanding principles of self-defense, which have traditionally been limited to the prevention of imminent serious injury or death.

In some ways, however, what is most alarming about the Florida law's presumptions is what they do *not* cover. On their face, these presumptions aggressively expand the castle doctrine, making it easier for people to claim the right to act in self-defense in their homes (and cars and tents, etc.) But there is one startling limitation to these presumptions that will make it harder for at least one class of people to seek protection under the law. According to s. 776.013(2)(a), the presumption of reasonable fear does not apply if "the person against whom the defensive force is used or threatened has the right to be in or is a lawful resident of the dwelling, residence, or vehicle, such as an owner, lessee, or titleholder." In other words, the presumption of reasonableness does not apply in situations where deadly force is used against a cohabitant. According to Koons (2006), "By disallowing the presumption for cohabitants, the legislative scheme significantly disfavors women who live with battering men."

This exception does not just exclude domestic violence victims from the benefits of the statute. It undermines the limited progress that was made in their right to engage in self-defense. As discussed above, victims of domestic violence—mostly women—have historically been denied the privilege of the castle doctrine. Instead, they have been expected to retreat even when retreat would clearly not save them from danger. In 1999 Florida's Supreme Court recognized the injustice of this. In its opinion in *Weiand v. State*, the Court quoted extensively from domestic violence experts:

> Imposition of the duty to retreat on a battered woman who finds herself the target of a unilateral, unprovoked attack in her own home is inherently unfair. During repeated instances of past abuse, she has "retreated," only to be caught, dragged back inside, and severely beaten again. If she manages to escape, other hurdles confront her. Where will she go if she has no money, no transportation, and if her children are left behind in the "care" of an enraged man?[8]

By denying the presumption of reasonable fear to a class of citizens with one of the strongest claims to it, Florida's stand-your-ground law actually undermines the limited protections afforded domestic violence victims in *Weiand*.

Strangely enough, some scholars have nonetheless insisted that the real problem with Florida's stand-your-ground law is that it empowers domestic violence victims to an alarming degree. This may be due to a misreading of the statute, particularly the language in 776.013(a) that follows the exception for cohabitants: "and there is not an injunction for protection from domestic violence or a written pretrial supervision order of no contact against that person." This confusingly worded section may lead a casual reader to conclude that the presumption of reasonable fear *will* apply to a domestic violence victim if she has obtained an order of protection against her cohabitant. But the section actually states only that the presumption of reasonableness in using deadly force *does not* apply against a co-habitant against whom there is no order of protection or no contact order; it does not state that the presumption of reasonableness in using deadly force against a co-habitant against whom there is an order of protection or no contact *does* apply.[9]

What is more, the law's chief architect herself made it abundantly clear that the stand-your-ground law was not meant to aid domestic violence victims.[10] When asked to confirm that stand-your-ground was not intended to apply in domestic violence situations, Marion Hammer responded affirmatively. Hammer explained, "You can't simply take action against an estranged spouse who breaks into the home if they own the home. You have to be under attack in those situations." In other words, a man can presume that a stranger trying to open his door intends to do him harm and is thus presumed to be justified in using deadly force, but a battered wife cannot presume that her abusive husband breaking down the door intends to harm her. She cannot presume this even if he has promised to kill her if she locks him out one more time, or if he has told her he will beat her to death if she ever tries to leave him. She is supposed to wait until the moment he rushes at her with a gun or a knife before she is allowed to use deadly force—notwithstanding the fact that such force will almost certainly come too late.[11]

Interestingly, the Florida law includes one other presumption in 776.013(4), which might contradict the exception discussed above: "A person who unlawfully and by force enters or attempts to enter a person's dwelling, residence, or occupied vehicle is presumed to be doing so with the intent to commit an unlawful act involving force or violence." On its face, it seems that a domestic violence victim might be able to take advantage of this presumption against an abusive partner, though this may simply be an inadvertent consequence of poor drafting. How this presumption would be read in light of the exception provision of 776.013(2) remains to be seen. Regardless, while this presumption might sound reasonable on its face, it is worth keeping in mind cases that involve confused, drunken, or mentally ill individuals attempting to open doors to what they believe are their homes or homes of friends.

iii. Immunity

Many of the states that have passed stand-your-ground laws include both criminal and civil immunity provisions. In the criminal context, this seemingly converts self-defense from an affirmative defense to be proven at trial to absolute immunity from arrest or even investigation.

Civil immunity provisions prohibit a person who has used justifiable force from being sued for any deaths or injuries that resulted from this use of force, including to bystanders. This is significant particularly in combination with the elimination of a duty to retreat in public, as deadly confrontations in public pose greater risks of injury or death to a greater number of people. These civil immunity provisions mean that a person can avoid liability for injuring or killing people even if the choice to engage in the deadly confrontation was reckless or grossly negligent (see Randolph 2014).

Florida's law provides both criminal and civil immunity for individuals who use justifiable force. The law states that a person who uses justifiable force "is justified in such conduct and is immune from criminal prosecution and civil action for the use or threatened use of such force." The law defines "criminal prosecution" as "arresting, detaining in custody, and charging or prosecuting the defendant." The law claims, unconvincingly, that a law enforcement agency "may use standard procedures for investigating" the use or threatened use of deadly force despite the fact that police cannot arrest, detain, or charge the defendant.

In 2014 the Florida legislature added a clause to the law that allows a person found to have acted in self-defense to request that their record be expunged. Such a provision could have dramatic effects on the press's ability to research and report on these cases. The *Tampa Bay Times*, which conducted a comprehensive study of over a hundred stand-your-ground cases, relied in part on court records to complete its review. The database it produced caused some consternation on the part of stand-your-ground proponents, as it highlighted many uncomfortable facts about the kinds of suspects and cases that were receiving stand-your-ground immunity. The *Times* criticized the new measure, arguing that it will effectively prevent the media from gathering information for similar projects (Sickler 2014).

b. The Effects of Stand-Your-Ground: Florida

Florida's stand-your-ground law was presented to the public as a necessary measure to protect "innocent people" (Megale 2013). Like other states with stand-your-ground laws, Florida saw an increase in homicides since passing the law (Vendatam 2013). The *Tampa Bay Times*'s review of over a hundred fatal stand-your-ground cases in Florida found that nearly half of those invoking self-defense had been arrested at least three times—many for violent offenses—before they killed someone (Stanley and Humburg 2012). More than a third had previously threatened someone with a gun or illegally carried a weapon. Some of them have been able to use the law to escape punishment for more than one homicide. For example, Tavarious

China Smith, a drug-dealing two-time killer, walked free both times under stand-your-ground (Stanley and Humburg 2012). So far from having a deterrent effect on crime, the law is proving to be a great benefit to repeat criminals.

One of the men who successfully used the law was Maurice Moorer. Moorer had a history of being violent with his wife, once beating her in the head and twice threatening her with guns. Not long after she divorced Moorer and started dating someone new, police were called to Moorer's home to investigate a homicide. Moorer had shot his ex-wife's boyfriend fourteen times while the unarmed man sat in his car. According to prosecutors, they couldn't find a way to disprove Moorer's claim of self-defense given the new law, which, they said, "cheapens human life" (Stanley and Humburg 2012). The law has also been successfully used by individuals who killed to protect their property. In 2012 Greyston Garcia chased down a man he believed had stolen his car radio and stabbed the alleged thief to death. A judge threw out the case against Garcia, finding that because the man Garcia was chasing had swung a bag full of car radios at Garcia, Garcia was justified under stand-your-ground in stabbing him in response.[12]

With regard to racial disparities, the *Tampa Bay Times* study revealed that a defendant who killed a black victim had a 73 percent chance of getting a dismissal, compared to a 59 percent chance for those who killed white victims (Stanley and Humburg 2012). Regardless of legal outcomes in particular cases, the "shoot-first" mentality of stand-your-ground arguably contributed to the deaths of several young black men, including Trayvon Martin and Jordan Davis. While Michael Dunn was found guilty of first-degree murder in the shooting of Davis (unlike Zimmerman, who was acquitted in the killing of Trayvon Martin) the conviction does not alter the fact that a young black man died over an altercation about loud music (McCormack 2014). Florida state senator Dwight Bullard commented directly on the racial implications of stand-your-ground when he expressed his "continued hope that we pursue the eradication of this unjust law for no other reason than, as an African American male, the idea that we are creating a precedent in which the lives of African American men are summarily devalued in a society, that over its existence, has placed monetary value on those same lives but now has gotten to a point where that same life has zero value is overly problematic" (ABA Report, 31). In addition to Trayvon Martin and Jordan Davis, 24 other children and teenagers have been killed in stand-your-ground cases as of 2014. One defendant attempted (unsuccessfully) to raise the defense for the shooting of a nine-year-old child (Leber and Flatow 2014).

With regard to gender, stand-your-ground laws have had no deterrent effect on intimate partner violence or sexual assault. The fact that George

Zimmerman was investigated twice for domestic violence in 2013, suffering no consequences for either of the incidents, suggests that the violence he showed on the night of Trayvon Martin's death was not uncharacteristic, and that racist and sexist aggression are often intertwined (Strasser 2013). A less famous stand-your-ground case than Zimmernan's, and one with very different results, made it abundantly clear that the law has done nothing to improve the lot of women who use defensive force against abusive partners (Franks 2014).

Marissa Alexander, an African American woman, fought back when her estranged husband, Rico Gray, attacked her in their shared home in 2010. Gray flew into a jealous rage after looking through Alexander's cell phone. Gray called Alexander a "whore" and a "bitch" and told her, "[i]f I can't have you, nobody [is] going to have you." After he refused Alexander's demand that he leave, Alexander attempted to leave but found that the garage door would not open. Realizing that she would have to return to the house, Alexander grabbed her gun from her truck and returned to the kitchen where, she asserts, Gray threatened her life. Alexander fired a shot into the ceiling to scare him off. Gray left with his two children, all of them unharmed.

Alexander's first attempt to claim immunity under stand-your-ground was denied, and she was charged with three counts of aggravated assault. The jury sentenced Alexander, who had recently given birth, to twenty years in prison after deliberating for eleven minutes. On appeal, a judge ruled that the jury had been improperly instructed regarding self-defense and granted Alexander a new trial. Alexander asked for a new stand-your-ground hearing and was denied (MSNBC 2014). In November 2014, Alexander accepted a plea deal that would allow her to be released in January 2015 (NPR 2014). Alexander was denied the protection of stand-your-ground despite the fact that she was personally knowledgeable of her attacker's long history of violence against women. He had been arrested twice before on misdemeanor charges of domestic battery and Alexander had once obtained a protective order against him. Gray had once pushed Alexander so hard that she fell backward and hit her head on the bathtub and admitted that he told Alexander that "if she ever cheated on [him, he] would kill her." Gray himself swore in a deposition that Alexander's version of events that day was true, though he later changed his story.

The fact that Alexander was unable to seek protection under stand-your-ground is not only a strong sign that the law disfavors women who defend themselves against abusers. Her case suggests that the law is in fact on the side of the abusers. Alexandr's case sends the message that victims of abuse are not allowed to fight back. They must simply leave or succumb to the abuse, even if it costs them their lives. For those truly concerned with the right to self-defense, Alexander's case should be an outrage.

With regard to clarifying the law enforcement response to justifiable uses of force, the law's criminal immunity provision has created considerable confusion among law enforcement with regard to investigating uses of deadly force. In the wake of the Trayvon Martin shooting, Sanford Police Chief Bill Lee stated that the law prevented him from arresting George Zimmerman (Franks 2014, 1117). He and other law enforcement officials clearly interpret the law to mean that they are prevented from making arrests in situations where individuals have plausible claims of self-defense. This deviates considerably from the traditional arrest standard, according to which law enforcement determines whether probable cause exists to believe a crime has been committed or is being committed. An arrest is a very preliminary step in a criminal investigation, allowing for a suspect to be detained and questioned. An arrest does not mean that charges will be filed, to say nothing of whether the defendant will have to stand trial. Even if charges are filed and the state moves forward with prosecution, the defendant is entitled to raise defenses, including affirmative defenses such as self-defense. In other words, an individual who has acted in self-defense has many opportunities to demonstrate that his actions were justified and avoid being punished by the state. The stand-your-ground law implies that a suspect does not even have to undergo the very preliminary step of arrest unless there is probable cause to believe that his claim of self-defense is not true—a striking departure from established procedure. This raises serious questions about institutional competence. Law enforcement officials are trained to determine probable cause; they are not trained to make legal conclusions about what were previously considered affirmative defenses. Before stand-your-ground, there was already reason to be concerned about the broad discretion law enforcement officials have in determining probable cause, especially considering institutional bias. After stand-your-ground, there is even more reason to worry that bias will affect determinations of arrest and incentivize officers to allow suspects to go free even when there are indications that they acted unlawfully.[13]

In short, the effects of Florida's stand-your-ground law have been an increase in homicides, protection for repeat criminals, aggravated racial and gender disparities, and heightened confusion created by the immunity provisions for the use of justifiable force. Perhaps unsurprisingly given these effects, 60 percent of Floridians want the law to be amended (ABA Report, 18).

c. The Effects of Stand-Your-Ground: Nationwide

The cumulative effects of stand-your-ground laws across the nation have been similar to those in Florida. Studies have shown that the laws have no deterrent effect on crime and encourage escalation in confrontations (Cheng and Hoekstra 2012). Other studies demonstrate that states experienced a

7.1 percent increase in homicides after adopting stand-your-ground laws (McClellan and Tekin 2012). Experts note that stand-your-ground laws in some states allow individuals more freedom to use deadly force than soldiers in combat situations:

> US service members operating in the most hostile environments . . . must consider the feasibility of less than lethal action when confronting threats on today's nonlinear battlefield. It is troubling that under Stand Your Ground, there are less restrictions imposed on US service members using deadly force when they return to the United States than when they are deployed in a combat environment. (Jenks, ABA Report, 27–28)

Several cases illustrate the troubling public perception that stand-your-ground laws give people a license to kill in non-lethal situations. Again, whether the killers in such cases are ultimately vindicated by the law does not provide the full picture: the equally important question is what violent people think the law entitles them to do.

Consider first the case of Joe Horn, a Texas stand-your-ground incident from 2007. Sixty-one-year-old Horn observed two men burglarizing his neighbor's home. In his 911 call, he suggested that he should go out and shoot the men. The operator advised him repeatedly to stay inside, telling Horn that "property isn't worth killing anyone over." Horn responded, "The laws have been changed in this country since September the first, and you know it," referring to Texas's version of the stand-your-ground law, which had passed on September 1, 2007 (Texas Penal Code §§ 9.41, 9.42, and 9.43). Horn left his house with his shotgun; in the 911 call he is heard confronting the suspects, saying, "Move, and you're dead," immediately followed by the sounds of three shotgun blasts. When Horn got back on the phone with the operator, he shouted, "They came in the front yard with me, man, I had no choice!" A plainclothes police detective who had arrived at the scene saw Horn shoot both men in the back, but did not arrest Horn. Police later identified the dead men as Colombian nationals with criminal records. A grand jury was convened in Horn's case, but no charges were brought against him (Ellick 2008). Horn was hailed as a "hero" by many in Texas and elsewhere (Rogers and Lezor 2008).

In 2010, also in Texas, Raul Rodriguez shot Kelly Danaher during a birthday party for Danaher's wife and three-year-old daughter. Rodriguez was angered by the loud music from the party and walked down the street to Danaher's house. Rodriguez brought a video camera and a gun with him. Rodriguez began filming the party and arguing with Danaher and others. At some point, Rodriguez pulled out his gun and threatened to shoot Danaher. Rodriguez then said into his video camera, "I'm in fear for my life; my life is in danger." A few moments later, he shot Danaher, who bled to death in his driveway. Rodriguez argued that he had acted within his rights under Texas's stand-your-ground law. A jury disagreed, finding Rodriguez guilty of murder (Stangeland 2012), but Rodriguez was granted a new trial on appeal (Rogers 2014).

In Minnesota, 65-year-old Byron Smith shot two unarmed teenagers to death as they descended into his basement on Thanksgiving Day 2012. Smith was waiting in his basement with a gun, snacks, a tarp, and an audio recorder after experiencing several break-ins. The *Washington Post* published a detailed account of what happened based on the audio recording and media reports:

> [Nick] Brady falls down the basement stairs. "You're dead," Smith tells him. . . . Almost immediately after the first shooting, the rustling of a tarp is heard, then a dragging sound and labored breathing. Smith said he had moved the boy's body to a workshop in the basement to keep his blood from staining the carpet. . . . The audio continues with the sound of a gun being reloaded. About 11 minutes pass between the two shootings, local reports say. [Haile] Kifer's footsteps are heard on the stairs and she calls out quietly, "Nick?" Then comes the sound of more shots. She falls down the stairs. "Oh, sorry about that," Smith tells her. She screams, "Oh my God!" Then more shots. Smith tells her, "You're dying," and calls her a "bitch," the AP reported.
>
> After more labored breathing and another dragging sound, Smith calls her "bitch" again. He told authorities that after he moved her, he noticed she was still gasping and didn't want her to suffer, so he fired under her chin with a .22-caliber handgun. . . . Smith told investigators the last time he fired was "a good clean finishing shot" and "she gave out the death twitch." (Beaver 2014)

Smith told no one about the killings until the following day. He claimed he was fearful after previous break-ins and that he acted in self-defense. Smith was convicted of first-degree murder (ABC Eyewitness News 2014).

Racial disparities in the criminal justice system, while present in all states, are higher in stand-your-ground states than others: a white shooter killing a black victim is 350 percent more likely to be found justified than if the same shooter killed a white victim (ABA Report, 22). Rev. Leonard Leach of Mt. Hebron Missionary Baptist Church in Texas observed that stand-your-ground laws promote a deadly combination of prejudice and arrogance:

> This law . . . exacerbates the tension that already exists between persons and classes who are different from us and individuals with whom we have strained relationships. It accommodates the unfounded fear on the part of those who may harbor unresolved anxieties. It perpetuates a foolish bravado of those who feel a bold security when they have a gun in their hand, and it exonerates an arrogance and/or ignorance. (ABA Report, 30)

With regard to gender inequality in self-defense, there has been no indication that the proliferation of stand-your-ground laws has done anything to deter rapists, stalkers, harassers, or other perpetrators from engaging in abuse. There is also no indication that they have provided protection for women with plausible claims of self-defense against abusive partners. In fact, the evidence has suggested the opposite: in statements that echo Marion Hammer, South Carolina prosecutors have explicitly stated that stand-your-ground laws do not apply to domestic violence victims. The statement came after a judge actually ruled in favor of a domestic violence victim on the basis of that state's version of stand-your-ground. In November 2012, Whitlee Jones was attempting to leave her partner, Eric Lee, after he punched her and dragged her down the street by her hair. As she gathered up her belongings and tried to exit the house, Lee blocked her way. Jones stabbed him, and Lee died. The case's lead prosecutor, Assistant Solicitor Culver Kidd, stated that "[The Legislature's] intent . . . was to provide law-abiding citizens greater protections from external threats in the form of intruders and attackers. . . . We believe that applying the statute so that its reach into our homes and personal relationships is inconsistent with [its] wording and intent" (Kutner 2014). Kidd is correct, as South Carolina's law is closely modeled on Florida's and includes the same deliberate exclusions of domestic violence victims.

As to the goal of providing uniformity in immunity proceedings and limiting arbitrary decisions about justifiable force, the American Bar Association Task Force found that when faced with virtually identical fact patterns, "different judges arrived at opposing decisions, with one defendant receiving immunity, while his counterpart receiving a tough sentence elsewhere" (ABA Report, 29), while "[p]olice on the street are unclear when the immunity statute applies and therein the new law impedes their ability to arrest and detain suspects. In some jurisdictions, police officers even stopped investigating shootings involving self-defense claims. . . . Police officers are frustrated that SYG law is being used as a loophole by repeat offenders. . . ." (ABA Report, 27). Forcing police officers to make legal assessments they are not trained to make also means that officers will rely on their subjective intuitions about a case, leading to unpredictable and likely biased results (Randolph 2014, 620).

As Dr. Jerry Ratcliffe, professor and chair of the Department of Criminal Justice at Temple University and Director of the Center for Security and Crimes Science, summed up the effects of stand-your-ground laws:

> If our aim is to increase criminal justice system costs, increase medical costs, increase racial tension, maintain our high adolescent death rate and put police officers at greater risk then this is good legislation, but if we are to use science and data and logic and analysis to drive sensible public policy then there is no reliable and credible evidence to support laws that encourage stand your ground and shoot your neighbor. These laws are playing to a Second Amendment ideology that has no roadblocks and [/or] reliable scientific or evidential support. These laws are not solving a problem, they are creating one. (ABA Report, 25)

Standing Up for Self-Defense

Wayne LaPierre is famous for asserting that "the only thing that stops a bad guy with a gun is a good guy with a gun" (Overby 2012). Stand-your-ground laws, created and promoted by the National Rifle Association and backed by powerful corporate interests, spread this delusional claim all over the country. The results are grim: more gun use, more aggression, and more deaths, none of which has had the slightest deterrent effect on crime rates. LaPierre made this statement in an interview only one week after a man shot and killed twenty children and six adults, as well as his own mother, in Newtown, Connecticut. The laws have widened the gap between the powerful and the marginalized, endangering vulnerable communities while reinforcing the privileges of those least at risk. Stand-your-ground proponents have cynically exploited Americans' unreflective and irrational fear of crime, carefully avoiding any acknowledgment of the racism, sexism, and classism that structures criminal victimization and violence.

The right to self-defense, if it means anything, must mean more than a single-minded focus on blunt instruments of death. It should take into account and evaluate the actual realities of violence: who uses it, how, and why. The average American has statistically very little reason to fear crime, and those at the top of the current social hierarchy have even less. Wealthy white men have never been the primary targets of violent crime, yet it is their interests and their view of the world that now dominate not only the legal but the social understanding of self-defense. The right to self-defense has been hijacked by the gun rights movement, which in turn has been hijacked by the most privileged members of our society. The NRA benefits from keeping Americans in a constant state of fear: a fearful population is a consumer population, and the incessant message that only guns can save us will keep the bullets and the money flowing.

But the right to self-defense should not be based on fear. It should be based on an intelligible principle of autonomy, which must in turn be based on equality and justice and efficiency. The one thing that proponents of stand-your-ground have right is that self-defense doctrine and practice is in dire need of reform. Their solution, however, creates only increased violence, anxiety, and injustice. Other solutions are possible, and their time is nigh.

Notes

1. "Though mass shootings make an outsize psychological impact, they are a tiny fraction of the nation's overall gun violence, which takes more than 30,000 lives annually" (Follman 2014).
2. "[N]ot one of 62 mass shootings in the United States over the last 30 years has been stopped [by an armed civilian]. More broadly, attempts by armed civilians to intervene in shooting rampages are rare—and are successful even more rarely" (Follman 2012).
3. "[R]esearch by the Harvard Injury Control Center determined that most purported self-defense gun uses involved the escalation of arguments, which is not what a civilized society would want to promote" (ABA Report, 33).
4. "Persons in poor households at or below the Federal Poverty Level (FPL) (39.8 per 1,000) had more than double the rate of violent victimization as persons in high-income households (16.9 per 1,000) for the period 2008–12. Serious violence (rape or sexual assault, robbery and aggravated assault) accounted for a greater percentage of violence among persons in poor households (38 percent) than in high-income households (27 percent)" (Bureau of Justice Statistics 2014).
5. National Center for Injury Prevention and Control (2010, 18) puts the number at 1,270,000. This figure is considerably higher than the number reported by the National Crime Victimization Survey, which counted 188,380 rapes in 2010 (Truman 2011). There is compelling evidence demonstrating that the NCVS's study is badly flawed (including lack of privacy controls and a definition of rape that excludes incapacitation) and that the CDC study is far more accurate.
6. "A staggering portion of violence against women is fatal, and a key driver of these homicides is access to guns. From 2001 through 2012, 6,410 women were murdered in the United States by an intimate partner using a gun—more than the total number of U.S. troops killed in action during the entirety of the Iraq and Afghanistan wars combined. Guns are used in fatal intimate partner violence more than any other weapon: Of all the women killed by intimate

partners during this period, 55 percent were killed with guns" (Gerney and Parsons 2014, 1).

7. "Witnesses opined that Pennsylvania was able to draft a better law because of its intense study of the perceived pitfalls that Florida and Texas experienced with its [sic] laws" (ABA, 16).

8. This case overruled *State v. Bobbitt*, which had held that "the privilege not to retreat, premised on the maxim that every man's home is his castle which he is entitled to protect from invasion, does not apply here where both Bobbitt and her husband had equal rights to be in the 'castle' and neither had the legal right to eject the other."

9. For any of this even to be relevant, one would also have to assume that protective orders are common, easily obtained, and timely. But that is not the case. Many victims are reluctant to seek protective orders out of fear of escalation, financial dependency, or lack of knowledge; courts do not issue protective orders on demand; many domestic violence situations escalate suddenly.

10. Legal scholar Joshua Dressler claims that "the NRA and women's groups worked closely in alliance" on Florida's stand-your-ground law, but offers no support for this claim. Given Hammer's clear statements on the subject, it would be very surprising if there were any (Franks, 1115).

11. "A decision—or even a threat—to leave can trigger lethal violence. Because domestic violence is marked by power and control, attempting to exit a room may be considered 'disobedience,' spurring escalated violence. . . . Trying to exit past a raging man may be the final move of a woman seeking only to avoid violence. Killing a battering man may be the safest available alternative" (Koons 2006, 658–659).

12. Garcia was killed not long after by a stray bullet from a suspected gang shootout (Leibowitz 2012).

13. "Law enforcement officers . . . are not trained to conduct the legal analysis required by such determinations of immunity, and the statute provides absolutely no guidance. Unfortunately, immunity will be granted based on an officer's individual assessment rather than pursuant to a uniform decision-making process" (Megale 2010).

References

ABC Eyewitness News. 2014. "Byron Smith's Attorney to Appeal Guilty Verdict." (April 19). http://kstp.com/article/stories/s3417138.shtml.

American Bar Association, National Taskforce on Stand Your Ground Laws. 2014. "Preliminary Report and Recommendations" (August 8).

Baum, Katrina. 2003. *Juvenile Victimization and Offending, 1993–2003.* Bureau of Justice Statistics, Special Crime Report, National Crime Victimization Survey.

Bender, Michael C. 2012. "Marion Hammer, the NRA's Most Powerful Weapon." *Bloomberg Businessweek* (May 7). http://www.businessweek.com/articles/2012-05-17/marion-hammer-the-nras-most-powerful-weapon.

Bernstein, Anita. 2013. "What's Wrong with Stereotyping?" *Arizona Law Review* 55.

Bever, Lindsey. 2014. "'You're Dead.' Chilling Audio of Minnesota Homeowner Repeatedly Shooting Unarmed Intruders." *Washington Post* (April 23). http://www.washingtonpost.com/news/morning-mix/wp/2014/04/23/youre-dead-chilling-audio-of-minnesota-homeowner-repeatedly-shooting-unarmed-intruders/?tid=pm_national_pop.

Bureau of Justice Statistics. 2012. "Criminal Victimization," Table 7 (October).

Catalano, Shannan. 2007. "Intimate Partner Violence in the United States." US Department of Justice. http://bjs.ojp.usdoj.gov/content/pub/pdf/ipvus.pdf.

Center for Individual Freedom. 2005. "Interview with Marion Hammer." (November 3).

Centers for Disease Control and Prevention. 2008. "Adverse Health Conditions and Health Risk Behaviors Associated with Intimate Partner Violence in the United States." *Weekly Report* (February). http://www.cdc.gov/mmwr/pdf/wk/mm5705.pdf.

CBS News. 2012 (June 29). http://www.cbsnews.com/news/greyston-garcia-who-won-fla-stand-your-ground-case-killed-in-suspected-gang-crossfire.

Cheng, Chen, and Mark Hoekstra. 2012. "Does Strengthening Self-Defense Law Deter Crime or Escalate Violence? Evidence from Expansions to Castle Doctrine." *Journal of Human Resources* 48.

Children's Safety Network National Injury and Violence Prevention Center. 2010. "The Cost of Gun Violence."

Cook, Philip J., and Jens Ludwig. 2000. *Gun Violence: The Real Costs*. New York: Oxford University Press.

Department of Justice, Bureau of Justice Statistics. 2005. "Family Violence Statistics: Including Statistics on Strangers and Acquaintances." http://bjs.ojp.usdoj.gov/content/pub/pdf/fvs02.pdf.

District of Columbia v. Heller. 2008 (128 S. Ct. 2783).

Ellick, Adam B. 2008. "Grand Jury Clears Texan in Killing of 2 Burglars." *New York Times* (July 1), A19.

Follman, Mark. 2012. "Do Armed Civilians Stop Mass Shooters? Actually, No." *Mother Jones* (December 19). http://motherjonew.com/politics/2012/12/armed-civilians-do-not-stop-mass-shootings.

Franks, Mary Anne. 2014. "Real Men Advance, Real Women Retreat: Stand Your Ground, Battered Women's Syndrome, and Violence as Male Privilege." *Miami Law Review* 68: 1099, 1100.

Gardner, Thomas, and Terry Anderson. 2014. *Criminal Law*. Independence, KY: Cengage Learning.

Gerney, Arkadi, and Chelsea Parsons. 2014. "Women Under the Gun: How Gun Violence Affects Women and 4 Policy Solutions to Better Protect Them." Center for American Progress (June).

Gillespie, Cynthia K. 1990. *Justifiable Homicide: Battered Women, Self-Defense, and the Law*. Columbus, OH: Ohio State University Press.

Grossman, Dave. 1996. *On Killing: The Psychological Cost of Learning to Kill in War and Society*. Back Bay Books.

Harrell, Erika. 2012. *Crime Against Persons with Disabilities, 2009-2012*. Bureau of Justice Statistics. http://www/bjs.gov/index.cfm?ty=pbdetail&iid=4884.

Hickey, Eric. 2003. *Encyclopedia of Murder and Violent Crime*. Thousand Oaks, CA: SAGE Publications.

Jacobsen, Carol. 2007. "When Justice Is Battered." *Solidarity*. http://www.solidarity -us.org/site/node/729.

Johnson, Nicholas. 2014. *The Black Tradition of Arms*. Amherst, NY: Prometheus Books.

Jones, Jeffery M. 2013. "Men, Married, Southerners Most Likely to Be Gun Owners." Gallup (February 1). http://gallup.com/poll/160223/men-married -southerners-likely-gun-owners.aspx.

Jonsson, Patrik. 2014a. "Michael Dunn Loud-Music Life Sentence: A Corrective on Stand Your Ground Laws?" *Christian Science Monitor* (October 18). http:// www.csmonitor.com/USA/Justice/2014/1018/Michael-Dunn-loud-music-life -sentence-a-corrective-on-stand-your-ground-laws-video.

Jonsson, Patrik. 2014b. "Trayvon Martin Killing in Florida Puts Stand Your Ground Law on Trial." *Christian Science Monitor* (March 16). http://www.csmonitor .com/USA/Justice/2012/0316/trayvon-martin-killing-in-florida-puts-Stand -Your-Ground-law-on-trial.

Koons, Judith. 2006. "Gunsmoke and Legal Mirrors: Women Surviving Intimate Battery and Deadly Legal Doctrines." *Journal of Law and Policy* 14.

Kopel, David. 2014. "Stand Your Ground Had Nothing to Do with the Dunn Verdict in Florida." *Washington Post* (February 17). http://www.washingtonpost .com/news/volokh-conspiracy/wp/2014/02/17/stand-your-ground-had-nothing -to-do-with-the-dunn-verdict-in-florida.

Kutner, Jenny. 2014. "Stand Whose Ground? How a Criminal Loophole Gives Domestic Abusers All the Rights." *Salon* (October 15). http://www.salon .com/2014/10/15/stand_whose_ground_how_a_criminal_loophole_gives _domestic_abusers_all_the_rights.

Leber, Rebecca, and Nicole Flatow. 2014. "Five Disturbing Facts About Stand Your Ground on the Second Anniversary of Trayvon Martin's Death." *Think Progress* (February 26). http://thinkprogress.org/justice/2014/02/26/3332391 /trayvon-martin-years.

Lee, Cynthia. 2003. *Murder and the Reasonable Man*. New York: New York University Press.

Lee, Cynthia. 2013. "Making Race Salient: Trayvon Martin and Implicit Bias in a Not Yet Post-Racial Society." *North Carolina Law Review* 91: 1555– 1612.

Leibowitz, Barry. 2012. "Greyston Garcia, Who Won Fla. 'Stand Your Ground' Case, Killed in Suspected Gang Crossfire." CBS News (June 29). http://www .cbsnews.com/news/greystone-garcia-who-won-fla-stand-your-ground-case -killed-in-suspected-gang-crossfire.

Lopez, German. 2014. "Open Carry Laws Didn't Stop Cops From Killing Tamir Rice or John Crawford." *Vox* (December 13). http://www.vox.com/2014/12/13/7384813/black-open-carry.

Ludwig, Jens, P. J. Cook, and T. W. Smith. 1998. "The Gender Gap in Reporting Household Gun Ownership." *American Journal of Public Health* 87.

Malcolm X Grassroots Movement. 2013. "Operation Ghetto Storm: 2012 Annual Report on the Extrajudicial Killings of 313 Black People by Police, Security Guards, and Vigilantes" (April). https://mxgm.org/wp-content/uploads/2013/04/Operation-Ghetto-Storm.pdf.

McClellan, Chandler, and Erdal Tekin. 2012. "Stand Your Ground Laws and Homicides." Institute for the Study of Labor. Discussion Paper Series 3-39.

McCormack, Simon. 2014. "Michael Dunn Found Guilty of First-Degree Murder in Killing of Jordan Davis." *Huffington Post* (October 1). http://www.huffingtonpost.com/2014/10/01/michael-dunn-guilty_n_5913926.html.

Megale, Elizabeth B. 2010. "Deadly Combinations: How Self-Defense Pairing Immunity with a Presumption of Fear Allow Criminals to 'Get Away With Murder.'" *American Journal of Trial Advocacy* 105.

Megale, Elizabeth B. 2013. "Disaster Unaverted: Reconciling the Desire for a Safe and Secure State with the Grim Realities of Stand Your Ground." *American Journal of Trial Advocacy* 37.

Montgomery, Ben. 2012. "Florida 'Stand Your Ground' Law Was Born of 2004 Case, But Story Has Been Distorted." *Tampa Bay Times* (April 14).

MSNBC. 2014. "Marissa Alexander Denied New Stand Your Ground Hearing" (July 21). http://www.msnbc.coom/msnbc.marissa-alexander-denied-new-stand-your-ground-hearing.

National Center for Injury Prevention and Control. 2010. "National Intimate Partner and Sexual Violence Survey: Intimate Partner Violence in the United States." http://www.cdc.gov/violenceprevention/pdf/nisvs_report2010-a.pdf.

National Public Radio. 2014. "Florida Woman In Stand Your Ground Case Accepts Plea Deal" (November 25). http://www.npr.org/blogs/thetwo-way/2014/11/25/366567307/florida-woman-in-stand-your-ground-case-accepts-plea-deal.

Nichols, John. 2012. "How ALEC Took Florida's 'License to Kill' Law National." *The Nation* (March 20).

Overby, Peter. 2012. "NRA: 'Only Thing That Stops a Bad Guy With a Gun Is a Good Guy With a Gun." National Public Radio (December 21). http://www.npr.org/2012/12/21/167824766/nra-only-thing-that-stops-a-bad-guy-with-a-gun-is-a-good-guy-with-a-gun.

Payne, B. Keith. 2006. "Weapon Bias: Split-Second Decisions and Unintended Stereotyping." *Current Directions in Psychological Science* 15 (December).

Prince, Joshua. "Firearm Law Attorney." ABA Report, 25.

Randolph, Jennifer. 2014. "How to Get Away with Murder: Criminal and Civil Immunity Provisions in 'Stand Your Ground' Legislation." *Seton Hall Law Review* 44.

Rape, Abuse, and Incest National Network. http://www.rainn.org/statistics (accessed April 18, 2014).

Richardson, L. Song, and Phillip Atiba Goff. 2012. "Self-Defense and the Suspicion Heuristic." _Iowa Law Review_ 293.

Rogers, Brian. 2014. "Court Overturns 'Stand Your Ground' Conviction." _Houston Chronicle_ (December 18). http://chron.com/news/houston-texas/article/Court-overturns-stand-your-ground-conviction-5966621.php.

Rogers, Brian, and Dale Lezor. 2008. "Joe Horn Cleared By Grand Jury in Pasadena Shootings." _Houston Chronicle_ (June 30). http://chron.com/neighborhood/pasadena-news/article.Joe-Horn-cleared-by-grand-jury-in-Pasadena-1587004.php.

Schorsch, Peter, Senator Don Gatz, and Representative Matt Gaetz. 2012. "Op-ed: Standing Up for 'Stand Your Ground." SaintPetersBlog (May 2). http://www.saintpetersblog.com/sen-don-gaetz-rep-matt-gaetz-op-ed-standing-up-for-stand-your-ground.

Solotaroff, Paul. 2013. "A Most American Way to Die." _Rolling Stone_ (April 25). http://www.rollingstone.cm/culture/news/jordan-davis-stand-your-grounds-latest-victim-20130425.

Stangeland, Brooke. 2012. "Self-Defense or Murder? What Drove Man to Kill Neighbor." ABC News (September 14). http://abcnews.go.com/US/defense-murder-drove-man-kill-neighbor/story?id=17226874&singlePage=true.

Stanley, Kameel, and Connie Humburg. 2012. "Many Killers Who Go Free with Florida 'Stand Your Ground' Law Have History of Violence." _Tampa Bay Times_ (July 20).

Strasser, Annie-Rose. 2013. "What George Zimmerman's Story Can Teach Us About Domestic Abusers." _Think Progress_ (November 19). http://thinkprogress.org/health/2013/11/19/2966281/zimmerman-domestic-violence.

Sugarmann, Josh. 2014. "Murder Rate for Black Americans Is Four Times the National Average." _Huffington Post_ (January 31). http://www.huffingtonpost.com/josh-sugarmann/murder-rate-for-blackame_b_4702228.html.

Truman, Jennifer. 2010. _National Crime Victimization Survey_. Department of Justice Publication No. 235508. http://bjs.gov/content/pub/pdf/cv10.pdf.

Van Sickler, Michael. 2014. "Amendment to Bill Expanding 'Stand Your Ground' Would Limit Access to Court Records." _Tampa Bay Times_ (March 19).

Vendatam, Shankar. 2013. "'Stand Your Ground' Linked to Increase in Homicides." National Public Radio (January 2). http://www.npr.org/2013/01/02/167984117/stand-your-ground-linked-to-increase-in-homicide.

Waldman, Michael. 2014. _The Second Amendment: A Biography_. New York: Simon and Schuster.

Weinstein, Adam. 2012. "How the NRA and Its Allies Helped Spread a Radical Gun Law Nationwide." _Mother Jones_ (June 7).

CHAPTER SIX

Gun Violence Reduction Strategies

Sean Maddan

Introduction

In late October 2014, Jaylen Fryberg, a freshman high school student at Marysville-Pilchuck High School in Washington, text invited several friends to the school cafeteria. Once the five individuals were seated at a table, Jaylen approached the table, pulled out a .40-caliber pistol, and opened fire on the victims. Zoe Galasso and Gia Soriano were killed; Shaylee Chuckulnaskit died of her wounds later at the hospital. The assault ended when a teacher at the school confronted and helped to subdue Jaylen. It is unclear what made Jaylen Fryberg ambush his friends. He was described as a popular student and had even been named the homecoming prince the previous week. Such high-profile shootings continue to occur with worrying frequency. The gun-related murder of nine people at the Emanuel American Methodist Episcopal Church in Charleston, South Carolina, in June 2015 and the shooting of eleven people, two of whom died, in a movie theater in Lafayette, Louisiana, in July 2015 are two tragic examples.

There has been an increase in mass shootings over the last 30 years. However, while many view mass shootings as the prototype of gun violence, these types of murder are, in fact, atypical. Media coverage gives the false impression that such homicides are prevalent due to the extended media emphasis placed on mass shooting violence; cable news networks will spend several days on mass shootings to fill air time and increase revenue. In reality, the most common nexus of guns, violence, and crime occurs at the street level in relation to situational homicides, robbery, and gang activity. In 2014 the vast majority of murders were attributable to street crime rather than mass shooting incidents. Whether through mass shootings or day-to-day street crimes, a central focus of public policy is to decrease the violence, especially lethal violence, associated with guns.

The United States is the most armed nation in the world and hence a key goal of public policy is keeping guns out of violent encounters (Cook and Ludwig 2000). This objective can be difficult. T. W. Smith noted that 40 percent of households have a gun and 22 percent of households have handguns, gun ownership is greater among males than females, gun ownership is greater in rural areas, among married individuals, among the middle-aged, varies little by education, increases with household income, and is more likely to occur amongst those with conservative/Republican political leanings (Smith 2000).Very few individuals (around 10 percent) carry firearms away from the home. The proportion of households with a firearm has tended to decrease in recent years (Smith 2000). The type of firearms that people own has been changing; long guns (rifles or shotguns) are on the decline, while ownership of handguns has been steadily increasing (Smith 2000).

The gun ownership patterns of U.S. citizens are arguably the root of the high levels of gun violence and firearm related crimes experienced every year (LaPierre 1994). Each year the United States has an inordinate number of homicides and violent crimes (Cook and Ludwig 2000). What is unique to the United States is the fact that the majority of these violent acts involve guns, specifically handguns (Cook and Ludwig 2000). A homicide rate that far surpasses other developed nations implies that guns help to intensify violent crimes. Cook and Ludwig argue that the "importance of guns in routine fights and robberies is that they intensify violence, increasing the likelihood of death. Because guns increase the scope and lethality of violence, keeping them away from violent encounters is a vital public goal" (Cook and Ludwig 2000, 5). Guns have been responsible for more than a million deaths since 1965 (Cook and Ludwig 2000). Because of these numbers, it is important to create and/or utilize policies that will impact the use of guns during the commission of violent criminal acts.

This chapter examines the nexus of guns, gun crime, and gun violence reduction policies in the United States. The purpose is to evaluate the impact of the various forms of gun control policy that have been utilized to curb gun crime. This chapter evaluates the various gun violence reduction strategies across a continuum from practices that impinge greatly on the individual rights of citizens to policies that have very limited impact on individual liberties. The gun violence reduction polices evaluated here are gun abolition, the regulation of gun dealers, gun buyback programs, the effectiveness of concealed-carry legislation, enhanced prosecution efforts, and directed police patrol strategies. Before this discussion can begin, the next section evaluates the nature and scope of gun crime in America.

Firearm Crime in the United States

According to Renshaw (1981), from 1973 to 1980, guns were present in 11 percent of all violent crimes and 32 percent of all armed incidents. Over this same time period, offenders were more likely to use guns in homicides than any other kind of violent crime; offenders were equally likely to use a gun in rapes, robberies, or aggravated assaults (Renshaw 1981). Zawitz (1995) notes that 57 percent of homicides were completed with a handgun, 3 percent with rifles, and 5 percent with shotguns. Further, 25 percent of rapes, sexual assaults, aggravated assaults, and robberies were completed by armed offenders. Rand and colleagues (1986) report that armed offenders were responsible for a total of 24 million victimizations from 1973 to 1982. Other than a peak in 1993, these percentages and numbers are largely the same, although overall gun-related crime rates have decreased heavily since 1993 (Cook and Ludwig 2000).

Firearms are also associated with crime in indirect ways. For instance, guns are associated with higher completion rates of crime (Rand, DeBerry, and Klaus 1986). Timrots and Rand (1987) indicated that offenders utilized a weapon in a quarter of all non-stranger crimes and a third of all stranger crimes; offenders who used guns on their targets typically did not know the victims. Male and black individuals predominated as victims of gun crime (Rand, DeBerry, and Klaus 1986). In addition, gun offenses typically involved multiple victims. Offenders usually did not shoot the victim; in 4 percent of the cases offenders did shoot a victim and in 21 percent the offender merely fired the weapon at the victim.

In terms of protection, three of four victims of violent crimes did something to protect themselves from the offender; self-defense was less likely in offenses involving strangers (Timrots and Rand 1987). Across all forms of self-defense by eventual victims, the least common method of protection for a violent crime was the display of a gun or other weapon (Timrots and Rand 1987).

Harlow (2001) examined the firearm usage of offenders by evaluating a sample of prisoners in the United States. Harlow noted that very few offenders currently in prison used, carried, or possessed a firearm in the commission of their current convicted offense in both the federal (18 percent) and state (15 percent) systems; less than 10 percent of the prisoners used a gun in their most current offense. Gun offenders were typically male, young, and equally likely to be either first time offenders or recidivists; however, there were differences among these different types of individuals in how they obtained their guns (Harlow 2001, 9).

Firearm Offender Characteristics

In the most exhaustive survey of gun criminals, Wright and Rossi (1986) and Wright (1986) described the typical gun offender. The survey of 1,800 convicted criminals (felony and male offenders) in ten states, assumed to resemble the overall state prison population, asked offenders how and why they obtained, carried, and utilized guns in their criminal activities. The research also examined where offenders acquired their guns, firearm preferences and motivations, and their responses to various types of proposed gun control policies. The first key finding of their survey indicates that half of the sample had carried a gun in at least one crime. The gun-carrying criminals could be grouped into those who had used a gun once in a crime, those who used guns sporadically, those who were handgun predators, and those who were shotgun predators. Of the entire group of offenders, those classified as handgun or shotgun predators (20 percent of all offenders in the sample) were the most active criminals in terms of total number of crimes reported.

Wright and Rossi (1986) evaluated the nature of the criminal firearms market. More than three quarters of the sample had owned guns at some point; 79 percent of these owned at least one handgun. Most of these offenders did not get their guns through traditional retailers. Most of the guns criminals acquired were through informal transactions (the black market) and theft. Because of this, most of the sample suggested that they would have no trouble getting a firearm upon release from prison. Indeed, half the prisoners in the study had stolen a gun at least once; most had stolen more than once. Most of these thefts were from private residences. For these offenders, gun theft appeared to be opportunistic as most offenders did not actively seek to steal the weapons, but just "happened upon them." The purpose of these gun thefts was usually to sell or trade the stolen piece. Thus, gun control in terms of tightening retailer practices would likely have no reductive effects on gun crime (Wright 1986).

Wright and Rossi (1986) also determined the criminal demand for firearms in their survey. Not only did offenders in this sample prefer to carry guns, but they preferred to carry large, well made weapons. Less than a third of the sample carried what would be considered a "Saturday Night

Special." In addition, the more the offender used a weapon in crimes, the more likely they were to carry quality weapons (greater accuracy and fire-power, and better construction). Offenders were able to get such weapons for the modest price of $100 to $200. Purging the market of cheap hand-guns (especially the Saturday Night Special) would have a limited impact on gun crime.

With regard to the motivation of offenders to carry weapons, the pri-mary rationale of offenders in the Wright and Rossi (1986) sample is that it is easier to commit a crime when the offender is armed. As well, offenders in this sample were largely raised around guns and have thus used/owned guns all their lives. The majority of individuals kept their guns loaded and had actually fired the guns (often in some cases) at other people. Wright (1986) suggested that over half the offenders had fired a weapon at someone at some time; likewise, half the sample suggested that they had been fired upon at some point. The decision to carry a firearm is argued to be a lifestyle decision of being a criminal (Wright and Rossi 1986). These offenders then used firearms mostly as self-protection (58 percent of the sample) as at least two-fifths of offenders had encoun-tered an armed victim. Being in this lifestyle, the majority of offenders carry guns even when they do not intend to engage in a criminal act.

The most surprising findings by Wright and Rossi (1986) revolved around what offenders thought of various gun control strategies. When asked about the cost of cheap handguns increasing beyond their financial means, the prisoners suggested that they would then borrow or steal the weapons they desired. When asked about a potential ban on small, cheap handguns, the offenders said they would carry bigger and more expensive weapons. In response to a complete ban on all handguns, the respondents argued that they would carry sawed-off long guns (rifles or shotguns). The direct conclusion taken from this sample is that "where there is a will, there is a way." Criminal gun offenders would adapt according to whatever policy scenario was enacted.

Juvenile Offenders and Guns

It is important to distinguish between adult and juvenile gun crime. As Rosenfeld's work (2000) indicates, adult homicides were actually decreas-ing between 1980 and 1995, a time when homicide rates, and gun homi-cides specifically, were increasing dramatically. Sheley and Wright (1995) further examined the characteristics of firearm offenders in relation to ju-veniles in the early 1990s. At the time, violent crime was peaking at an all time high and juvenile offenders were taking much of the blame for these offense increases. Sheley and Wright conducted survey research on two purposive samples of juveniles. The first sample was selected from incarcerated juveniles (835 male inmates in six correctional facilities) and the second sample was selected from inner-city high school students (758 male students from 10 inner-city high schools); both samples were collected in California, Illinois, Louisiana, and New Jersey. The survey instrument focused on respondents' exposure to guns (obtaining, possession, carrying, and rationale for possession and carrying), crime, violence, drug activity, and gang membership.

In relation to the inmate sample, 86 percent had owned a firearm sometime in their life and 73 percent owned three or more guns. According to Sheley and Wright (1995), the revolver was the most commonly owned gun. In relation to the student sample, 30 percent had owned a firearm sometime in their life. The most common gun possessed by this sample again was the revolver. Both samples denoted the importance of firepower, quality, difficulty in tracing, ease of shooting, and accuracy as key features guns should possess. Thus, gun ownership was relatively common among the juveniles in this research.

Sheley and Wright (1995) suggest that the primary motivation for the high incidence of gun ownership and carrying in the two samples was related to protection. Since both samples came from major cities, most of the respondents indicated that they had been shot, shot at, or stabbed at some point in their lives; in addition, the vast majority had been threatened with serious physical violence at least once in their lives. The protection motivation also lies at the heart of the link between guns and drugs. While the correlation between drug usage and gun ownership/carrying patterns was tenuous, Sheley and Wright (1995) found that those who sold drugs were much more likely to have and carry firearms.

Finally, Sheley and Wright found that 74 percent of the inmates and 39 percent of the students were affiliated with gangs, which is an important finding because gangs display high levels of gun possession, carrying, and usage. Sheley and Wright's research indicated that both gang and non-gang members in their samples had high levels of gun possession. They argued that gang members are more visible than their non-gang counterparts (especially in the early 1990s), giving them an air of being more dangerous and more likely to engage in gun-related crime than individual juveniles who utilized guns in their individual criminality.

Now that we have examined the nature of gun crime and gun offenders in the United States, the next section evaluates the various policies that have acted as gun violence reduction strategies in the United States during the last half century.

Gun Violence Reduction Strategies and Crime

According to Wright and Rossi (1986), most gun violence reduction strategies can be seen in relation to two basic approaches: "(1) attempts to interdict the acquisition of handguns by persons with criminal backgrounds or tendencies; and (2) attempts to deter criminals from using handguns by raising the costs of doing so." Cook and Ludwig (2000) argue that "Given that guns may be used for both good and ill, the goal of gun policy in the United States has been [mostly] to reduce the flow of guns to the highest-risk groups while preserving access for most people." This section examines the various gun violence reduction strategies that have been implemented in the United States. The policies evaluated here revolve around gun abolition, the regulation of gun retailers, gun buyback programs, concealed carry laws, enhanced prosecution strategies, and directed police patrols.

Gun Abolition

The most extreme approach to gun violence reduction strategies is the banning of guns (Walker 2006). Policies to ban handguns are indicative of several strategies including "the outlawing of possession, outlawing bullets, prohibiting the manufacture/sale of guns and banning certain types of guns" (Walker 2006, 197). Gun bans are more easily advocated than implemented into a meaningful policy.

Kaplan (1981), examining the utility of gun prohibition, suggested that one of the key points to address in enacting laws is a consideration of how many individuals will follow or not follow the law. Comparing gun prohibition to drug prohibition, Kaplan determined that gun prohibition would be a difficult task that would inevitably result in failure. It is accepted that alcohol prohibition in the United States from 1920 to 1933 was a failure. In both prohibition cases, large numbers of people think they are justified in breaking the law. There is a serious issue also with prohibiting something before a large enough body of the population engages in that illegal behavior. This is especially problematic for guns because many individuals own firearms. Kaplan suggested that a large number of gun owners would ignore any such prohibition and in breaking the law would run little risk of being caught. Finally, it is problematic for all laws when a single law can criminalize a very large portion of the population. This fact may well lead individuals, who possess outlawed firearms, to feel alienated and to be more likely to engage in wider criminal activity. The ramifications of this situation could be exceptionally expensive, especially for the criminal justice system.

Kaplan (1981) argues that society would be forced to take one of three courses if there were not voluntary compliance. First, more money would have to be pumped into the criminal justice system for enforcement and punishment. Second, other types of offenders would be treated more leniently so that the criminal justice system could adequately handle the new class of gun offenders. Third, and inevitably, gun possession would be treated as marijuana possession is today. Kaplan argues that this latter case would yield selective enforcement, further adding to the racial/ethnic strains already placed on the criminal justice system. Most importantly, the majority of gun owners are legitimate, law-abiding citizens who do not use their guns in the commission of criminal acts.

With all of the philosophical and logistical issues with gun abolition notwithstanding, the District of Columbia in 1975 passed the most widespread ban on guns seen in the United States to that point. The D.C. ban (ultimately ruled unconstitutional in 1998 by the U.S. Supreme Court in *District of Columbia v. Heller*) was designed to reduce the number of firearm-related crimes and to monitor more effectively firearm trafficking. The District of Columbia banned guns for everyone except law enforcement officers and those who registered under an older D.C. law or registered with the chief of police; both of the latter were rare. Despite these loopholes, the final D.C. gun ban statute was still much weaker than it could have been. In 1980 an evaluation conducted by the U.S. Conference of Mayors suggested the ban was a complete success in terms of reducing gun crime in the District. This study would be the only one to fully support the impact of the D.C. gun ban. The primary problem with the study was the use of unacceptable control groups and the use of crime rates rather than raw scores. Jones suggests that the actual impact of the law was uncertain (Jones 1981).

Research by Loftin and colleagues (1991) indicates, through an interrupted time series analysis, a partial impact of the D.C. law on gun homicides and suicides. However, Britt and colleagues (1996) questioned the use of the interrupted time series analysis in their review of the D.C. Gun Law. Utilizing Baltimore, Maryland, as a control group, Britt and colleagues (1996) re-evaluated Loftin and colleagues' work utilizing the law's effective date at both sites. The results indicated that there was no impact of the law in the District. Indeed, Britt and colleagues found a greater drop in homicides in Baltimore where there was no such restrictive law. McDowall and colleagues responded to the critique of their original work. Re-analyzing their own work and Britt and colleagues' data, McDowall and colleagues (1996) argued that all Baltimore's homicides, gun and non-gun, decreased at the same rate, whereas the same did not happen in the District. Britt and colleagues' (1996) rejoinder further added to the uncertainty in interpreting the results of these complementary research articles.

Determining the impact of gun abolition on gun crime and gun violence is difficult for several reasons. First, the nature of the conflicting outcomes of the research makes it difficult to determine if city- or district-wide bans have any impact on gun crime and violence. Depending on the time series analysis from Loftin and colleagues or Britt and colleagues, one can garner support or refutation of the gun ban in Washington, D.C. At best, the empirical results can be considered inconclusive. Second, even when bans are put in place, they have little impact on the total number of guns currently in circulation. It is estimated that there are more than 300 million guns currently in circulation in the United States, which indicates that there is approximately one gun for every single one of the roughly 320 citizens in the United States. The number of firearms increases by roughly five million guns every year through new manufacturing.

Third, what is more important when it comes to city-wide bans on firearms is the Constitution's Second Amendment. While there has been a debate over the meaning of the Second Amendment, in the two Supreme Court decisions in *District of Columbia v. Heller* (554 US 570, 2008) and *McDonald v. Chicago* (561 US 742, 2010), the Court has decided that the possession of guns is an individual right. The Court in both decisions noted that people have the right to possess guns for legitimate purposes, primarily in relation to self-defense. Hence, both decisions ruled that gun bans in Washington, D.C., and the states are unconstitutional. Thus, banning guns is completely unfeasible, making it a poor policy choice when trying to reduce the amount of violence associated with firearms.

Regulating Gun Dealers

Criminals tend to acquire their guns from a variety of sources; the primary gun market, straw purchases from legitimate dealers, private sales, the black market, and theft are all places where criminals can obtain firearms (Wright and Rossi 1986; Wellford, Pepper, and Petrie 2004). One gun violence reduction strategy suggests that the way to curb criminals from getting weapons is through making laws that hold gun dealers more accountable for distributing guns to criminals. By restricting availability through retailers and increasing the cost of guns (Wright and Rossi 1986), it is hypothesized that both gun crime and gun violence will decrease.

The primary manner of regulating dealers historically has been an increase in licensing fees and making sure that federal firearms licensees (FFLs) sold a set number of firearms every year. In 1993 and 1994, these types of provisions helped to decrease the overall number of FFLs by half; a majority of these FFLs had used the license to buy guns only for personal use (Koper 2002). Koper's analyses led him to argue that neither of these provisional mandates affected gun crime rates, even though they occurred at the same time a drop in gun crime/violence was recorded. Koper indicated that those who surrendered their license were less likely to be linked to criminal guns through ATF traces than some of the FFLs that remained in business.

An alternate manner of regulating legitimate gun dealers is through the implementation of waiting periods. Wayne LaPierre (1994) outlined the underlying rationale behind waiting periods as keeping the guns away from criminals, keeping guns away from other undesirables (mentally-ill or mentally-handicapped), and halting crimes of passion. Because a large percentage of criminals acquire their guns from the secondary market or by stealing them, waiting periods have a limited impact on gun crime/violence; LaPierre argued that these policies largely affect only the law-abiding citizen (LaPierre 1994). LaPierre suggested that instantaneous record checks are both quicker and more effective than waiting periods. His arguments have largely proven correct as instantaneous record checks are the way most FFLs conduct business today.

Research indicates that only a small number of FFLs are responsible for a large number of crime gun traces (Wellford, Pepper, and Petrie 2004). These FFLs are high-volume dealers, which suggests that some guns sold are falling through the cracks so to speak. Because of these high-volume dealers, and the fact that guns are so readily available through other means, the impact of regulating the primary gun market appears to be limited (Braga et al. 2002). Only a small number of FFLs selling guns illegally will be detected this way. Punishing these offenders is important, but it will affect gun crime and gun violence only narrowly. Regulating dealers does not appear to be an overly effective strategy for dealing with gun crime due to the existence of the black market and those offenders who will steal guns when they need them.

Gun Buyback Programs

Another strategy geared toward gun violence reduction can be found in some local governments' attempts to buy guns from citizens in an effort to reduce the availability of firearms. This strategy does not impact any individual rights. As noted above, there are millions of guns in circulation throughout the United States in addition to the millions of firearms manufactured each year. The rationale behind gun buyback programs suggests that the government can buy guns from citizens, which will have an indirect impact on the black market and stolen guns that are used in crime and gun-related violence. The people who surrender guns are not required to identify themselves, so even offenders are encouraged to hand in any guns they wish to rid themselves of. All of the guns that are received are recorded and then destroyed.

There is little research on these types of policies. In one example of research on a gun buyback in Seattle, Callahan and colleagues (1994) utilized a mixed methodology to examine data from surveys of individuals who turned in guns, official data, and telephone interviews with the public to ascertain the effectiveness of the Seattle program. Callahan and colleagues found that the majority of firearms turned in were both operational and were handguns. The weapons were primarily owned for protection or had been received as a gift; the majority of individuals still owned guns that they did not turn in. The primary reasons for turning in guns were for either safe disposal of the gun or to receive quick cash. While the majority of the public was supportive of the program, Callahan and colleagues' findings indicated that the program had no statistically significant impact on violent crimes or overall deaths in Seattle. This evaluation was typical of other evaluations completed on various gun buyback programs throughout the United States (Wellford, Pepper, and Petrie 2004).

Although popular with the public, research findings have largely dismissed as ineffective these types of gun violence reduction programs (Wellford, Pepper, and Petrie 2004). Wellford and colleagues outlined the key problems associated with gun buyback programs. First, the guns that are typically surrendered are the least likely to be used in the commission of crimes. Second, replacement guns are so easy to obtain that it is unlikely that gun buyback programs result in an actual decline of guns on the streets. Third, the "likelihood that any gun will be used in a crime in any given year is low" (Wellford, Pepper, and Petrie 2004). The authors calculated the odds of a particular gun being involved in a homicide at 1 in 10,000. Thus, gun buyback programs are theoretically and empirically limited in combating gun-related violent crime.

Concealed Carry Laws

One of the most controversial mechanisms for combatting gun violence is to place guns in the hands of more citizens. In this scenario, rather than removing or banning guns, more citizens have guns in an effort to deter would-be criminals from engaging in gun crime and violence. The "more guns, less crime" hypothesis was developed and researched by Lott (2000) and Mustard and Lott (1997). Their hypothesis claims that when citizens have legal access to carrying guns, criminals who prey on citizens will be more likely to be deterred from engaging in serious forms of person-to-person criminality because criminals "are motivated by self preservation" (Lott 2000, 8). When guns are concealed, criminals are then unable to evaluate whether or not a potential victim is armed. According to Lott, in 98 percent of all cases where people use guns defensively, they only have to brandish the weapon.

The primary question that Lott addressed in his research was "will allowing citizens to carry concealed handguns mean that otherwise law-abiding citizens will harm each other? Or will the threat of self-defense by citizens armed with guns primarily deter criminals?" (Lott 2000, 10). Lott assumes that criminals are inherently a rational group, and therefore allowing citizens to carry guns will reduce the incidence of violent crimes. To examine these research questions and the "more guns, less crime argument," Lott evaluated the crime rates across the United States with regard to the 33 states that have non-discretionary rules or no permit requirements for concealed weapons compared to the other 17 states that have discretionary gun carrying rules (10) or states forbidding concealed handguns (7). Lott's research utilized both states and counties as units or measurement.

Lott discovered that states with non-discretionary rules or no permit requirements were likely to have less violent crime (Lott 2000). Most importantly, concealed handguns in particular had a significant impact on homicide. This finding held across the state and county levels, although magnitude of effects was greater at the county level. The effect of concealed handgun laws on county level violent crime varied by population, population density, per capita income, and percentage of African Americans in the county. The effect was more pronounced in urban areas, where females and minorities gained the most from concealed handgun laws.

Lott also concluded that concealed handgun laws had an impact across non-violent and other types of crime. He argued that mass public shootings were less likely in states with lenient concealed handgun policies (Lott 2000). Lott's results also supported the claim that concealed handgun laws had an effect on property offenses. In addition, Lott argued that waiting periods and background checks have no crime reduction benefits. Most importantly, Lott argued that those who carry concealed weapons legally do not commit either murder or other types of crimes. Lott concluded: "If the rest of the country had adopted right-to-carry concealed-handgun provisions in 1992, about 1,500 murders and 4,000 rapes would have been avoided" (Lott 2000, 159).

Lott made many claims about the impact of "shall issue" concealed handgun laws, and many researchers have taken Lott's research to task for poor methodology, incomplete data collection, and faulty inferences derived from his data analyses. Although a great deal of research has been conducted to both support and refute Lott's conclusions, the most explicit challenge to Lott's claims comes from Donohue (2003). Donohue lists three primary concerns with Lott's research: (1) Lott and Mustard and Lott do not take into account the rising crack epidemic of the 1980s in their analysis (model mis-specification); (2) the adoption of shall-issue laws does not randomly occur across states (possible treatment effect threat to validity and coding errors); and (3) the use of strong reliance on country level data. To evaluate these concerns, Donohue utilized five more years of data in addition to the Lott and Mustard data. To increase the power of his findings, Donohue also introduced time lag and lead variables to better gauge the impact of concealed carry laws.

The primary problem addressed by the Donohue analyses involved the county level data. The problem with county level data is the number of missing cases, especially in relation to Uniform Crime Reporting data; many counties have little to no crime (at least that is reported). But even when there is not a problem with missing data, many rural counties are omitted from analyses because these counties do not experience any homicides in the course of a year. There is also the problem with the data analyses themselves. Depending on the regression models employed, county and state level data caused instability in the magnitude of effects. Thus, the robustness of the analytic techniques in relation to the data is questionable across all analyses that Lot and Mustard present.

While Lott and Mustard argued that individuals licensed to carry concealed handguns are unlikely to engage in homicide and other serious criminality, Donohue (2003) suggests that these individuals still contribute to the overall murder rate. The first mechanism by which concealed carry laws affect the homicide rate is that if criminals are aware that members of the public are armed, they themselves will more likely carry guns and will be willing to use them more quickly, which can result in more murders. This is a reasonable conclusion, given that Lott argued that offenders are basically rational. The second mechanism by which concealed carry laws affect homicide rates is through gun theft. A sizeable portion of guns used in crimes every year are stolen and therefore an increased number of individuals carrying firearms will result in a larger population from which to steal guns (Donohue 2003). Therefore, liberalized concealed carry laws could contribute to the overall homicide rate and other forms of gun related violent crime.

At this point research on the impact of concealed carry laws has largely abated. This is especially true in light of the decreases in crime since 1994.

The predominance of the empirical research and critiques suggest that Lott's research is problematic. Although an interesting idea, the "more guns, less crime" hypothesis has largely been dismissed due to the lack of precision in the data and statistical analyses employed. Giving citizens the right to carry concealed handguns does not appear to impact the crime rate in the United States.

Enhanced Prosecution

Another method of decreasing gun crime and gun violence comes in the form of specialized prosecution and mandatory minimum and longer sentences. It is suggested that these mandatory sentences will deter offenders from carrying weapons in the commission of crimes because if they are caught with the weapon, more jail time can be added to the sentence they would have received for the original crime. This type of gun control policy is politically attractive because it does not target legitimate gun owners and users. These gun control policies extend back to the 1970s, but the empirical investigation of these policies still leads to debates over their effectiveness.

One of the very first enhanced prosecution policies occurred in Massachusetts with the Bartley-Fox Gun Law. Bartley-Fox mandated a one-year minimum prison sentence for those who carried a gun. Although carrying was the wording of the statute, it was the use of guns in crime that was implied by the law. Utilizing a time-series analysis of the program, Pierce and Bowers (1981) came to several conclusions. First, while the law did have an impact on gun assaults, the researchers found that non-gun assaults increased. Second, the law was accompanied by a decrease in gun robberies. Most importantly, the law coincided with a significant decline in gun homicides. Finally, while Pierce and Bowers found these statistically significant declines across various forms of gun crime, they concluded that these results were not the result of the Bartley-Fox Gun Law. What affected the various gun crime types most was the publicity associated with the law. The law, through a vigorous media campaign, alerted individuals to the severity and certainty of punishments associated with carrying a gun or using a gun in the commission of a crime.

Although the law in Massachusetts was viewed positively and received empirical support, research in other areas has not shown similar success. Loftin and McDowall (1981) evaluated a similar enhanced prosecution law in Michigan, where offenders who used a gun in a crime would get a mandatory two-year prison term. While the mandatory minimum was more severe in Michigan, Loftin and McDowall found that the law had no statistically significant impact on the incidence of gun crime (gun homicides, gun robberies, and gun assaults) in Detroit.

One reason given for the insignificant results that Loftin and McDowall reported was that prosecutors were not necessarily applying the mandatory minimum sentences to offenders in Michigan. Although this conclusion was largely speculation in Michigan, the same effects were seen in California in research Lizotte and Zatz (1986) conducted. Lizotte and Zatz had more follow-up data, which allowed them to conclude definitively that prosecutors were not utilizing the laws and hence gun crime rates were not decreasing as was hypothesized.

McDowall and colleagues (1992) analyzed mandatory sentencing laws for gun crimes in Detroit, Jacksonville, Miami, Philadelphia, Pittsburgh, and Tampa. Because the disaggregated analyses of mandatory minimum sentences had largely displayed statistically insignificant results across previous studies, McDowall and colleagues aggregated the data from these sites to evaluate the overall effect of mandatory minimum laws for gun crime in these six cities located in three different states. Utilizing interrupted time series analyses, the researchers found support for the earlier Pierce and Bowers study in Boston. Homicides were reduced across cities, but McDowall and colleagues (1992) concluded that the effect is based on the public announcement of the laws, not the laws themselves. Unfortunately, the results were also indicative of the earlier Loftin and McDowall and Lizotte and Zatz studies that showed no impact of the laws on gun robberies and gun assaults.

Project Exile, conducted in Richmond, Virginia, is a recent example of a crime reduction initiative rooted in enhanced prosecution techniques (Raphael and Ludwig 2003). Exile is an advance over prior prosecution-oriented efforts to curb gun crime because myriad criminal justice agencies have contributed resources to the program. It is a collaborative effort between law enforcement and prosecutors, which has received wide support. Richmond law enforcement and the regional U.S. attorney's office worked together to impose a zero tolerance approach on gun crimes. Both the state of Virginia and the federal government have penalties for gun offenses. In many states, federal penalties for felon-in-possession of firearms (FIP) as well as drug offenses that involve a firearm are much stricter than those enforced by the state (Wintemute 2000, 72). In order to virtually guarantee a sentence enhancement, Richmond law enforcement, trained in federal law enforcement statutes and practices, ultimately worked together with the U.S. attorney to prosecute offenders in the federal system.

Utilizing the sentencing enhancement approach appears to be effective. In addition to the federal system applying longer prison stays, the penalty is still more severe. For example, unlike Virginia, the federal court is able to sentence the offender to an out-of-state prison. Also, the federal system denies bail to gun offenders more frequently than state systems. Therefore, it is not simply sentence enhancements or an advertisement campaign stressing a zero tolerance attitude. Rather, it is an effective combination of state and federal resources that seek swift, certain, and severe punishments for gun crimes.

As stated earlier with sentence enhancements, it is generally argued that (1) the incapacitated offender is unable to commit additional crimes, and (2) potential offenders will be deterred from committing crimes with a gun. Ideally, both scenarios result in a lower incidence of gun crime. Project Exile enjoyed support from both sides of the gun control issue. As noted earlier, Exile's popularity and attractiveness stems from widespread public support for sentence enhancements, mandatory sentences, and harsher punishments to criminals who commit crimes with firearms (Wright, Rossi, and Daly 1994). These approaches to reducing gun violence pose no threat or potential additional costs to legitimate gun owners.

Raphael and Ludwig (2003) note that Project Exile has been declared a success story across a spectrum that ranges from the National Rifle Association (NRA) to Virginians Against Gun Violence. This effort, which began in February 1997, received widespread support for a number of reasons. First, there was a 40 percent reduction in gun homicides from 1997 to 1998 (Raphael and Ludwig 2003). Second, the policy is especially attractive when a 40 percent reduction in gun homicides is combined with program that is consistent with public opinion and that is likely to receive support from the legitimate gun subculture.

Although Project Exile has been given wide support, little systematic evaluation, outside of Raphael and Ludwig, has been devoted to the program's effectiveness. A 40 percent reduction in homicide the year after the project began is certainly worthy of mention, but what is equally noteworthy is that Richmond witnessed a 40 percent increase in homicides the year before the program was implemented (Raphael and Ludwig 2003). Furthermore, cities with the largest increases in homicides during the 1980s and early 1990s, such as Richmond, were the same cities that witnessed the largest decreases in the late 1990s regardless of Project Exile. In other words:

> The impressive declines in gun homicide rates in Richmond around the time of Project Exile can be almost entirely explained by the fact that the city had unusually large increases in gun homicides through the mid 1990s, and that cities with larger-than-average increases in gun homicide

rates subsequently experienced unusually large declines. (Raphael and Ludwig 2003)

Unfortunately, there is little empirical evidence to support Project Exile's alleged success. Raphael and Ludwig allude to the fact that if a program happens to be introduced at a time when the downside of a crime cycle is expected, the public has a tendency to label the intervention an extraordinary success. Conversely, when potentially worthwhile interventions are introduced at a time when the crime cycle is expected to peak, it seems that the public tends to view the intervention, prematurely and superficially, a failure.

The research on the efficacy of mandatory minimum sentences and sentencing enhancements is not entirely positive. The results largely indicated that mandatory minimum sentences do not have an impact on gun crime. Although the Exile strategy utilized more interagency cooperation, it did not have an exceptional effect on gun crime (Ludwig 2005). While the laws themselves do not appear to have had an impact, what does seem to have been supported across all of the studies on sentencing policies is the impact of the publicity which informed the public of the ramifications of carrying or utilizing a gun in the course of committing a criminal act.

Directed Police Patrol Strategies

A relatively recent strategy to curb gun crime comes from the law enforcement community. Through New York's Compstat (complaint statistics) program of the late 1980s, it was determined that law enforcement could influence the crime rate through identifying high crime areas and then attacking those areas with a concentrated police presence until the crime decreased or was displaced to other areas. Eck and Maguire (2000) argued that, when attempting to reduce crime, the number of police officers is not as important as the way in which law enforcement resources are allocated. This approach to curbing the overall crime rate was quickly put to work in confronting gun crime in particular.

The first attempt to curb gun crime through directed law enforcement patrols occurred in Kansas City in the early 1990s. The Kansas City Gun Experiment (KCGE) was based on the assumption that additional patrols in a given area could result in increased gun seizures and a reduction in gun crime and violence. Sherman and colleagues (1995, 98) matched two patrol beats that had exceptionally high crime rates as well as an exceptionally high number of homicides and a high frequency of drive-by shootings. In the experiment, the target district received extra patrols focused on gun crime over a 29-week period in 1992. The control district received the same amount of patrol and police presence that it had always received; there was no reduction in law enforcement services.

The impact of the KCGE was evaluated by an examination of data about gun seizures, crime reports, calls served, and arrest records. Time series analyses were utilized to explore the results. Gun seizures in the target area were up dramatically; it was estimated that one gun was seized every 84 hours and one gun was seized for every 28 traffic stops. This data should be tempered by the observation that many guns were seized for "safekeeping" (a process where officers seize a gun when they think violence could ensue). Most of the guns seized for safekeeping were later returned. The findings also indicated that gun crimes decreased in the target area over the course of the experiment. While there were more seizures and less crime in the target district, there were similar declines in the control beat on a smaller scale, and so there were no statistically significant differences between the two districts. The one significant finding for Sherman and colleagues was that fear of crime decreased greatly in the target site. Although the results of the project did not attain statistical significance, the KCGE did show larger decreases in gun crime and an increase in guns seized in the target area along with a reduction in the fear of crime. These results were largely cost effective in that officers were not just randomly patrolling a beat but were focused on a specific area in relation to a particular type of crime.

One threat to the historical validity of Sherman and colleagues' (1995) results was two preexisting initiatives to curb gun crime in Kansas City. The first was the door-to-door gun patrol. This program had officers going to homes in high crime areas and informing residents of a crackdown on gun carrying and asking residents to call a hotline to report the illegal carrying of firearms. Although only two calls were received, the impact of the public being notified appeared to cause a decrease in gun carrying, much like the public notification in sentencing enhancements indicated in the previous section. The only individuals arrested for illegally carrying guns were from outside that district, which suggests limited success for this program. The second program involved body language training for officers so that they could determine if someone is carrying a gun. Although this program resulted in few arrests, the knowledge that officers had received the training could have ultimately trickled down to residents in the area. Thus, although both programs seemed to be largely ineffective, they still could have influenced the results of the KCGE.

Due to the mostly positive results of analyses on the Kansas City Gun Experiment, Boston law enforcement attempted an enhanced version of the KCGE. Boston's Operation Ceasefire began in 1995 and the implementation of what is known as the Operation Ceasefire strategy was started in the spring of 1996 (Braga and colleagues 2001). The two major features of Operation Ceasefire included (1) a proactive effort by law enforcement to target the illegal firearms market and (2) the establishment of systematic and prominent strategies for deterring violence. Due to the existence of the Boston Gun Project, the law enforcement aspect of Operation Ceasefire was already in position when the program began.

The Boston Gun Project was a problem-oriented policing strategy that was primarily concerned with reducing homicides among youth in Boston (Braga et al. 2001). Put simply, in a problem-oriented approach, police focus on assessing the specific problem at hand, such as gun crime among youth. Subsequently, the description of the problem and knowledge about the nature of the problem are used in order to take more effective action. Once police respond, the nature of the problem alters but does not vanish. A second round of assessment begins and interventions based on that particular assessment are made (Braga et al. 2001). Although the current example of problem-oriented policing is specific to Boston, this iterative process is inherent in the problem-oriented policing approach in general. This process continued as an effective method to target the ever-changing characteristics of crime. The Boston Gun Project responded to the increase in youth homicide incidents from 1984 to 1994. Given the Boston Gun Project's multilateral task, the response was aggressive. Research over this time period indicated that the increase in youth homicide was shown to be entirely firearm related (Cook and Laub 1998). Guns and gun crime needed to be the focus in order to address the increases in youth homicides.

The Boston Gun Project was not simply an effort conducted by the Boston Police Department. Much like Virginia's Project Exile discussed above, many other components and resources were employed in order to identify and prosecute gun offenders. Key participants in the Boston Gun Project included federal agencies such as the U.S. attorney and state efforts by the Massachusetts Department of Youth Services and the Massachusetts State Police. Local efforts such as the sheriffs' departments and community efforts were also involved in the systematic response. Operation Ceasefire built on the strengths of the unprecedented collaboration involved in the Boston Gun Project, and in so doing, firmly established the proactive law enforcement feature of the operation.

The second major feature of Operation Ceasefire is that it also sought to be a deterrent strategy. Ceasefire used features of Project Exile to enhance prosecutions of gun criminals, which would lead to specific deterrence for gun offenders who are imprisoned for longer sentences. Firearm prosecutions are also likely to send a clear message to potential gun offenders with regard to the consequences of gun crime. This type of strategy is known as general deterrence. Both types of deterrence should ideally lead to fewer gun crimes.

In order for general deterrence to function, the potential gun-offending population must be aware of the consequences of committing gun-related crimes as well as the new system under which their jurisdiction was operating. Operation Ceasefire sought to establish this general deterrence by the "advertising of the law enforcement strategy and the personalized nature of its application" (Braga et al. 2001, 201). The media campaign focused on the target population by making explicit cause-and-effect statements between the targeted types of behavior as well as the sharp criminal justice system responses to them. As opposed to targeting all youth in Boston, youths involved in gangs were the primary target (Braga et al. 2001). The media dissemination strategy targeted gangs that were likely to be involved specifically in violent crime.

In their evaluation of Operation Ceasefire, Braga and colleagues (2001) compared Boston's youth violence before and after the implementation of the intervention. They also analyzed several other cities' youth violence, which had no such intervention, as comparison groups. They found that most cities showed a decline in youth violence at about the time of the intervention. However, the nature of Boston's decline was greater and more abrupt than in cities that showed a general decline at the same time. From the point of evaluating Operation Ceasefire and given the unique character of Boston's decline, there is reason to believe that Boston's crime reduction was distinct from the other cities' declines. The distinction was attributed to Operation Ceasefire. Braga and colleagues concluded that "Operation Ceasefire was likely responsible for a substantial reduction in youth homicide and youth gun violence in the city" (Braga et al. 2001, 220).

More generally, the relatively rare collaborative effort and the problem-oriented policing used in Operation Ceasefire showed real promise. This new collaboration of various types of practitioners and academics yielded a range of innovations in targeting gun crime. Indeed, the joint efforts in Boston were arguably successful and, as a result of bridging various gaps between research and practice, operations were definitely improved (Braga et al. 2001, 220). The real key to success for Ceasefire, through a diverse effort, lies in the assessment phase of Boston's particular violence problem. The success of Operation Ceasefire is due largely to empirically assessing the problem and responding appropriately to changes in gun crime and gun violence.

The cumulative research on directed police patrol strategies in the Kansas City Gun Experiment and Boston's Operation Ceasefire indicate a successful gun violence reduction strategy. Indeed, directed patrol strategies have been argued to be the most successful manner of combating gun crime (Walker 2006). With the success of the directed patrol research, perceived to be a function of interagency cooperation, especially in Boston between law enforcement and the U.S. attorney's office, it was quickly concluded that a combination of directed patrol strategies and aggressive sentencing would be even more effective in combating gun crime. And so was born the Project Safe Neighborhoods Initiative.

Project Safe Neighborhoods (PSN), unlike Operation Ceasefire and Project Exile, is a national gun violence reduction strategy; the PSN design, however, takes lessons from both these previous efforts. In particular, it is the collaboration of various governmental agencies and community level efforts that have been defined as vital elements in order to have a significant effect on reducing crime. PSN has five core elements: (1) partnership, (2) strategic planning, (3) training, (4) community outreach and public awareness, and (5) accountability.

The first component of PSN is partnership. The design of PSN first recognizes that a collaborative effort between agencies must be formed in the name of public safety. In particular, all law enforcement agencies from the same judicial districts are headed by their respective U.S. attorney. Cooperating collectively, agencies enact a uniform approach to reducing gun crime in the district. It is not simply collaboration, but the combination of resources that allows for an aggressive approach to reducing gun crime. Ideally, the results of the committed resources will be greater than the sum of the parts.

As stated in the discussion of Boston's Operation Ceasefire, one of the key components in the program's effectiveness is not simply collaboration, but knowing the specific nature of the problem and allowing the collective efforts to be applied adequately. The second component of PSN, known as strategic planning, is included in the overall operation. In achieving the strategic planning component of PSN, the U.S. attorney's office first assesses the nature and scope of the district-specific gun crime problem through empirical investigation. Once researchers have identified the problem and the most significant areas in need of intervention are identified, a systematic and targeted effort is employed to combat that problem. In short, the strategic planning component was only the first step in the iterative problem-oriented policing strategy. Because the collaboration inherent in the design of PSN transcends the traditional scope of law enforcement agencies, the third component of PSN addresses training. The PSN initiative sought to reduce gun violence on a number of fronts. Each participating agency needs to be aware not only of their position within the larger scheme of the operation, but also of the current laws and the nature of the problem with which they were concerned. Various training opportunities were offered through PSN to all involved criminal justice system agents, the research partner, and the media partner. The goals of this component, among others, include becoming familiar with the proper search and seizure procedures necessary to successfully prosecute offenders. Training in firearms identification, the nature of gun trafficking, safety issues, and evidence management were also key components in making PSN a success. Furthermore, because the U.S. attorney was more adequately able to plan and organize training sessions, participants were encouraged to offer training sessions at the local levels. This latitude allowed the various U.S. attorneys' offices to play a stronger role in gun crime reduction at the local level. In addition, the U.S. attorney was able to execute discretion and was subsequently able to target locales that may be in more need of thorough training.

The fourth component of PSN is outreach; this component is entirely at the local and community levels of the jurisdiction. In order to more effectively target gun crime in communities, the community itself was an asset that could not be overlooked. Within the outreach component was the goal of public awareness. The heart of the outreach component seeks to educate the community and in so doing, deter potential offenders. This awareness is twofold. First, citizens are made aware of the collaborative effort against gun violence. This aspect also sought to educate the public both on the fact that their law enforcement agencies were actively seeking to make their neighborhoods safer and the ways in which the tactic was being employed. This component of PSN allowed for the residents to become actively involved with the overall goal of safe neighborhoods. Second, a byproduct of awareness in the community is an opportunity to increase deterrence. By educating the public through various brochures and advertisement campaigns (the media partner), potential gun offenders are made aware of the vigilant effort the authorities had given toward reducing gun crime.

The fifth component of PSN is accountability. This component can be viewed in the same spirit of problem-oriented policing. As was discussed with Project Exile, there is no final intervention that will result in total gun crime eradication. There may be interventions that are effective given a particular gun problem, but officials must realize that once the intervention is implemented, the nature of the gun crime problem is likely to change in response to that intervention. Therefore, the accountability component should involve an ongoing evaluation of the tactics employed and taking the time to redefine the nature of the resulting gun problem.

For instance, crime data will need to be analyzed in order to identify any changes or trends in crime that warrant adjustments in the intervention tactics.

It should be noted that in light of evidence that shows no statistically significant effect of Project Exile, the five components outlined above do have some major strengths. In particular, the project is not simply intended to achieve just one of the five goals. Rather, the collective operation of the five components of PSN as well as the unprecedented collaboration inherent in the project is where the strength lies. In order for PSN to have a positive effect, each aspect must be fully functioning. For example, outlining an elaborate goal in a large geographic area is meaningless if there are no collective resources available to achieve the objective. Similarly, governmental collaboration without direction is of little constructive use, but multifaceted efforts linked by a common goal can achieve results of critical mass.

An overall evaluation of PSN is very difficult to complete because each district's target area(s) incorporated an individually tailored strategy for dealing with the gun crime unique to that area. Most of the published individual evaluations of specific PSN programs seem to indicate success. While gun crime prosecutions increased across all districts, lower gun crimes are reported in the Southern District of Alabama, in the Middle District of Alabama, the Eastern District of Missouri, and Lowell, the District of Massachusetts (O'Shea 2007; McGarrell et al. 2007; Decker et al. 2005; Decker et al. 2007; McDevitt et al. 2007; Braga et al. 2008). Indeed, in the case of Lowell, Massachusetts, Braga and colleagues (2008) argued that the "pulling levers" approach resulted in a substantial decrease in gun assaults and gun homicides. Rosenfeld and colleagues (2005) did not examine PSN per se, but their later evaluation of Exile, Operation Ceasefire, and Compstat indicated the successful reduction of homicide rates in Richmond, Boston, and New York.

The overall national program evaluation by McGarrell and colleagues (2009) illustrated the success of PSN. They suggested that cities in which PSN was implemented witnessed a reduction in violent crime; comparing violent crime in 82 target sites to 170 non-target sites, McGarrell and colleagues found that violent crime decreased substantially. From a sample of PSN sites, McGarrell and colleagues conducted in-depth analyses of gun crime in those cities. Their results indicated statistically significant decreases in gun-related violence in the sample of nine PSN sites.

Not all of the reviews of PSN have been positive. Berk (2005) vigorously attacked Rosenfeld and colleagues' flawed methodology and causal inferences in evaluating Exile, Operation Ceasefire, and Compstat. Even Ludwig's

(2005) evaluation was less positive than his and Raphael's earlier work on the impact of Project Exile, which serves as the basis of PSN. Ludwig argued that the emphasis of PSN should have been on targeted law enforcement practices rather than on enhanced prosecution. After outlining the funding for PSN, where more than $360 million was spent on sentencing efforts (over a third of the total budget), Ludwig evaluated the various tactical elements of PSN. According to Ludwig, Exile and enhanced sentencing practices do not have a "supernormal" effect on gun crime; in other words, the effect is not much larger than expected if the criminal justice system did nothing at all. Ludwig recommended that combating gun crime should reside with law enforcement, especially since gun violence is concentrated within a small subset of citizens and neighborhoods within a given area. Because of this, the impact of law enforcement strategies can have a much more pronounced effect than Exile's sentencing strategies (a better risk-return combination).

Conclusion

According to Cook and Ludwig (2000, 11), "medical expenses and lost productivity make up very little of the societal burden of gun violence." Rather, the key costs associated with gun crime and gun violence are related to criminal justice and security expenditures to prevent gun crime. It is hypothesized that crime costs the criminal justice system $2 billion more than would be expended in the absence of gun-related crime. Even more money is lost when intangible costs are considered. Using contingent valuation survey methods, Cook and Ludwig estimated that Americans would be willing to pay $80 billion a year to eliminate the use of guns in violent crimes (Cook and Ludwig 2000). This estimate suggests that gun crime and gun violence is a very important issue that the bulk of citizens want addressed.

Unfortunately there is a good deal of debate about how to contain gun-related violence. Moore (1981) argued that gun control policy must strike a balance between the legitimate use of guns and a reduction in the illegal use of guns. One side of the debate emphasizes that the majority of guns are utilized for legal purposes; the other side focuses on evidence that links the widespread availability of guns and violent crime. According to Moore, gun control policies have focused on particular weapons (assault rifles or Saturday night specials) and harsh penalties for those who use guns in the commission of crimes.

Zimring and Hawkins (1996, 1997) suggest that crime and violence are often considered to be closely linked. They argue that this conception is incorrect and inevitably influences criminal justice policy toward violent crime in an unhelpful way. The basis for this perspective is that the vast majority of crime in the United States is non-violent (more than 80 percent). According to Zimring and Hawkins, "there is no reason to assume that the people who commit violent criminal acts are indistinguishable from the sorts of people who commit nonviolent criminal acts" (1996, 44). If the U.S. crime rate is compared with most of the other industrialized nations, those rates are largely similar across those nations. Where the United States differs from other nations is in the rate of violent crime. The United States surpasses many countries with regard to rates of violent crime. A specific example is rates of robbery. In most countries analyzed by Zimring and Hawkins, robbery generally results in no harm to the victim; however, in the United States the victim is likely to be injured when the victim resists the robbery, does not cooperate with the robber, or does not hand over money or property.

Based on these observations, Zimring and Hawkins (1996) argue that making general crime control policies to address both violent and nonviolent crimes is likely to be unsuccessful. They suggest that viewing violence as a crime problem creates a narrow perspective and focus. If violence is seen only as a crime problem, then if the usual tools and processes of the criminal justice system are applied, they may well have no impact; and if violence is seen only as a crime problem, sources of violence are only evaluated through the caseload of the criminal justice system, especially the courts. Many of the conditions that generate violence will be ignored. There is also a diffusion of focus when violence is considered to be only a crime problem. The vast range of criminal behavior is not violent. As Zimring and Hawkins note, "if only 15 percent of crime involves violence, a general anti-crime policy will miss the target (if violence is the target) 85 percent of the time" (1996, 67). Finally, Zimring and Hawkins denote the "paradox" of the crime crackdown. As the fear of violence produces a campaign against crime, criminal justice resources toward violent criminals tend to decrease.

In terms of the majority of crime control policies considered here, these programs can largely be considered failures. The reason that most of these policies are failures is that they consider gun crime to be a crime problem. The policies associated with gun bans, gun regulation, and gun buybacks have been shown to be irrelevant in curbing gun crime. Total gun bans are generally unfeasible due to the sheer numbers of guns in circulation and the empirical evidence indicates inconclusive results on the effectiveness of gun bans. More importantly for gun bans, recent court decisions indicate that gun bans are unconstitutional. Bans on substances (for instance, marijuana) and vice (for instance, gambling and prostitution) have had similar results. Regulating legitimate gun dealers can only have a minimal impact on gun crimes because only a few FFLs are a source for the majority of guns that get into the hands of criminals. The same types of regulations used against hospitals and pharmacies indicate similar results. The vast majority of gun, and drug, offenders get their guns, or drugs, from illegitimate sources. The empirical research on gun buyback programs indicates abysmal failure substantively, although communities seem to have positive attitudes toward these programs. A similar policy used by police agencies is traffic ticket amnesty days, where individuals who have traffic citations can pay without the threat of being arrested.

Sentencing enhancement strategies are utilized across the criminal justice system with regard to various forms of criminality. Career criminal sentencing enhancements, as well as drug enhancements and violent crime enhancements, are all mechanisms to increase prison sentences beyond the penalty for the actual criminal offense. Mandatory minimum sentencing and prosecution strategies found in the Project Safe Neighborhoods initiative have been shown to be either ineffective or have only modest effects on gun crime. The bulk of the research appears to indicate that any impacts associated with the application of mandatory minimum sentences comes from the announcement of these programs, not the programs themselves. Thus, sentencing enhancement strategies do not appear to be a comprehensive means of controlling gun crime in the United States.

One gun control program that lies outside of Zimring and Hawkins's conceptions of gun crime is concealed carry laws. Under the "more guns, less crime" thesis, gun crime should decrease with more gun carrying by private citizens. The empirical evidence does not support this contention. Concealed carry laws do not decrease crime substantially, especially in light of crime trends, violent and nonviolent, that have been decreasing since 1994.

The only gun control policy aimed at reducing the level of crime in the United States and supported by the empirical literature is directed patrol strategies. Directed patrol, especially in Boston's Operation Ceasefire and PSN's partial use of directed patrol, appear to have the greatest benefits in reducing the incidence of gun-related crime.

Future Policy Directions

The remainder of this chapter examines several gun violence reduction strategies that might have an impact on violent crime in the future. The programs noted here include extensions of directed police patrol strategies, tracking private sales, personalizing weapons, and the collection of better data from various criminal justice agencies and businesses. These strategies have the best chance of curbing violent gun crime for the remainder of the twenty-first century.

Cook and Ludwig (2000) argue for an increase in the use of directed patrols. Because of the perceived successes of Boston's Operation Ceasefire and, to a limited extent, the Project Safe Neighborhoods Initiative, directed patrols to combat gun crime should be continued because they appear to have a good chance of reducing various forms of violent gun crime. The one way to tweak these types of programs is to include an announcement campaign in a coordinated effort to decrease gun crime.

Second, Cook and Ludwig note that one focus of gun control policy that has not been explored is the tracking of private sales, also known as universal background checks. If these types of sales could be regulated, it would hold owners accountable for selling, loaning, or giving firearms to would-be offenders. This policy change could be accomplished by mandating that all firearms sales be channeled through federally licensed dealers, making the FFLs responsible for a role they already have through the transfer of weapons they sell on a regular basis. Cook and Ludwig (2000) estimate that this strategy could impact the transfer of two million guns per year. The primary problem with this approach is that the gun lobby would be adamantly opposed to the perceived infringement of gun rights. Therefore, although this approach has the ability to impede criminals from obtaining firearms, it would undoubtedly be controversial. In addition, it would take one to two generations to account for the multitude of guns that are currently available from private parties.

Third, in relation to emerging technology, the personalization of weapons will be important in curbing gun crime. As Cook and Ludwig note, the personalizing of weapons through technological developments will nullify the ability of criminals to steal weapons and then use them in the commission of crimes. This is important as the black market and gun theft is responsible for a significant number of gun transfers every year. Emerging gun personalization technology, using fingerprints, could have a substantial effect on gun crimes.

Finally, data is very limited and decentralized when it comes to guns, gun tracking, and gun crime. Cook and Ludwig argue for an expansion of criminal justice data to track guns, gun crime, and gun seizures. Not only does data need to be expanded to allow criminologists to better explore the relationship among firearms, criminals, and gun-related crime, the data that is collected by various federal and state agencies need to be better coordinated so that various agency databases can be integrated to further the goal of combating violent gun crime in the United States.

References

Berk, R. A. 2005. "Knowing When to Fold 'em: An Essay on Evaluating the Impact of Ceasefire, Compstat, and Exile." *Criminology and Public Policy* 4: 451–466.

Braga, A. A., P. K. Cook, D. M. Kennedy, and M. H. Moore. 2002. "The Illegal Supply of Firearms." *Crime and Justice* 29: 319–352.

Braga, A. A., D. M. Kennedy, E. J. Waring, and A. M. Piehl. 2001. "Problem-Oriented Policing, Deterrence, and Youth Violence: An Evaluation of Boston's Operation Ceasefire." *Journal of Research in Crime and Delinquency* 38: 195–225.

Braga, A. A., G. L. Pierce, J. McDevitt, B. J. Bond, and S. Cronin. 2008. "The Strategic Prevention of Gun Violence among Gang-Involved Offenders." *Justice Quarterly* 25: 132–162.

Britt, C. L., G. Kleck, and D. J. Bordua. 1996. "A Reassessment of the D.C. Gun Law: Some Cautionary Notes on the Use of Interrupted Time Series Designs for Policy Impact Assessment." *Law and Society Review* 30: 361–380.

Callahan, C. M., F. P. Rivara, and T. D. Koepsell. 1994. "Money for Guns: Evaluation of the Seattle Gun Buy-Back Program." *Public Health Reports* 109: 472–477.

Cook, P. J., and J. H. Laub. 1998. "The Unprecedented Epidemic in Youth Violence." In *Crime and Justice: An Annual Review of Research*. Edited by M. Tonry. Chicago: University of Chicago Press.

Cook, P. J., and J. Ludwig. 2000. *Gun Violence: The Real Costs*. New York: Oxford University Press.

Decker, S. H., G. D. Curry, S. Catalano, A. Watkins, and L. Green. 2005. *Strategic Approaches to Community Safety Initiative (SACSI) in St. Louis*. Washington, DC: US Department of Justice.

Decker, S. H., B. M. Hueber, A. Watkins, L. Green, T. Bynum, and E. F. McGarrell. 2007. *Project Safe Neighborhoods: Strategic Interventions. Eastern District of Missouri: Case Study 7*. Washington, DC: US Department of Justice.

Donohue, J. J. 2003. "The Impact of Concealed-Carry Laws." In *Evaluating Gun Policy: Effects on Crime and Violence*. Edited by J. Ludwig and P. J. Cook. Washington, DC: Brookings Institution Press (287–325).

Eck, J. E., and E. Maguire. 2000. "Have Changes in Policing Reduced Violent Crime? An Assessment of the Evidence." In *The Crime Drop in America*. Edited by A. Blumstein and J. Wallman. Cambridge, MA: Cambridge University Press.

Harlow, C. W. 2001. *Firearm Use by Offenders*. Washington, DC: Bureau of Justice Statistics.

Jones, E. D. 1981. "The District of Columbia's 'Firearm Control Registration Act of 1975:' The Toughest Handgun Control Law in the United States—Or Is It?" *Annals of the Academy of Political and Social Science* 455: 138–149.

Kaplan, J. 1981. "The Wisdom of Gun Prohibition." *Annals of the Academy of Political and Social Science* 455: 11–23.

Koper, C. S. 2002. "Federal Legislation and Gun Markets: How Much Have Recent Reforms of the Federal Firearms Licensing System Reduced Criminal Gun Suppliers?" *Criminology and Public Policy* 1: 151–178.

LaPierre, W. 1994. *Guns, Crime, and Freedom.* Washington, DC: Regnery Publishing.

Lizotte, A. J., and M. S. Zatz. 1986. "The Use and Abuse of Sentence Enhancement for Firearms Offenses in California." *Law and Contemporary Problems* 49: 199–221.

Loftin, C., and D. McDowall. 1981. "'One with a Gun Gets You Two:' Mandatory Sentencing and Firearms Violence in Detroit." *Annals of the Academy of Political and Social Science* 455: 150–167.

Loftin, C., D. McDowall, B. Wiersema, and T. J. Cottey. 1991. "Effects of Restrictive Licensing of Handguns on Homicide and Suicide in the District of Columbia." *New England Journal of Medicine* 325: 1615–1630.

Lott, J. R., Jr. 2000. *More Guns, Less Crime: Understanding Crime and Gun Control Laws.* Second edition. Chicago: University of Chicago Press.

Lott, J. R., Jr., and D. B. Mustard. 1997. "Crime, Deterrence, and Right-to-Carry Concealed Handguns." *Journal of Legal Studies* 26:1–68.

Ludwig, J. 2005. "Better Gun Enforcement, Less Crime." *Criminology and Public Policy* 4: 677–716.

McDevitt, J., A. Bragga, S. Cronin, E. F. McGarrell, and T. Bynum. 2007. *Project Safe Neighborhoods: Strategic Interventions. Lowell, District of Massachusetts: Case Study 6.* Washington, DC: US Department of Justice.

McDowall, D., C. Loftin, and B. Wiersema. 1992. "A Comparative Study of the Preventive Effects of Mandatory Sentencing Laws for Gun Crimes." *Journal of Criminal Law and Criminology* 83: 378–394.

McGarrell, E. F., N. K. Hipple, N. Corsaro, E. Papanastos, E. Stevens, and J. Albritton. 2007. *Project Safe Neighborhoods: Strategic Interventions. Middle District of Alabama: Case Study 5.* Washington, DC: US Department of Justice.

McGarrell, E. F., H. K. Hipple, N. Corsaro, T. S. Bynum, H. Perez, C. A. Zimmerman, and M. Garmo. 2009. *Project Safe Neighborhoods: A National Program to Reduce Gun Crime—Final Project Report.* Washington, DC: US Department of Justice.

Moore, M. H. 1981. "Keeping Handguns from Criminal Offenders." *Annals of the Academy of Political and Social Science* 455: 92–109.

O'Shea, T. C. 2007. "Getting the Message Out: The Project Safe Neighborhoods Public-Private Partnership." *Police Quarterly* 10: 288–307.

Pierce, G. L., and W. J. Bowers. 1981. "The Bartley-Fox Gun Law's Short-Term Impact on Crime in Boston." *Annals of the Academy of Political and Social Science* 455: 120–137.

Rand, M. R., M. DeBerry, and P. Klaus. 1986. *The Use of Weapons in Committing Crimes.* Washington, DC: Bureau of Justice Statistics.

Raphael, S., and J. Ludwig. 2003. *Evaluating Gun Policy: Effects on Crime and Violence.* Washington, DC: Brookings Institution.

Renshaw, B. H. 1981. *Violent Crime in the United States.* Washington, DC: Bureau of Justice Statistics.

Rosenfeld, R. 2000. "Patterns in Adult Homicide: 1980–1995." In *The Crime Drop in America.* Edited by A. Blumstein and J. Wallman. Cambridge: Cambridge University Press, 130–163.

Rosenfeld, R., R. Fornango, and E. Baumer. 2005. "Did Ceasefire, Compstat, and Exile Reduce Homicide?" *Criminology and Public Policy* 2: 419–450.

Sheley, J. F., and J. D. Wright. 1995. *In the Line of Fire: Youth, Guns, and Violence in Urban America.* Hawthorne, NY: Aldine de Gruyter.

Sherman, L. W., J. W. Shaw, and D. P. Rogan. 1995. *The Kansas City Gun Experiment.* Washington, DC: National Institute of Justice.

Smith, T. W. 2000. *1999 National Gun Policy Survey of the National Opinion Research Center: Research Findings.* Chicago: University of Chicago Press.

Timrots, A. D., and M. R. Rand. 1987. *Violent Crime by Strangers and Nonstrangers.* Washington, DC: Bureau of Justice Statistics.

Walker, S. 2006. *Sense and Nonsense about Crime and Drugs.* Belmont, CA: Thompson Wadsworth.

Wellford, C. F., J. V. Pepper, and C. V. Petrie. 2004. *Firearms and Violence: A Critical Review.* Washington, DC: National Academies Press.

Wintemute, G. 2000. "Guns and Gun Violence." In *The Crime Drop in America.* Edited by A. Blumstein and J. Wallman. Cambridge: Cambridge University Press.

Wright, J. D. 1986. *The Armed Criminal in America.* Washington, DC: Bureau of Justice Statistics.

Wright, J. D., and P. H. Rossi. 1986. *Armed and Considered Dangerous: A Survey of Felons and Their Firearms.* Hawthorne, NY: Aldine de Gruyter.

Wright, J. D., P. H. Rossi, and K. Daly. 1994. *Under the Gun: Weapons, Crime, and Violence in America.* Hawthorne, NY: Aldine de Gruyter.

Zawitz, M. W. 1995. *Guns Used in Crime.* Washington, DC: Bureau of Justice Statistics.

Zimring, F. E., and G. Hawkins. 1996. "Is American Violence a Crime Problem?" *Duke Law Journal* 46: 43–72.

Zimring, F. E., and G. Hawkins. 1997. *Crime Is Not the Problem: Lethal Violence in America.* New York: Oxford University Press.

CHAPTER SEVEN

Background Checks for Purchasing Firearms

Glenn H. Utter

Researchers often have questioned the effectiveness of public policy, as well as the ability to measure accurately the consequences of policy change. Gun control measures are certainly no exception. Franklin E. Zimring (1975), evaluating the results of the Gun Control Act of 1968 (GCA) after the law had been in effect for five years, noted the obvious flaw in the law's intent to keep firearms out of the hands of individuals in prohibited categories, such as convicted felons, "mental defectives," and drug users. In the Senate Report (No. 90-1097) on the Gun Control Act, the objectives of the legislation were described: "The principal purposes . . . are to aid in making it possible to keep firearms out of the hands of those not legally entitled to possess them because of age, criminal background, or incompetency, and to assist law enforcement authorities in the States and their subdivisions in combating the increasing prevalence of crime in the United States."

However, under the law as originally passed, gun dealers, lacking any mechanism for verifying the truthfulness of purchasers' statements, essentially took the word of customers that they were not disqualified from acquiring a firearm. The only means of enforcing the restrictions would involve law enforcement discovering (perhaps through investigating a robbery or shooting) that the law breaker possessed a firearm that had been acquired by making false statements on the form he or she was required to complete. Zimring stated that an alternative to this highly questionable and inefficient process would involve "creating separate screening procedures"

(153). Anticipating the Brady Law, he suggested the establishment of a system in which dealers submitted information about prospective purchases to a federal agency, which would check a "central record file" to determine whether the customer was eligible to purchase a firearm. Given the status of electronic databases at the time, Zimring concluded that background checks would require an extended waiting period before a firearm transfer could proceed, and referred to such a proposed background check system as "cumbersome" (153). Zimring concluded that the system of regulation that the 1968 law established was "of limited use in making firearms more difficult for ineligible classes to obtain, but the federal prohibitions and record-keeping requirement made it possible to convict persons ineligible to have guns if they were later apprehended with a firearm" (153). The law became potentially useful only after the fact, focusing on prosecution of violators after a crime had been committed. There might be a minimal deterrent effect produced by the awareness on the part of violators that they possessed a firearm illegally and that they could be prosecuted for that violation alone at some indeterminate future time.

Zimring noted that since passage of the Gun Control Act in 1968, gun violence rates and the proportion of violent acts committed with firearms had increased significantly. He attributed this increase in part to handgun ownership becoming a "subcultural institution" in larger cities "which are the main arena of American violence" (195). Given the role of handguns in violent acts, Zimring asserted that further action on gun control required a focus on handguns. He was critical of the decentralized process by which records of gun sales are kept by dealers (197). Given the limitations of the 1968 law, and referring to Congress as a policy-making institution, he concluded that "the Gun Control Act of 1968 may stand as an example of the blind leading the blind" (198).

Legislative History

If certain individuals are to be prohibited from owning or purchasing a firearm, a process for identifying such individuals would obviously have to be developed. Prior to passage of the Brady Handgun Violence Prevention Act in 1993, no such system at the national level existed. The Federal Firearms Act of 1938 (52 Stat. 1250) required that, for the modest fee of one dollar, firearm manufacturers, importers, and dealers obtain a federal firearms license from the Internal Revenue Service. The law mandated that federally licensed dealers maintain records of the names and addresses of those who purchased firearms and prohibited firearm sales to individuals known by a federally licensed firearm dealer to be fugitives from justice, felons, under indictment for a felony, or prohibited by state law from purchasing firearms (Cook and Goss 2014, 99). However, no procedure for determining such information was included in the law.

Supporters worked for seven years to bring about congressional passage of the Brady Bill, which supporters hoped would remedy the weaknesses that Zimring observed in the Gun Control Act of 1968. In February 1987 a bill to require background checks and a waiting period for the purchase of a handgun was first introduced in Congress, but faced strong opposition from President Ronald Reagan and other influential public figures as well as gun rights organizations such as the National Rifle Association (NRA). Although the bill reached the floor of the U.S. House of Representatives in September 1988, strong NRA opposition, including the submission of amendments to the bill by congressional opponents, doomed the legislative effort (Vizzard 2000, 134). Representative Bill McCollum, a strong supporter of gun rights, introduced an alternative proposal, supported by the NRA, that called for the attorney general to create an instant criminal background check system that involved firearms dealers accessing a computer database maintained by the Justice Department in order to determine the eligibility of individuals to purchase a firearm (Patterson and Eakins 1998, 55). The House of Representatives approved McCollum's substitute bill, thus effectively killing the original proposal. In 1990 the bill again came before Congress. The House and Senate passed different versions of the legislation, but although a conference committee reached a compromise, which the House approved, opponents in the Senate mounted a successful filibuster effort and the legislation failed once again.

Following the 1992 election, in which Bill Clinton was elected president, the bill to institute background checks for firearm purchases again came before Congress. During the 1992 presidential campaign, Clinton had expressed support for passage of the proposal. With the backing of various interests, including legal and medical associations, trade unions, and law enforcement organizations, the prospects for the legislation were revived. James Brady, President Ronald Reagan's press secretary who was severely wounded during an attempt in 1981 to assassinate the president, became a vocal supporter, along with his wife Sarah, of the legislation, which became known as the Brady Bill. Brady often referred to the difficulties he faced as a victim of gun violence, for instance commenting that the aggravation that members of Congress experienced due to the lobbying of the NRA did not compare to the aggravation he experienced each day (Patterson and Eakins 1998, 56).

The House voted in favor of the legislation, as did the Senate. However, the Senate approved an amendment to the bill that called for an end to the five-day waiting period after five years and the establishment of an instant background check system (Vizzard 2000, 136). The amendment became part of the final bill after a conference committee resolved differences between the House and Senate versions. Representative Bill McCollum proposed an amendment that would preempt states from instituting their own waiting periods after the instant check system became operational, but the House rejected this amendment (Patterson and Eakins 1998, 57). Each chamber approved the legislation on November 24, and President Clinton signed the bill on November 30, 1993.

The resulting law, a product of compromise between supporters and opponents, included a waiting period of five days before a handgun purchase could be completed. Called a "cooling-off period," the waiting period, in addition to allowing time to run background checks, was intended to discourage purchases in the heat of the moment and by those who might be contemplating suicide. However, the waiting period would continue only for five years, at which time the Justice Department would begin an instant check system. The inclusion of an expiration date for the waiting period certainly was a compromise for supporters of the legislation. One of the goals of gun control advocates was to deter rash purchases of firearms that could be used in highly emotional circumstances, such as suicide and quarrels between intimate partners. Therefore, limiting the waiting period represented a weakening of a significant goal of supporters. However, gun rights advocates argued that individuals, in imminent need of protection, would not be able to acquire a firearm when most needed if they were required to delay the purchase. They also emphasized the inconvenience a waiting period would be for law-abiding citizens when making a firearm purchase.

In order to gain congressional passage of the Brady Act, gun control supporters followed a strategy of accommodating the concerns of gun rights advocates, a tactic that subsequently resulted in a weakened system for limiting firearms sales to law-abiding citizens and preventing the acquisition of firearms by certain prohibited groups originally defined in the Gun Control Act of 1968. A key weakness in the legislation was that the bill applied only to the sale of handguns by federally licensed firearm dealers, thus excluding any transfers by private persons, which amounted to an estimated 40 percent of firearm transfers each year (Wintemute 2013, 20). As William Vizzard (2000, 134) concludes, "This [limitation] greatly reduced any potential inconvenience to the vast majority of gun owners, but also created a massive hole in the buyer-screening system." Vizzard also notes that, at least initially, the law mandated that federal firearms licensees send information about buyers to local law enforcement officers instead of to a centralized federal agency, a policy that reduced concerns among gun rights supporters about expanding the power of the federal government. Therefore, checks were being conducted by thousands of state and local agencies without the uniformity of policy application that the federal government could provide.

Jay Printz, sheriff of Ravilli County, Montana, and Richard Mack, sheriff of Graham County, Arizona, challenged the federal mandate that they conduct background checks, arguing that the mandate was unconstitutional. In 1997 the U.S. Supreme Court, in *Printz v. United States* (521 US 898, 1997), declared this background check system an unconstitutional violation of the Tenth Amendment to the U.S. Constitution in that the federal government required local officials to carry out a federal policy and hence violated the federal system of governing that allotted a level of independence to states from the national government. The decision ultimately was interpreted to have minimal effect on the conduct of background checks, given that the federal Department of Justice in November 1998 initiated the permanent provisions of the Brady Law establishing the National Instant Criminal Background Check System (NICS). However, due to the *Printz* decision, the federal government could not mandate that state and local governments provide records to the NICS, and must rely on the voluntary participation of these governments (Price and Norris 2008, 123). The federal government was severely limited in the length of time (ultimately just 24 hours) that background check information resulting from approved purchases could be maintained by the federal government.

Operation of the Brady Law

The Brady Law established the legal requirement that federally licensed firearms dealers initiate a background check to determine whether a prospective firearm purchaser is prohibited from acquiring a gun. The act originally contained two sections: 102(a), an interim section, and 102(b), a permanent section. According to the interim section, to go into effect 90 days after the bill was enacted, and ending five years (60 months) following enactment, the firearms dealer (transferer) was required to receive from the purchaser (transferee) a statement containing the name, address, and date of birth as this information appears on a valid identification document of the transferee. The document must contain a photograph of the transferee and a description of the identification used [section 102(a)(s)(3)]. The dealer is required to verify the identification of the purchaser by examining the document. The dealer must then provide "notice of the contents of the statement to the chief law enforcement officer of the place of residence of the transferee" [section 102(a)(s)(1)(A)(i)(III-IV)]. The law then mandates that the chief law enforcement officer make a reasonable effort to complete a criminal background check on the purchaser within five business days. If no disqualifying information has been discovered, the firearm transfer may continue.

The purchaser may also present to the dealer a statement issued by the chief law enforcement officer of the purchaser's place of residence stating that the purchaser requires possession of a handgun for self-protection and for protection of the immediate family, a provision that reflects the concerns of gun rights advocates that individuals have quick access, if need be, to the means of self-protection. The purchaser also may present to the dealer a permit that allows the purchaser to acquire and possess a handgun. The permit must have been issued not more than five years prior to the current purchase, and the prospective purchaser has not subsequently forfeited the right to purchase a firearm, such as by committing an action that places the transferee in one of the prohibited categories. Further provisions in the Act allow the purchase if conducting a background check is impractical due to insufficient law enforcement personnel, the remoteness of the dealer's premises, or the lack of communications facilities at the location of the business.

Additional categories of those prohibited from purchasing a firearm have been approved by Congress. The Violent Crime Control Act of 1994 prohibited the purchase or possession of a firearm by anyone subject to a restraining order protecting an intimate partner or a child of an intimate partner (Price and Norris 2008, 128). In 1996 Congress passed the Lautenberg Amendment, named for Senator Frank Lautenberg (D-NJ), the sponsor of the measure, which prohibited the purchase or possession of a firearm by persons who have been convicted of a misdemeanor crime of domestic violence (Cook and Goss 2014, 106).

Vizzard (2000, 136) concludes that "the Brady bill did not constitute a significant policy change." Although the law established a national standard for determining the eligibility requirements for purchasing a firearm, Vizzard claims that "the bill failed to take advantage of the reporting process to establish a national gun-sales registry" because records were to be kept by firearm dealers themselves. However, had such a gun registry been included in the bill, undoubtedly gun rights supporters, led by the National Rifle Association and other gun rights organizations, would have lobbied fiercely—and certainly successfully—to defeat the legislation.

The Gun Control Act of 1968 (82 Stat. 1213), which replaced the Federal Firearms Act of 1938, included prohibitions on the sale of firearms to certain excluded groups, including the sale of long-gun ammunition to anyone under 18 years of age, or handgun ammunition to any person less than 21 years of age.

Firearms Transactions Record (Form 4473)

(available at https://atf.gov/content/firearms/firearms-industry/applications-eform-4473)

Anyone who has purchased a firearm from a federally licensed firearms dealer has filled out a Form 4473, the Firearms Transaction Record. Section A of the form requires the purchaser to provide basic information, including his or her full name, current residence address (number and street, city, county, state, and zip code), place of birth (U.S. city and state, or foreign country), height, weight, gender, and birth date. Providing the purchaser's social security number is optional (question 8), but the form states that including it "will help prevent misidentification." Under certain circumstances, a purchaser will acquire a "unique personal identification number" issued by the Federal Bureau of Investigation NICS Voluntary Appeal File which can be provided in response to question 9. As the instructions for question 9 state, "For purchasers approved to have information maintained about them in the FBI NICS Voluntary Appeal File, NICS will provide them with a Unique Personal Identification Number, which the buyer should record in question 9. The licensee [dealer] may be asked to provide the UPIN to NICS or the State." Question 10 asks whether the applicant is Hispanic or Latino (10a) and further asks for race classification (10b). Crucial eligibility criteria to purchase a firearm are determined in question 11, beginning with whether the applicant is the actual buyer. The form states, "If you are not the actual buyer, the dealer cannot transfer the firearm(s) to you." Thus the form makes clear to a potential "straw purchaser"—someone who intends to acquire a firearm for someone else who is disqualified from purchasing a gun—that such an act is illegal. Questions 11b through 11k include the list of disqualifying conditions. Answering "yes" to any of these prohibits the applicant from purchasing a firearm.

Currently, Congress has determined that ten categories of individuals are prohibited from purchasing a firearm from a federally licensed firearm dealer, including any person who:

1. is under indictment for, or has been convicted of, a crime punishable by imprisonment for more than one year;
2. is a fugitive from justice;

3. is an unlawful user of, or addicted to, a controlled substance;
4. has been adjudicated as a "mental defective" or has been committed to a mental institution;
5. is an illegal alien or has been admitted to the United States under a non-immigrant visa;
6. was dishonorably discharged from the U.S. Armed Forces;
7. has renounced U.S. citizenship;
8. is subject to a court order restraining him or her from harassing, stalking, or threatening an intimate partner or child;
9. has been convicted of a misdemeanor crime of domestic violence;
10. is under age 18 for a long gun purchase or under age 21 for a handgun purchase. (Lee, Frandsen, Naglich, and Lauver 2010)

Question 13 asks for the purchaser's state of residence, and question 14 asks for country of citizenship. If the applicant is not a U.S. citizen, question 15 requests the applicant's "U.S.-issued alien number or admission number." On lines 16 and 17 the purchaser signs and dates the form, certifying that the answers provided "are true, correct, and complete."

The firearm seller completes Section B of the form. The seller identifies the type of gun being transferred (handgun, long gun, or "other"), whether the sale is occurring at a gun show, and if so, the name and location of the event, the type of identification the purchaser has shown to the dealer, including the expiration date and possible other identification documents. On line 21a the seller registers the date on which the seller transmitted the purchaser's information provided in Section A to the NICS or to the state agency (if a point of contact state), and, "if provided," records the NICS or state transaction number on line 21b. On line 21c, the dealer records the initial response the NICS or "the appropriate state agency" provided (either Proceed [with the transaction], Denied, Cancelled, or Delayed (for up to three days). If a delay occurs, it is usually to allow greater time to complete the background check. After three business days, even if there is no response from the system, the dealer may continue with the sale. However, such delays have proven infrequent, with more than 95 percent of checks completed within a few minutes (Spitzer 2015, 159). If the NICS has issued a "Proceed" response, the dealer may conclude the sale and then record that response and the date it was received on line 21e. Lines 22 and 23 deal with the situation in which a National Firearms Act firearm (for instance, an automatic weapon) is involved, or if the purchaser has shown a valid firearm permit issued by the state in which the transaction occurred, which in some states may substitute for a NICS background check (see Table 7.1).

Table 7.1 State Policies on Firearm Purchases

State	Point of Contact	Private Sellers	Waiting Period	Gun Purchase Limit	NICS Exempt with State Permit
Alabama	NO	NO	NO	NO	NO
Alaska	NO	NO	NO	NO	YES
Arizona	NO	NO	NO	NO	YES
Arkansas	NO	NO	NO	NO	YES
California	YES	YES	YES (10 days, all firearms)	YES (one handgun every 30 days)	YES (Entertainment Firearms Permit only)
Colorado	YES	YES	NO	NO	NO
Connecticut	YES	YES (Gun shows)	NO	NO	NO
Delaware	NO	YES	NO	NO	NO
Florida	YES	NO	YES (3 days, handguns)	NO	NO
Georgia	NO	NO	NO	NO	YES
Hawaii	YES	YES	YES (14 days, all firearms)	NO	YES
Idaho	NO	NO	NO	NO	YES
Illinois	YES	YES (Gun shows)	YES (24 hours, long guns; 72 hours, handguns)	NO	NO
Indiana	NO	NO	NO	NO	NO
Iowa	Partial (handguns)	YES (handguns)	YES (3 days, handguns)	NO	YES
Kansas	NO	NO	NO	NO	YES

(Continued)

Table 7.1 *(Continued)*

State	Point of Contact	Private Sellers	Waiting Period	Gun Purchase Limit	NICS Exempt with State Permit
Kentucky	NO	NO	NO	NO	YES
Louisiana	NO	NO	NO	NO	NO
Maine	NO	NO	NO	NO	NO
Maryland	Partial (handguns & assault weapons)	YES	YES (7 days, handguns)	YES (one handgun or assault weapon every 30 days)	NO
Massachusetts	NO—but requires a state license	NO	NO	YES (private sellers limited to 4 gun sales per year)	NO
Michigan	Partial (handguns)	NO	NO	NO	YES
Minnesota	NO	NO	NO	NO	NO
Mississippi	NO	NO	NO	NO	YES
Missouri	NO	NO	NO	NO	NO
Montana	NO	NO	NO	NO	YES
Nebraska	Partial (handguns)	YES (handguns)	NO	NO	YES
Nevada	YES	NO	NO	NO	YES
New Hampshire	Partial (handguns)	NO	NO	NO	NO
New Jersey	YES	NO	YES (7 days, handguns)	YES (one handgun every 30 days)	NO
New Mexico	NO	NO	NO	NO	NO
New York	NO	YES	NO	NO	NO

State	Partial (handguns)				
North Carolina	NO	YES (handguns)	NO	NO	YES
North Dakota	NO	NO	NO	NO	YES
Ohio	NO	NO	NO	NO	NO
Oklahoma	NO	NO	NO	NO	NO
Oregon	YES	NO	NO	NO	NO
Pennsylvania	YES	YES (handguns)	NO	NO	NO
Rhode Island	NO	YES	YES (7 days, all firearms)	NO	NO
South Carolina	NO	NO	NO	NO	YES
South Dakota	NO	NO	NO	NO	NO
Tennessee	YES	NO	NO	NO	NO
Texas	NO	NO	NO	NO	YES
Utah	YES	NO	NO	NO	YES
Vermont	NO	NO	NO	NO	NO
Virginia	YES	NO	NO	YES (one gun per month, 1993–2012)	NO
Washington	Partial (handguns)	NO	NO	NO	YES
West Virginia	NO	NO	NO	NO	YES
Wisconsin	YES	NO	YES (48 hours, handguns)	NO	NO
Wyoming	NO	NO	NO	NO	YES

In Section C, the purchaser is asked to sign the form once more if the firearm transfer occurs on a date different from that on which the purchaser initially signed Section A. In Section D, the dealer records the firearms being transferred to the buyer, including the name of the manufacturer and/or importer, the model number and serial number of each firearm, the type of gun, and the caliber or gauge. If the purchaser receives multiple firearms, the dealer (licensee) is instructed to complete ATF Form 3310.4 (available at https://www.atf.gov/firearms/faq/licenses-conduct-of-business .html#atf-f-3310-4). That form's instructions state: "This form is to be used by licensees to report all transactions in which an unlicensed person [private purchaser] acquired two or more pistols or revolvers or any combination of pistols or revolvers totaling two or more at one time or during five consecutive business days." In addition to the name of the recipient ("transferee") of the firearms, the dealer must report the recipient's residence address, ethnicity ("Hispanic or Latino" or "Not Hispanic or Latino"), race, and date and place of birth. If the buyer is "authorized to act on behalf of a corporation, company, association, partnership or other such business entity," the dealer is instructed to provide the name and address of that organization.

On line 33 of Form 4473, the dealer certifies that answers provided in Sections B and D are "True, correct, and complete," and that on the basis of information the purchaser provided, "it is my belief that it is not unlawful for me to sell, deliver, transport, or otherwise dispose of the firearm(s) on this form to the person identified in Section A."

The background check system relies on three major data sources: the NICS Index, the Interstate Identification Index (III), and the National Crime Information Center (NCIC). The NICS Index includes disqualifying records on those—including persons dishonorably discharged from the military, adjudicated a mental defective, or convicted of immigration violations—who would not be included in the III or NCIC data sources. The Interstate Identification Index contains criminal history records of those arrested and convicted of felonies and certain serious misdemeanors. The NCIC includes law enforcement files of fugitives and, among others, individuals subject to restraining orders. This data source also contains the Violent Gang and Terrorist Organization File (VGTOF). In 2009 the Federal Bureau of Investigation created a file for "known and appropriately suspected terrorists (KST) (Krouse 2012, 81). Krouse states that "Effective February 2004 the Brady background check system was changed to include a terrorist watch list check and to alert NICS staff when a prospective firearms transferee or permit applicant is potentially identified as a known or suspected terrorist." However, the U.S. attorney general has no statutory authority to employ the terrorist watch list as a screening device for prospective firearms buyers (Krouse 2012, 82). Certain legislators have expressed skepticism about using the terrorist watch list to disqualify individuals from purchasing firearms—the so-called Terrorist Gap proposal. Opponents, such as Senator Lindsey Graham (R-SC), have noted that a legal determination of disqualification, such as a felony conviction in a court, differed significantly from a terrorist watch list that an intelligence analyst has created, without any formal legal sanction resulting from the due process of law. Nonetheless, supporters of adding people placed on the terrorist watch list to the records of those prohibited from purchasing or possessing a firearm argue that such persons may represent a real danger and should not be allowed to purchase firearms.

The Brady Law contains a provision that prohibits the sharing of a background check record with any other federal or state agency, and also prohibits using the Brady background check system as a national registry of firearms or firearm owners (Krouse 2012, 82). Gun rights groups were successful in preventing what they consider a totally unacceptable outcome: the possibility that background checks might be used to establish a de facto firearm registry. Beginning in 2003, a limitation on the information that the Bureau of Alcohol, Tobacco, Firearms, and Explosives could provide to state and local governments or to make public generally was introduced as an amendment to the Justice Department appropriations. It was called the Tiahrt amendment after Todd Tiahrt (R-KS), the congressman who introduced the measure. Among other things, the amendment formalized the policy of the George W. Bush administration of destroying the National Instant Criminal Background Check records after twenty-four hours. Opponents argued that deleting the records so quickly made it more difficult to discover false statements on the background check form and to determine if the persons purchasing firearms are the true recipients, or "straw purchases." Gun rights organizations, on the other hand, supported the amendment as a guarantee against a national gun registry and as a way of protecting gun dealers from excessive civil suits.

Limitations and Criticisms of Background Check Policy

Some gun rights advocates as well as gun control supporters have criticized the Brady background check system because the law requires only federal firearms licensees to run background checks. Prosecutions under the Brady Law are relatively rare. John R. Lott Jr. (2011), noted author of *More Guns, Less Crime*, estimates that the number of cases referred to prosecutors is extremely low, and the number of convictions in cases that went forward in 2010 was even lower: "only 32 convictions or pleas [sic] agreements." Just 13 of those convictions involved falsified information on the Firearms Transaction Record form 4473, which Lott calculates at 0.018 percent of the 71,010 denials in 2009. Lott states that the NICS denies gun purchases of many people who erroneously have been identified as included in one or more of the prohibited categories because they have the same name as someone legitimately in the record. However, the background check Form 4473 allows, but does not require, prospective purchasers to provide their social security number, which certainly would eliminate many false positives. According to Lott, for 2009 the NICS issued 71,010 denials. He quotes a U.S. Department of Justice report indicating that 66,329 (93 percent) of the denials "did not meet referral guidelines or were overturned after review by Brady operations or after the FBI received additional information." When additional false positives were discovered among those cases referred for further examination, Lott estimates a false positive rate of 94.2 percent.

The National Rifle Association also has criticized the Brady Law for the low number of prosecutions [at least during Bill Clinton's presidency (Henigan 2009, 146–147)]. Dennis Henigan, vice president for law and policy at the Brady Center to Prevent Gun Violence, states that convictions are rare because it is "difficult to prove that the prohibited person was aware of the prohibition and intentionally lied." In addition to preventing sales to prohibited persons who attempt to purchase a firearm from a federally licensed firearm dealer, the Brady Law can act as a deterrent in that many prohibited persons may not attempt to purchase a firearm from a federally licensed firearms dealer, knowing that they will likely be turned away and may be arrested for making false statements on Form 4473. In response, gun rights advocates argue that only "law-abiding" persons will conduct firearms transfers through a licensed firearms dealer, and that those with criminal intent, or those prohibited under law from purchasing a firearm will simply forgo the firearms dealer's background check by finding alternative sources. However, although gun rights advocates often consider the check as such ineffective in reducing the violent crime rate, gun control supporters argue that acquiring a firearm other than from a licensed dealer is more difficult than it is thought to be. They conclude that many disqualified persons, facing the background check roadblock, will simply not acquire a firearm from private persons who are not required to conduct a background check through the NICS. Gun control supporters also argue that the system can be made even more effective by extending the background check requirement to sales between private persons.

Soon after implementation of the Brady Law, James B. Jacobs and Kimberly A. Potter (1995) conducted an evaluation of the law and its prospects for success. According to Jacobs and Potter, reliance on federally licensed firearms dealers to enforce the law constitutes one difficulty with the legislation. They refer to the regulatory system as "all smoke and mirrors" (104). Any person wishing to receive a license must submit to the Bureau of Alcohol, Tobacco, Firearms, and Explosives a photograph and fingerprints, complete and sign an application stating that he or she is not disqualified from purchasing and possessing firearms, and provide a business name, location, and business hours (104). Unless the ATF discovers a false or inaccurate statement on the application, the bureau must issue a license. The authors note that, at that time, the ATF had to rely on limited information to determine relevant background information about the applicant. They observe that many licensees (nearly 300,000 at that time) do not operate a business, but wish to have the ability to purchase firearms through the mail (1995, 105–106). However, by 2013 the number of federally licensed dealers had declined to about 65,000, due largely to the increase in the fee charged to acquire a license to $200, with an annual renewal cost of $90 (Spitzer 2015, 159; 2012, 515).

Jacobs and Potter identify as a second difficulty with the Brady Law that a prospective firearm purchaser is not required to provide fingerprints, a surer form of identification than a piece of identification with a photograph. The authors observe that "There is a brisk market in such documents" (106) and that a dealer, provided with a poor photo, may nonetheless be hesitant to alienate a customer and lose a sale. Associated with problems of identification of the purchaser is a third difficulty: the possibility that the true purchaser might use a "straw man"—someone who is not prohibited from purchasing a firearm—to complete the purchase and then hand over the firearm to the disqualified person.

A fourth difficulty, which Jacobs and Potter consider the most significant (already mentioned above), is that the background check system applies only to federally licensed dealers and excludes the secondary market, which involves purchases "from a street dealer, friend, relative, or person advertising in the newspaper" (107). This limitation of the law has continued to attract the attention of those who want to make the background check more effective by expanding the system to cover such transfers not currently covered by the Brady law.

Josh Sugarmann and Kristen Rand of the Violence Policy Center, who support more stringent regulation of firearms, have expressed reservations about the Brady Law, calling background checks "for the most part nugatory in stopping firearms misuse" (Sugarmann and Rand 1997, 9). They offer three criticisms of the background check system. First, they state that those who are legally prohibited from purchasing a firearm from a federally licensed dealer seldom attempt to purchase a firearm from such a dealer. Instead, they find alternative sources for guns, including from private sellers, through straw man purchases, or by stealing them. Second, Sugarmann and Rand question the notion that the population can be neatly divided into two categories: those with a felony record and the "law-abiding." They argue that many have been arrested for serious crimes, but for various reasons have never been convicted and therefore are still legally eligible to purchase a firearm, even though they are at increased risk of committing violent crimes. Third, they assert that background checks have little effect in preventing suicides or gun-related violence among friends and family members because weapons used in such actions usually can be legally purchased prior to any suicide attempt or violent confrontation.

Don B. Kates (2005), a civil liberties attorney, gun rights advocate, and critic of background checks, argues that legal attempts to keep firearms out of the hands of those who commit violent crimes are doomed to failure. He mentions state laws, passed from the 1920s to the present, as well as the federal Gun Control Act of 1968, as examples of such failed attempts, concluding that "The crime history of 20th-century America makes it obvious that these laws are regularly flouted" (2005, 317). However, Kates fails to mention that the Gun Control Act, and likely most of the state provisions, lacked any effective enforcement mechanism such as a system of criminal background checks. Although not specifically mentioning the Brady Law, Kates, in agreement with many gun control supporters, argues that those prohibited from acquiring a firearm can avail themselves of many alternative sources: "Just as we are largely unable to prevent [aberrants] from committing murders so are we largely unable to prevent them from getting illegal guns" (323). Kates takes a further step in his argument against the objectives of gun control supporters, stating that "Attempting to disarm the general population will make things much worse" (324), which is a goal that most supporters of restrictions on firearm acquisition and possession undoubtedly do not advocate. Kates claims that those with criminal intent will be undeterred by legal restrictions on firearm acquisition from committing violent crimes and therefore basically law-abiding citizens who are potential victims of such crimes must not be denied the means of defending themselves. Kates shifts his focus between attempts to deny firearm acquisition by likely criminals and attempts to deny firearm ownership to all citizens (disarming the general population), a far more radical proposal that the U.S. Supreme Court [in *District of Columbia v. Heller* (554 US 270, 2008), and *McDonald v. Chicago* (561 US 742, 2010)] has declared unconstitutional and that the vast majority of gun control advocates does not support. Nonetheless, Kates's argument provides the clearest case against policies that attempt to keep firearms out of the hands of those most likely to commit violent crimes because ultimately the law-abiding citizen, and hence the potential victim of violent crime, may be denied the means of self-protection.

Lott's (2011) focus is on those potential purchasers who are inconvenienced by the background check system. In addition to the possibility of being falsely categorized as ineligible to purchase a firearm, many may face delayed responses from the NICS. Lott notes that eight percent of background checks do not result in immediate responses and that two-thirds of those delayed checks take as long as three days (the legal time limit for checks) to resolve. Gun control advocates have two major responses to Lott's criticism of the NICS. With regard to the inconvenience imposed on law-abiding citizens, James S. Brady, the presidential press secretary who was seriously wounded in the 1981 assassination attempt on President Ronald Reagan, commented about the argument regarding the background check being an inconvenience for firearm purchasers, "I need help getting out of bed, help taking a shower and help getting dressed, and—damn it—I need help going to the bathroom. I guess I'm paying for their inconvenience" (quoted in Barron 2014, A1). Gun rights supporters might counter, at least in part, that the person who shot Brady would not have been denied the purchase of a handgun under the NICS. The second response of gun control supporters, as mentioned previously, is that a key claim for the success of the NICS is the number of gun purchases by prohibited individuals that likely have been deterred by the background check requirement. The success of the deterrence effect depends on how easily a prohibited person can find alternative sources of firearms, which has led gun control advocates to support a comprehensive background check system (to be discussed later).

The Effect of the Background Check Policy on Violent Crime

Accurately determining the consequences (positive or negative—whether intended or not) of a given policy change can be extremely difficult and complex. The purpose of the federal mandate requiring federal firearms licensees to conduct background checks on prospective firearms purchasers, instituted by the Brady Law, is ultimately to reduce the rate of firearms-related violence—noting, as does the National Rifle Association's Institute for Legislative Action (1999)—that a large proportion of violent crimes do not involve firearms. In 1999, the NRAILA provided the estimate that fewer than 30 percent of violent crimes involve the use of firearms. One measure of the law's effectiveness is the percentage of applications (Form 4473) that are rejected as the result of the NICS check. William J. Krouse (2012, 29) observes that from December 1998 through 2009, of more than 95 million background checks conducted, the system rejected 1.6 million purchases, resulting in a denial rate of 1.68 percent. A measure that researchers are ultimately unable to use is the number of persons who, because they would fail the background check, did not attempt to purchase a firearm from a federally licensed firearms dealer. Determining the deterrent effect of the background check suffers from the same difficulty of any measure of deterrence: it is dependent on the non-occurrence of an event, whether that event is military aggression in international relations or in the present case the attempt to purchase a firearm.

Those critical of the Brady Law—both gun control supporters as well as gun rights advocates—argue that many of those deterred by the Brady Law requirement find a way around the background check restriction by acquiring firearms in the so-called secondary market. They acquire firearms from a private person who is not required to run a background check, or they steal guns, or have someone else, who can pass the background check (a "straw purchaser"), purchase a gun for them. Many gun rights supporters conclude that background checks represent a futile attempt to reduce gun-related violence while inconveniencing law-abiding purchasers; alternatively, advocates of gun control claim that the NICS has had some effect in reducing gun-related violence. For instance, the Violence Policy Center (2015) reported that analysis of 2013 data from the Centers for Disease Control and Prevention's National Center for Injury Prevention and Control indicated that states with "weak gun violence prevention laws and higher rates of gun ownership" (for instance, Alaska and Louisiana) have the "highest overall gun death rates in the nation." In contrast, states with stricter firearm laws and lower gun ownership rates (such as Hawaii and Massachusetts) have much lower rates of gun-related fatalities. Sumner, Layde, and Guse (2008), in a study of the association between firearm death rates and background checks conducted by different levels of government (federal, state, and local) from 2002 to 2004, concluded that the use of local-level agencies (for instance, police or sheriff's departments) resulted in a 27 percent lower suicide rate.

The most complex measure of the effectiveness of the background check policy is whether firearm-related violence declined, increased, or was not affected by the policy's application. At best, researchers employ a quasi-experimental research design, which must involve the statistical control of other variables such as region of the country, general level of crime, and drug related violations of the law, that might influence the level of violence independently of, or in concert with, the background checks process. Gary Kleck (1997), generally considered a critic of gun control measures, concludes his extensive analysis of firearms and gun control by stating that "most technically sound evidence indicates that most types of gun control have no measurable effect, for good or ill, on rates of most types of crime and violence." However, he mentions exceptions to this conclusion: measures that include background checks "appear to reduce rates of homicide and perhaps suicide"; banning gun possession by criminals "may reduce robbery and aggravated assault"; banning possession by the mentally ill "appears to reduce homicide and suicide"; local licensing of gun dealers "may reduce robbery, aggravated assault, and suicide"; mandatory penalties for illegal gun carrying "may reduce robbery;" and enhanced penalties for using a gun in the commission of a crime "may reduce homicide, robbery and rape" (Kleck 1997, 377).

Gun rights supporters continue to emphasize that the background check system—along with other limitations on firearm ownership—restricts the right of law-abiding citizens to purchase a firearm while at the same time those who would fail the background check find alternative sources for acquiring firearms. Hence, so goes the argument, we should expect no change in the rate of gun-related violence, or even expect an increase due to the advantage that law-breakers have over the average citizen who may be discouraged from purchasing a firearm due to the paperwork involved and possible delays, given that firearms can be used for defense and deterrence against crime as well as instruments of criminal activity. Kevin M. Cunningham, a lawyer working for the National Rifle Association, has argued that the Brady Law is "simply unworkable" because "criminals do not, to any appreciable degree, buy handguns from federally licensed firearms dealers" (Cunningham 1994, 59, 61; quoted in Henigan 2009, 14). However, Dennis Henigan argues that "the effectiveness of the Brady Act in curbing retail sales to criminals does not depend on the willingness of prospective murderers to obey the law" (Henigan 2009, 43) because, although there are alternative sources for firearms, such individuals, Henigan argues, find it relatively difficult to acquire firearms illegally. Henigan also claims that the Brady Law has been a key factor in the decline in violent crime, stating that, although violent crime rates began to decline just prior to passage of the Brady Act, "the use of firearms in violent crime did not begin its sharp decline until Brady's inaugural year of 1994" (2009, 44). This assertion undoubtedly is based on a relatively crude measurement that does not take into account other variables that could influence levels of violent crime.

NICS Improvement Amendments Act of 2007

The shooting at the Virginia Polytechnic Institute and State University, in which a mentally deranged student shot and killed 32 other students and teachers and wounded seventeen others, raised concerns in many quarters about the efficiency of the NICS in determining those who should be prevented from acquiring firearms. Many states were not providing the system with adequate data on the categories of individuals who were legally disqualified from purchasing a firearm—among them persons who have been adjudicated as mentally incompetent. Soon after the tragedy, Congress acted to improve the National Instant Criminal Background Check System. William J. Krouse (2012, 102) states that the resulting law "amends and strengthens a provision of the Brady Handgun Violence Prevention Act . . . that requires federal agencies to provide, and the Attorney General to secure, any government records with information relevant to determining the eligibility of a person to receive a firearm for inclusion in databases queried by NICS." Representative Carolyn McCarthy (D-NY), whose husband was murdered in 1993 by a gunman on the Long Island Railroad, was one of the key sponsors of the NICS Improvement Amendments Act. Representative Lamar Smith (R-TX) and John D. Dingall (D-MI), who had served as a member of the board of the National Rifle Association and who acted as a liaison with the NRA, co-sponsored the bill. Smith's support represented the bipartisan backing for the measure (Plank and Urbina 2007, A20). Wayne LaPierre, executive vice president of the NRA, expressed the support of his gun rights organization for greater efficiency in placing mental health records into the NICS. However, gun rights organizations were not unified in supporting the bill. Larry Pratt, executive director of Gun Owners of America, stated that his organization was concerned that the legislation would result in the denial of a civil liberty "without due process" (Luo 2007, A16). Some mental health officials (for instance, Price and Norris 2014) also raised questions about the bill, expressing concern that the legislation would weaken privacy laws and might not include provisions recognizing that people could be cured of their mental illness (Luo 2007, A16). Others expressed concern that veterans who have been diagnosed with post-traumatic stress disorder (PTSD) might be disqualified from acquiring a firearm. However, supporters of the legislation responded that such a diagnosis would not lead to disqualification (Krouse 2012, 104).

Concerns were also raised that people might not seek assistance for psychological difficulties if, as a result, they could be restricted from purchasing or possessing a firearm, perceiving such a restriction as a form of punishment. Federal law (Title 27, Code of Federal Regulations, section 478.1) states that the term "adjudicated a mental defective" involves a ruling by a court, board, commission, or other lawful authority that a person "as a result of marked subnormal intelligence or mental illness, incompetency, condition, or disease: (1) is a danger to himself or others, or (2) lacks the mental capacity to manage his own affairs. The term also includes (1) a finding of insanity by a court in a criminal case and (2) those persons found incompetent to stand trial or found not guilty by reason of lack of mental responsibility . . ." (Krouse 2012, 104).

In expressing its support for the Improvement Act bill, the NRA's Institute for Legislative Action focused comments primarily on the protection of the individual's right to acquire and possess a firearm (National Rifle Association, Institute for Legislative Action 2007). The Institute responded to the claim made by other gun rights groups that the legislation would prevent thousands of people from possessing a firearm, stating that "This is not true." The Institute asserted that the act would in fact expand gun rights because it "would allow some people now unfairly prohibited from owning guns to have their rights restored, and to have their names removed from the instant check system." At the insistence of the NRA, the bill included the right of any person to appeal inclusion in the NICS database, and also the right of appeal to have a person's right to possess firearms restored.

The Institute stated that gun ownership rights could be denied only if a person "is a danger to himself or others, or lacks the capacity to manage his own affairs." The organization noted that the legislation required all federal agencies that "impose mental health adjudications or commitments" to establish a procedure for "relief from disabilities." An individual would have the opportunity under the proposed law to correct any error in such adjudication, either through an appeal to the agency involved, or by way of the court system. If the appeal is granted, the prohibition on gun ownership must be removed. The Institute also emphasized the mandate that any state receiving funding under the legislation would be required to establish a relief from disabilities program for mental adjudications and commitments. If relief is granted, the state action would remove the individual from the federal record prohibiting gun possession. The Institute also expressed support for the bill because, by requiring federal agencies and participating states to provide more complete records, the background check system would be more complete and more accurate in determining which individuals should be included in the data bank of those prohibited from possessing firearms.

In addition, the Institute supported the legislation because it would require the removal of "expired, incorrect or otherwise irrelevant records."

The legislation also would prohibit any federal government fees charged for background checks, and mandate a Government Accountability Office audit of funds already allocated for improvements in the gathering of criminal history data.

In an obvious response to other gun rights organizations as well as mental health groups that opposed the legislation, the Institute emphasized that current federal law as well as the proposed legislation do not preclude gun possession by anyone who has voluntarily received psychological counseling or on their own initiative entered a hospital for mental health assistance. Only those, the Institute repeated, who are "adjudicated as a mental defective" or "committed to any mental institute" could be denied firearm ownership. Any person voluntarily seeking treatment for alcohol or drug use would not be included in the NICS records. Those engaged in recent illegal drug use, indicating that they are still involved with drug-related activity, are prohibited from possessing firearms. The Institute concluded: "No person who needs help for a mental health or substance abuse problem should be deterred from seeking that help due to fear of losing Second Amendment rights."

The Brady Campaign to Prevent Gun Violence, although opposed to NRA-supported provisions that were added to the legislation, ultimately supported the bill. Paul Helmke, then president of the organization, commented that "An imperfect bill is better than no bill at all" (Luo 2011, A1). However, a coalition of three groups supporting gun control measures (the Violence Policy Center, the Coalition to Stop Gun Violence, and the Legal Community Against Gun Violence) issued a statement conveying their concerns with the NICS Improvement Amendments Act. They stated that the NRA had succeeded in making "last-minute changes" to the bill before the House vote on June 13, 2007 (Violence Policy Center 2007a) and argued that the legislation would create "a new, more restrictive standard" for submitting records to the NICS from federal agencies. The press release from the three groups stated that federal commitment records could not be submitted to the NICS unless the records indicate that an individual "is a danger to himself or others or lacks the capacity to manage his own affairs." The groups opposed to the bill argued that the prior standard prohibited anyone involuntarily committed to an institution from acquiring a firearm. In addition, the groups asserted, records already submitted to the NICS that did not meet the new standard would be removed.

The gun control groups raised objections to the bill's re-establishment of a "relief from disabilities" mechanism, mentioning the expense of such a program—which Congress had defunded in 1993. The groups also mentioned their apprehension over a provision allowing veterans currently prohibited from possessing firearms—approximately 80,000 individuals—to petition for restoration of gun rights.

The House of Representatives passed the bill on June 13, 2007, the Senate approved the bill on December 20 of that year, and President George W. Bush signed the legislation into law on January 8, 2008. The law offers states financial assistance to gather and release to the NICS all records related to determining whether prospective firearms purchases can proceed. Among the databases of greatest concern, given recent tragic shootings, were the maintenance of mental health records, including the names of those adjudicated as mentally defective or those committed to mental institutions (Price and Norris 2008). The law granted to the attorney general the authority to award grant funds to states to use in improving their ability to report relevant information to the NICS (Law Center to Prevent Gun Violence 2012).

Following final passage of the NICS Improvement Amendments Act, Kirsten Rand, legislative director of the Violence Policy Center, stated: "The bill is now nothing more than a gun lobby wish list. It will waste millions of taxpayer dollars restoring the gun privileges of persons previously determined to present a danger to themselves or others. Once a solution, the bill is now part of the problem" (Violence Policy Center 2007b).

Five years after passage of the NICS Improvement Amendments Act, Michael S. Schmidt and Charlie Savage (2012) reported in the *New York Times* that state submissions to the FBI database of mentally ill individuals had been disappointing. Some states, such as New York, had submitted more than 100,000 names, but 19 states had submitted fewer than 100. Schmidt and Savage stated that, according to a 2012 report from the Government Accountability Office, the number of mental health records submitted by states had increased from approximately 126,000 in 2004 to 1.2 million in 2011. However, just twelve states contributed most to the increase, while 30 states were not providing any noncriminal records. Schmidt and Savage reported that the incomplete database resulted in "violent felons, fugitives and the mentally ill being able to buy firearms when the FBI cannot determine the person's history during a three-day waiting period."

The Bureau of Justice Statistics (2014) reported on the practices some 22 states have instituted for improving record reporting to the NICS. These states received grants through the NICS Improvement Amendments Act Record Improvement Program (NARIP). For instance, Florida received a 1.5 million dollar grant for the Florida Department of Law Enforcement (FDLE) to, among other goals, increase staff for the Firearm Purchase Program (FPP) in order to handle more efficiently the entry of information into the state's online Firearms Eligibility System, and to hire staff to enter data into the state's Mental Competency (MECOM) database. Illinois also received a $1.5 million grant for the Illinois Criminal Justice Information Authority (ICJIA), which in turn provides funds to the Illinois State Police (ISP) for the continuing process of automating the submission of disqualifying records to the NICS index.

Michael Luo (2011) reported on a *New York Times* investigation of the NICS Improvement Amendments Act mandate that the states wishing to receive federal grants to improve reporting of records to the system are required to establish a relief from disability process for those wishing to have their right to acquire and possess firearms restored. Federal agencies are also required to establish a rights restoration process, which the Department of Veterans Affairs completed in November 2010. More than 100,000 veterans at that time were prohibited from possessing a firearm because they had been determined by the agency to be mentally incompetent. Luo reported that, following passage of the Improvements Act, more than twenty state legislatures passed restoration laws, granting authority largely to state courts to grant gun rights to appellants. The *New York Times* investigation concluded that the guidelines established in many states proved to be vague, with minimal criteria for determining background information for each case. When judges made a decision, they sometimes (but not always) required a doctor's note, which often involved a general practitioner rather than a mental health professional. Even mental health professionals have difficulty predicting the potential for violence in an individual case. Mental health experts such as Jeffrey Swanson have been able to provide overall data for people with mental illness and the incidence of violent acts (Grady 2013, A19). In one study, Swanson reported that 33 percent of individuals with "serious mental illness" had past instances of violent behavior, compared to 15 percent of people with no "major mental disorder" (Luo 2011, A1). He found the highest rate of past violent behavior—64 percent—among those with both major mental disorders and a history of substance abuse.

The law contains provisions intended to encourage state officials to submit to the U.S. attorney general those records that involve information about individuals included in categories of persons not qualified to acquire or possess a firearm. Of special importance are records involving domestic violence misdemeanor convictions, restraining orders involving "harassing, stalking, or threatening an intimate partner or child of such intimate partner" (Krouse 2012, 15), as well as mental health judgments. To encourage states to provide more complete records, the law authorizes the attorney general to waive the requirement of a state to match grant funding if the state makes an effort to provide records to the NICS system. The attorney general also has the authority to reduce a law enforcement assistance grant if a state fails to comply sufficiently with the objective of computerizing records that would disqualify certain individuals from purchasing firearms. With passage of the NICS Improvements Amendments Act of 2007, Congress authorized the attorney general to grant additional funds to states to continue the improvement of electronic record access. The Bureau of Justice Statistics has called this grant program the NICS Act Record Improvement Program (NARIP) (Krouse 2012, 32).

Before passing the Improvement Amendments Act, Congress had authorized the grant program, National Criminal History Improvement Program (NCHIP) in 1968 to enhance the completeness of the nation's criminal history records that would ultimately prove relevant to disqualifying conditions for purchasing a firearm, especially those involving felony convictions. States receive grants through the Bureau of Justice Statistics (BJS) to update and computerize such records (Krouse 30) and to make the information more completely and readily available to such federal criminal justice databases as the NICS Index, the Interstate Identification Index (III), the National Sex Offender Registry (NSOR), and the National Crime Information Center (NCIC) (Krouse 2012, 30). Despite the NCHIP program, several states failed to submit to the FBI any records of persons adjudicated to be "mentally defective" (Krouse 31). Often, state laws regarding patients' rights and privacy have discouraged the submission of mental health records.

Some states have taken steps to enhance their background check policies. For instance, with passage of the Secure Ammunition and Firearms Enforcement (SAFE) Act in 2013, New York became one of the stricter states in prohibiting mentally unstable individuals and those in other restricted categories from purchasing or possessing firearms. The SAFE Act mandates that doctors, psychologists, and other medical personnel send mental evaluation reports to county health officials, who, if they assent to the evaluations, enter the names into the Division of Criminal Justice Services database of those prohibited from purchasing a firearm. They are required to report any person "likely to engage in conduct that would result in serious harm to self or others" (Hartocollis 2014, 1), which represents a much broader criterion than the requirement, contained in federal law, that a person be adjudicated as mentally incompetent or be involuntarily institutionalized. The information is maintained in the database for five years. If a person entered in the database is found to possess a gun permit, which is required to purchase a handgun in New York, the law directs officials to revoke the license and impound all of the individual's firearms.

By October 2014 the names of more than 40,000 New York residents had been placed on the list of prohibited persons due to mental health issues. Critics of the new policy noted that any procedures for determining the likelihood of a person becoming violent is far from scientifically reliable (Price and Norris 2008, 125). Some mental health workers have expressed concern that the New York mandate to report the names of mental patients—as well as federal government policies—could possibly discourage some from voluntarily seeking help from a doctor or psychologist. Others noted gaps in the legislation. For instance, in areas of the state other than New York City, an individual on the list of prohibited persons may purchase a long gun without a permit, assuming that the individual would satisfy the less restrictive criteria of the NICS. In addition, there is no clearly established process for enforcing the confiscation of firearms from a prohibited person. The National Rifle Association has criticized New York's procedures regarding those determined to be mentally unstable, calling for a "process of adjudication" in order to prevent any "capricious" or "malicious" determination of prohibited status (Hartocollis 2014, 21).

In addition to assuring more efficient transmission of relevant disqualifying records from state governments, President Barack Obama acted to improve the gathering of relevant data in the executive branch of the federal government. In January 2013 President Obama ordered the attorney general to offer federal agencies guidance in identifying and sharing with the National Instant Criminal Background Check System "relevant Federal records" (Obama 2013). The affected agencies are to submit a report to the Department of Justice providing information about the availability of applicable records and a plan for implementing the provision of such information to the NICS. The memorandum instructed the relevant agencies to submit a report to the president via the attorney general containing information about the types of records to be shared with the NICS and the number of records that have been submitted to databases accessible to the NICS. The president's memorandum also established a NICS Consultation and Coordination Working Group composed of representatives from various agencies, including the departments of Defense, Veterans Affairs, and Homeland Security, and chaired by the attorney general, which is to determine whether an agency possesses relevant records that should be made available to the NICS.

Congress has not taken any action to expand the NICS to other avenues for purchasing firearms, and therefore a large proportion of firearms transfers—estimated to involve up to 40 percent of transactions each year; Cook and Goss (2014, 81) estimate that unlicensed sellers "make 25 percent to 50 percent of gun vendors at gun shows"—still are not subject to a criminal background check, except in those few states that have instituted a comprehensive, or universal, check. Organizations supporting gun control speculate that an expanded criminal background check system would prohibit several thousand more firearm transactions to disqualified individuals each year (Educational Fund to Stop Gun Violence 2002, 9).

Comprehensive Background Check Proposal

The proposal for a universal (comprehensive) background check requirement contains two provisions. First, the proposed legislation would mandate that only those licensed by the federal government, including importers, manufacturers, dealers, and collectors, may sell, deliver, or transfer a firearm to someone who is not a federal firearms licensee. Therefore, all firearms transfers by private individuals must be conducted through a licensed dealer. Such a restriction would apply to the widely reported estimate of 40 percent of firearm transfers that currently occur between private persons.

The second provision of the proposed legislation applies to the transfer of firearms as a gift, bequest, or transfer to a close family member, or possibly to a loan of a firearm to a person known to the lender for a lawful purpose, and for a limited period of time (perhaps 30 days). Just how effective a universal background check system would be is an open question, especially with the proviso regarding close family members.

Contrary to the dismissal by many gun rights supporters as well as gun control supporters, of legal efforts to prohibit firearm ownership to certain groups of people likely to commit violent crimes, Garen Wintemute (2013) argues that background checks for firearm transfers have had some positive effects and that they could be made much more effective by broadening their application beyond federally licensed firearms dealers to cover private sales and transfers in order to prevent prohibited individuals from acquiring guns. Similar to Jeffrey R. Snyder's (1997) use of Florida as the model for concealed carry policy, Wintemute commends California's policy regarding comprehensive background checks, calling it a "suitable model" for other states as well as for a nation-wide procedure established by the federal government. Since 1991 California has conducted comprehensive background checks for firearm transfers. The state also has in place a now-limited ten-day waiting period before a transfer can be completed (12). Wintemute observes that the more restrictive policy for firearm purchases apparently has not discouraged purchases by qualified individuals, reporting average firearms sales increases of more than 15 percent per year over a recent five-year period (12). Wintemute undoubtedly reports this figure in response to the argument that background checks, whether intentionally meant to or not, discourage firearm acquisition by law-abiding citizens.

Wintemute argues that the lack of decisive statistical evidence that the Brady Law mandate for background checks has led to reductions in violent crimes can be attributed to a lack of checks of the many firearm transfers each year that occur without a background check and also without a centralized record of sales. Such records are kept by federally licensed firearms dealers, but not by private sellers. Wintemute argues that firearm trafficking—the illegal transfer of firearms to prohibited persons and for the purpose of illegal activities—could be more effectively restricted if more comprehensive background checks and record-keeping were established. In California, private transfers (except among family members) involve the seller finalizing the sale through a federally licensed dealer, who initiates a background check of the purchaser and keeps a record of the transfer. If a firearm is used in a crime, the weapon can be traced to the more recent purchaser rather than to the first person who acquired the weapon from a federally licensed dealer. Wintemute terms this procedure creating the "missing links in the chain of evidence" between the initial retail purchaser and the criminal from whom the weapon was recovered (23–24).

Currently twelve states have instituted some form of comprehensive background checks (see Table 7.1). In California, federally licensed firearms retailers may charge ten dollars per firearm for serving as a transfer agent for private sales of firearms (12). Dealers then are responsible for conducting the background check on the prospective firearm recipient. The purchaser may take possession of the firearm only after California's ten-day waiting period requirement has expired. However, in August 2014 a federal judge invalidated the waiting period for those who currently own a firearm and for those who already possess a permit to own a gun.

Wintemute addresses certain difficulties and costs often attributed to comprehensive background checks. As mentioned above, a major criticism is that background checks make firearm transfers "less convenient" (36). In response, Wintemute argues that such checks are similar to current airport security screening, which represents a relatively minor hindrance that results in a safer and more secure civil aviation system. He also mentions the financial costs of universal checks as another possible limitation. Wintemute concludes that the "great majority of individuals" will recognize the value of such checks in deterring violent crime, and asserts that the ten-dollar fee in California "has proved satisfactory" (36). Wintemute recognizes that a national background check on private transfers, if instituted on the national level, might overload the present computerized NICS system. His solution is to extend the three-day waiting period presently allowed to complete delayed checks and thus permit additional time to conduct background checks. However, it is uncertain whether instituting an extension of the waiting period would be politically feasible, given likely opposition from gun rights supporters who would certainly consider such delays an additional burden on law-abiding citizens.

Wintemute (2013, 2) recommends that a comprehensive background check policy should not exempt those holding a concealed weapon permit or other firearm license from a background check because "a small but important fraction of such individuals" are actually prohibited from purchasing a firearm, having been included in one of the prohibited categories since receiving the permit. Another difficulty with a comprehensive background check system involves the archiving of data and the resulting concern for privacy. Wintemute responds that, as with the current procedure, the identification of buyer and seller would be kept in the retailer's records and released to law enforcement only if required for a criminal investigation (37). As a final difficulty, Wintemute mentions the constitutionality of comprehensive background checks: would the U.S. Supreme Court find that such checks pass "constitutional muster"? He refers to a recent analysis (Rosenthal and Winkler 2013) which concludes that the courts would view comprehensive checks as furthering a "compelling government interest"—preventing violence—and hence would find such checks constitutional (37).

The Future of Background Checks

Criticisms of the National Instant Criminal Background Check System notwithstanding, background checks will continue. It appears clear to a large majority of citizens as well as public officials that there are certain categories of individuals who should be prohibited from possessing firearms. How successful the NICS is will depend to a large extent on how extensive will be the cooperation of the 50 states with the federal government in providing relevant data to the system, and also on the proportion of gun transfers each year that occur without a background check. Just how restrictive categories are defined and how individuals might remove themselves from a category will undoubtedly remain a matter of contention, with policy views determined to a great extent by which values are emphasized: the right of individuals to keep and bear arms or the safety and security of the community from those who would use firearms to commit violent crimes or to do harm to themselves.

References

Barron, James. 2014. "Taking a Bullet, Gaining a Cause." *New York Times* (August 5): A1.

Bureau of Alcohol, Tobacco, Firearms, and Explosives. 2012. *State Laws and Published Ordinances—Firearms.* Thirty-first edition. Washington, DC: U.S. Government Printing Office.

Bureau of Justice Statistics. 2014. "Promising Practices by States for Improved Record Keeping." http://www.bjs.gov/index.cfm?ty=tp&tid=491#promising.

Cunningham, Kevin M. 1994. "When Gun Control Meets the Constitution." *Journal of Civil Rights and Economic Development* 10 (1). http://scholarship.law .stjohns.edu/jcred/vol10/iss1/4 (accessed February 25, 2013).

Educational Fund to Stop Gun Violence. 2002. "Closing Illegal Gun Markets: Extending Criminal Background Checks to All Gun Sales." http://efsgv.org (accessed February 25, 2015).

Ekstrand, Laurie E., and Randolph C. Hite. 2000. *Gun Control: Implementation of the National Instant Criminal Background Check System.* Washington, DC: United States General Accounting Office.

Grady, Denise. 2013. "Signs May Be Evident in Hindsight, but Predicting Violent Behavior Is Tough." *New York Times* (September 19): A19.

Hahn, Robert A., Okeg Bilukha, Alex Crosby, Mindy T. Fullilove, Akiva Liberman, Eve Moscicki, Susan Snyder, Farris Tuma, and Peter A. Briss. 2005. "Firearms Laws and the Reduction of Violence: A Systematic Review." *American Journal of Preventive Medicine* 28 (2S1): 40–71.

Hartocollis, Anemona. 2014. "Mental Reports Put Thousands on New York's No-Guns List." *New York Times* (October 19): A1.

Henigan, Dennis A. 2009. *Lethal Logic: Exploding the Myths That Paralyze American Gun Policy.* Washington, DC: Potomac Books.

Jacobs, James B., and Kimberly A. Potter. 1995. "Keeping Guns out of the 'Wrong' Hands: The Brady Law and the Limits of Regulation." *Journal of Criminal Law and Criminology* 86 (Fall): 93–120.

Kates, Don B. 2005. "The Hopelessness of Trying to Disarm the Kinds of People Who Murder." *Bridges* 12 (Fall/Winter): 313–330.

Kleck, Gary. 1997. *Targeting Guns: Firearms and Their Control.* New York: Aldine de Gruyter.

Krouse, William J. 2012. *Gun Control Legislation.* Washington, DC: Congressional Research Service.

Law Center to Prevent Gun Violence. 2012. "Key Congressional Acts Related to Firearms." http://smartgunlaws.org/key-federal-acts-regarding-guns.

Lee, Akkina D., Ronald J. Frandsen, Dave Naglich, and Gene A. Lauver. 2013. *Background Checks for Firearm Transfers, 2010—Statistical Tables.* Bureau of Justice Statistics (February 12). http://www.bjs.gov/index.cfm?ty=pbdetail&iid=4596 (accessed February 25, 2015).

National Rifle Association, Institute for Legislative Action. 1999. "The 'Brady Handgun Violence Prevention Act:' Does It Live Up to Its Name?" (July 28). http://nraila.org/articles/19990728/the-brady-handgun-violence-prevention-a (accessed February 24, 2015).

National Rifle Association, Institute of Legislative Action. 2007. "The NICS Improvement Bill: Myth and Reality" (October 5). https://www.nraila.org/articles/20071005/the-nics-improvement-bill-myth-and-rea (accessed February 24, 2015).

Obama, Barack. 2013. "Presidential Memorandum: Improving Availability of Relevant Executive Branch Records to the National Instant Criminal Background Check System" (January 16). http://www.whitehouse.gov/the-press-office/2013/01/16/presidential-memorandum-improving-availability-relevant-executive-branch (accessed February 25, 2015).

Patterson, Samuel C., and Keith R. Eakins. 1998. "Congress and Gun Control." In John M. Bruce and Clyde Wilcox, editors. *The Changing Politics of Gun Control.* Lanham, MD: Rowman and Littlefield.

Price, Marilyn, and Donna N. Norris. 2008. "National Instant Criminal Background Improvement Act: Implications for Persons With Mental Illness." *Journal of the Academic of Psychiatry and the Law* 36 (March): 123–130.

Rosenthal, Lawrence E., and Adam Winkler. 2013. "The Scope of Regulatory Authority under the Second Amendment." In Daniel W. Webster and Jon S. Vernick, editors. *Reducing Gun Violence in America: Informing Policy with Evidence and Analysis.* Baltimore, MD: Johns Hopkins University Press, 225–236.

Schmidt, Michael S., and Charlie Savage. 2012. "Gaps in F.B.I. Data Undercut Background Checks for Guns." *New York Times* (December 21): A1.

Snyder, Jeffrey R. 1997. "Fighting Back: Self-Defense and the Right to Carry a Handgun." Cato Institute Policy Analysis 284 (October 22). http://www.cato.org/publications/policy-analysis/fighting-back-crime-selfdefense-right-carry-handgun (accessed February 25, 2015).

Spitzer, Robert J. 2012. "Licensing." In *Guns in American Society.* Gregg Lee Carter, editor. Santa Barbara, CA: ABC-CLIO.

Spitzer, Robert J. 2015. *The Politics of Gun Control.* Sixth edition. Boulder, CO: Paradigm Publishers.

Sugarmann, Josh, and Kristen Rand. 1997. *Cease Fire: A Comprehensive Strategy to Reduce Forearms Violence.* Washington, DC: Violence Policy Center.

Sumner, Steven A., Peter M. Layde, and Clare E. Guse. 2008. "Firearm Death Rates and Association with Level of Firearm Purchase Background Check." *American Journal of Preventive Medicine* 35 (6).

Violence Policy Center. 2007a. "National Gun Violence Prevention Groups Voice Concern About Cancerous Components of Bill to Improve Gun Background Checks." https://www.vpc.org/press/0707csgv.htm. (accessed November 15, 2014).

Violence Policy Center. 2007b. "Gun Lobby Hijacks Bill Intended to Improve Gun Buyer Background Checks" (December 19). https://www.vpc.org/press/0712nics .htm (accessed November 15, 2014).

Vizzard, William J. 2000. *Shots in the Dark: The Policy, Politics, and Symbolism of Gun Control*. Lanham, MD: Rowman and Littlefield.

Wintemute, Garen. 2013. *Background Checks for Firearm Transfers: Assessment and Recommendations*. Sacramento, CA: Violence Prevention Research Program, University of California at Davis School of Medicine.

Zimring, Franklin E. 1975. "Firearms and Federal Law: The Gun Control Act of 1968." *Journal of Legal Studies* 4: 133–198.

CHAPTER EIGHT

Seeking Common Ground: Perspective of a Gun Control Supporter

Paul Helmke

Introduction—How I Got Involved with the Gun Issue

One of the first letters I wrote when I became the head of the Brady Campaign and Brady Center to Prevent Gun Violence was to Wayne LaPierre, the executive vice president of the National Rifle Association. I asked LaPierre if he'd be willing to meet with me—with or without staff; whenever and wherever he preferred; publicly or privately—to see if there were any areas where we might be able to find agreement, or areas where our positions and interests weren't that far apart, regarding gun policy. He never responded to my letter.

As a lawyer and then as a politician and mayor in Fort Wayne, Indiana, I had never shied away from conflict and controversy, but had always felt that it was better to seek common ground and find areas where adversaries could agree to move forward whenever possible rather than squander time, money, and progress on unnecessary battles. Since I did not consider myself virulently "anti-gun" or believe that we needed to "take everybody's guns away," it seemed to me that there might be some significant areas where potential agreement could be possible. Guns were not a part of my family life growing up, but I earned my NRA "Marksmanship" and "Pro-Marksmanship" badges at camp when I was in grade school, had friends who went hunting with their fathers, and engaged in my share of make-believe Davy Crockett, Cowboys and Indians, and Civil War shoot-outs. My mother's father, who was a machine-gunner in World War I, and her older brother, would occasionally bring us game they had shot. My father and his father had both been elected as county prosecutor and I often heard their stories about guns used by criminals and by law enforcement.

When I was about to start high school, I was stunned to see a story on the local television news that one of my best friends from grade school had been shot and seriously wounded at a home of an acquaintance. One teenage boy found his older brother's gun and decided to "scare" Scott by pointing it at him and threatening to shoot. Scott turned to leave and was shot in the back; he survived, but an eighth of an inch either way would have led to death or paralysis. It was clear to me that the lessons I had learned about gun safety at camp were not something that others necessarily followed.

As an undergraduate majoring in Political Science at Indiana University in the late 1960s, I wrote a paper on how votes for or against the Gun Control Act of 1968 impacted the U.S. Senate races that year and followed closely the high-profile shootings and outbreaks of urban and rural violence throughout the country. While raising issues and leading rallies and protests as student body president at IU, I worried about rumors of groups bringing guns to campus and later the fall-out from the National Guard shootings and four student deaths at Kent State University.

It was not until I was elected mayor, however, that I started focusing directly on the issue of gun violence. A month after my election, but before I took office, one of our police recruits was shot and killed during a training scenario outside of the state. The city's training officer had loaded his weapon during the lunch break and forgot to unload it when the training started up again. Having an African American recruit killed by a white officer led to racial tensions in our city and showed me that even well-trained individuals could make fatal mistakes when carrying firearms.

An influx of crack cocaine and gang wars were leading to increases in violence in my city when I took office, and we responded with raids on drug houses, increased taxes to hire more police officers, instituted partnerships with neighborhood groups and faith-based institutions, responded with our versions of "broken-window" and "community-oriented policing" and "community-oriented government" strategies, and generally tried anything we thought could help make the city safer. When one of the drug dealers was killed by law enforcement in one of our first drug house raids, I started to get death threats. Still, it wasn't long before I started to walk neighborhoods in all parts of the city and go to community meetings without protection to demonstrate the basic safety of the city.

But there were still too many shootings. I got the call from my police chief in the middle of the night when one of our police officers was shot and killed by her husband, also a police officer, when the loaded gun they kept next to their bed for their protection discharged during a domestic quarrel. I went to the hospital when a minister's son was shot in the head from a drive-by shooting when he was waiting to be picked up from a YMCA branch. I met with relatives of shooting victims and went to prayer vigils at the scenes of the violence.

As we implemented a number of law enforcement and community strategies, I learned from my police command and others how weak the gun laws were in our state and country. I decided to support the efforts of Jim and Sarah Brady to require gun sellers to perform background checks on their gun buyers to see if they were "prohibited purchasers" as defined by the Gun Control Act of 1968 and not just rely on the buyer's word concerning his or her status. When my police officers told me how they were out-gunned in responding to a bank robbery at a strip mall, I supported efforts to try and restrict access to weapons that were particularly dangerous because of the number of rounds that could be fired quickly and powerfully.

Because of my "law and order" and public safety concerns, I participated in news conferences in Washington, D.C., Indianapolis, and Fort Wayne with the Bradys, other mayors, law enforcement representatives, and top elected and appointed officials to try to do something about the weak and nearly non-existent laws to help reduce gun violence. I pushed these issues with elected officials at all levels of government and was happy to see the Brady Bill become law, and later to sit on the platform on the South Lawn of the White House along with other mayors like Rudy Giuliani for New York City and with the heads of groups like the National Sheriffs Association when President William Clinton signed the Crime Bill. Having legislation that provided for more police, the establishment of the Community Oriented Policing Services (COPS) office, increased efforts on domestic violence, and restrictions on "assault weapons" and high capacity ammunition magazines seemed like a good thing for my community as well as the country.

Crime rates and violence began to drop in my city and across the country in the mid-1990s, but efforts to strengthen gun laws further remained controversial and police tactics became more of a concern in Fort Wayne and elsewhere. I was often questioned about my stance on gun issues during my U.S. Senate primary campaign in Indiana in 1998. My success in winning the Republican nomination that year showed that my positions were not as politically toxic as some argued, particularly when I explained those positions in connection with an overall crime-fighting strategy. After the Columbine shootings in 1999, I continued to speak out for stronger gun laws but national legislation failed to pass.

When I left office after twelve years as mayor at the beginning of 2000 and returned to the practice of law, I continued to follow gun violence and crime prevention issues—noticing particularly candidate George W. Bush's support for the "assault weapon ban" and trigger locks during the presidential debates that year. After 9/11, I was more involved in matters surrounding communications interoperability for public safety providers and threat assessments for state and local governments but still followed discussions and debates concerning guns.

In 2006, with a Republican president and Congress, the Bradys and the Board of Directors for the Brady Campaign and Brady Center to Prevent Gun Violence asked me to sign on to a five-year term to head their organization beginning that July. I knew it would be tough to get legislation passed at the national level—efforts to renew the "Assault Weapon Ban" had been unsuccessful less than two years earlier—but this was still an issue that was very important to me and I hoped that my background might help lead to some progress.

Finding Common Ground

And so I wrote Wayne LaPierre to see if there might be some common ground. When he didn't respond, I'd mention the letter to his staff when I saw them at television interviews or meetings when we had been asked to present our positions on current gun issues—and still I got no response. When I finally had joint television appearances with LaPierre after the U.S. Supreme Court decisions voiding near-total gun bans in Washington, D.C., and then Chicago, I asked him directly on-air about sitting down to find common ground, particularly in view of language in those decisions indicating that many restrictions on guns were "presumptively lawful." Once again, LaPierre ignored my request and refused to consider any attempt to identify areas of agreement.

The tragedy here is not just the continuing level of gun violence in this country—approximately 32 gun murders, 51 gun suicides, 1 or 2 fatal gun accidents, and 183 non-fatal gun injuries every day in this country, along with the related medical and hospital costs, lost wages and productivity, and continuing burden and grief for families and caregivers—but the fact that it shouldn't be that hard to reach some level of agreement on measures to reduce gun violence without "trampling" on anyone's constitutional rights or unduly restricting anyone's legitimate need or desire to hunt with guns, collect guns, or have guns for the personal protection.

Why LaPierre didn't want to discuss trying to find common ground and why we aren't able to reach a governing consensus on measures to reduce gun violence involves issues of organizational self-preservation and perpetuation, fundraising, politics, fear-mongering, and paranoia. Richard Feldman, in the next chapter of this volume, correctly focuses on long-held suspicions of opposing agendas and "identity politics" as additional reasons LaPierre might have had for not wanting to meet with me. This approach to the issue means that the fight will go on indefinitely and that common ground will never be found. Unlike other "hot-button" or "wedge" issues, however, as long as we make it clear that we're not talking about "banning all guns" (which is not a position that I or any of the organizations I've worked with takes), or saying that there should be *no* restrictions of any sort on guns and gun ownership (which I don't believe is the case with anyone, as far as I know, on the "other" side with whom I've ever debated gun issues), there should be a lot of room here for compromise.

If anything, the decisions by the U.S. Supreme Court in *Heller* and *McDonald* should make it easier to find common ground. Those decisions make it clear that "[like] most rights, the right secured by the Second Amendment, is not unlimited" and that some restrictions on who gets guns, how guns are sold, how guns are stored, where guns can be taken, when guns can be carried, and what kinds of guns are available are "presumptively lawful." Where we draw the specific lines on these categories described by Justice Scalia in Section III of the *Heller* case and reinforced by Justice Alito in the *McDonald* case might still be subject to court scrutiny, but they are also good topics for discussion, debate, and potential compromise.

Background Checks

Perhaps the area where it should be easiest to reach agreement is with regard to background checks—Brady's signature issue. If we all (or nearly all) agree that not everyone should be able to possess or buy a gun, then we should want to design and develop a system to try and keep these particular people from easily getting guns. For a good background check system to have any chance of being effective, we need to look at: (1) who should be on the list of "prohibited purchasers"; (2) how we get that list of individuals into an accessible database; and (3) how we make sure that data base is checked before nearly all guns are sold or transferred.

Prohibited Purchasers:

The current list of "prohibited purchasers" is focused mainly on felons, mentally dangerous individuals, and those subject to domestic violence restraining orders. In addition, there are restrictions on individuals dishonorably discharged from the military, non-citizens, and drug abusers. The main issue here is how these different categories are defined, and whether new categories should be added or current categories deleted or redefined.

For example, it might make sense to add some violent misdemeanants to the list of prohibited purchasers since an individual who has been convicted of being violent is not someone most of us would want to have a gun. Conversely, while a convicted felon has arguably shown a blatant disregard for following the law, an argument might be made that tax evaders or some other felons might not be the sorts of individuals who we need to bar from gun ownership. It is encouraging that Richard agrees that we need a "more intelligent standard" here.

The mentally dangerous category (described in the statute as "mental defective") has received a lot of attention in recent years. Many people don't realize that the category currently is basically concerned with only those who have been found officially by a court or a court-like body to be a danger to themselves or others or have been similarly declared or found to be incompetent. The category does not include those who have only sought treatment for different types or levels of mental illness. As Richard points out, more money is needed to deal with mental health issues. At the same time, instead of blaming mental illness for most of our gun violence problems, we need to be aware of studies showing that only 4 percent of the violence is tied to mental health issues. While a number of high-profile mass shooters have been described as mentally dangerous, very few of them technically fit this legal category at the time they did their shooting. How to write a definition that includes these types of potential killers is one of the challenges we should be facing.

Another major issue with the mentally dangerous category is how someone gets off the prohibited purchaser list once the individual is no longer considered dangerous. Unless one considers being mentally dangerous always incurable, there should be some process for individuals to get off the prohibited list. How that change in status should be determined (by a doctor or a court or some other way), and how the removal process should work, is another area where parties to the gun violence debate should be able to find some common ground. Restraining orders in domestic violence cases are sometimes challenged because of questions about notice and opportunities to be heard, as well as by steps some law enforcement personnel use to enforce the orders by seizing guns. Absent gun registration provisions, it is often difficult to know who really "owns" a gun that may have been moved or transferred to a different person or place in response to a restraining order. Whether or not a restraining order has been issued or is still in place and its correct status reflected in the data base can cause problems in making this category of prohibited purchaser effective.

The "drug abuser" category is one that could be the most effective in keeping questionable people from being able to buy a gun legally depending on how the category is defined. Indeed, the studies on the connection between mental health problems and shootings show that alcohol abuse and drug use (and past violent behavior) are much more important as predictors of future gun violence. There have been some proposals to expand the regulatory definition from anyone who has been arrested for a drug offense in the last year to anyone arrested in the last five years. While I have concerns with equating arrest with guilt, particularly when there has been plenty of time for a court disposition of an arrest, there may be other ways to tighten up the definition here. Maybe ask if anyone has used illegal drugs (particularly since the statute uses the phrase "unlawful user of . . . any controlled substance") within a certain time period or been arrested within a certain time period and then require a drug test of some sort for those individuals? Maybe do something similar for individuals who fit other criteria indicating drug use or alcohol abuse? There may be issues here with effectiveness and time delays, but tighter definitions could make a positive difference.

Since 9/11, there have been proposals to add some of the different lists of individuals of concern to the Department of Homeland Security to the list of individuals prohibited from buying and owning guns. If someone is on a "terrorist watch list" or even a "no-fly" list, is this really a person who we should let buy guns easily though legal channels? As Richard indicates, the objection to these proposals is that no one knows for sure who is on these lists and why, whether we want to let these people know that they are on the lists, mistakes on the lists, and no clear procedures for challenging the list and getting off the list. This isn't a "simple" issue, but it is an area that should be discussed to see if some agreement can be reached so known terrorists can't easily amass arsenals to be used against us.

Database Records

Even with a good list of people we consider too dangerous, that list does no one any good unless the names are submitted to and readily accessible in a database available to gun sellers. One of the major lessons we learned from the Virginia Tech massacre on April 16, 2007, was how our background check system does not work properly when the names of prohibited purchasers are not submitted to the database by the states. The Virginia Tech shooter had been found by a Virginia court to be a danger to himself or others. Virginia did not submit his name to the database, however, because they had a state policy to submit only the names of those found to be dangerous by a court and ordered to undergo in-house treatment, which had not been ordered for this individual. The shooter twice (because Virginia had a one-gun-a-month law) went to buy a gun from a federally licensed dealer and both times he passed the background check because of the state's failure to submit the information. If the information had been submitted, the sales would not have occurred.

After this information came out, we learned that only an estimated 10–20 percent of the records of mentally dangerous individuals had been submitted by the states to the background check database. My home state of Indiana had submitted only one such record at this time. New York State had submitted only four such records. In addition, it was estimated that 20–25 percent of the felon records were missing along with a significant number of individuals subject to restraining orders. Background checks cannot work properly if the records of prohibited purchasers are not in the database checked by gun sellers.

Following Virginia Tech, the Brady Campaign and I supported legislation proposed by Representative Carolyn McCarthy from New York to create incentives to the states to have them submit more records along with disincentives if they didn't. Many in the Gun Violence Prevention (GVP) movement were opposed to this legislation because it also established procedures for individuals to get off the prohibited-person list, particularly individuals in the Veterans Administration system who had been declared incompetent to manage their own affairs and directly receive their VA checks. At the same time, the NRA remained silent or gave token tepid support to the legislation. My support was based on the fact that I did not consider mental dangerousness to be a permanent condition, and because I felt that getting significantly more names of prohibited purchasers into the data base outweighed any problems with a much smaller number of individuals possibly coming out of the system. The legislation passed the House a few months after the shootings in Blacksburg and finally made it through the Senate eight months after that tragic day. Senator Edward Kennedy called me in December before agreement was reached to make sure I was happy with the final compromise worked out by Senator Tom Coburn on behalf of the NRA and Senator Chuck Schumer and Kennedy's office on behalf of the GVP movement. The legislation went through on a voice vote and was signed quietly by President George W. Bush in early January of 2008.

Because of this legislation, many more records have been added to the background check data base. Much more needs to be done, but now there is a stronger framework on which to build. Both Brady and the NRA were involved in allowing this to be passed. If the GVP movement had not been able to help get anything passed after Virginia Tech, and if we had been unwilling to work with Congresswoman McCarthy, one of our strongest allies on the Hill, I'm not sure if we would ever have been able to advance any legislation for a number of years. Compromise can be controversial and messy, but is needed to make progress.

"Private Seller" Loophole

Even with a good list of potentially dangerous individuals, and even if all those records are in a readily accessible data base to gun sellers, a background check system will be ineffective if a significant number of sellers are not required to perform these background checks. Since no records are kept of sales that occur without background checks, we have to rely on estimates but most of those who have examined the issue have concluded that somewhere close to 40 percent of all gun sales occur without a background check.

The big loophole here is that only federally licensed dealers are covered by the Brady Law on background checks. So-called private sellers who transfer guns from their own "collections" are not required to do background checks. Since the passage of the Brady Law, this loophole has been exploited, particularly at gun shows in many states, to allow sellers to transfer hundreds of guns week after week without any paperwork or background checks. While federally licensed gun stores who do background checks have brick-and-mortar places of business, and have to do their own advertising and pay the normal costs of daily operations, these "private sellers" can rely on gun show promoters to provide them a venue, advertising, and a walk-in clientele, all with less paperwork for (and fewer taxes collected from) their customers.

Over 2.2 million prohibited purchases have been stopped by the Brady Law since the start of the instant check data base in 1998. While I agree with Richard that much more needs to be done to penalize those who have attempted to buy guns and have been stopped, the process still has made it harder for people we've defined as dangerous from getting weapons. Why we allow an easy alternative for prohibited purchasers to get guns from "private sellers" makes no sense to me.

This problem could be fixed by requiring background checks for nearly all sales (perhaps with exceptions for immediate family members and other limited categories). States like California have figured out how to make this work operationally, and fears that requiring these background checks would put gun shows in California out of business have been proven to be unfounded. For other non-exempt private sales, ways can certainly be found to get a background check done at nearby gun stores or through other means in a timely fashion that don't unnecessarily burden any of involved parties. This is where the different sides to this issue could work together to close some of the current loopholes and fix some of the current problems. Richard's proposed "Gun Show Preservation and Protection Act" is a good example of something that both sides might be willing to support. Again, there might be arguments about the details and the definitions, but it has the potential of reducing the easy access to guns by individuals society considers dangerous without unduly burdening legitimate purchasers. If the NRA let elected officials know that something like this was acceptable, we'd start seeing real progress on this issue.

One of the most frustrating things for me is to read statements from some of the elected officials saying they are voting against an effort to improve the background check system by saying that there are problems with the existing system. Yes, there are problems. It has done good things but needs strengthening. So let's try to fix these problems, not perpetuate them.

Yes, even with a strong improved background check system, dangerous people may still find ways to get guns. But we put laws on the books not just to stop bad people from doing bad things, but also to make a point as to what a civilized society expects from its members and also so we have something additional to charge them with when they get caught. And, as Richard points out, these gun charges needed to be treated seriously by prosecutors and courts. The fact that people break laws is not a good argument for getting rid of those laws, but should be the reason for constantly looking at ways to strengthen those laws and make them more effective.

Public Gun Carrying

One of the biggest issues pushed by the gun rights movement over the past 20 years has been expanding concealed carry to more states, changing "may issue" states with regard to carry permits to "shall issue" states, fighting restrictions on places where guns are not allowed, and promoting and encouraging "open carry" of guns. While efforts to fight this have been largely unsuccessful in most states, the GVP community has been able to block the push in the U.S. Congress for automatic national reciprocity of concealed carry permits. This issue is unlikely to go away soon and is one where finding common ground might be possible.

As I write this, the courts have not ruled definitively on whether or not there is a constitutional right to carry guns outside the home. Both the *Heller* and *McDonald* cases dealt just with having a gun in the home for self-defense, and the language in those decisions seems to indicate that most limits on carrying guns in public would be approved. References to "19th-century courts" finding "prohibitions on carrying concealed weapons" to be "lawful under the Second Amendment or state analogues," as well as specific support for restrictions on bringing guns to "sensitive places" tends to make this a policy issue rather than a constitutional one.

Much of the policy debate here revolves around whether having more guns being carried in public makes us safer or puts us more at risk. To those in the GVP movement, the risks of having more guns in public places clearly outweigh the benefits. We cite research showing that those who carry guns are four times more likely to be attacked than those without a gun (although this may be an indicator that those who carry are often in neighborhoods or businesses with increased risks) and highlight every story about an accidental or negligent shooting by a legal gun carrier. Gun rights activists argue that "gun-free zones" become targets of opportunity for bad people and that states with permissive gun carry laws have less crime, often ignoring or marginalizing any information to the contrary.

My biggest concern with gun carriers is whether they fully understand the risks and responsibilities involved in bringing that gun into the public sphere. If someone has a gun at home, they may put the residents of and visitors to that home at increased risk (since a gun in the home, according to some studies, is twenty-one times more likely to harm someone legitimately in the home than an intruder), but individuals can choose not to go to these homes. When the gun owner brings the gun out of the home, all of us have to live with the consequences.

The problem is that some states require little or no training on gun safety, gun laws, gun use and misuse, when to shoot, and so on. I've known people who have been able to get concealed carry permits without ever touching a gun. Some states do little more than requiring an application and a processing fee. This is bad enough policy for those who live in or visit these states, but when other states give reciprocity to those permits, the situation gets even worse.

One possible way to find common ground on gun carry would be to agree to some minimum training and testing standards for anyone who wanted to carry a gun outside of the home. I am happy that Richard appears to agree with this for individuals wishing to carry "in other states under federal law" as part of an "'enhanced' state carry license." Having stricter requirements to get a permit would make it more likely that the gun would not be misused. Combine this with a more extensive background check than what is required just to buy a gun, and regular renewals, and most of those on opposing sides of the gun issue might feel somewhat satisfied.

One of the related issues here is what role local law enforcement should have in granting a carry permit. When I was mayor, there were people the police knew were involved in selling drugs or running gangs, or were dangerous in some other way, but whom we never had enough evidence against for an arrest. It seems we would want these law enforcement professionals to be able to provide some say and input, whether final or advisory, on whether someone could legally carry a gun in public. For those who are concerned that no one would ever get a permit unless they were well-connected, we could establish some sort of review or appeal procedure. Otherwise, we may be giving passes for dangerous people to carry guns legally in public. While Richard says he is confused by this position, arguing that criminals and "[c]razy people" won't bother with getting a permit, it still makes no sense to me for government agencies to issue permits to people whom local law enforcement have legitimate reason to believe have been engaged in violent criminal enterprises or are dangerously mentally ill.

Another issue raised here is whether the procedures for granting a permit to carry might also be translatable in some degree to buying guns. Many gun rights advocates strongly oppose licensing of gun owners and registration of guns, but many of these people seemingly have no problem with obtaining a carry permit. If we had licensing of gun owners, we could help make sure that individuals with guns knew the risks and responsibilities of gun ownership. If we required guns to be registered, then we would know which individual actually owned and was responsible for which gun.

Even with an agreed-upon process for permitting gun carry, there is still an issue whether there are places that should be off-limits to guns. Gun rights advocates argue that so-called gun-free zones have become targets of opportunity for mass shooters. GVP advocates argue that we need to keep all guns not in the hands of law enforcement or private security out of these places for safety reasons.

There are a number of problems with allowing guns in places like schools and government buildings (the two specific areas mentioned in the *Heller* decision as locations where guns could presumptively be prohibited). These are both areas where it may be difficult to keep a gun secure.

School and building lockers, dorm rooms and business offices, student backpacks and lobbyist briefcases, teachers' or legislators' desks provide very little secure storage for a gun. In the event of a shooting, law enforcement would have real problems in these venues knowing who the "good guys with guns" were and who the "bad guys" were. Without real up-to-date training, the "good guy" could easily end up being an early victim or end up injuring innocent bystanders. After all, even police officers only hit their target 20 percent of the time in active shooter situations—and this is something they practice. There are concerns too with the gun being taken— approximately 20 percent of the time when a police officer is shot, it is with that officer's or his or her partner's gun. No one wants to be a "helpless" victim, but adding another shooter to a chaotic and traumatic situation has the potential to add more injuries and deaths for the innocent.

It is not clear how the "open carry" debate fits into this whole discussion. Historically there were fewer restrictions on those who carried openly than those who concealed their weapons. Those who promote "open carry" now seem to have as their main objective getting others used to and comfortable with guns in public. It seems that this actually might be a counterproductive. GVP groups have gotten good publicity by pressuring retailers like Starbucks and Target to keep guns out of their properties. Police are very likely, with good reason, to be suspicious and concerned about individuals displaying guns in public places.

The continuing battles on gun carry could be resolved if there were basic criteria for who should be allowed to take guns into public places, what places could be placed off limits to these guns, and how those guns could be carried. Absolutist approaches have not worked well so compromise makes sense.

Limits on Types of Guns and Ammunition

The most controversial topic in the gun debate has always seemed to be efforts to limit specific types of guns. The so-called Assault Weapons Ban, which was in effect from 1994 to 2004, spurred a lot of debate, evasion, and criticism. The gun rights movement mocked opponents by saying they just were opposed to "scary looking" guns. Definitions were problematic because gun manufacturers could change or modify features to take their guns out of the ban. The grandfathering of existing weapons meeting the definition meant that the effectiveness of the ban was always going to be called into question.

Again, the constitutionality of any similar "ban" is a bit unclear, although Justice Scalia's opinion in *Heller* did endorse restrictions on "dangerous and unusual" weapons. How this squares with his comments about weapons in "common use" is yet to be seen, but the Court seems to have squarely rejected an "any weapon is okay" approach. Historically, there have been restrictions—but not bans—on fully automatic weapons and machine guns since the 1930s. Given the changes in guns since the Depression Era, the question now should be whether there are any guns which should be treated more like machine guns than handguns or hunting rifles. If the opposing sides on these issues could sit down and discuss which guns are particularly "dangerous and unusual" and should be treated differently, and what those differences should be, then maybe this issue too could get resolved.

We've placed some limits on plastic guns because they are easier to hide. When this issue came before Congress in the late 1980s, the support was overwhelming. Technology has made this a concern once again. With advances in 3-D printing, we need to look more at how and if we can keep these weapons out of circulation.

The main objection to "assault weapons" (and gun sellers have long used that phrase as well as those seeking to place limits on these guns) is the number of rounds they are able to fire quickly. Many of the public don't understand the difference between semi-automatic and fully-automatic weapons, and that is seen as helping those who want restrictions, but being able to fire thirty rounds with a trigger-twitch in fifteen seconds is something that is a legitimate topic of concern. The question is whether these semi-automatics are more like machine guns or traditional hunting rifles. If we agree that they are somewhere in-between, maybe we need a commensurate level of restriction.

While Justice Scalia dismissed concerns about whether "small arms could be useful against modern day bombers and tanks," there are some in the gun rights movement who want a lot more than traditional "small arms." Where do .50-caliber rifles capable of incapacitating a helicopter or a plane on the ground at long range fit into the discussion? As technology increases the range, lethality, and speed of weapons, do we continue to treat them not just like the flintlocks of the Founders' era, but even the guns of the 1930s or 1960s when gun restrictions first started being adopted by Congress?

Perhaps one specific topic for review is the size of the ammunition magazine. Many forget that the 1994–2004 "Assault Weapons Ban" also limited new ammunition magazines to ten rounds. Again, there were issues with grandfathered items, but these restrictions may have had more impact than the restrictions on various types of guns. Those guns could be modified, but a size restriction on the magazine impacted all of the guns. Since the main concern with the "assault weapon" was the number of rounds that could be fired quickly, the magazine limits meant there had to be at least some break in shooting after ten bullets.

The Tucson shootings in January 2011 that left Congresswoman Gabby Giffords seriously injured help show the significance of magazine limits. The shooter in that instance had a magazine that held thirty-one bullets. He was tackled when he went to change magazines. While gun enthusiasts talk about how quickly and easily these magazines can be changed, not every "bad guy" is a gun expert, and even if they are skilled, the process is a lot harder when people are dying and screaming and running and there is blood on the ground. The nine-year-old girl and some of the other victims may well have survived if the shooter had been forced to put in a new magazine after ten rounds rather than thirty-one. Similarly, it has been reported that ten or eleven students were able to escape harm at Sandy Hook in December 2012 when the shooter there had to change ammunition magazines.

When we tried to publicize this issue at Brady, we talked about putting restrictions on "assault clips." I got criticism from those who said that phrase was inaccurate, but most of the public thinks of *TIME* or *Sports Illustrated* when someone mentions "magazines," and we felt the use of "assault" not only recalled "assault weapons" but also accurately described what was happening when someone could fire thirty rounds at a target or targets in close to fifteen seconds. In our view at Brady, the only reason someone needed to be able to fire more than ten rounds quickly was if they were trying to kill a lot of people. If they were just concerned about self-defense, they had more than enough fire power with a ten-round magazine.

One of the arguments against this proposal that Richard advances is that an individual could just carry another gun (or two) and thus have more rounds to fire. As with many of these topics and proposals, there is no perfect of foolproof solution. But I've always argued that just because someone can find a way around a restriction doesn't mean we should make it easy for them. Multiple guns may be more difficult to carry and shoot. It might make sense to argue about the exact number of rounds we allow in a magazine, but right now there is no limit. There should be room for some compromise on this issue.

People can be killed and injured in a lot of different ways and that is always going to be the case. But some methods are more lethal and dangerous than others. I always tell people we had people injured by drive-by shootings when I was mayor, but never by drive-by knifings. There are differences in things that can and do cause harm. We should be able to reach agreement to limit some guns and some ammunition magazines to make it a little less likely that more people can be killed at a distance very quickly from modern weapons.

Safer Guns

While new technology has made guns more dangerous in many ways, it also has the potential to make guns safer if folks would be willing to work together. Possibilities for safer guns include "smart guns" that can be fired only by an owner-authorized user, new versions of trigger locks, and bullet-in-the chamber indicators. Technology also helps make "micro-stamping" a real possibility so markings on ejected cartridges can be used to help identify the last legal owner of guns used at crime scenes.

The main objection to these and other new features is that they are un-workable or unreliable, but that usually can be said about almost any new feature connected to any product. This is where testing and innovation should come into play. Instead, the gun lobby reflexively opposes anything new that might be considered a safety feature, perhaps because they are afraid it might lead to a higher cost for the gun or new legal requirements regarding guns.

We should stop being afraid of new innovations, just as we should stop choking research on gun violence and possible interventions to reduce current levels of violence. The trench warfare over any new idea or prod-uct or topic of research ends up serving only the status quo. We would all benefit from new looks at some of these old battles.

Gun Trafficking Laws

Individuals who traffic in the illegal sale of guns shouldn't have the sup-port of anyone involved in the debate over gun policy. But still, the laws to fight illegal gun sales are notoriously weak. When we view proposals or suggestions on changes to existing laws with automatic opposition be-cause of the source of the idea, we help guarantee the continuance of an ineffective enforcement program.

There was legitimate outrage over the "Fast and Furious" operation in-volving attempted "sting" sales on guns going from border states to Mexico a few years ago, and the hidden video shown on network television of individuals carrying boxes of guns out to their cars and trucks shocked many people. Part of the tragedy here, however, is that it was totally legal to buy all these guns as long as the buyer was not a prohibited purchaser and totally legal to resell them to others as long as the seller had no actual knowledge that the buyer was not a prohibited purchaser. It may have been illegal to take the guns across the border, but it was not illegal to take them to the border.

When we allow someone to buy dozens of similar weapons at one time, are we really surprised that those guns get sold out of the trunk or "off the books" to all sorts of purchasers? When someone can buy any number of guns one day, saying they are for their own possession, and then sell them to someone else the next day saying that they changed their mind, are we surprised that we don't do a better job stopping "straw purchasers"? When we have no way of clearly proving who owns a gun because the guns do not need to be registered in anyone's name and private sales do not require any paperwork, are we surprised when it is almost impossible to show that a prohibited person has a gun illegally, or that a gun traced to a crime belonged to the last owner of record?

We could look at restricting the number of guns that could be bought at one time. Some might argue that "one gun a month" is too restrictive, but are they willing to suggest another number instead of continuing to have no limits? We could require mandatory reporting of lost or stolen guns, not to hassle legal gun owners, but as a way to frustrate gun trafficking. We could work to develop standards of practice, if not regulations, for gun dealers to help stop straw purchasing.

While Richard argues against proposals to limit multiple sales, he does make an important proposal which would help stop gun trafficking with his discussion of stolen firearms. In my talks about gun violence prevention, I make the point that one of the main things burglars look for in homes are guns—arguably making homes with a gun a more attractive target (assuming an empty house) than those without a gun. Richard's suggestion that firearm retailers check the list of reported stolen guns when buying used guns as a way to make it harder for thieves and fences to "unload" these "'hot' firearms" could go a long way to combating gun trafficking. These are the sorts of ideas that could be brought to the table and perhaps become policy if more individuals and groups involved with the gun issue were willing to sit down and try to find common ground.

Conclusion

If Wayne LaPierre isn't willing to sit down to discuss whether we can find common ground, then NRA members, elected officials who seek the NRA's endorsement, and gun owners in general need to pressure their leaders at the NRA and in other groups to do this for them. Gun violence is a serious problem in this country. While we will never be able to end all violence, we can take steps to reduce it.

Guns are legal and are here to stay. The challenge is how to make it harder for those guns to go from being a legal product to something that easily gets into the hands of dangerous people. Different strategies may be needed for individuals who want guns for criminal purposes, those who are dangerously mentally ill, and those who are likely to use guns negligently and irresponsibly. No system is perfect, but if we are willing to sit down and seek common ground, we can make our country a safer place.

CHAPTER NINE

Seeking Common Ground: Perspective of a Gun Rights Supporter

Richard Feldman

Prequel

Absolutes in life are few and far between while infinite gradations of gray abound. The ideology and intensity of the debate within the firearm/civil liberties issue cluster mask many hidden opportunities for reasoned analysis, synthesis, and skillful legislative, societal, or regulatory improvement. Dialogue between opposing positions within this broad debate is stilted due to *identity politics* and the understandable distrust generated by years of semantic name-calling, premeditated demonization, and divergent political agendas on both sides. Intentional or contrived misunderstandings of terminology and a focus on power over functional public policy lead to a "gundamentalist" line in the sand on the "pro-gun rights" side and a disingenuous hoplophobic approach masquerading as "common sense" violence reduction proponents on the other "gun control" side.

Introduction: How I Got Involved with the Gun Issue

Thirty years ago my first position involving firearms was representing the National Rifle Association. I came from a non-gun, suburban northeast household where the term "gun control" simply implied "keeping guns out of the *wrong* hands." I had then assumed that the possession of a gun (particularly a handgun) was not inherently dangerous per se, yet the term "*gun control*" came to be equated with restricting the manufacture, sale, and use of (hand) guns for as many people as possible. The presumption is that the fewer guns in existence, the lower the likelihood that they would be available for criminals, the mentally disturbed, and unsupervised juveniles. As a hypothesis it suggests a logical relationship (and herein lies the rub). Upon closer examination the theory is specious regarding the very problems that the model is supposed to explain while simultaneously creating numerous (if unintended) political conditions for the intelligent discussion and creation of policy initiatives that might well have a salubrious impact upon those fuzzily identified problems. Looking at this differently, one can ask, "Who supports providing access to firearms for violent predatory criminals, the mentally deranged, or unsupervised juveniles?" No one ever raises his or her hand in agreement! Thus, if the broadest question within this debate is carefully crafted, there appears to be considerable unanimity in purpose. The devil, of course, is always in the details! Until and unless we delineate our terms precisely we can't even know whether we're discussing the same subject or if our purported differences are real or fancied. The warden explained it well in *Cool Hand Luke*—"What we have here is a failure to communicate." Precisely!

My training in handguns was courtesy of the Cambridge police department prior to law school in the late 1970s. Obtaining a handgun lawfully in eastern (urban) Massachusetts required some effort even then. Illegally acquiring a gun then or now is significantly easier. My "V-8" moment as a rookie was at a crime scene of a robbery at a small bodega that had been robbed repeatedly. The owner told me that the chief refused to "sign-off" on his handgun license. Upon some checking I uncovered a common truth about many senior law enforcement officials that certainly extends to many politicians—"We're OK . . . you're not!" Indeed the inconvenient history of "gun control" in America is the history of racism, sexism, and elitism. That grocery store owner was an immigrant, a naturalized citizen who spoke with a thick accent and simply didn't conform to the superficial perceptions that the chief had on who was proper to own a handgun and who was not. It was a defining event for me and I started reading the literature on this issue, coming across a book by civil rights attorney Don Kates entitled *Gun Control, the Liberal Skeptics Speak Out*. He takes a decidedly left-of-center, libertarian look at the balancing of firearm rights and responsibilities within the context of our democratic republic. Liberals historically were and generally are skeptical of government intrusion into individual freedoms—except as it applies to gun ownership. The burden of proof on regulations into personal liberty should be on the state to show why a restriction is both necessary and effective. Conservatives typically "support the police" (on crime issues), except when it came to gun rights. They parroted that if the police felt restrained by Miranda warnings, well the goal was to make the police more effective so they were against those mandated warnings! Why should a free people make their top priority serving the interests of the police? Aren't the cops supposed to protect the rights of the people? Shouldn't our broad orientation be to maximize freedom for the citizens, not to minimize it so as to convenience the police?

My key take-away in my brief stint on the job was that "there is never a cop around when you (civilians) need one," because if there was, you wouldn't need one! Most agree that violent felons don't commit crimes in front of uniformed police officers. Thus, when you're alone, you are on your own! The job of the police is to catch the criminals after the fact. Black-letter law is unequivocal in that; when confronted by immediate deadly force, individuals have the lawful right to use deadly force to protect themselves. What value is this right if the police chief can deny you the very means to protect/enforce that right? That makes the right meaningless!

I began to see the "gun control" mantra as a subterfuge for limiting the ability of ordinary citizens to possess the same level of protection that the police and politicians are accustomed to. The gun is never the problem. The question is always, "In whose hands are the guns and how did they acquire them?" Even the "gundamentalists" support gun control—for violent predatory criminals—so why are we arguing about the "what," instead of the "who" and the "how"?

Common Ground

In the prior chapter Paul Helmke discusses how Wayne LaPierre (the National Rifle Association's executive vice president) never responded to his requests for a meeting. I know Paul; he's a smart guy. When our terminology is imprecise and the stakes are very high, internal politics often trumps policy and certainly public posturing. From a gun rights perspective, sitting down with the leader of a group that (arguably) never met a gun restriction it didn't like is akin to breaking bread with a robber who wants to take your possessions and asks, "Why not meet me halfway and just give me your wallet so I'm not forced to take it and your jewelry?" "Be reasonable," the robber says, "just give me some of your money and I'll go away." It's the quintessential meeting between the wolf and the shepherd. "You have all those sheep, I don't want them all, just some of them."

What incentives does the shepherd have to hold this discussion? This may not be fair, but that's precisely how gun owners see this conference about "common ground." If the shepherd spends his time negotiating with the wolf, how long before the owner of the herd decides to fire the shepherd and hire one who spends his time guarding the flock? You don't have to agree with this analysis, just understand the perspective. Many of us in the gun rights movement remember groups like the Coalition to Stop Gun Violence once had a different and more poignant (honest?) name, the National Coalition to Ban Handguns. Turns out that gun owners are very suspicious of wolves in sheep's clothing.

This exemplifies another hurdle in modern America—the "identity politics" problem. If you identify strongly with a group or politician, you are quite understandably increasingly more likely to go along with that group on any allied issue. If you can't stand some politician (and who doesn't?) you're predisposed to oppose any position espoused by that person even before you consider the merits. I admit my guilt. The Brady Campaign prior to Paul Helmke was called Handgun Control Inc. (HCI). They had the tagline *"keeping guns out of the wrong hands."* I was a lobbyist for their opponents; I didn't like that tagline, because I opposed what HCI supported. But that tagline is exactly correct! We all want to keep guns out of the wrong hands, even if our definition of who is "wrong" varies considerably. Identity politics is a powerful motivating factor in legislation lobbying, social and cultural positioning, and largely under-reported and unrecognized as a formidable organizing tool. Perhaps now Paul Helmke better understands why Wayne LaPierre had plenty of robust reasons not to meet with him. As Marlon Brando would say in the Godfather, "It's not personal, it's business."

Background Check Issue Cluster

This issue began (nationally) since the 1968 Gun Control Act. That law required a federal firearms licensee (FFL) to obtain information on Form 4473 of the buyer who upon signing the form committed perjury if they lied and now possesses the firearm unlawfully. The Brady Handgun Violence Prevention Act of 1994 requires the FFL to obtain (generally) a NICS background check run by the FBI or state law enforcement prior to that transfer to verify the authenticity of the information. The firearm industry supported the background check requirement because it protected the retail dealer who previously would transfer a gun (unknowingly) to a customer with no check into the veracity of the allegations sworn to on Form 4473. The law coincided with the computerization and instant access of data allowing for a (usually) seamless check, and rapid government response for the sale to conclude. It also forced jurisdictions everywhere to update and clean the disposition of cases in their system which was an additional benefit to citizens who might have been unaware of the record errors and its substantial impacts upon their employment and credit possibilities. The law required, within the commercial industry, that persons unknown to one another (retailer and seller) would have a background check run at the time of transfer from the licensed dealer to the consumer/buyer. I personally and enthusiastically supported this law in my testimony before the House Subcommittee on Crime in the fall of 1993 on behalf of the firearm industry (American Shooting Sports Council).

The law had no effect on "private sales" transactions because that was not under federal law and it left those decisions to the states. Thus, if you and I live in the same state (state law being silent) a person-to-person (non-FFL) transfer is perfectly lawful whether at a gun show, at a flea market, from a newspaper or internet sales, or a transfer between father and son, two co-workers who happen to be police officers, or two neighbors who each happen to work at the district attorney's office prosecuting felons. Thus these "private sales" are of two very distinct types, namely those between (a) persons who do *not* know each other and (b) between those who *do* in fact know each other due to their being relatives, friends, co-workers, or neighbors. This is a critical dividing line delineating the key identified problem of transfers between individuals who have no reasonable expectation of knowing anything about the backgrounds of each other. Proceeding cautiously, deliberately, and carefully, this important line can be drawn without inflaming the determined opposition from those (myself included) who oppose government background checks for transfers when the seller personally knows the buyer. In addition many of us are suspicious that the real reason (true or false) is for the government to build a list of all gun owners, possibly outlawing or crippling gun shows and thereby discouraging the firearm heritage and cultural outlet for millions of Americans. Following the Wiki leaks and other National Security Agency revelations, can anyone honestly say that the government doesn't routinely lie to us citizens?

The proponents of universal background checks always claim that to ensure that the buyer meets the federal requirements, all transfers should undergo the National Instant Criminal Background Check System (NICS) check. Here is my "compromise" solution. Let's call it the "Gun Show Preservation and Protection Act." What gun rights group would oppose that? It would set up a new FFL license category for gun show promoters allowing them to run the NICS checks at gun shows. It would give sellers of firearms who transfer any gun under the NICS check system the same protection under federal law that manufacturers and retailers have under the Protection of Lawful Commerce in Arms Act (note the valuable and nonpenal incentive). It would exclude from the mandated requirements firearm transfers between family members, friends, co-workers, and neighbors known to the seller for more than one year, but it wouldn't provide the liability protection extended to the industry. So if I sell my gun to a friend who decides to rob a bank that afternoon with his new pistol I too can be sued. Had I taken the gun to an FFL to do the transfer I could have been excluded from the lawsuit from the start, but if I just transfer the gun I'm subject to court inquiry into what I knew and when I knew it. Instead of arguing endlessly over what the perfect system should be, why don't we support a pretty good one that takes into account the legitimate concerns both sides have? Opponents of this cite the fact that criminals also have friends. This is true, but if you possess a gun illegally, what reason would there be not to sell it to another criminal? Can anyone imagine a gangbanger concerned that his transfer of the gun to a fellow gang member would be a violation of the Gun Control Act of 1968?

Prohibited Purchasers

In the prior chapter Paul brings up an important point that's never had a good public evaluation. We generally prohibit convicted felons from lawful firearm ownership, but misdemeanor convictions, even for multiple violent felony arrests plea bargained down to misdemeanors, are no bar to firearm purchases. His point is basic. Why do we prohibit non-violent felons but tolerate violent misdemeanors lawfully acquiring guns? Indeed, the conviction for the same act may be a felony in one state and a misdemeanor in a bordering jurisdiction and vice versa. Aren't we smarter than this? Can't we devise a more intelligent standard with a review process after ten or more years following the punishment for the return of one's firearm civil liberties?

The prohibition for those "adjudicated mentally insane" avoids the crux of the most difficult category of firearm misusages. Crazy people will do insane and dangerous things and we as a society have neglected and avoided our responsibility to provide help for them. This will cost money, which we have chosen to spend on other things while blaming gun laws and gun owners whenever any new horrific tragedy arises. The media relentlessly ask why the gun rights organizations don't take on a policy and leadership role on this issue. Exactly what expertise does the NRA have on mental health? Why should any gun rights group lead a fight when the mental health community is either silent or befuddled? Where is the American Psychological Association? Why doesn't Congress or the president convene meetings to craft answers from them? At the very least our thought process ought to be to do the least harm by encouraging people to seek psychological help. We ought not discourage troubled individuals from seeking help by contemplating a law that leads to the cessation of their Second Amendment freedoms at least right at the outset.

Perhaps the biggest bugaboo in the entire criminal justice/firearm conversation revolves around drugs. Our war on drugs has cost billions of dollars and tens of thousands of lives. On this issue perhaps we should consider the old maxim, "When you're in a hole, STOP DIGGING!" The fight over drugs, not just marijuana but all drugs, misses the identical point that alcohol prohibition led to—the cure is far worse than the problem! Ask the retired professionals from LEAP (Law Enforcement Against Prohibition). They are unanimous that the war on drugs leads to more drug misuse, more gun violence, and more ruined lives with huge societal costs. For the record, Jack Cole, one of their founders and a retired New Jersey State Police drug enforcement specialist, states that there have been a number of law-enforcement victories; "the cost of heroin has gone down and the purity has gone way up."

Another set of issues within this discussion is whether people on the terrorist watch list should be denied buying guns by law. This sounds perfectly rational on the surface, but once again, the devil truly is in the details. Who is on the terrorist watchlist, how did they get there, and how does one get removed? Depending on which list we are talking about there may be a million people on some form of watch list. Former senator Ted Kennedy found himself on the Transportation Security Administration "no-fly" list and had a heck of a time getting removed—and he was a powerful, recognizable, influential U.S. senator! The counter intuitive truth, according to every experienced law enforcement official I've spoken with (off the record), is that a real terrorist is highly unlikely to walk into a gun shop and submit to a NICS check before obtaining guns. If a real terrorist was that stupid, the last thing we should do is alert them that they didn't pass the background check! That unlikely moment is called "actionable intelligence." If a terrorist attempts to buy fifteen Barrett semi-automatic rifles, that would be the perfect moment to begin intensive surveillance and figure out what's going on, not pat ourselves on the head and congratulate ourselves for preventing the transfer of those guns from a legitimate source. These issues are never as simple as they initially appear and the answers are always more convoluted and nuanced once you know "the rest of the story."

Database Records

When it comes to databases the old maxim "GIGO" still holds—garbage in, garbage out. Records are only as helpful as their accuracy. We continue to make a serious mistake of assuming that any time a prohibited person is stopped from a firearm purchase we have prevented a potential harm. While it's true that the purchase may be denied at the gun shop, why do we congratulate ourselves that the tragedy was avoided? Preventing dangerous mentally challenged persons through NICS checks from a new firearm purchase works much better than thwarting intentional criminal acquisitions. All we have done is relocate the purchase for intentional "bad guys" from a legitimate source to an illegitimate one. The past twenty years, history of the Brady Law is rather sad when we look at how few prosecutions there have been for prohibited persons attempting to buy guns from legitimate sources. Any prosecutor will tell you (and criminals know this) that the first thing thrown out for a plea bargain is the "felon in possession" charge. What is the message to the criminals? It shouts, "We really don't care about the gun laws."

Stolen Firearms

This aspect of the gun issue gets virtually no policy discussion, rather surprisingly. Where do criminals obtain most of their guns? Is it by going through background checks at gun stores with fake identification or using "straw man" purchases? No. Is it by going to gun shows and buying from non-FFL sellers? No. Do they clandestinely manufacture guns side by side with their meth labs? No. THEY STEAL THEM! The statistics on firearm theft have been fairly consistent over the past twenty years. Criminals steal in excess of a half a million firearms every year. There aren't 500,000 criminal gun misusages annually so what happens to those guns? The majority of them are resold back into the legitimate channels.

What do burglars steal? Forty years ago they stole TVs and stereos along with cash, jewelry, drugs, and guns, anything they could fence or easily dispose of. No one steals televisions anymore. This is how the illicit system operates. If you burglarize homes you're bound to know a couple of fences who are all too happy to buy those guns for pennies on the dollar. Any fence knows enough to take the stolen property a state or two away from the area and try to sell them back to a dealer who is excited about buying used guns—that's where retail shops have high profit margins (used, not stolen, guns). When a dealer buys a gun he/she puts it into their "A & D" book (acquisition and disposition). If we were to add one small, computerized step to this process the entire market in stolen guns would become far more difficult and problematical for lawbreakers. Ninety-nine percent of store-front firearm retailers organize their books on computer. As a dealer enters the serial number, the make and model of the gun, why not automatically have the system check the NCIC list of reported stolen guns? By the third entry with a positive hit of a reported firearm most local police would be interested in paying the seller an immediate visit and inquiring exactly how they acquired those guns reported as stolen. Word of mouth being what it is, in short order fences wouldn't be too eager to buy "hot" firearms and thieves wouldn't be so enamored with stealing them if they can't unload them easily. Add to this some incentive for gun owners such as, keep the serial numbers of your guns and if reported you will get those guns returned when located. Alternately to the retailer, if the guns aren't reported as stolen and you innocently buy them, you aren't ever liable to their rightful owner or their insurance company should the theft and your sale subsequently be discovered and reported.

This orientation is critically important and always overlooked during discussions of prospective firearm legislation. You don't have to make it illegal for the owner not to report the theft; his economic interest alone will encourage him to do so. The insurance companies will require those serial numbers in order to collect the insurance, so gun owners will have a financial incentive to keep the numbers and make police reports without threat of penalty for doing so! Will this prevent the future theft of all firearms? No, but it will reduce the enticements for theft and add a degree of hindrances to illegal dealers that will have the intended results! Gun owners oppose mandatory reporting because they just don't want to be victimized twice; once for the theft and then for the failure to report the theft. Inducements, not criminal mandates, work better, are far more politically acceptable, and lead to the identical policy location. On the other hand, crafting regulations and laws that gun owners actually would support (or at least won't oppose) prevents presidential hand wringing, congressional news conferences, and editorial bashing based on doctrinaire, ancient perceptions.

Concealed Carry, Open Carry

This is the issue that's likely to come up in Congress over the next ten years. The Senate already passed a version of this to mandate every state recognizing the carry permit of other states. Open carry when out in the woods is fine. It is legal in many places but that doesn't make it smart or a great idea, just a legal one. The whole purpose in carrying a handgun is self-defense. If the bad guy knows you have one you will be the first one attacked, the element of surprise being lost. No state legislature is going to seriously reconsider their state's "shall issue" laws. Some states like New Hampshire require a $10 payment, no training, and they issue that concealed carry license, indeed they must issue it to just about anyone. Some states like Texas are "shall issue" but they require actual training and a modicum of instruction on the law of deadly force, a good idea in my view. The gun harm reduction community should view the national carry debate as a last best line of defense. Handled thoughtfully (something rarely done in this deliberation) it's an opportunity to have some useful requirements for the carrying of concealed firearms from state to state. A smart approach wouldn't seek to change any of the current state reciprocity agreements. It would mandate training standards and once met, state authorities would issue an "enhanced" state carry license allowing that now better trained citizen to carry in other states under federal law.

In the previous chapter Paul discusses the possibility that we might end up giving "passes for dangerous people to carry guns in public." Frankly that statement confuses me. Criminals carry in public all the time and we don't (seriously) expect them to fill out official permission forms to carry concealed. Crazy people also carry guns and misuse them in horrible tragedies (frequently in "gun free zones"). I can't imagine Paul is suggesting that denying a lunatic a carry license will be an effective tool in preventing them from murdering a dozen people at a shopping mall or on school property. Terrorists won't be applying for them either. Paul must be postulating that there is some subgroup of individuals that can lawfully buy guns but ought not (even with training) be allowed to lawfully carry the legal guns they lawfully continue to own. Making public policy for that group shouldn't prevent us from establishing norms for the 99.8 percent of us that don't fall into that category. Trying to satisfy every conceivable permutation and situational problem prevents society from making important decisions affecting the bulk of the population. I can always craft a "what if" situation that might not have happened "but for." This is what law professors are supposed to do. Nevertheless, good policy enacted is far better than perfect policy endlessly debated.

Limits on Types of Guns and Ammunition

The technical debate over "good guns" and "bad guns," "assault weapons" versus non–assault weapons, has to be the most spurious debilitating and downright silliest debate points within the confines of this issue. My definition for an assault weapon is simple—"any loaded firearm pointed at me is an assault weapon while any loaded firearm in my hands is a defensive device." The gun doesn't make itself an "assault" or a "defensive" tool, the user does! That's the whole point! It's never the gun, but in whose hands are the guns. That's what matters. Even the 1994 federal law called the guns "semi-automatic" assault weapons, a complete contradiction in technical terminology. If it can't fire fully automatically it can't be a true "assault weapon." This dialogue truly is the holy grail of stupid. Which would be worse, facing a thug with grandfather's 12-gauge shotgun loaded with four rounds of double 0 buck or a 9mm rifle with a forward magazine, a flash suppresser, bayonet lug attachment, barrel shroud, and eleven rounds in the magazine? Obviously this is a trick question! Dead is dead, and being killed with a shotgun is only marginally different than being killed with a rifle, so why are we wasting valuable time over such irrelevant distinctions?

There are more than 100 million (probably much more) higher-capacity magazines (over ten rounds) lawfully owned in America. Think about this: the New York Secure Ammunition and Firearms Enforcement (SAFE) Act (enacted in 2013 after the Newtown, Connecticut, shooting) makes it illegal to possess a pistol loaded with more than seven rounds in the magazine. Compare and contrast with this: a licensed handgun owner in New York may have a pistol in each hand with seven bullets in the magazine and one in the chamber for a total of sixteen rounds ready for firing. Should that same licensed citizen possess an empty twenty-round magazine and no pistol, they would now be committing a major felony. Is it really surprising that gun owners across this country are suspicious of politicians espousing claims of "safety" with the resulting focus on the mechanical device of licensed citizens rather than the smaller and admittedly dangerous class of intentional criminals?

In the prior chapter Paul Helmke questions why "the only reason someone needed to be able to fire more than ten rounds quickly was if they were trying to kill a lot of people." Every police officer in this country carries a sidearm with more than ten rounds, yet I am of the distinct view that rarely do any of them desire "to kill a lot of people." Yes, police are generally better trained than the average gun owner, so why do they need more rounds than a suburban housewife encountering three burglars breaking into her home if they are so well trained? When fire breaks out, water is a good thing to have on hand, and in that scenario more is better for police and civilians!

Smart Guns

We can make a gun today that will never be misused, so long as we manufacture it without the firing pin! Then again it can't be used and it really wouldn't be a "gun" if it can't fire. There have been mechanical safety devices for more than one hundred years available with firearms. Ultimately the most important safety device for a firearm is the brain of the operator of that device. Relying on mechanical or computer technology, while useful in certain situations, can be catastrophic in others. The more the safety devices and fail safes, the greater the likelihood of a critical problem when you need it most. The unstated problem with this particular issue is "distrust." The anti-gun community has been behind a push for "smart guns" for some of the wrong reasons. They are correct that it would increase the cost of firearms. Many gun owners would like to own a gun that knows when to fire and when the operator really didn't mean to fire it. We'd like to carry that gun even if it costs double the price, but why would we want, need, or buy that technology for the dozens of other handguns that sit in our safes and are never carried for protection? Why don't the gun harm prevention folks ever really support firearm safety education? Doesn't society owe an obligation to teach our children some basic safety rules so that we can prevent accidents? Actions have consequences and our perceptions are based upon our assessment of those activities.

Gun Trafficking Laws

Here is yet another issue that "cuts" one way superficially and appears entirely differently upon closer examination. Over the past twenty years in order to control illegal trafficking some proposals have included "one gun a month." When a buyer purchases two or more handguns from a licensee, that FFL holder must fill out a "multiple sales form." A copy of that multiple sales form is sent to the local (or state) police and to the Bureau of Alcohol, Tobacco, Firearms, and Explosives (ATF). In the 1990s gangbangers would send (typically) a girlfriend (no criminal history) into a gun shop to purchase several guns at one time. I sat through a hearing in Congress listening to several buyers who thought this was legal. Too bad the multiple sales form doesn't require a signature by the buyer alerting them to the fact that they are now on a special list or will be should any of these guns show up being traced from a crime scene. The dilemma became apparent in one meeting with then Philadelphia Mayor Ed Rendell where the one-gun-a-month proposal again came to the fore. Ask any senior ATF agent what the single most important investigative lead is on gun running and they will tell you, "Oh, it's the multiple sales form." As we explained to the mayors, "Eliminate multiple sales, and you eliminate the single most important investigative lead the police have in tracking gun runners." Once again, the more you know, the more complicated the task becomes in crafting methods to combat the problems without interfering either with law enforcement techniques or legitimate buyers. Of course in a "one-gun-a-month" jurisdiction, you can send seven people to the same gun shop to each buy one gun and then nobody is the wiser.

Conclusion

Gun violence is only a problem when committed against innocent people. Gun violence against predatory persons is a blessing in the absence of other alternatives. There are almost as many guns in civilian hands as there are people in the United States. What is sorely lacking in the debate over firearms is an appreciation of whose ox is being gored. Public opinion polls are mixed on many of the specifics of this controversy but one thing stands clear: when gun owners feel that their rights to own firearms for any lawful purpose are on the table, politicians beware! Every time there is a "dust-up" on guns and elected officials tout the latest poll that shows 80 percent of voters support restricting this or banning that, I can confidently assert the following: "Congressman, you don't have to worry about the 80 percent that approves of your proposal, because they aren't going to support you or oppose you based on your vote on this issue. You'd best be concerned with the 20 percent who disagree with you, because they are the activist gun owners who care about their Second Amendment rights and a hefty percentage of them actually will vote for you or against you based upon what you do on this legislation." On the other hand, elected officials who forget about an important constituency always appear in shock on election night when they discover that gun owners care deeply enough about their guns to make this a defining issue. It's an acutely subliminal concern and it's not about guns on this level; it's about trust, and a government or a politician that no longer trusts his constituents is no longer worthy of their trust in return.

To millions and millions of American gun owners it's never been exclusively about guns—it's about freedom, and being against that freedom is an uncomfortably dangerous position for elected officials to find themselves in come the first Tuesday after the first Monday in November. Voters and pundits who lack the nuanced understanding that we've discussed here just can't believe or accept as "fair" that a relatively small percentage of voters can actually make such an important difference in the outcome of American politics. Democracy is a messy business, but the alternative is terrifyingly ugly, leading us back to the origins of the Second Amendment with our struggle against rule by the British Crown, who most assuredly thought it knew what was in our best interests whether we agreed or not.

Index

About the Editor and Contributors

The Editor

Glenn H. Utter (PhD, University of Buffalo) is distinguished professor emeritus at Lamar University, Beaumont, Texas. He is the author, co-author, and editor of several books, including *Encyclopedia of Gun Control and Gun Rights* (2011), *Youth and Political Participation* (2012), *Culture Wars in America: A Documentary and Reference Guide* (2010), *Campaign and Election Reform* (2008), and *Mainline Christians and U.S. Public Policy* (2007).

The Contributors

Richard Feldman (JD, Vermont Law School) is a former lobbyist and regional political director for the National Rifle Association (NRA). He is author of *Ricochet: Confessions of a Gun Lobbyist* (2008), in which he recounts the NRA's rise as an effective lobbying organization and recounts the key moments in the organization's history. Feldman was a Ronald Reagan appointee to the Commerce Department and served as executive director of the American Shooting Sports Council (ASSC), until 2000 the trade association of the firearms industry. Feldman currently is the president of the Independent Firearm Owners Association.

Mary Anne Franks (JD, Harvard Law School) is associate professor of law at the University of Miami School of Law, Coral Gables, Florida. Her research interests include cyberlaw, bias-free speech, privacy, and self-defense. Franks's scholarship has appeared in several academic journals, including the *UCLA Law Review*, the *California Law Review*, and the *Columbia Journal of Law and Gender*. She publishes frequently in popular periodicals such as the *Atlantic* and the *Huffington Post*, and often serves as a source for the mass media.

Paul Helmke (JD, Yale University) is professor of practice and director of the Civic Leaders Living-Learning Center in the School of Public and Environmental Affairs at Indiana University, Bloomington, Indiana. He served three terms as mayor of Fort Wayne, Indiana (1988–1999). In 2006 Helmke became president of the Brady Campaign to Prevent Gun Violence, a position he held until 2011. Following the Virginia Tech shooting in 2007, he frequently appeared on television news programs urging the adoption of more stringent gun control measures. Helmke moved to Indiana University in 2013.

Sean Maddan (PhD, University of Nebraska) is associate professor of criminology and criminal justice at the University of Tampa in Tampa, Florida. He has published several articles in academic journals and co-authored the textbooks *Statistics in Criminology and Criminal Justice: Analysis and Interpretation* (2012) and *Understanding Statistics for the Social Sciences, Criminal Justice, and Criminology* (2011). He is also the author of *The Labeling of Sex Offenders: The Unintended Consequences of the Best Intentioned Public Policies* (2008).

Glenn E. Meyer (PhD, University of Buffalo) is professor of psychology at Trinity University, San Antonio, Texas. He is author and co-author of several journal articles on experimental research dealing with the legal implications of the self-defense use of firearms by legally-armed citizens.

Michael C. Powell (MPA, Grand Canyon University, Phoenix, Arizona) is police lieutenant at McNeese State University, Lake Charles, Louisiana. Powell has served in several law enforcement positions, including chief of police for the Forks, Washington, police department, and has been certified as an instructor in several law enforcement specialties. He is currently completing a master of science degree in Criminal Justice at McNeese State University.

Amanda J. Reinke (PhD candidate, Department of Anthropology and the Certificate Program on Disasters, Displacement, and Human Rights at the University of Tennessee, Knoxville.) She has coauthored a peer-reviewed article on African children's right to participate in their own protection.

Saundra J. Ribando (DPA, University of Alabama) is professor of political science and director of the Center for Public Service at Georgia Regents University, Augusta, Georgia. She has focused recent research on the effects that university consolidation has on the faculty and culture of the organization, and has co-authored a journal article on the subject ("Change Happens: Assessing the Initial Impact of a University Consolidation on Faculty," *Public Personnel Management*, March 2015).

Robert L. Spinks (MS, University of Cincinnati) is chief of police and adjunct instructor in the criminal justice program at McNeese State University, Lake Charles, Louisiana. In more than 30 years of criminal justice experience, he has served in various positions, including as a police officer, police chief, and director of public safety. Spinks is certified as an instructor in several law enforcement specialties and served as a consultant and trainer for more than 45 law enforcement agencies in the Pacific Northwest.

Ronald D. Stephens (EdD, University of Southern California) is chair in school safety, Graduate School of Education and Psychology at Pepperdine University, Los Angeles, California, and executive director of the National School Safety Center. He serves as executive editor of *School Safety*, a leading school crime prevention journal. Stephens has presented lectures on school safety to more than 500 public groups and organizations, has served as guest lecturer at many universities, and has been a consultant to numerous school districts.